SEMINAL

HEALTH, SOCIETY, AND INEQUALITY SERIES

General Editor: Jennifer A. Reich

The Third Net: The Hidden System of Migrant Health Care
Lisa Sun-Hee Park, Erin Hoekstra, and Anthony M. Jimenez

The Reproduction of Inequality: How Class Shapes the Pregnant Body and Infant Health
Katherine Mason

Elder Care in Crisis: How the Social Safety Net Fails Families
Emily K. Abel

Toxic Sexual Politics: Toxicology, Environmental Poisons, and Queer Feminist Futures
Melina Packer

Seminal: On Sperm, Health, and Politics
Edited by Rene Almeling, Lisa Campo-Engelstein, and Brian T. Nguyen

Seminal

On Sperm, Health, and Politics

Edited by
Rene Almeling,
Lisa Campo-Engelstein,
and Brian T. Nguyen

NEW YORK UNIVERSITY PRESS
New York

NEW YORK UNIVERSITY PRESS
New York
www.nyupress.org

© 2025 by New York University
All rights reserved

Please contact the Library of Congress for Cataloging-in-Publication data.

ISBN: 9781479834068 (hardback)
ISBN: 9781479834082 (paperback)
ISBN: 9781479834112 (library ebook)
ISBN: 9781479834105 (consumer ebook)

This book is printed on acid-free paper, and its binding materials are chosen for strength and durability. We strive to use environmentally responsible suppliers and materials to the greatest extent possible in publishing our books.

The manufacturer's authorized representative in the EU for product safety is Mare Nostrum Group B.V., Mauritskade 21D, 1091 GC Amsterdam, The Netherlands.
Email: gpsr@mare-nostrum.co.uk.

Manufactured in the United States of America

10 9 8 7 6 5 4 3 2 1

Also available as an ebook

CONTENTS

List of Figures   ix

List of Abbreviations   xi

Introduction: Complexities at the Nexus of Sperm, Health, and Politics   1
   Rene Almeling, Lisa Campo-Engelstein, and Brian T. Nguyen

PART I: INCORPORATING SPERM

1. An Ob-Gyn Reflects on How to Incorporate Sperm into Health and Politics   21
   Brian T. Nguyen

2. The Challenges of Focusing on Men without Centering Men in Reproductive Health, Rights, and Justice   29
   Jennifer A. Reich

3. A Preventive Care Approach to Meeting Male Adolescents' Sexual and Reproductive Health Care Needs   36
   Arik V. Marcell

4. "Healthy Masculinity" Is Not a Feminist Strategy for Sperm, Health, and Politics   54
   Tristan Bridges

5. Introducing a Stratified Reproductive Justice Framework for Sperm, Health, and Politics   61
   Krystale E. Littlejohn

PART II: COUNTING SPERM

6. Male Infertility Is a Public Health Problem   71
   Christopher De Jonge

7. How Male Infertility Diagnosis and Treatment Evolved
   over the Last Two Decades   84
   Stanton Honig

8. Sperm Counts in Crises   90
   Marion Boulicault

9. Sperm as Sentinel   103
   Janelle Lamoreaux

10. Sperm Banks and the Shortage of Black Sperm Donors   107
    Alyssa M. Newman

    PART III: MAKING SPERM

11. State Surveillance and the Politics of Paternity   113
    Lynne Haney

12. Caught Between Sperm and Transition Care   121
    Jeremy A. Gottlieb

13. Whose Sperm Is Worthy? How Eugenics Promotes
    the Control of Transgender People's Reproduction   134
    Stef M. Shuster

14. Do Young Men Care about Their Fertility?   140
    David L. Bell

15. In Vitro Gametogenesis as a Window into Sperm Health
    and Politics   145
    Anne Le Goff

    PART IV: STOPPING SPERM

16. Biological Fables, Vasectomies, and the Future of Sperm
    after *Roe*   157
    Andréa Becker

17. Contraception, Male Engagement, and
    Reproductive Identity   166
    Logan Nickels

18. Gendered Language, Pregnant Bodies, and Male
    Contraceptive Development   174
    Fabian Hennig

19. Shepherding Sperm in Catholic Health Systems   190
    Lori Freedman

PART V: REGULATING SPERM

20. Examining the Politics, Ethics, and Legality of Anonymity
    in Gamete Donation   199
    Rebecca W. O'Connor

21. Masculinity, Eugenics, and American Family Stories   205
    Karen Weingarten

22. Technoscientific Reproduction, Queer Sperm, and the
    Politics of Masculinity   215
    Meredith P. Field

23. Too Much or Not Enough? Genetic Testing of Sperm Donors   223
    Michelle J. Bayefsky

24. Developing a Reproductive Justice Approach to Regulating
    Formal and Informal Sperm Donation   228
    Naomi Cahn and Sonia M. Suter

25. The High Stakes of Gamete Regulation in a
    Post-*Dobbs* World   243
    Courtney G. Joslin, Katherine L. Kraschel, and Douglas NeJaime

PART VI: EMBODYING SPERM

26. Why Men Are Missing from Discussions of Infertility and
    What to Do about It   255
    William D. Petok

27. Sperm Troubles and Infertility Technologies in the
    Middle East and Arab America   261
    Marcia C. Inhorn

28. Sex, Gender, and the Biological and Mental "Load"
    of Reproduction   273
    Julie Bindeman

29. Direct-to-Consumer Digital Health, Hybrid Masculinities,
    and the "Straighting" of Sexual Intimacy   280
    Ben Curran Wills

30. Speculating about Sperm for Trans Reproductive Futures   288
    Carlo Sariego

    Acknowledgments   299

    About the Editors   301

    About the Contributors   303

    Index   317

LIST OF FIGURES

Figure I.1: Conceptual diagram of bodies as the result of multilayered biological and social processes 4

Figure 1.1: The EMERGE (Expanding Male Engagement in Reproductive and Gender Equity) Framework 24

Figure 3.1: Socioecological framework that influences young male's sexual and reproductive health and care 38

Figure 6.1: Male Reproductive Health Ecosystem (Barratt et al. 2018) 77

Figure 27.1: Intracytoplasmic sperm injection (ICSI) 266

Figure 27.2: ICSI being performed by an embryologist in Beirut, Lebanon 268

LIST OF ABBREVIATIONS

AMA: American Medical Association
ART: Assisted Reproductive Technologies
ASRM: American Society for Reproductive Medicine
CDC: Centers for Disease Control and Prevention
DIY: Do-it-yourself
DNA: Deoxyribonucleic acid
ED: Erectile dysfunction
FDA: Food and Drug Administration
HIPAA: Health Insurance Portability and Accountability Act
HIV: Human immunodeficiency virus
HPV: Human papillomavirus
ICSI: Intracytoplasmic sperm injection
IPSC: Induced pluripotent stem cells
IVF: In vitro fertilization
IVG: In vitro gametogenesis
JAMA: Journal of the American Medical Association
LGBTQ+: Lesbian, Gay, Bi, Trans, Queer, Plus
MRHI: Male Reproductive Health Initiative
NIH: National Institutes of Health
OB-GYN: Obstetrics and Gynecology, or obstetrician-gynecologist
SRH: Sexual and Reproductive Health
STI: Sexually transmitted infection
UN: United Nations
UPA: Uniform Parentage Act
WHO: World Health Organization
WPATH: World Professional Association for Transgender Health

Introduction

Complexities at the Nexus of Sperm, Health, and Politics

RENE ALMELING, LISA CAMPO-ENGELSTEIN, AND
BRIAN T. NGUYEN

For many people, hearing the word *sperm* will call to mind topics related to reproduction, fertility, and sexuality; images of sperm meeting egg; concerns about sperm count; or risks of sexually transmitted infections, to name just a few. Type *sperm* into Google, and the search results include listicles like "Everything You Need to Know about Sperm" and commonly asked questions, such as "Where does sperm come from?," "How often should a man release sperm?," and "How many drops of sperm is needed to get pregnant?" These queries, too, are usually rooted in understandings of sperm as reproductive or sexual, or both.[1]

With this book, we seek to place sperm in two additional contexts: health and politics. In part, we are responding to a surge of recent research piecing together the relationship between sperm and health. For example, there is growing evidence that the age and health of male bodies can affect their sperm and, in turn, reproductive outcomes, such as miscarriage and the risk of childhood illnesses (Almeling 2020; Kimmins et al. 2023). In addition, there are renewed efforts to finally develop new methods of male contraception beyond the condom and vasectomy, including by nonprofit organizations and a bevy of start-ups banking on men's willingness to share the work of preventing unwanted pregnancies (Campo-Engelstein, Kaufman, and Parker 2019; Nguyen and Jacobsohn 2023; Oudshoorn 2003). Scientists continue to debate whether global sperm counts are dropping and, if so, by how much and due to which causes (Boulicault et al. 2022; Levine et al. 2017; Levine et al. 2023). And beyond the realm of reproductive health, there is an emerging approach to sperm as an easily accessible biomarker of current and future health, an indicator of risks for a wide range of ailments beyond infertility, including mortality (Kasman, Del Giudice, and Eisenberg 2020).

Scholars have demonstrated that any time we are talking about bodies and health, we are also talking about politics (e.g., Epstein 2022; Foucault 1980; Roberts 1997). The politics of how bodies are categorized: On what basis is a body considered to be male? How does the presence or absence of sperm influence such categorizations? The politics of how health is defined: What constitutes a "healthy" body? To what extent is responsibility for health assigned to individuals or their circumstances? The politics of gender and reproduction: What is the future of bodily autonomy following the Supreme Court's evisceration of a federal right to abortion and unending legislative attacks on trans and nonbinary people? The politics of decisions determining who has access to the basics, not only for health but life itself—to food, shelter, and clean water? In the contemporary United States, each and every one of these processes, from the cellular to the societal, are riven by deeply rooted and intersecting inequalities, such as those associated with socioeconomic status, racism, sexism, homophobia, and ableism (e.g., Collins 2015; Glenn 1999).

In our own work as, respectively, a sociologist, a bioethicist, and a physician-scientist, we have encountered numerous complexities at the nexus of sperm, health, and politics. Our goal in this volume is to advance a conversation about how these three nouns have been—and could or should be—related to one another. We convened a broad array of experts—social scientists, physicians, historians, philosophers, scientists, and policymakers—to share their views about the most pressing issues at the intersections of sperm, health, and politics in contemporary America. Each drafted a short "think piece," and we gathered for a daylong meeting to workshop the essays. The goal was not consensus, but generative, collaborative, and profoundly interdisciplinary discussion and feedback, after which everyone revised their essay. The final think pieces are collected in the pages that follow and range across a wide variety of issues, from the specter of eugenics to contemporary incarnations of masculinity, from the oldest questions about male infertility to the latest technological developments for creating sperm, from concerns about the effects of environmental toxins to approaches for regulating sperm markets, and from novel ideas about how to better educate youth to strategies for incorporating male reproductive and sexual health into the medical system—all the while attending to the enormous variation in how individuals understand and experience sperm. In this introduction, we orient the reader to the many complexities that arise when addressing these and other issues before providing a guide to navigating the essays, which together offer an unprecedented and kaleidoscopic view of the relationship between sperm, health, and politics.

What Is Sperm?

Before we go any further, we have to raise what might seem like a basic question: "What is sperm?" A quick glance at a dictionary will reveal a simple description of a "male reproductive cell" or a "gamete," often noting that it can "unite with" or "fertilize" an egg in order to "produce young."[2] And, certainly, sperm is a biological entity, a form of bodily material, but it is not only that. Decades of research by social scientists and historians demonstrate that all bodily processes and body parts are both fundamentally biological *and* fundamentally social. That is, it is not possible to see or study or discuss or experience sperm outside of sociality, apart from the historical processes and cultural norms that shape how it is made meaningful (Almeling 2011; Daniels 2006; Mamo 2007; Martin 1991; Mohr 2018; Moore 2007; Thompson 2005; Tober 2018; Wahlberg 2018).

Indeed, sperm is not any one thing. From the perspective of individuals or institutions at different times and in different places, it can be sexual or reproductive, or both, or neither. It can be sacred. It can be waste. Its presence can be exhilarating or devastating. Its absence can be exhilarating or devastating. It can be a matter of complete indifference.

As an illustration of how sperm is both biological and social, consider the metaphor of nested dolls. Rene Almeling borrowed this metaphor from Anne Fausto-Sterling (2000, 254) and applied it first to reproduction (Almeling 2015) and here to sperm (see figure 1.1). Considering sperm, or any bodily process or body part, as the outcome of multilayered biological and social processes involves appreciating the indissoluble links between genetic and cellular processes, through individual

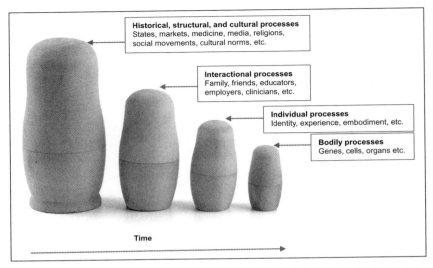

Figure I.1: Conceptual diagram of bodies as the result of multilayered biological and social processes.

and interactional processes, all the way to historical and structural processes. There is an "etc." at the end of each list in figure I.1 to highlight the incompleteness of these lists.

If one imagines each of the layers—each doll—to be neither entirely malleable nor fully rigid, the nested dolls metaphor is useful because it shows that a change in the shape of any one biological or social process will reverberate, altering the shape of all the other layers, inwards and outwards. In addition, a focus on process incorporates an emphasis on time, both in terms of an individual's life course and longer-range historical processes, stretching from the past into the future.

The Complex Health Politics of Sperm

It is because sperm is both biological and social that these tiny cells can provoke such big questions. Here we sketch some of the major complexities that arise when considering the health-related and political aspects of sperm, which include how to understand sperm in relation to sex and gender; how sperm has and has not been incorporated into health and health care; how racialized, gendered, and class-based inequalities intertwine to influence the health politics of sperm; and debates about focusing on sperm in the context of contemporary reproductive politics in the United States. The reader will find each of these core themes, along with many others, refracted through the various essays in this volume.

Sperm in Relation to Sex and Gender

This book began as a book about male reproductive and sexual health. We were interested in bringing together scholars and clinicians working on topics such as male infertility, male contraception, and paternal effects on reproductive outcomes. While it is easy to identify connections between each of these topics, in practice, there are few people working on them, and they typically do not know one another. As a result, we went through the effort of organizing an in-person workshop, where everyone could gather in a single room and attempt to converse across enormously disparate fields, from reproductive biology to literature and anthropology to regulatory law.

But almost as soon as we identified the theme for the workshop—"male reproductive and sexual health"—we became uneasy about the adjective "male." On the one hand, we felt the need to specify *male* because the default adjective in front of terms like infertility, contraception, and reproductive outcomes is usually *female*, even if it is not stated. On the other hand, we were fully aware of the important efforts by gender scholars and advocates for trans and nonbinary people to challenge traditional categories of sex and gender (e.g., Currah 2022; Schilt and Lagos 2017). By "traditional," we refer to the following set of assumptions: that sex is a binary category in which bodies are either female or male, that female bodies have eggs and male bodies have sperm, and that females identify as women and males identify as men. These are cultural beliefs about the human body, and they can be found everywhere from high school textbooks to biomedical research agendas and bathroom architecture.

We reject this set of assumptions, recognizing that there is wide variation in bodily configurations and identities. Human bodies and their genes, chromosomes, gametes, and genitalia do not fit neatly into two categories, and there is no easy congruence between an individual's body and their gender identity, much less their sexual practices, reproductive plans, or beliefs about health. To offer just a few examples of how complex the relationship between sperm, sex, and gender can be, consider a person assigned male at birth who, as an adult, identifies as a man (i.e., a cisgender man) but whose body does not make sperm; a person assigned female at birth who now identifies as a transman whose body never made sperm; or a person assigned male at birth who identifies as nonbinary whose body does make sperm.

It was respect for just how complicated and variable the relation between bodies, gender, reproductivity, and sexuality can be that led us to reframe the workshop (and this book) as being about *sperm*. Our sense was that it was more precise to refer to cells and not have to use the words male or men or even masculinity.[3] Indeed, one goal of this volume is to unsettle assumptions about what sperm is, what kinds of bodies it can be found within, and how people experience it. But the turn to sperm raised questions of its own, including a concern about focusing solely on cells and not the fully formed individuals in which it is found, each with their own lives, hopes, and dreams. Many of the essays grapple with these issues, offering different analytical perspectives on how social processes around sex and gender shape approaches to sperm in a range of settings, from everyday interactions to the clinic.

Incorporating Sperm into Health and Health Care

Even as we work to challenge assumptions about the relationship between sperm, sex, and gender, we are cognizant that both the culture and institutions of the US health care system are still largely organized around the belief that there are two separate sexes. Following decades of activism by women's health advocates, federal agencies like the National Institutes of Health began requiring in the 1990s that women be included in medical research. Today medical students and medical researchers are urged to consider "sex as a biological variable" in *any* studies of vertebrate animals (i.e., animals with a backbone, including humans, reptiles, amphibians, and birds) (NIH 2023). While rooted in a crucial effort to ensure that biomedical research does not focus solely on male bodies and male cells, it also reinforces the notion that there are just two kinds of sexed bodies and that the sex of a body will usually matter for whatever bodily process is being studied (Richardson 2022; Springer, Mager

Stellman, and Jordan-Young 2012). The sociologist Steven Epstein (2007) has dubbed this the "inclusion and difference paradigm." Female bodies are now systematically *included* in medical research, but on the basis of an assumption that their bodies are *different*.

One of the primary ways that female bodies are routinely distinguished from male bodies in health and health care is in terms of their reproductivity. Scholars have documented how biomedical research and clinical practice oriented to reproduction tends to focus on female bodies (e.g., Ginsburg and Rapp 1995; Inhorn et al. 2009), to the extent that "women's health" was long equated with "reproductive health" (Waggoner 2017). Pregnancy, too, is a biological and social process, and cultural beliefs about women as "naturally" oriented to family and children coalesced with scientific hypotheses about the enduring significance of everything they did before, during, and after pregnancy (Richardson 2021; Valdez 2021).

Meanwhile, there has been little attention to male reproductive health. Few research dollars have been devoted to examining how the age and health of male bodies might affect their sperm and, in turn, their children's health. There are usually not warnings on medications or cigarettes about their potential effects on male fertility. Clinicians do not routinely inquire about the reproductive plans of their male patients, and public health officials do not urge men to take care of themselves for the sake of their future children. As Almeling argues in her book *GUYnecology: The Missing Science of Men's Reproductive Health* (2020), this *in*attention is rooted in a binary approach to the human body: a focus on the reproductive health of female bodies has been accompanied by an assumption that the health of male bodies, and sperm in particular, does not matter for reproductive outcomes.

Now, more and more research points to the significance of paternal age, smoking, and other toxic exposures for male fertility and children's health (for a review, see Kimmins et al. 2023). Simultaneously, there are renewed and intensifying efforts to develop new contraceptive technologies that work in and on male bodies, not just the elusive "male pill" but a wide range of creative approaches to stopping sperm without permanently altering a man's fertility (Male Contraceptive Initiative 2024). And, acknowledging how patriarchal dynamics can stymie women's access to reproductive and sexual health services around the world, global health officials are working to incorporate messaging about "men as partners" into their metrics and initiatives (e.g., ICRW and Promundo 2017; Adamou et al. 2017; Wegner et al. 1998). Each of these developments has contributed to calls to more fully incorporate sperm, male bodies, and men into the conceptualization and provision of reproductive and sexual health.

Yet, the question of just how to do so does not have a clear answer. Given the cultural associations of reproductive health with female bodies, it will take a great deal of effort across many sectors—everything from high school sex education and medical curricula to corporate boardrooms and newsrooms—to create more knowledge about sperm, to develop clinical approaches to sperm-related problems, and more generally to improve awareness of the relationship between sperm and health. Many of the think pieces in this collection take up these challenges and offer potential approaches for where, when, and how to more fully integrate sperm into health and health care in the United States.

Sperm in the Context of Intersecting Inequalities

Thus far, we have concentrated on issues related to sex and gender, but a full analysis of sperm, health, and politics requires that we grapple with the myriad ways that social processes around gender intersect with massive economic and racialized inequalities in this country. The United States is one of the wealthiest countries in the world (World Bank 2022), and yet half a million people live on the street (Henry et al. 2021), one out of every seven children resides in a home where there is not enough food to eat (Coleman-Jensen et al. 2020, 5), and tens of millions cannot get medical care when they need it, often due to cost (HHS, n.d.). Within each of these terrible social facts, there is racialized disparity. Indeed, systemic racism and racialized discrimination remain as virulent as ever, producing clear effects in outcomes across health, education, occupation, housing, and incarceration (for reviews on each topic, respectively, see Cloud et al. 2023; Domina, Penner, and Penner 2017; Pager and Shepherd 2008; Williams, Lawrence, and Davis 2019).

So when considering how sperm relates to conceptualizations of sex and gender, we must also think about the social processes through which bodies are categorized not only as male and female but also "Black," "White," "Asian," and so on. And although biological categories of race have been thoroughly debunked (e.g. Duster 2003; Roberts 2011), the lifelong effects of living in a racist society can have measurable health effects—physical, mental, and societal—that contribute to racialized health inequalities (e.g., Homan, Brown, and King 2021; Krieger 2005). When considering how to incorporate sperm into health and health care, we have to address the social determinants of health that are far beyond any one individual's control (Healthy People 2023), the huge disparities in access to health care providers, and the racialized differences in quality of care once people make it to the clinic (Fiscella and Sanders 2016; Smedley, Stith, and Nelson 2003).

None of these are small problems, and the list does not stop there. One of our concerns about fostering connections between "sperm" and "health" is the well-documented tendency of health- and medicine-focused approaches to concentrate attention at the level of the individual, to make the health of any one body a matter of individual choices rather than attending to how it is also a product of historical, structural, and cultural processes (think back to the nested dolls). This is perhaps especially relevant in the United States, where a cultural belief in individualism runs deep and is one reason we have a weaker social safety net than most high-income countries (Valente 2019). Making health a matter of individual responsibility is often associated with a tendency to blame and stigmatize those who cannot achieve health, and sometimes even to surveil and punish, especially those who are already marginalized (e.g., Mitchell et al. 2021). In a country where racism and poverty preclude a significant proportion of the population from accessing basic resources—housing, food, clean water, health care—we must proceed very cautiously in pairing sperm and health.

Sperm in the Context of Contemporary Reproductive Politics

We assembled these essays during an especially fraught period for reproductive politics in the United States. After forty years of a federally protected right to abortion, the Supreme Court overturned *Roe v. Wade* in the summer of 2022. It is certainly true that the *right* to abortion did not guarantee *access* to abortion, especially for those with limited ability to pay for this out-of-pocket procedure or in states where there were few providers (Cohen and Joffe 2020). But the court's decision did radically reshape American law, and there is no question about just how dire the current landscape is: thirteen states and counting have banned abortion (Alan Guttmacher Institute 2024), creating enormous hardship for anyone who is pregnant and does not want to be, as well as their families, friends, and clinicians (Foster 2021). Additionally, with new assaults on access to contraception, gender-affirming care, and in vitro fertilization, clinicians are encountering numerous challenges in following basic standards of care as they navigate constantly fluctuating laws and regulations.

As a result, any effort to link sperm and politics must also contend with the enormous threats to individual rights to pursue and avoid pregnancy. We stand with every advocate and scholar working toward a vision of reproductive justice, which underscores the significance of bodily autonomy in people's decisions *not to have* children as well as their decisions *to have* children and *to parent* their children in a safe environment (Luna and Luker 2013; Ross and Solinger 2017). This framework was initially developed in the 1990s by organizations led by women of color, such as SisterSong, and it has been crucial in broadening the goals of reproductive advocacy from a focus on contraception and abortion to a wider range of related issues, such as forced and coercive sterilization (Roberts 1997; Sariego 2025), the effects of mass incarceration on health and family life (Wildeman and Wang 2017), and the abrogation of parental rights by the child welfare system (Reich 2005; Roberts 2022), all of which disproportionately affect poor individuals and people of color.

Like reproductive health, reproductive rights and reproductive justice have largely been conceptualized with women in mind, with the goal of ensuring bodily autonomy before, during, and after pregnancy. Let us be clear: we consider these rights to be completely sacrosanct. We have no patience for the Supreme Court or state legislatures or men's rights groups or any others who seek to exert power over the reproductive decision-making of women and people who can become pregnant. In raising the question of how to think about the relationship between sperm and reproductive politics, we aim for an expansive approach to considering the various possibilities of what reproductive justice might be for those who produce sperm, but always with a firm limit in place that ensures the bodily autonomy of pregnancy-capable people.

Overview of the Book

This volume encompasses a range of insightful—and often provocative—discussions of these and many other complexities at the nexus of sperm, health, and politics, with a focus on the United States. Think pieces by experts from various scholarly disciplines and medical specialties tackle crucial questions about the prospect of attending to "male" reproductive and sexual health in the context of enormous social and political changes in this country. Our interdisciplinary approach is rooted in an understanding of sperm as both fundamentally biological and fundamentally social, and we have grouped the essays into six sections. Each essay stands on its own, even as they are in conversation across the breadth of the volume. Readers are welcome to read from first to last or skip around based on their interests.

The set of think pieces in part 1 examines the possibilities for *incorporating sperm* into conceptualizations of health and gender, the American health care system, and reproductive politics, all while avoiding pitfalls such as reifying masculinity or further entrenching intersecting inequalities. Part 2 takes up long-standing debates about *counting sperm* and male fertility, offering a range of perspectives about its relation to reproduction, medicine, markets, and the environment. Essays in part 3 contemplate *making sperm* in ways that are both bodily and cultural, analyzing how states, medical guidelines, gendered and racialized identities, and emerging technologies come together to constitute these cells. Part 4 focuses on the social and technological processes of *stopping sperm*, with several essays on different forms of male contraception and one about how sperm is managed in Catholic medical facilities. Efforts in *regulating sperm* have primarily concentrated on sperm donation and sperm banks, and each think piece in part 5 examines a different facet of these policies, with several focused on donor anonymity and the implications of the Supreme Court's decision in *Dobbs v. Jackson Women's Health Organization*. Part 6, on *embodying sperm*, could have contained an infinite number of essays, given all the variation in how sperm is embodied and experienced. It offers a sampling of perspectives, from those of cis men grappling with infertility to approaches centering queer and trans individuals.

In assembling this seminal set of essays, we hope to inspire new thinking and new approaches to sperm, health, and politics. While no edited volume can be fully comprehensive, our intent is for the think pieces to be of use to:

- social scientific and humanistic scholars who research and teach courses in areas related to gender, race, sexuality, health, medicine, bodies, and reproduction;
- biomedical researchers focused on various aspects of human reproduction, infertility and fertility, contraceptive technologies, abortion, and medically assisted reproduction;
- clinicians in obstetrics and gynecology, urology, adolescent medicine, andrology, sexual health, endocrinology, pediatrics, internal medicine, and preventive medicine;
- public health advocates and policymakers who work on issues related to reproductive and sexual health; and
- students and members of the general public who want to learn more about any and all of these issues.

Keeping in mind the range of audiences we hope to reach and noting variation in how different fields use terminology, we have asked each author to be clear with their language, whether field-specific jargon or terms related to gender (such as male, men, cis men, etc.). We did not attempt to standardize the use of such terms across the essays but have made every effort to ensure that the text reflects our aims of being accessible and inclusive.

Ultimately, our goal with this volume is to contribute to a more reproductively just society by generating novel interdisciplinary approaches to improving the reproductive and sexual health of *all* people.

NOTES

1 Results of Google searches for "sperm" conducted on June 1, 2023, and November 22, 2023.
2 *Merriam-Webster.com Dictionary*, s.v. "sperm," accessed December 5, 2024, https://www.merriam-webster.com/dictionary/sperm.

3 On masculinity and health, see, e.g., Rosenfeld and Faircloth 2006; Wentzell 2013; White et al. 2023.

REFERENCES

Adamou, Bridgit, Brittany S. Iskarpatyoti, Chris B. O. Agala, and Carolina Mejia. 2017. *Male Engagement in Family Planning: Gaps in Monitoring and Evaluation.* Chapel Hill: Measure Evaluation and US Agency for International Development.

Alan Guttmacher Institute. 2024. "State Policies on Abortion." July 29, 2024. https://www.guttmacher.org/state-policy/explore/state-policies-later-abortions.

Almeling, Rene. 2011. *Sex Cells: The Medical Market for Eggs and Sperm.* Berkeley: University of California Press.

Almeling, Rene. 2015. "Reproduction." *Annual Review of Sociology* 41 (1): 423–42. https://doi.org/10.1146/annurev-soc-073014-112258.

Almeling, Rene. 2020. *GUYnecology: The Missing Science of Men's Reproductive Health.* Oakland: University of California Press.

Boulicault, Marion, Meg Perret, Jonathon Galka, Alex Borsa, Annika Gompers, Meredith Reiches, and Sarah Richardson. 2022. "The Future of Sperm: A Biovariability Framework for Understanding Global Sperm Count Trends." *Human Fertility* 25 (5): 888–902. https://doi.org/10.1080/14647273.2021.1917778.

Campo-Engelstein, Lisa, Suzanne Kaufman, and Wendy M. Parker. 2019. "Where Is the Pill for the 'Reproductive Man?': A Content Analysis of Contemporary US Newspaper Articles." *Men and Masculinities* 22 (2): 360–79. https://doi.org/10.1177/1097184X17707990.

Cloud, David H., Ilana R. Garcia-Grossman, Andrea Armstrong, and Brie Williams. 2023. "Public Health and Prisons: Priorities in the Age of Mass Incarceration." *Annual Review of Public Health* 44 (1): 407–28. https://doi.org/10.1146/annurev-publhealth-071521-034016.

Cohen, David S., and Carole Joffe. 2020. *Obstacle Course: The Everyday Struggle to Get an Abortion in America.* Berkeley: University of California Press.

Coleman-Jensen, Alisha, Matthew P. Rabbitt, Christian A. Gregory, and Anita Singh. 2020. "Statistical Supplement to Household Food Security in the United States in 2019." Economic Research Service, US Department of Agriculture, September 2020. www.ers.usda.gov.

Collins, Patricia Hill. 2015. "Intersectionality's Definitional Dilemmas." *Annual Review of Sociology* 41 (1): 1–20. https://doi.org/10.1146/annurev-soc-073014-112142.

Currah, Paisely. 2022. *Sex Is as Sex Does: Governing Transgender Identity.* New York: New York University Press.

Daniels, Cynthia. 2006. *Exposing Men: The Science and Politics of Male Reproduction.* New York: Oxford University Press.

Domina, Thurston, Andrew Penner, and Emily Penner. 2017. "Categorical Inequality: Schools as Sorting Machines." *Annual Review of Sociology* 43 (1): 311–30. https://doi.org/10.1146/annurev-soc-060116-053354.

Duster, Troy. 2003. *Backdoor to Eugenics*. 2nd ed. New York: Routledge.
Epstein, Steven. 2007. *Inclusion: The Politics of Difference in Medical Research*. Chicago: University of Chicago Press.
Epstein, Steven. 2022. *The Quest for Sexual Health: How an Elusive Ideal has Transformed Science, Politics, and Everyday Life*. Chicago: University of Chicago Press.
Fausto-Sterling, Anne. 2000. *Sexing the Body: Gender Politics and the Construction of the Body*. New York: Basic Books.
Fiscella, Kevin, and Mechelle R. Sanders. 2016. "Racial and Ethnic Disparities in the Quality of Health Care." *Annual Review of Public Health* 37 (1): 375–94. https://doi.org/10.1146/annurev-publhealth-032315-021439.
Foster, Diana Greene. 2021. *The Turnaway Study: The Cost of Denying Women Access to Abortion*. New York: Scribner.
Foucault, Michel. 1980. *The History of Sexuality*. New York: Vintage Books.
Ginsburg, Faye, and Rayna Rapp. 1995. *Conceiving the New World Order: The Global Politics of Reproduction*. Berkeley: University of California Press.
Glenn, Evelyn Nakano. 1999. "The Social Construction and Institutionalization of Gender and Race: An Integrative Framework." In *Revisioning Gender*, edited by Myra Marx Ferree, Judith Lorber, and Beth Hess. Thousand Oaks, CA: SAGE.
Health and Human Services (HHS). n.d. "Health Care Access and Quality." Healthy People 2030, US Department of Health and Human Services. Accessed August 2023. https://health.gov.
Healthy People. 2023. "Social Determinants of Health." Healthy People 2030, US Department of Health and Human Services. Accessed August 2023. https://health.gov.
Henry, Meghan, Tanya de Sousa, Caroline Roddey, Swati Gayen, and Thomas Joe Bednar. 2021. *2020 Annual Homeless Assessment Report*. N.p.: US Department of Housing and Urban Development.
Homan, Patricia, Tyson H. Brown, and Brittany King. 2021. "Structural Intersectionality as a New Direction for Health Disparities Research." *Journal of Health and Social Behavior* 62 (3): 350–70. https://doi.org/10.1177/00221465211032947.
Inhorn, Marcia, Tine Tjornhoj-Thomsen, Helene Goldberg, and Maruska la Cour Mosegaard, eds. 2009. *Reconceiving the Second Sex: Men, Masculinity, and Reproduction*. New York: Berghahn Books.
Smedley, Brian D., Adrienne Y. Stith, and Alan R. Nelson, eds. 2003. *Unequal Treatment: Confronting Racial and Ethnic Disparities in Health Care*. Institute of Medicine. Washington, DC: National Academies Press.
International Center for Research on Women (ICRW) and Promundo 2017. *Engaging Men and Boys to Achieve Gender Equality: How can we build on what we have learned?* Washington, DC: International Center for Research on Women and Instituto Promundo. https://www.icrw.org.
Kasman, Alex M., Francesco Del Giudice, and Michael L. Eisenberg. 2020. "New Insights to Guide Patient Care: The Bidirectional Relationship Between Male Infertility and Male Health." *Fertility and Sterility* 113 (3): 469–77. https://doi.org/10.1016/j.fertnstert.2020.01.002.

Kimmins, Sarah, Richard A. Anderson, Christopher L. R. Barratt, Hermann M. Behre, Sarah R. Catford, Christopher J. De Jonge, Geraldine Delbes et al. 2023. "Frequency, Morbidity and Equity: The Case for Increased Research on Male Fertility." *Nature Reviews Urology* 21 (2): 102–24. https://doi.org/10.1038/s41585-023-00820-4.

Krieger, Nancy. 2005. "Stormy Weather: Race, Gene Expression, and the Science of Health Disparities." *American Journal of Public Health* 95 (12): 2155–60.

Levine, Hagai, Niels Jørgensen, Anderson Martino-Andrade, Jamie Mendiola, Dan Weksler-Derri, Irina Mindlis, Rachel Pinotti, and Shanna H. Swan. 2017. "Temporal Trends in Sperm Count: A Systematic Review and Meta-regression Analysis." *Human Reproduction Update* 23 (6): 646–59. https://doi.org/10.1093/humupd/dmx022.

Levine, Hagai, Niels Jørgensen, Anderson Martino-Andrade, Jaime Mendiola, Dan Weksler-Derri, Maya Jolles, Rachel Pinotti, and Shanna H Swan. 2023. "Temporal Trends in Sperm Count: A Systematic Review and Meta-regression Analysis of Samples Collected Globally in the 20th and 21st Centuries." *Human Reproduction Update* 29 (2): 157–76. https://doi.org/10.1093/humupd/dmac035.

Luna, Zakiya, and Kristin Luker. 2013. "Reproductive Justice." *Annual Review of Law and Social Science* 9:327–52. https://doi.org/10.1146/annurev-lawsocsci-102612-134037.

Male Contraceptive Initiative. 2024. "What is in Development." www.malecontraceptive.org.

Mamo, Laura. 2007. *Queering Reproduction: Achieving Pregnancy in the Age of Technoscience*. Durham, NC: Duke University Press.

Martin, Emily. 1991. "The Egg and the Sperm: How Science Has Constructed a Romance Based on Stereotypical Male-Female Roles." *Signs* 16:485–501.

Mitchell, Uchechi A., Akemi Nishida, Faith E. Fletcher, and Yamilé Molina. 2021. "The Long Arm of Oppression: How Structural Stigma against Marginalized Communities Perpetuates Within-Group Health Disparities." *Health Education & Behavior* 48 (3): 342–51. https://doi.org/10.1177/10901981211011927.

Mohr, Sebastian. 2018. *Being a Sperm Donor: Masculinity, Sexuality, and Biosociality in Denmark*. New York: Berghahn Books.

Moore, Lisa Jean. 2007. *Sperm Counts: Overcome by Man's Most Precious Fluid*. New York: New York University Press.

Nguyen, Brian T., and Tamar L. Jacobsohn. 2023. "Men's Willingness to Use Novel Male Contraception is Linked to Gender-Equitable Attitudes: Results from an Exploratory Online Survey." *Contraception* 123:110001. https://doi.org/10.1016/j.contraception.2023.110001.

National Institutes of Health (NIH). 2023. "NIH Policy on Sex as a Biological Variable." https://orwh.od.nih.gov.

Oudshoorn, Nelly. 2003. *The Male Pill: A Biography of a Technology in the Making*. Durham, NC: Duke University Press.

Pager, Devah, and Hana Shepherd. 2008. "The Sociology of Discrimination: Racial Discrimination in Employment, Housing, Credit, and Consumer Markets." *Annual Review of Sociology* 34:181–209.

Reich, Jennifer. 2005. *Fixing Families: Parents, Power, and the Child Welfare System.* New York: Routledge.

Richardson, Sarah. 2021. *The Maternal Imprint.* Chicago: University of Chicago Press.

Richardson, Sarah. 2022. "Sex Contextualism." *Philosophy, Theory, and Practice in Biology* 14 (2). https://doi.org/10.3998/ptpbio.2096.

Roberts, Dorothy. 1997. *Killing the Black Body: Race, Reproduction and the Meaning of Liberty.* New York: Pantheon.

Roberts, Dorothy. 2011. *Fatal Invention: How Science, Politics, and Big Business Recreate Race in the Twenty-first Century.* New York: New Press.

Roberts, Dorothy. 2022. *Torn Apart: How the Child Welfare System Destroys Black Families—and How Abolition Can Build a Safer World.* New York: Basic Books.

Rosenfeld, Dana, and Christopher Faircloth, eds. 2006. *Medicalized Masculinities.* Philadelphia: Temple University Press.

Ross, Loretta, and Rickie Solinger. 2017. *Reproductive Justice: An Introduction.* Berkeley: University of California Press.

Sariego, Carlo. 2025. "Birth Rights and Wrongs: Reproductive Outsiders in Azar v. Garza (2018) and Madrigal v. Quilligan (1978)." *Signs: Journal of Women in Culture and Society* 50 (2): 343–368.

Schilt, Kristen, and Danya Lagos. 2017. "The Development of Transgender Studies in Sociology." *Annual Review of Sociology* 43 (1): 425–43. https://doi.org/10.1146/annurev-soc-060116-053348.

Springer, Kristen W., Jeanne Mager Stellman, and Rebecca M. Jordan-Young. 2012. "Beyond a Catalogue of Differences: A Theoretical Frame and Good Practice Guidelines for Researching Sex/Gender in Human Health." *Social Science & Medicine* 74 (11): 1817–24. https://doi.org/10.1016/j.socscimed.2011.05.033.

Thompson, Charis. 2005. *Making Parents: The Ontological Choreography of Reproductive Technologies.* Cambridge, MA: MIT Press.

Tober, Diane. 2018. *Romancing the Sperm: Shifting Biopolitics and the Making of Modern Families.* New Brunswick, NJ: Rutgers University Press.

Valdez, Natali. 2021. *Weighing the Future: Race, Science, and Pregnancy Trials in the Postgenomic Era.* Oakland: University of California Press.

Valente, Samantha. 2019. "Safety Nets: An International Comparison." *New Labor Forum* 28 (2): 44–50. https://doi.org/10.1177/1095796019838824.

Waggoner, Miranda. 2017. *The Zero Trimester: Pre-Pregnancy Care and the Politics of Reproductive Risk.* Oakland: University of California Press.

Wahlberg, Ayo. 2018. *Good Quality: The Routinization of Sperm Banking in China.* Berkeley: University of California Press.

Wegner, Mary Nell, Evelyn Landry, David Wilkinson, and Joanne Tzanis. 1998. "Men as Partners in Reproductive Health: From Issues to Action." *International Family Planning Perspectives* 24 (1): 38–42. https://doi.org/10.2307/2991918.

Wentzell, Emily A. 2013. *Maturing Masculinities: Aging, Chronic Illness, and Viagra in Mexico.* Durham, NC: Duke University Press.

White, Alan, Raewyn Connell, Derek M. Griffith, and Peter Baker. 2023. "Defining 'Men's Health': Towards a More Inclusive Definition." *International Journal of Men's Social and Community Health* 6 (1): e1–9. https://doi.org/10.22374/ijmsch.v6i1.100.

Wildeman, Christopher, and Emily A. Wang. 2017. "Mass Incarceration, Public Health, and Widening Inequality in the USA." *The Lancet* 389 (10077): 1,464–74. https://doi.org/10.1016/s0140-6736(17)30259-3.

Williams, David R., Jourdyn A. Lawrence, and Brigette A. Davis. 2019. "Racism and Health: Evidence and Needed Research." *Annual Review of Public Health* 40 (1): 105–25. https://doi.org/10.1146/annurev-publhealth-040218-043750.

World Bank. 2022. "DataBank: Nominal GDP and Per Capita GDP." World Bank. Accessed August 2022.

PART I

Incorporating Sperm

1

An Ob-Gyn Reflects on How to Incorporate Sperm into Health and Politics

BRIAN T. NGUYEN

As a male obstetrician-gynecologist at a university-affiliated, safety net hospital and tertiary referral center, I provide high-level, evidence-based health care aimed at optimizing the health of a primarily low-income, marginalized population of female patients. Caring for female patients, however, has also given me the opportunity to see how gendered inequalities structure their reproductive lives and how gender influences the problems and pathologies they face.

In any given week, I will tell a patient that her pregnancy is failing, abnormal, or even life-threatening. These patients will commonly need surgery, the blood loss from which can rival those encountered in trauma fields. I will diagnose young patients with sexually transmitted infections that may prevent them from ever becoming pregnant. I will diagnose pregnancies in patients who had never wanted to have sex. I will perform routine cervical cancer screenings that are awkward and invasive. I will recommend contraceptive methods that prioritize the prevention of pregnancy over the prevention of pain.

I never anticipated that my weeks would be consumed with managing so much of my patient's anxiety, anguish, and anger. I never knew that being female, or having a uterus, could be the primary cause of these feelings. These are episodes that women commonly experience alone even if they are in relationships with men, and in some cases, these episodes may be perpetrated by male partners. Even if men or male partners are made aware of these painful experiences, their awareness is sometimes abstract at best, shaped by a society that has never considered these to be anything other than "women's issues."

People who cannot become pregnant may be unable to grasp the full extent of the physical and socioeconomic burdens of pregnancy. Indeed, this has been the case with many male policymakers who have centered the fetus over the female patient, turning something deeply personal into something political. With *Dobbs v. Jackson Women's Health Organization*, the Supreme Court of the United States overturned federal protections for abortion based on subjective interpretations of the Constitution rather than the lived experiences of women nationwide. This decision set forth a series of state-wide abortion restrictions across the United States, enacted primarily by privileged white men seated within the safety and security of state legislatures. However, the political entanglement of sexual and reproductive health can be attributed not to these men alone, but rather to the concatenation of pervasive gendered social inequalities and a health care system that creates gendered silos for sexual and reproductive health.

As an obstetrician-gynecologist, I am an expert in sex and reproduction. While a large proportion of both women's and men's lives frequently entails the pursuit of recreational and procreative sex and the prevention of unwanted pregnancy as heterosexual couples, my patients are limited to females. Even if they might benefit from sexual and reproductive health services, their male partners do not have access to my expertise. Moreover, there are no clinicians to whom I can refer male partners with certainty that they will receive the same level of comprehensive care. Primary care physicians are the mainstay of preventive health care for men in the United States, yet they rarely provide preconception and contraceptive counseling. Urologists and andrologists are specialists who manage more acute conditions (e.g., erectile dysfunction, kidney stones, cancer) and who primarily provide office procedures and surgeries. For men wanting to better understand their behavioral and genetic contributions to pregnancy outcomes, or for those seeking contraceptives to prevent an unwanted pregnancy, options remain exceedingly limited and underexplored by both science and industry.

The lack of experts in male sexual and reproductive health compounds early lessons that many men hear in school and from the media that they have little to contribute or act on with respect to sexual and reproductive health. Early on in their education, when young men are separated from young women and receive separate, gender-specific sex education, they are indirectly and incorrectly taught that they do not need to understand women's bodies and women's experiences of menses, contraception, and pregnancy.

Gender equity is not possible unless the field of sexual and reproductive health expands to include research and interventions aimed at cis men and male bodies to the same degree that they have addressed cis women and female bodies. As an obstetrician-gynecologist, I recognized that the numerous facets of sexual and reproductive health that we routinely discussed with our female patients could be relevant to men and their male partners. To that end, I developed the EMERGE Lab as a thinktank aimed at producing research that reexamines the relevance of traditionally "female" sexual and reproductive health screenings and services to men and reimagines a role for men's inclusion in ways that improve sexual and reproductive health for all. EMERGE stands for Expanding Male Engagement in Reproductive and Gender Equity and is guided by a framework that systematically characterizes the range of sexual and reproductive health relevant to men based upon the sexual and reproductive health-related care already being offered to women (see figure 1.1). In contrast to currently held notions of men's sexual and reproductive health, which revolve around sexual dysfunction and prostate and testicular cancers, the EMERGE framework expands the scope significantly. Figure 1.1 offers several examples of gendered issues in sexual and reproductive health.

Sexually Transmitted Infections

Despite the availability and accessibility of methods for both treating and preventing sexually transmitted infections, rates in the United States continue to rise. Condoms are underused by men in new sexual relationships (Nguyen and Violette 2022), yet the United States Preventive Services Task Force has not made any recommendations for the screening of young men for gonorrhea and chlamydia. Meanwhile, they recommend that women under the age of twenty-four years have annual screening (Davidson et al. 2021). The lack of recommendation is related

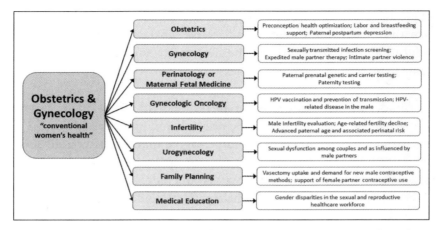

Figure 1.1: The EMERGE (Expanding Male Engagement in Reproductive and Gender Equity) Framework characterizes the range of sexual and reproductive health relevant to men based upon the sexual and reproductive health care already being offered to women. More information is available at https://theEMERGELab.com.

to a lack of resources and research to demonstrate that men carry and transmit sexually transmitted infections.

Human Papillomavirus Vaccination

Human papillomavirus (HPV) vaccination rates among young men continue to trail behind those of young women, despite overwhelming evidence that HPV can cause penile, anal, and oropharyngeal cancers and despite recent changes to the Food and Drug Administration's labeling that recognize the benefit of the vaccine regardless of gender. Given the prevalence of cervical cancer screening in the United States, HPV-related oropharyngeal cancers are expected to become more prevalent than cervical cancers, shifting the disproportionate impact of HPV-related disease to men (Schmeler and Sturgis 2016). This can be prevented, however, via comprehensive campaigns that emphasize the changing burden of disease and the importance of vaccinating young men and male partners. Indeed, HPV vaccine uptake among young men is greatest when they receive messaging that informs them of both how the vaccine prevents male-specific HPV-related illness and how it minimizes HPV transmission, protecting their female partners (Bonafide and Vanable 2015).

Contraception

Contraceptive options for men remain limited to condoms and vasectomies. Despite research dating back to the middle of the twentieth century, there remains no method of hormonal male contraception on the market. Without a method of reversible, medical contraception available for men, pregnancy prevention has almost exclusively become a female burden. Pharmaceutical companies are reluctant to invest in male methods, citing concerns that men would not be interested, forgetting that when condoms were the only method available, that men were both invested in and primarily in control of their use. However, men's views on gender-equitable behavior are changing in ways that prompt greater demand for male contraception and reproductive responsibility (Nguyen and Jacobsohn 2023). With several hormonal male contraceptive methods in active human clinical trials, as well as surveys demonstrating their acceptability even in early stages (Nguyen et al. 2020; Nguyen, Yuen, et al. 2021), our health care system has yet to consider the ideal health care provider to take on the responsibility of providing male contraception to men (Jacobsohn et al. 2022).

Pregnancy and Preconception Care

As pregnancy occurs in female bodies, health care providers appropriately focus on the maternal factors that influence pregnancy outcomes. Men's contributions are of secondary importance, as evidenced by (1) health insurance policies that do not cover paternal genetic testing (Nguyen, Campo-Engelstein, et al. 2023; Nguyen, Mazza, and Nguyen 2023), (2) the lack of programs aimed at assisting with behavioral change at the time of pregnancy, such as smoking cessation and mental health care, which are known to improve maternal and child outcomes, and (3) an increasing attention to the association between men's age, sperm quality, and pregnancy outcomes, independent of the age of their female partner (Nguyen, Chang, and Bendikson 2019). Attention to these issues could influence men to consider their own health as it pertains to reproductive outcomes and the welfare of their families.

Childbirth

Childbirth can be one of the most powerful, life-changing events that an individual can experience. However, the medical system's focus on the birthing person rather than what is often a couple experiencing the birth, or even, in some cases, the system's contempt for male partners, can affect men's engagement in the process and prevent them from stepping into supportive, caretaking roles for their partner and child. Further, when men are denied paid paternity leave or disincentivized to take their full allotment, their female partners assume childcare responsibility by default. This can lead to the further ossification of gender roles over time, such that men lose awareness of the challenges of childcare.

Unplanned Pregnancy and Abortion

Unaware of the dangers of pregnancy and the challenges of childcare, when men become involved in an unintended pregnancy, they may lack the empathy needed to recognize that any decisions about the pregnancy should be those of his female partner. Even for men who are supportive of their partner's abortion, they may also experience feelings of stigma and shame, which are sometimes felt by their female partners (Nguyen et al. 2018). Yet without the same educational framing provided to their female partners by health care providers and their peers, men may not recognize how commonly other men become involved in an abortion and thus how essential these services are. Taken further, men may not realize the importance of their vocal advocacy for abortion until their partner's ability to obtain one is threatened (Haridasani Gupta 2022).

Permanent Contraception

Even though vasectomy is a cheaper, safer, and more effective method of sterilization or permanent contraception than tubal ligation, it remains underutilized. When couples reach their desired family size, the female partner is more likely to undergo surgery, with few couples ever considering vasectomy as an option. Those who want to obtain a vasectomy are disincentivized by federal policies that provide coverage for tubal ligation to the exclusion of vasectomy (Nguyen, Long, et al. 2021). In such a way, men are completely unable to participate in pregnancy planning such that their exclusion and disengagement becomes a social norm.

* * *

It is important to note that these recommendations are not aimed at the diversion of resources already allocated to female sexual and reproductive health, nor are they intended to prioritize the rights of men over those of women. Instead, my goal is to encourage a consideration of how sexual and reproductive health are relevant to and interrelated among *all* individuals. My hope is that this approach will alleviate disproportionate burdens of reproductivity for women, but of course men would benefit in terms of their own health and lives as well.

In sum, the EMERGE framework is a culmination of several years of clinical practice in obstetrics and gynecology, and even more years spent advocating for women's health and reproductive rights. Women's health and reproductive rights cannot be protected without a cultural shift that acknowledges men's sexual and reproductive health-related vulnerabilities and responsibilities.

REFERENCES

Bonafide, Katherine E., and Peter A. Vanable. 2015. "Male Human Papillomavirus Vaccine Acceptance Is Enhanced by a Brief Intervention That Emphasizes Both Male-Specific Vaccine Benefits and Altruistic Motives." *Sexually Transmitted Diseases* 42 (2):76–80. https://doi.org/10.1097/olq.0000000000000226.

Davidson, Karina W., Michael J. Barry, Carol M. Mangione, Michael Cabana, Aaron B. Caughey, Esa M. Davis, Katrina E. Donahue et al. 2021. "Screening for Chlamydia and Gonorrhea: US Preventive Services Task Force Recommendation Statement." *JAMA* 326 (10): 949–56. https://doi.org/10.1001/jama.2021.14081.

Jacobsohn, Tamar, Brian T. Nguyen, Jill E. Brown, Arthi Thirumalai, Michael Massone, Stephanie T. Page, Christina Wang, Jeffrey Kroopnick, and Diana L. Blithe. 2022. "Male Contraception Is Coming: Who Do Men Want to Prescribe Their Birth Control?" *Contraception* 115:44–48. https://doi.org/10.1016/j.contraception.2022.04.014.

Haridasani Gupta, Alisha. 2022. "The Voices of Men Affected by Abortion." *New York Times*, June 25, 2022. www.nytimes.com.

Nguyen, Brian T., Erica J. Chang, and Kristin A. Bendikson. 2019. "Advanced Paternal Age and the Risk of Spontaneous Abortion: An Analysis of the Combined 2011–2013 and 2013–2015 National Survey of Family Growth." *American Journal of Obstetrics and Gynecology* 221 (5): 476.e1–476.e7. https://doi.org/10.1016/j.ajog.2019.05.028.

Nguyen, Brian T., Maritza T. Farrant, Bradley D. Anawalt, Fiona Yuen, Arthi Thirumalai, John K. Amory, Ronald S. Swerdloff et al. 2020. "Acceptability of Oral Dimethandrolone Undecanoate in a 28-Day Placebo-Controlled Trial of a Hormonal Male Contraceptive Prototype." *Contraception* 102 (1): 52–57. https://doi.org/10.1016/j.contraception.2020.04.006.

Nguyen, Brian T., Luciana E. Hebert, Sara L. Newton, and Melissa L. Gilliam. 2018. "Supporting Women at the Time of Abortion: A Mixed-Methods Study of Male Partner Experiences and Perspectives." *Perspectives on Sexual and Reproductive Health* 50 (2): 75–83. https://doi.org/10.1363/psrh.12059.

Nguyen, Brian T., and Tamar L. Jacobsohn. 2023. "Men's Willingness to Use Novel Male Contraception Is Linked to Gender-Equitable Attitudes: Results from an Exploratory Online Survey." *Contraception* 123:110001. https://doi.org/10.1016/j.contraception.2023.110001.

Nguyen, Brian T., Minica Long, Nina Petrosyan, Dayna Grundy, Brisa Mahoney, and Katrina J. Heyrana. 2021. "Access to Male Sexual and Reproductive Health Services in Publicly Funded California Clinics in 2018." *Contraception* 104 (2): 165–69. https://doi.org/10.1016/j.contraception.2021.04.004.

Nguyen, Brian T., and Caroline Violette. 2022. "Condom Use at Coitarche Among Men in Non-Steady Relationships in the United States, 2006–2013." *Journal of Adolescent Health* 70 (1): 127–32. https://doi.org/10.1016/j.jadohealth.2021.06.027.

Nguyen, Brian T., Fiona Yuen, Maritza Farrant, Arthi Thirumalai, Frances Fernando, John K. Amory, Ronald S. Swerdloff et al. 2021. "Acceptability of the Oral Hormonal Male Contraceptive Prototype, 11β-Methyl-19-Nortestosterone Dodecylcarbonate (11β-MNTDC), in a 28-Day Placebo-Controlled Trial." *Contraception* 104 (5): 531–37. https://doi.org/10.1016/j.contraception.2021.06.009.

Nguyen, Michelle T., Lisa Campo-Engelstein, Richard H. Lee, and Brian T. Nguyen. 2023. "An Ethical Argument for Health Insurance Coverage of Paternal Prenatal Genetic Testing." *Obstetrics and Gynecology* 141 (1): 11–14. https://doi.org/10.1097/aog.0000000000005018.

Nguyen, Michelle T., Genevieve Mazza, and Brian T. Nguyen. 2023. "The Completion of Indicated Paternal Prenatal Genetic and Carrier Testing at a Public Hospital in Los Angeles, California." *Genetics in Medicine Open* 1 (1): 100831. https://doi.org/10.1016/j.gimo.2023.100831.

Schmeler, Kathleen M., and Erich M. Sturgis. 2016. "Expanding the Benefits of HPV Vaccination to Boys and Men." *The Lancet* 387 (10030): 1,798–99. https://doi.org/10.1016/s0140-6736(16)30314-2.

2

The Challenges of Focusing on Men without Centering Men in Reproductive Health, Rights, and Justice

JENNIFER A. REICH

How do we understand men as invested in reproductive rights and justice and as having an experience as potentially procreative people within a social landscape that for women is politically fraught, contentious, and even life-threatening? This question has challenged me since I first wrote about men's experiences with abortion about two decades ago (Reich and Brindis 2006; Reich 2008). Recognizing that some men have feelings when a pregnancy they coconceived is terminated, I aimed to walk an analytical tightrope on which I could argue that their experiences deserved examination, even as I did not want to argue that they deserved new legal rights to determine pregnancy outcomes or significant investment in programs for them that might deplete other resources that support women. This research project was also unusual in that several men who volunteered to be interviewed later explained how their partner had not really been pregnant or had, as they understood it, lied and claimed to be pregnant in order to manipulate them. These aspiring research participants had not actually had an experience of pregnancy or abortion, and yet they insisted their experience was the same as other men in my study who had actually coconceived a fetus in a terminated pregnancy.

I did not include these data in the study, but their stories serve as a powerful reminder that while men may have a socially or emotionally significant experience of unintended pregnancy and abortion, they do not have an *embodied* experience. At the same time, their roles as potentially procreative beings who may love and care for women highlight how much they could contribute to efforts to support reproductive health, choice, and justice. In this essay, I examine these tensions as they manifest in contexts ranging from abortion to maternal mortality to preventative care to think through the challenges and possibilities of involving men—by which I mean cisgender and most often heterosexual men—in research and policy on reproduction without placing them at the center of such considerations.

Questions of men's role can feel particularly salient when thinking about abortion, especially when considering the range of legal strategies men have employed during the past several decades to gain control of abortion decisions, even in the face of Supreme Court rulings that clarified the primacy of women's abortion decision over that of her partner's (see *Planned Parenthood of Southeastern Pennsylvania v. Casey* [1992]). Men have sought court orders to prevent legal abortion (Weiss 2022). Men have set up estates for embryos and have sued clinics for wrongful death (Santa Cruz 2022), even when the pregnant woman was a minor (Associated Press 2019). In 2022, New Hampshire saw an unsuccessful bill that would have allowed "a man claiming to be the father of an unborn child to seek an injunction to force a woman to maintain her pregnancy, potentially against her wishes" (*WMUR9-ABC* 2022). Each of these examples provides a reminder of the stakes of offering men meaningful involvement in abortion without allowing them greater control over women's decisions about their bodies. Now that the US Supreme Court has removed constitutional protections to seek an abortion (see *Dobbs v. Jackson Women's Health Organization* 2022), these efforts to erode women's access to abortion are only likely to increase and may become more successful.

However, abortion is not the only topic that gives rise to questions about men's involvement in reproduction. We should also be concerned about the risks facing women who would prefer to terminate a pregnancy but are forced to carry to term. In addition to the health risks of pregnancy itself, women's lives are often worse after giving birth when forced to carry to term. The Turnaway Study, which compared outcomes of women who obtained an abortion with those who were not able to access an abortion they wanted, found that women who had the abortion fared better on multiple dimensions, including having a higher credit score, being able to meet basic needs, and experiencing a reduction in physical violence (Foster 2021). Women denied access to abortion were more likely to be raising children alone and experiencing physical violence from the man involved in the pregnancy.

The stark truth is that for women who cannot access or are blocked from abortion services, pregnancy will likely increase their risk of violence. In fact, the leading cause of pregnancy-associated death in the United States is homicide. Pregnant and postpartum women are more than twice as likely to die by homicide than from either hemorrhage or hypertension-related disorders. In 2020, they were 35 percent more likely to be murdered than were nonpregnant or postpartum women (Wallace 2022). These rates are significantly higher for women of color: Black women face five times the risk of being murdered during or immediately after pregnancy as white women do (Tobin-Tyler 2022). In these ways, the stakes of women's autonomy and men's involvement can be quite literally questions of life or death. We must grapple with the fact that not all male involvement in reproduction and family life is positive.

Questions of how to meaningfully involve men in reproductive health, choice, and justice are also significant in pregnancies where women choose to continue to term. There is evidence that men's involvement in pregnancy may help to improve the health of women and infants. Women with an involved partner have lower rates of infant mortality and may get more support for quitting smoking during pregnancy (Alio et al. 2011; Martin et al. 2007). Having an involved male partner appears to lessen the impact of a women's adverse childhood events on negative birth outcomes (Testa and Jackson 2021).

Although the mechanisms by which men's involvement helps are complicated, the stakes are high. Take the issue of maternal mortality, where American women have the highest maternal mortality rate of any wealthy nation—triple the rate of any other country—with 23.8 deaths per 100,000 live births (Gunja 2022). When looking only at Black maternal mortality, the rate jumps to 55.3 deaths per 100,000 live births. Black women die at two to three times the rate of white women in childbirth (Hill, Artiga, and Ranji 2022), leaving partners, children, families, and communities without them. As the recent documentary *Aftershock* insists, "When a Black mother dies, there is a ripple effect." This film, which focuses on "a growing brotherhood of surviving Black fathers," illustrates in heartbreaking terms men's investment in maternal health, including their profound feelings of grief and loss and increased caregiving responsibilities. Yet, it would be a mistake to singularly focus advocacy and resources on addressing men's trauma and the challenges they face, since preventing women's deaths would ameliorate their struggles (Eiselt and Lee 2022).

The focus on the reproductive health of women and the consequent decentering of men does not require us to ignore men as sexual and reproductive beings. Yet acknowledging men's roles without making them central can lead to challenging conversations and limited successes. Take for example, the recommendations for screenings for sexually transmitted infections. The US Preventative Services Task Force recommends screening for chlamydia and gonorrhea in all sexually active women and pregnant persons but "concludes that the current evidence is insufficient to assess the balance of benefits and harms of screening for chlamydia and gonorrhea in men" (USPSTF 2021). The vaccine against human papillomavirus (HPV), a cause of cervical cancer as well as head, neck, throat, anal, and penile cancers, provides another example of how decentering men may leave women alone to carry the burden of preventative sexual and reproductive health. HPV is nearly ubiquitous; according to the Centers for Disease Control and Prevention, "HPV is so common that almost every sexually active person will get HPV at some point if they don't get vaccinated" (CDC 2022). When the vaccine was first licensed in 2006 in the United States for use in girls and women, Merck, the pharmaceutical company that developed it, aggressively marketed "girl power" in campaigns promising that girls could be "one less" case of cervical cancer (Wailoo et al. 2010).

Merck's campaign and federal approval solely for girls was problematic for several reasons. First, it ignored the demand from gay men who had long asked for more support in preventing HPV-related anal cancers (Mamo and Epstein 2014). Second, it erased boys' and men's roles in sexual health. In 2009, federal agencies changed their recommendations to include boys and men. The rationale was that vaccinating boys and men could help to prevent HPV spread and prevent cancer in women. However, this change did not increase boys' use. That changed in 2020, when the HPV vaccine was again reclassified as key to preventing oropharyngeal cancer, which is more common in men. As the vaccine was redefined as a direct benefit to the men who used it—including boys and men imagined to be exclusively sexually active with women—use went up in a way it had not when the goal was for men to help protect women (Lu et al. 2022; Sherman and Nailer 2018; Lacombe-Duncan, Newman, and Baiden 2018). The history of the HPV vaccine, how it has been marketed, and its uptake reveal just how challenging it can be to engage men as allies in women's reproductive and sexual health. It also leaves open the question of how a future male contraceptive method will be marketed as being in men's self-interest, even as the direct benefits are likely to be most significant for women.

These dynamics are reinforced by policy. The decision to exclude male contraception, including safe and reliable methods like vasectomy, from the contraceptive coverage mandate in the Affordable Care Act is a reminder that reproductive health care is not preventative care for men in the way it is for women and those capable of pregnancy who risk pregnancy-related complications and death. The lack of contraceptive coverage for men implicitly defines pregnancy prevention, just like screening for sexually transmitted infections, as the sole responsibility of women. This is unfortunate, given that many women endure side effects with contraception (Littlejohn 2013), with almost half of women using reversible contraceptive methods discontinuing a method at some point because of dissatisfaction with it (Moreau, Cleland, and Trussell 2007). Covering the costs of contraception incurred by men who want to support women's efforts to avoid pregnancy would in fact be good policy and could underpin a cultural understanding that men who want to advocate for women, even when they seemingly do not directly benefit, should be supported in their efforts to do so.

Women face an increasingly punitive world when it comes to reproduction, which is most harsh for women of color and those from low-income backgrounds. Denial of contraception and abortion, arrest and prosecution for perinatal substance use (Paltrow 2022), threat to child custody for refusing medical care, or blame when babies are born with disabilities (Blum 2007) are all ways that women stand alone in their reproductive lives. Men too are affected by lack of abortion and contraceptive services, may also use illicit substances, and parent children with disabilities—but they typically do not endure the same sanctions, even as they may face exposure to state surveillance, limits on their ability to be involved with their children, and expectations for financial support that often exceed their means. Research on boys and men should engage complex questions of their sexual and procreative possibilities, barriers, and experiences. Yet, researchers must continue to consider how their work fits into a resource-limited, increasingly punitive landscape that women and those capable of carrying pregnancies face. Focusing on men cannot and should not decenter those who inescapably face the greatest responsibility for reproduction, even as men's role in reproduction deserves examination.

REFERENCES

Alio, Amina P., Alfred K. Mbah, Jennifer L. Kornosky, Deanna Wathington, Phillip J. Marty, and Hamisu M. Salihu. 2011. "Assessing the Impact of Paternal Involvement on Racial/Ethnic Disparities in Infant Mortality Rates." *Journal of Community Health* 36 (1): 63–68. https://doi.org/10.1007/s10900-010-9280-3.

Associated Press. 2019. "Man Sues Abortion Clinic after Teenage Girlfriend Terminates Pregnancy." *KRCA3*, March 8, 2019. https://www.kcra.com.

Blum, Linda. 2007. "Mother-Blame in the Prozac Nation: Raising Kids with Invisible Disabilities." *Gender & Society* 21 (2): 202–26.

Centers for Disease Control and Prevention (CDC). 2022. "Genital HPV Infection—Basic Fact Sheet." Centers for Disease Control and Prevention. Last modified April 22, 2022. https://www.cdc.gov.

Eiselt, Paula, and Tonya Lewis Lee, dirs. 2022. *Aftershock*. Produced by Paula Eiselt and Tonya Lewis Lee, released January 23, 2022.

Foster, Diana Greene. 2021. *The Turnaway Study: Ten Years, A Thousand Women, and the Consequences of Having—or Being Denied—an Abortion*. New York: Scribner.

Gunja, Munira Z. 2022. "Health and Health Care for Women of Reproductive Age." *Commonwealth Fund*, April 5, 2022.

Hill, Latoya, Samantha Artiga, and Usha Ranji. 2022. "Racial Disparities in Maternal and Infant Health: Current Status and Efforts to Address Them." *Kaiser Family Foundation*, November 1, 2022. www.kff.org.

Lacombe-Duncan, Ashley, Peter A. Newman, and Philip Baiden. 2018. "Human Papillomavirus Vaccine Acceptability and Decision-Making among Adolescent Boys and Parents: A Meta-ethnography of Qualitative Studies." *Vaccine* 36 (19): 2,545–58. https://doi.org/10.1016/j.vaccine.2018.02.079.

Littlejohn, Krystale E. 2013. "'It's Those Pills That Are Ruining Me': Gender and the Social Meanings of Hormonal Contraceptive Side Effects." *Gender & Society* 27 (6): 843–63. https://doi.org/10.1177/0891243213504033.

Lu, Peng-Jun, David Yankey, Benjamin Fredua, Mei-Chun Hung, Natalie Sterrett, Lauri E. Markowitz, and Laurie D. Elam-Evans. 2022. "Human Papillomavirus Vaccination Trends Among Adolescents: 2015 to 2020." *Pediatrics* 150 (1). https://doi.org/10.1542/peds.2022-056597.

Mamo, Laura, and Steven Epstein. 2014. "The Pharmaceuticalization of Sexual Risk: Vaccine Development and the New Politics of Cancer Prevention." *Social Science & Medicine* 101:155–65.
Martin, Laurie T., Michelle J. McNamara, Alyssa S. Milot, Tamara Halle, and Elizabeth C. Hair. 2007. "The Effects of Father Involvement during Pregnancy on Receipt of Prenatal Care and Maternal Smoking." *Maternal Child Health Journal* 11 (6): 595–602. https://doi.org/10.1007/s10995-007-0209-0.
Moreau, Caroline, Kelly Cleland, and James Trussell. 2007. "Contraceptive Discontinuation Attributed to Method Dissatisfaction in the United States." *Contraception* 76 (4): 267–72.
Paltrow, Lynn M. 2022. "*Roe v Wade* and the new Jane Crow: Reproductive Rights in the Age of Mass Incarceration." *American Journal of Public Health* 112 (9): 1313–17.
Reich, Jennifer A. 2008. "Not Ready to Fill His Father's Shoes: A Masculinist Discourse of Abortion." *Men and Masculinities* 11 (1): 3–21.
Reich, Jennifer, and Claire Brindis. 2006. "Conceiving Risk and Responsibility: A Qualitative Examination of Men's Experiences of Unintended Pregnancy and Abortion." *International Journal of Men's Health* 5 (2): 133–52.
Santa Cruz, Nicole. 2022. "Her Ex-Husband Is Suing a Clinic Over the Abortion She Had Four Years Ago." *ProPublica*, July 15, 2022. www.propublica.org.
Sherman, Susan Mary, and Emma Nailer. 2018. "Attitudes Towards and Knowledge about Human Papillomavirus (HPV) and the HPV Vaccination in Parents of Teenage Boys in the UK." *PLOS ONE* 13 (4): e0195801.
Testa, Alexander, and Dylan B. Jackson. 2021. "Maternal Adverse Childhood Experiences, Paternal Involvement, and Infant Health." *Journal of Pediatrics* 236:157–163.e1. https://doi.org/10.1016/j.jpeds.2021.04.031.
Tobin-Tyler, Elizabeth. 2022. "A Grim New Reality—Intimate-Partner Violence after Dobbs and Bruen." *New England Journal of Medicine* 387 (14): 1247–49. https://doi.org/10.1056/nejmp2209696.
United States Preventative Services Task Force (USPSTF). 2021. "Final Recommendation Statement: Chlamydia and Gonorrhea: Screening." Last modified September 7, 2021. www.uspreventiveservicestaskforce.org.
Wailoo, Keith, Julie Livingston, Steven Epstein, and Robert Aronowitz, eds. 2010. *Three Shots at Prevention: The HPV Vaccine and the Politics of Medicine's Simple Solutions*. Baltimore, MD: Johns Hopkins University Press.
Wallace, Maeve E. 2022. "Trends in Pregnancy-Associated Homicide, United States, 2020." *American Journal of Public Health* 112 (9): 1333–36. https://doi.org/10.2105/ajph.2022.306937.
Weiss, David. 2022. "Man Sues to Stop Ex-girlfriend from Having Abortion Plains Township Man Wins an Injunction to Halt Procedure Until a Judge Can Decide." *Times Leader*, July 30, 2022. www.timesleader.com.
WMUR9-ABC. 2022. "New Hampshire House Bill Would Allow Men to Sue, Prevent Women Seeking Abortion." February 9, 2022. www.wmur.com.

3

A Preventive Care Approach to Meeting Male Adolescents' Sexual and Reproductive Health Care Needs

ARIK V. MARCELL

Sexual and reproductive health (SRH) is defined as "a state of physical, mental and social well-being and not merely absence of disease, dysfunction or infirmity in all matters relating to the reproductive system and to its functions and processes" (UN 1994; WHO 2006). This definition is holistic and comprehensive, underscoring that males along with females "have the right to be informed and access safe, effective, affordable, and acceptable family planning methods of choice and appropriate healthcare services" (UN 1994).

Contemporary preventive care guidelines recommend that primary care providers deliver sexual and reproductive health care to all young males aged twelve and older (Gavin et al. 2014; Hagan et al. 2017), including services to prevent sexually transmitted infections, HIV, unintended pregnancy, and reproductive-related cancers. Primary care providers are also tasked with promoting reproductive life plans, preconception care, and healthy sexual development and relationships and reducing sexual problems and infertility (Marcell et al. 2015). Yet, young males receive comparatively less comprehensive sex education than their female counterparts and are rarely asked about and counseled on sexual behavior as part of clinical care (Alexander et al. 2016; Alexander et al. 2014; Lafferty et al. 2002; Lafferty et al. 2001). *Why do we continue to fail to meet male adolescents' sexual and reproductive health education and care needs?*

We can look at an annual well visit with one of my adolescent male patients to illustrate some of the issues that require fixing. During his visit, this seventeen-year-old male shared that he was nine years old when he first had sex. He was home alone and a slightly older girl began to touch him during unsupervised play. He explained that he did not know what sex was at the time, but it felt good. Since then, he said, he continued to seek out that pleasurable feeling and that he would probably be on a different path now if it had not happened. More than ten sexual partners later, he had just learned his current partner was pregnant, and it was not planned. His partner wanted to continue the pregnancy, but he expressed concerns about how having a child now would interfere with his plans for school and work. He had no experience caring for infants and no idea what to do with a baby after it was born. At the end of the visit, he joked how this unplanned pregnancy was a wake-up call for him and that he hoped to talk about birth control with his partner. He reflected that no doctor had ever talked with him before about these kinds of issues, and he was grateful to be able to do so.

This young man's experience is not atypical. Adolescent males across the nation experience early sexual experiences, a lack of comprehensive sexual and reproductive health (SRH) education, personal SRH risk trajectories, challenges in social interactions about SRH, and a lack of evidence-based SRH health care. An example of this trend is that inconsistent and incorrect condom use and the use of less effective methods contribute to high rates of sexually transmitted infections, especially for racial, ethnic, and sexual minority males, as well as unintended pregnancy (CDC 2020a, 2020b; Finer and Zolna 2016; Hamilton and Mathews 2016; Heywood et al. 2015; Lindberg, Sonfield, and Gemmill 2008; Martinez and Abma 2015; O'Donnell, O'Donnell, and Stueve 2001; Szucs et al. 2020). By not engaging adolescent males in comprehensive SRH education and care, we are failing to meet their needs *and* compromising their partners' SRH.

A Socioecological Approach

To better meet young men where they are, I propose a multilevel, socioecological approach to preventive care with a focus on sexual and reproductive health (see figure 3.1). Young men's *personal* behaviors and contexts are influenced by *social* (e.g., family, peers, intimate partners), *structural* (e.g., clinical settings), and *cultural* (e.g., socialization scripts) contexts (Bronfenbrenner 1979), each of which also influences the other. This multilevel approach will enable us to engage adolescent males in the normal growth and development process of adolescence, involve

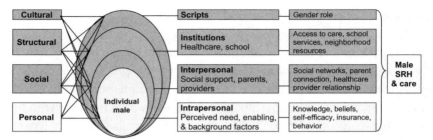

Figure 3.1: Socioecological framework that influences young male's sexual and reproductive health (SRH) and care.

them as critical partners in family planning, and improve their capacity for parenting and fathering, with impact on generational health.

Personal Context

At the personal level, the normal tasks of adolescent development for everyone include physical growth and development, sexual and gender identity formation, establishing intimacy and intimate relationships, and preparing for the future. Most research on male adolescents' sexual and reproductive health focuses on this personal level and, in particular, on males' sexual health behaviors. Most males report having had sex by age eighteen, and they experience high rates of sexually transmitted infections (including HIV) and unintended partner pregnancies (Abma and Martinez 2017; CDC 2020a, 2020b; Martinez et al. 2006). These general statistics mask significant disparities among racial, ethnic, and sexual minority males. Moreover, somewhere between 15 and 28 percent of mainly racial and ethnic minority males in metropolitan cities across the United States reported their first sex experience was at age twelve or younger, as compared to a national average rate of 8 percent (Lindberg, Maddow-Zimet, and Marcell 2019).

These striking findings make clear that we need to start sex education much earlier since most males are not receiving any sex education before their first sexual experience (Lindberg and Kantor 2022). And rather than just focusing on young men's sexual behaviors, we also need to know more about their awareness and knowledge of sexual and reproductive health. For example, work by Sonya Borrero et al. (2013) in the United States demonstrated young adult men had failing knowledge scores for every contraceptive method except for condoms. Young men's general awareness of what constitutes SRH, its importance and how to achieve it, needs to be examined and influenced. On a personal level, young men may lack awareness about affordable SRH services, feel anxious about getting tested for sexually transmitted infections, or unprepared to navigate conversations about positive test results or unwanted sexual encounters (Marcell et al. 2017). Young men may also not perceive the need to talk with a doctor about their sexual health. As noted by two young men I interviewed about how they make decisions to seek sexual health care: "If it's not an emergency . . . you don't want to go, or maybe you don't have time . . . , very simply you don't need to" and "If you're using a condom, there's no need for a clinic" (Marcell et al. 2017).

When young men do interact with clinicians, those from a variety of racial, ethnic, and sexual minority backgrounds want what all patients want: to have compassionate, respectful, caring doctors who will maintain confidentiality; to be able to choose the doctor they see; to feel they are understood and not judged by their clinician; and to have the clinician tell them what to expect before they do it, especially when it comes to the genital exam (Marcell et al. 2017). For example, one adolescent shared, "They're supposed to tell you before they do that. Like my doctor [says] 'I'm about to check your testicles. Is that okay?' Then I say 'Yes.' They're supposed to ask." (Marcell et al. 2017). These young men also discussed wanting to learn from their clinicians: "It would be good to know about your body so you can understand it better. Like, about sexuality—it would be good to learn about . . . how to control yourself, and how to be prepared . . . to be an adult" (Marcell et al. 2017).

We need to build a greater evidence base of successful approaches to connect young men to sexual and reproductive health care. One community-based and a few clinic-based quasi-experimental studies have shown promising results for increasing young men's access to SRH care (Fine et al. 2017; Kalmuss et al. 2008; Marcell et al. 2013; Raine et al. 2003). For example, one study found after expanding male services in a family planning clinic, the number of visits increased by 192 percent for male adolescents and 119 percent for adult males without affecting female patients' satisfaction with their care (Raine et al. 2003). We also need SRH educational interventions for young people with intellectual and physical disabilities, and especially for young males, since few have been developed and evaluated for this population despite a demonstrated need (Borawska-Charko, Rohleder, and Finlay 2017). Finally, young men also experience other SRH-related issues that also require further investigation, including comorbid health behaviors (e.g., substance use) and health conditions (e.g., depression), sexual health problems, intimate partner and sexual violence, and cancer (Kann et al. 2018; Laumann et al. 2009; Black et al. 2011; American Cancer Society 2007, 2011).

Social Context

Adult men typically have smaller social networks than adult women (Fischer and Oliker 1983). In keeping with this association, young men have smaller peer networks for sexual health information (Dolcini et al. 2012), leaving fewer opportunities for young men to talk about their health or receive feedback or direction from well-informed peers or adults. Indeed, many young men would like more credible sources of sexual and reproductive health information and education (Marcell et al. 2017). One young man noted, "Some people don't have a good role model or male role model at that. Your mother doesn't tell you everything . . . It's good for a male to explain to you, or somebody that had been through something, to sit down and talk to you: 'Like, it isn't good, to just be out and having sex with everybody'" (Marcell et al. 2017).

It is interesting to note that young men typically cite their mothers alongside health care providers as their most helpful sources for SRH information (Marcell et al. 2017). However, mothers point to their lack of knowledge and skills for discussing sex with their sons, and many would prefer that male role models or trained clinicians did so (Marcell et al. 2010). This is aligned with research that shows the quality of mothers' discussions about sex with their daughters is much greater than those with their sons (DiIorio, Kelley, and Hockenberry-Eaton 1999; Kirkman, Rosenthal, and Feldman 2002; Lefkowitz 2002). Although parent-based SRH interventions can be effective, they require more than just the "big talk," and parent-based SRH interventions are not always readily available (Martino et al. 2008).

At the social level, we need to ensure all parents, youth-supporting professionals, and peers have the requisite training and tools to talk about sexual and reproductive health with young men and connect them to needed care. One cause for optimism: the majority of young men believe they share equal responsibility with their partner for contraception decisions (Forste and Morgan 1998). And research shows when male partners are involved, females' contraception use is improved (Grady et al. 2010).

Cultural Context

As young men develop their identities, they are particularly vulnerable to the influence of sociocultural norms and scripts—masculinity. Boys are taught a "boy code" that includes being physically tough and competitive, not expressing emotion, avoiding seeking guidance, and accepting double standards about sexual behavior, including the expectation that men have sex early and often and that women should not. Indeed, studies show young men who endorse more traditional beliefs are at higher risk for engaging in problem behaviors, experiencing negative sexual health outcomes, and not using preventive health care services (Marcell et al. 2007; Pleck 1995). Young men reflect on how these cultural scripts impact their care-seeking experiences: "If I was a female or whatever I'd be [expected to be] in the clinic . . . I'm not that though" and "Yeah . . . it's females that go. Most likely females have a good relationship with the[ir] doctor. They talk to the[ir] doctor about anything" (Marcell et al. 2017).

Many factors reinforce these more traditional masculinity beliefs, including our history of colonization and violence, professional and organized sports, and the media. One study revealed that 12 percent of all teen media content was sexual and gendered in nature, primarily depicting men being obsessed with sex, sex defining one's manhood, and women being responsible for contraception, teen pregnancy, and preventing sexually transmitted infections (Hust, Brown, and L'Engle 2008).

The salience of masculinity beliefs during adolescence likely contributes to involuntary reductions in the size of young men's male peer friendship networks as they develop into men (Way 2013). Young men who begin to explore intimate partnerships may find it difficult to co-manage male friendships. Masculinity-inflected cultural scripts that involve being called "gay" by their peers can push young men away from same-sex friendships that were previously foundational social supports.

At the cultural level, innovative strategies are needed to promote multiple masculinities, sexualities, and care-use behaviors. There are many ways to be male. Such strategies would require partnering with public health programming and initiatives, the media, and other stakeholders to counteract and limit negative male portrayals and stereotypes. Teaching young people how to become media literate can help them learn how to minimize the negative impacts of more traditional and negative cultural gender roles.

Structural Context: Health Care

Structurally, deficiencies in the care of young men's sexual and reproductive health can be linked to the organization of the United States health care system where funding is disproportionately focused on maternal, infant, and child health. Professional associations such as the American College of Obstetrics and Gynecology (established 1951) and the North American Society for Pediatric and Adolescent Gynecology (established 1986) have organized care and toolkits for women's sexual and reproductive health in general and for young adult women specifically. Meanwhile, there is no one single specialty, professional organization, or federal agency focused solely on men's comprehensive SRH care across the lifespan; young men are often overlooked. While the American Medical Association and the American Academy of Pediatrics began organizing adolescent services in the mid-1990s (Green 1994), it was not until 2011 that the latter published its first clinical report on young men's SRH care and 2018 that the Society for Adolescent Health and Medicine published its first position statement advocating for young men's SRH care (Marcell et al. 2011; Santa Maria et al. 2018).

In the past decade, we also developed the first federal guidance on family planning and SRH care, titled *Providing Quality Family Planning Services*, that integrated recommendations for male sexual and reproductive health care throughout and included the needs of male adolescents. Published by the Office of Population Affairs and the Centers for Disease Control and Prevention, these clinical guidelines for Title X, a public health act enacted in 1970 dedicated to providing women and men comprehensive family planning and related services, make evidence-informed recommendations for the evaluation and care of four core services: contraception, basic infertility, preconception, and the prevention and treatment of sexually transmitted infections and HIV (Gavin et al. 2014; Marcell et al. 2015). The International Planned Parenthood Federation incorporated our recommendations in its first global guidance on men's sexual and reproductive health care and also included guidance on male reproductive system disorders; male support of prenatal, postnatal, and safe abortion care; and sexual and gender-based violence (Shand et al. 2017).

Past research demonstrates that few young men report getting needed SRH care (Alexander et al. 2014; Burstein et al. 2003; Chandra et al. 2011; Lafferty et al. 2002). Although the baseline of SRH care for female adolescents is not much better, far fewer male adolescents report being asked about sex, discussing puberty or birth control, or being counseled about sexual and reproductive health. For adolescents being seen as part of well-care, pediatricians spent only thirty-six seconds talking about sex, and this was two times less likely to happen when patients were male than female, raising further concerns about the quality of SRH care male adolescents receive (Alexander et al. 2014). Yet, it is still not clear how many young men are receiving quality SRH care, as we discussed in our report on providing quality services in this area. In a study conducted with sexually active male patients (ages fifteen to twenty-four) being seen in teen-focused clinics in Baltimore, I found that less than one in ten reported receipt of all recommended sexual and reproductive health care (Marcell et al. 2018). They mainly reported getting STI- and HIV-related care and being asked if they were sexually active; fewer young men reported being asked about their sexual orientation, receiving condoms, being counseled about family planning, or educated about emergency contraception.

There is a broad array of clinicians who see male adolescents for primary care but few established clinical, research, and public health training programs focus on men's SRH and even fewer on young men's SRH, which raises critical concern about the role of future clinicians, researchers, and public health practitioners in improving the state of male SRH. In particular, research suggests that female clinicians have greater discomfort taking sexual histories from male patients and in conducting male exams (Boekeloo et al. 2002; Lurie et al. 1998), despite other studies showing female clinicians provide better quality preventive care than male clinicians. Since most of the new primary care workforce is and will likely continue to be female clinicians (Goodman 2005; Hooker and Berlin, 2002), SRH education and skills development will be crucial for clinicians of all gender identities who will be working with patients of all gender identities.

The lack of health care infrastructure focused on male SRH has a range of consequences, from the personal to the political. On a policy level, there have been missed opportunities to expand men's preventive SRH coverage to include, for example, contraception coverage for men (such as vasectomy and condoms) as part of the Affordable Care Act (Sonfield 2002). It has also resulted in young men's own lack of familiarity with and skills in using health care, which has manifested in differential male and female preventive care visit patterns over the life course. Using a person-centered data analysis approach, together with colleagues, we showed that well-visit attendance substantially declined for fully half of males after age five (when vaccines are required for school entry), much earlier in time than has been previously described and as compared to the majority of females attending well visits across the same period (Van Eck et al. 2021). Also, among males whose well visits dropped off, one-third continued to be disconnected from preventive care through age seventeen, versus less than 10 percent of females over the same timeframe.

The bottom line is that we need to innovate in the health care system to better meet young men's sexual and reproductive health care needs. At a minimum, this will involve training all types of clinicians at all levels on the requisite skills to deliver quality SRH care to young men, especially in the context of primary care. In the longer term, this will involve making structural changes to the health care system to recognize the SRH needs of males across the life course, along with dedication of policies and funding to do so.

Structural Context: Sex Education

Another structural impediment to achieving men's sexual and reproductive health in the United States is the lack of a federal mandate for formal comprehensive sex education. Instead, what is taught is at the discretion of each state, school jurisdiction, and sometimes school principal. Consequently, little is known about the breadth and depth of sex education in this country. Data from the National Survey of Family Growth provides some basic information about what kinds of sex education young people receive at school, home, and in the clinical setting. We have shown that there are gender-based sex education discrepancies where more females than males learn about birth control at school and more males than females learn about condoms at home (Donaldson et al. 2013). However, when adolescents report receiving sex education from neither their parents nor schools, clinicians are not filling in the sex education gap (Donaldson et al. 2013).

Youth-supporting professionals, like school nurses, can play a role in connecting young men to sexual and reproductive health care (Dittus et al. 2018). Offering trainings to nonclinical, professional staff in community-based settings can also improve their ability to talk about SRH with young men and direct young men toward online resources for SRH care (Perin et al. 2019).

Improving Sexual and Reproductive Health, Healthcare, and Education for Young Males

Blaming individuals for their lack of engagement in sexual and reproductive health by making statements like "He just doesn't care" overlooks the multitude of contributing social and structural factors that need to be addressed. Few interventions have attended to the multiple contexts, including the personal, social, cultural, and structural levels needed to improve young men's SRH and access to care. One exception is Project Hombre, a quasi-experimental study conducted in favelas in Brazil (Pulerwitz, Barker, and Nascimento 2006). It used a "gender transformative approach" to examine whether promoting gender-equitable norms and behaviors among young men could reduce the risk of sexually transmitted infections. This study followed three communities of males aged fourteen to twenty-five over a one-year period. In the first community, young men received group education that aimed to transform gender inequity, address traditional masculine norms, and provide SRH education (personal- and social-level context). In the second community, the researchers produced a community-based, social marketing lifestyle campaign and engaged the health sector as an ally (cultural- and structural-level context). The third community served as a control group (although they received the intervention later). The results showed that in the first and second community, young men improved their attitudes toward inequitable gender norms over time, but in only the second community that had received both the personal- and social-level and structural- and cultural-level interventions were improvements seen in a number of key STI and HIV-related outcomes. We need to draw on the benefits of multilevel interventions, such as Project Hombre, and invest in multilevel strategies in the United States, since none exist, to improve young men's SRH and care use.

To summarize, let's return to the case of the young man I described at the beginning of this essay and ask: what can we do differently? We can do a better job ensuring he had comprehensive sexual and reproductive health education at home and at school, including being provided evidence-informed SRH care as well as related public health programming. He needed greater investment in educational and clinical programs that were cognizant of his SRH needs, including his need for caring and compassionate clinicians. We can also provide him opportunities to practice his skills navigating the health care system; engaging adolescent males in SRH care can also be used as a "clinical hook" to address their other health needs and help them develop critical health care use skills. We require strategies to more effectively engage him as an expectant father. Expectant fathers represent a population with no touchpoints in maternity care and in the health care and public health systems more broadly. Yet, a large body of research demonstrates involving fathers early in pregnancy can contribute to better infant, mother, and father health outcomes (Allen and Daly 2007; Palkovitz 1980; Sarkadi et al. 2008; Shorey, He, and Morelius 2016; Yargawa and Leonardi-Bee 2015). Finally, we could have better addressed all of his social determinants of health—conditions in the environments where people are born, live, learn, work, play, and age—that can affect a range of health outcomes and risks (Thornton et al. 2016).

To conclude, multiple levels of young men's socioecology influence their sexual and reproductive health and access to care. We need to identify strategies at each level to promote young men's SRH and care, including increasing awareness and knowledge among young men, their parents, and professionals who work with them. We need to better train clinicians to deliver quality sexual and reproductive health care to young men and invest in training the next generation of clinical, research, and public health experts focused on young men's SRH and care. We also need to make cultural shifts that can positively impact young men's SRH and care seeking and broaden the health system's reach across the life course for men's SRH. Finally, when considering young men's need for SRH and care, we need to ensure all young men are being considered regardless of their sex at birth, gender identity, sexual orientation, intellectual and physical ability, race, ethnicity, culture, socioeconomic status, religion, politics, and geography. The sexual and reproductive health field focused on men across the lifespan, inclusive of young men, is in its infancy, and we have many opportunities for investment and innovation.

REFERENCES

Abma, Joyce C., and Gladys M. Martinez. 2017. "Sexual Activity and Contraceptive Use among Teenagers in the United States, 2011–2015." *National Health Statistics Report* 104:1–23.

Alexander, Stewart C., Sharon L. Christ, J. Dennis Fortenberry, Katheryn I. Pollak, Truls Østbye, Terrill Bravender, and Cleveland G. Shields. 2016. "Identifying Types of Sex Conversations in Adolescent Health Maintenance Visits." *Sexual Health* 13 (1): 22–28. https://doi.org/10.1071/SH15080.

Alexander, Stewart C., J. Dennis Fortenberry, Katheryn I. Pollak, Terrill Bravender, J. Kelly Davis, Truls Ostbye, James A. Tulsky, Rowena J. Dolor, Cleveland G. Shields. 2014. "Sexuality Talk during Adolescent Health Maintenance Visits." *JAMA Pediatrics* 168 (2): 163–69. https://doi.org/10.1001/jamapediatrics.2013.4338.

Allen, Sarah, and Kerry Daly. 2007. *The Effects of Father Involvement: An Updated Research Summary of the Evidence.* Guelph, Ontario: Centre for Families, Work, and Well-Being, University of Guelph.

American Cancer Society. 2007. *Cancer Facts & Figures 2007.* Atlanta: American Cancer Society. www.cancer.org.

American Cancer Society. 2011. *Testicular Cancer: Can Testicular Cancer Be Found Early?* Atlanta: American Cancer Society. www.cancer.org.

Black, Michelle C., Kathleen C. Basile, Matthew J. Breiding, Sharon G. Smith, Mikel L. Walters, Melissa T. Merrick, Jierh Chen, and Mark R. Stevens. 2011. *The National Intimate Partner and Sexual Violence Survey (NISVS): 2010 Summary Report.* Atlanta: US Department of Health and Human Services. www.cdc.gov.

Boekeloo, B. O., M. H. Snyder, M. Bobbin, G. R. Burstein, D. Conley, T. C. Quinn, and J. M. Zenilman. 2002. "Provider Willingness to Screen All Sexually Active Adolescents for Chlamydia." *Sexually Transmitted Infections* 78 (5): 369–73. https://doi.org/10.1136/sti.78.5.369.

Borawska-Charko, Magdalena, Poul Rohleder, Mick W. L. Finlay. 2017. "The Sexual Health Knowledge of People with Intellectual Disabilities: A Review." *Sexuality Research and Social Policy* 14: 393–409.

Borrero, Sonya, Amy Farkas, Christine Dehlendorf, and Corinne H. Rocca. 2013. "Racial and Ethnic Differences in Men's Knowledge and Attitudes about Contraception." *Contraception* 88 (4): 532–38.

Bronfenbrenner, Urie. 1979. *The Ecology of Human Development*. Cambridge, MA: Harvard University Press.

Burstein, Gale R., Richard Lowry, Jonathan D. Klein, and John S. Santelli. 2003. "Missed Opportunities for Sexually Transmitted Diseases, Human Immunodeficiency Virus, and Pregnancy Prevention Services during Adolescent Health Supervision Visits." *Pediatrics* 111 (5): 996–1001. https://doi.org/10.1542/peds.111.5.996.

Centers for Disease Control and Prevention (CDC). 2020a. "Estimated HIV incidence in the United States, 2015–2019." *HIV Surveillance Supplemental Report* 26 (1).

Centers for Disease Control and Prevention (CDC). 2020b. *Sexually Transmitted Disease Surveillance, 2019*. Atlanta: US Department of Health and Human Services, Centers for Disease Control and Prevention, National Center for HIV, Viral Hepatitis, STD, and TB Prevention, Division of STD Prevention. www.cdc.gov.

Chandra, Anjani, William Mosher, Casey Copen, and Catlainn Sionean. 2011. "Sexual Behavior, Sexual Attraction, and Sexual Identity in the United States: Data from the 2006–2008 National Survey of Family Growth." *National Health Statistics Report* 3 (36): 1–36.

DiIorio, Colleen, Maureen Kelley, and Marilyn Hockenberry-Eaton. 1999. "Communication about Sexual Issues: Mothers, Fathers, and Friends." *Journal of Adolescent Health* 24 (3): 181–89. https://doi.org/10.1016/s1054-139x(98)00115-3.

Dittus, Patricia J., Christopher R. Harper, Jeffrey S. Becasen, Robin A. Donatello, and Ethier, K. A. 2018. "Structural Intervention with School Nurses Increases Receipt of Sexual Health Care among Male High School Students." *Journal of Adolescent Health* 62 (1): 52–58. https://doi.org/10.1016/j.jadohealth.2017.07.017.

Dolcini, M. Margaret, Joseph A. Catania, Gary W. Harper, Cherrie B. Boyer, and Kimberley A. Richards. 2012. "Sexual Health Information Networks: What Are Urban African American Youth Learning?" *Research in Human Development* 9 (1): 54–77. https://doi.org/10.1080/15427609.2012.654432.

Donaldson, Abigail A., Laura D. Lindberg, Jonathan M. Ellen, and Arik V. Marcell. 2013. "Receipt of Sexual Health Information from Parents, Teachers, and Healthcare Providers by Sexually Experienced U.S. Adolescents." *Journal of Adolescent Health* 53 (2): 235–40. https://doi.org/10.1016/j.jadohealth.2013.03.017.

Fine, David, Lee Warner, Sarah Salomon, and David M. Johnson. 2017. "Interventions to Increase Male Attendance and Testing for Sexually Transmitted Infections at

Publicly-Funded Family Planning Clinics." *Journal of Adolescent Health* 61 (1): 32–39. https://doi.org/10.1016/j.jadohealth.2017.03.011.

Finer, Lawrence B., and Mia R. Zolna. 2016. "Declines in Unintended Pregnancy in the United States, 2008–2011." *New England Journal of Medicine* 374 (9): 843–52. https://doi.org/10.1056/NEJMsa1506575.

Fischer, Claude S., and Stacey J. Oliker. 1983. "A Research Note on Friendship, Gender, and the Life Cycle." *Social Forces* 62 (1): 124–33. https://doi.org/10.2307/2578351.

Forste, Renata, and Julie Morgan. 1998. "How Relationships of U.S. Men Affect Contraceptive Use and Efforts to Prevent Sexually Transmitted Diseases." *Family Planning Perspectives* 30 (2): 56–62. https://doi.org/10.2307/2991660.

Gavin, Loretta, Susan Moskosky, Marion Carter, Kathryn Curtis, Emily Godfrey, Arik V. Marcell, Lauren Zapata. 2014. "Guidance for Providing Quality Family Planning Services: Recommendations of CDC and the U.S. Office of Population Affairs." *Morbidity and Mortality Weekly Report* 63 (4): 1–54.

Goodman, David C. 2005. "The Pediatrician Workforce: Current Status and Future Prospects." *Pediatrics* 116 (1): e156–73. https://doi.org/10.1542/peds.2005-0874.

Grady, William R, Daniel H. Klepinger, John O. Billy, and Lisa A. Cubbins. 2010. "The Role of Relationship Power in Couple Decisions about Contraception in the US." *Journal of Biosocial Science* 42 (3): 307–23. https://doi.org/10.1017/S0021932009990575.

Green, Morris, ed. 1994. *Bright Futures: Guidelines for Health Supervision of Infants, Children, & Adolescents*. Arlington, VA: National Center for Education in Maternal & Child Health.

Hagan, Joseph F. Jr., Judith S. Shaw, Paula M. Duncan, & eds. 2017. *Bright Futures: Guidelines for Health Supervision of Infants, Children, & Adolescents*. 4th ed. Elk Grove Village, IL: American Academy of Pediatrics.

Hamilton, Brady E., and T. J. Mathews. 2016. *Continued Declines in Teen Births in the United States, 2015*. NCHS Data Brief no. 259. Hyattsville, MD: National Center for Health Statistics.

Heywood, Wendy, Kent Patrick, Anthony M. A. Smith, & Marian K. Pitts. 2015. "Associations Between Early First Sexual Intercourse and Later Sexual and Reproductive Outcomes: A Systematic Review of Population-Based Data." *Archives of Sexual Behavior* 44 (3): 531–69. https://doi.org/10.1007/s10508-014-0374-3.

Hooker, Roderick S., and Linda E. Berlin. 2002. "Trends in the Supply of Physician Assistants and Nurse Practitioners in the United States." *Health Affairs* 21 (5): 174–81. https://doi.org/10.1377/hlthaff.21.5.174.

Hust, Stacey J. T., Jane D. Brown, and Kelly Ladin L'Engle. 2008. "Boys Will Be Boys and Girls Better Be Prepared: An Analysis of the Rare Sexual Health Messages in Young Adolescents' Media." *Mass Communication & Society* 11 (1): 3–23. https://doi.org/10.1080/15205430701668139.

Kalmuss, Debra, Bruce Armstrong, Molly Franks, Gabrielle Hecker, & Jessica Gonzalez. 2008. "Evaluation of a Community-Based Sexual Health Intervention for Young

Adult Latino and African-American Men." *Journal of Men's Health* 5 (4): 318–26. https://doi.org/10.1016/j.jomh.2008.08.003.

Kann, Laura, Tim McManus, William A. Harris, Shari L. Shanklin, Katherine H. Flint, Barbara Queen, Kathleen A. Ethier. 2018. "Youth Risk Behavior Surveillance—United States, 2017." *Morbidity and Mortality Weekly Report Surveillance Summary* 67 (8): 1–114. https://doi.org/10.15585/mmwr.ss6708a1.

Kirkman, Maggie, Doreen A. Rosenthal, and S. Shirley Feldman. 2002. "Talking to a Tiger: Fathers Reveal Their Difficulties in Communicating about Sexuality with Adolescents." *New Directions for Child and Adolescent Development* 97:57–74. https://doi.org/10.1002/cd.50.

Lafferty, William E., Lois Downey, Christine M. Holan, Alice Lind, William Kassler, Guoyu Tao, & Kathleen L. Irwin. 2002. "Provision of Sexual Health Services to Adolescent Enrollees in Medicaid Managed Care." *American Journal of Public Health* 92 (11): 1779–83. https://doi.org/10.2105/ajph.92.11.1779.

Lafferty, William E., Lois Downey, Anne W. Shields, Christine M. Holan, & Alice Lind. 2001. "Adolescent Enrollees in Medicaid Managed Care: The Provision of Well Care and Sexual Health Assessment." *Journal of Adolescent Health* 28 (6): 497–508. https://doi.org/10.1016/s1054-139x(00)00196-8.

Laumann, Edward O., Dale B. Glasseran, Raimundo C. S. Neves, and Edson D. Moreira Jr. 2009. "A Population-Based Survey of Sexual Activity, Sexual Problems and Associated Help-Seeking Behavior Patterns in Mature Adults in the United States of America." *International Journal of Impotence Research* 21 (3): 171–78. https://doi.org/10.1038/ijir.2009.7.

Lefkowitz, Eva S. 2002. "Beyond the Yes-No Question: Measuring Parent-Adolescent Communication about Sex." *New Directions for Child and Adolescent Development* 97:43–56. https://doi.org/10.1002/cd.49.

Lindberg, Laura D., and Leslie M. Kantor. 2022. "Adolescents' Receipt of Sex Education in a Nationally Representative Sample, 2011–2019." *Journal of Adolescent Health* 70 (2): 290–97. https://doi.org/10.1016/j.jadohealth.2021.08.027.

Lindberg, Laura D., Isaac Maddow-Zimet, and Arik V. Marcell. 2019. "Prevalence of Sexual Initiation Before Age 13 Years Among Male Adolescents and Young Adults in the United States." *JAMA Pediatrics* 173 (6): 553–60. https://doi.org/10.1001/jamapediatrics.2019.0458.

Lindberg, Laura D., Adam Sonfield, and Alison Gemmill. 2008. "Reassessing Adolescent Male Sexual and Reproductive Health in the United States: Research and Recommendations." *American Journal of Men's Health* 2 (1): 40–56. https://doi.org/10.1177/1557988307309460.

Lurie, Nicole, Karen Margolis, Paul G. McGovern, and Pamela Mink. 1998. "Physician Self-Report of Comfort and Skill in Providing Preventive Care to Patients of the Opposite Sex." *Archives of Family Medicine* 7 (2): 134–37. https://doi.org/10.1001/archfami.7.2.134.

Marcell, Arik V., Elizabeth Allan, Eric A. Clay, Catherine Watson, and Freya L. Sonenstein. 2013. "Effectiveness of a Brief Curriculum to Promote Condom and Health

Care Use Among Out-of-School Young Adult Males." *Perspectives on Sexual and Reproductive Health* 45 (1): 33–40. https://doi.org/10.1363/4503313.

Marcell, Arik V., Carol A. Ford, Joseph A. Pleck, and Freya L. Sonenstein. 2007. "Masculine Beliefs, Parental Communication, and Adolescent Males' Health Care Use." *Pediatrics* 119 (4): e965–74. https://doi.org/10.1542/peds.2006-1683.

Marcell, Arik V., Loretta E. Gavin, Susan B. Moskosky, Robert McKenna, and Anne M. Rompalo. 2015. "Developing Federal Clinical Care Recommendations for Men." Supplement, *American Journal of Preventive Medicine* 49 (2 Supp 1): S14–22. https://doi.org/10.1016/j.amepre.2015.03.006.

Marcell, Arik V., Susannah E. Gibbs, Nanlesta A. Pilgrim, Kathleen R. Page, Renata Arrington-Sanders, Jacky M. Jennings, Patricia J. Dittus. 2018. "Sexual and Reproductive Health Care Receipt Among Young Males Aged 15–24." *Journal of Adolescent Health* 62 (4): 382–89. https://doi.org/10.1016/j.jadohealth.2017.08.016.

Marcell, Arik V., Terry L. Howard, Keith Plowden, and Catherine Watson. 2010. "Exploring Women's Perceptions about Their Role in Supporting Partners' and Sons' Reproductive Health Care." *American Journal of Men's Health* 4 (4): 297–304. https://doi.org/10.1177/1557988309335822.

Marcell, Arik V., Anthony R. Morgan, Renata Sanders, Nicole Lunardi, Nanlesta A. Pilgrim, Jacky M. Jennings, Patricia J. Dittus. 2017. "The Socioecology of Sexual and Reproductive Health Care Use Among Young Urban Minority Males." *Journal of Adolescent Health* 60 (4): 402–10. https://doi.org/10.1016/j.jadohealth.2016.11.014.

Marcell, Arik V., Charles Wibbelsman, Warren M. Siegel, and and the Committee on Adolescence. 2011. "Male Adolescent Sexual and Reproductive Health Care: Clinical Report for the Committee on Adolescence. American Academy of Pediatrics." *Pediatrics* 128 (5): e1–19. https://doi.org/10.1542/peds.2011-2384.

Martinez, Gladys M., and Joyce C. Abma. 2015. *Sexual Activity, Contraceptive Use, and Childbearing of Teenagers Aged 15–19 in the United States*. NCHS Data Brief no. 209. Hyattsville, MD: National Center for Health Statistics

Martinez, Gladys M., Anjani Chandra, Joyce C. Abma, Jo Jones, and William D. Mosher. 2006. "Fertility, Contraception, and Fatherhood: Data on Men and Women from Cycle 6 (2002) of the 2002 National Survey of Family Growth." *Vital Health Statistics* 23 (26): 1–142.

Martino, Steven C., Marc N. Elliott, Rosalie Corona, David E. Kanouse, and Mark A. Schuster. 2008. "Beyond the "Big Talk": The Roles of Breadth and Repetition in Parent-Adolescent Communication about Sexual Topics." *Pediatrics* 121 (3): e612–18. https://doi.org/10.1542/peds.2007-2156.

O'Donnell, Lydia, Carl R. O'Donnell, and Ann Stueve. 2001. "Early Sexual Initiation and Subsequent Sex-Related Risks among Urban Minority Youth: The Reach for Health Study." *Family Planning Perspectives* 33 (6): 268–75.

Palkovitz, Rob. 1980. "Predictors of Involvement in First Time Fathers." PhD diss., Rutgers University. Proquest (8105035).

Perin, Jamie, Jacky M. Jennings, Renata Arrington-Sanders, Kahtleen R. Page, Penny S. Loosier, Patricia J. Dittus, and Arik V. Marcell. 2019. "Evaluation of an Adapted

Project Connect Community Based Intervention among Professionals Serving Young Minority Men." *Sexually Transmitted Disease* 46 (3): 165–71. https://doi.org/10.1097/OLQ.0000000000000977.

Pleck, Joseph H. 1995. "The Gender Role Strain Paradigm: An Update." In *A New Psychology of Men*, edited by R. F. Levant and W. S. Pollack. New York: Basic Books.

Pulerwitz, Julie, Gary Barker, Marcio Segundo, and Marcos Nascimento. 2006. *Promoting More Gender-Equitable Norms and Behaviors among Young Men as an HIV/AIDS Prevention Strategy*. Washington, DC: Population Council. https://pdf.usaid.gov.

Raine, Tina, Arik V. Marcell, Corinne H. Rocca, and Cynthia C. Harper. 2003. "The Other Half of the Equation: Serving Young Men in a Young Women's Reproductive Health Clinic." *Perspectives on Sexual and Reproductive Health* 35 (5): 208–14. https://doi.org/10.1363/psrh.35.208.03.

Santa Maria, Diane, Jason Rafferty, May Lau, Vincent Guilamo-Ramos, Kathleen Tebb, Nicholas Chadi, Anne-Emmanuelle Ambresin, Ellie Vyvyer, Arik V. Marcell. 2018. "Advocating for Adolescent and Young Adult Male Sexual and Reproductive Health: A Position Statement from the Society for Adolescent Health and Medicine." *Journal of Adolescent Health* 63 (5): 657–61. https://doi.org/10.1016/j.jadohealth.2018.08.007.

Sarkadi, Anna, Robert Kristiansson, Frank Oberklaid, and Sven Bremberg. 2008. "Fathers' Involvement and Children's Developmental Outcomes: A Systematic Review of Longitudinal Studies." *Acta Paediatrics* 97 (2): 153–58. https://doi.org/10.1111/j.1651-2227.2007.00572.x.

Shand, Tim, Jon Hopkins, Jameel Zamir, Arik V. Marcell, and Stephanie Perlson. 2017. *Global Sexual and Reproductive Health Service Package for Men and Adolescent Boys*. London; New York: IPPF; UNFPA. www.unfpa.org.

Shorey, Shefaly, Hong-Gu He, and Evalotte Morelius. 2016. "Skin-to-Skin Contact by Fathers and the Impact on Infant and Paternal Outcomes: An Integrative Review." *Midwifery* 40:207–17. https://doi.org/10.1016/j.midw.2016.07.007.

Sonfield, Adam. 2002. "Looking at Men's Sexual and Reproductive Health Needs." *Guttmacher Report on Public Policy* 5 (2): 7–10.

Szucs, Leigh E., Richard Lowry, Amy M. Fasula, Sanjana Pampati, Casy E. Copen, Khaleel S. Hussaini, Riley J. Steiner. 2020. "Condom and Contraceptive Use among Sexually Active High School Students—Youth Risk Behavior Survey, United States, 2019." *Morbidity and Mortality Weekly Report Supplement* 69 (1): 11–18. https://doi.org/10.15585/mmwr.su6901a2.

Thornton, Rachel L. J., Crystal M. Glover, Crystal W. Cené, et al. 2016. "Evaluating Strategies for Reducing Health Disparities by Addressing the Social Determinants of Health." *Health Affairs* 35 (8): 1416–23. https://doi.org/10.1377/hlthaff.2015.1357.

United Nations (UN). 1994. *Programme of Action. Adopted at the International Conference on Population and Development, Cairo*. N.p.: United Nations Population Fund, 2004

Van Eck, Kathryn, MadhuliThakkar, Pamela A. Matson, Lingxin Hao, and Arik V. Marcell. 2021. "Adolescents' Patterns of Well-Care Use Over Time: Who Stays Connected." *American Journal of Preventive Medicine* 60 (5): e221–29. https://doi.org/10.1016/j.amepre.2020.12.008.

Way, Niobe. 2013. "Boys' Friendships During Adolescence: Intimacy, Desire, and Loss." *Journal of Research on Adolescence* 23 (2): 201–13. https://doi.org/10.1111/jora.12047.

World Health Organization (WHO). 2006. *Defining Sexual Health: Report of a Technical Consultation on Sexual Health, 28–31 January 2002*. Geneva, Switzerland: World Health Organization.

Yargawa, Judith, and Jo Leonardi-Bee. 2015. "Male Involvement and Maternal Health Outcomes: Systematic Review and Meta-analysis." *Journal of Epidemiology and Community Health* 69 (6): 604–12. https://doi.org/10.1136/jech-2014-204784.

4

"Healthy Masculinity" Is Not a Feminist Strategy for Sperm, Health, and Politics

TRISTAN BRIDGES

A little over five years ago, I was sitting in an urgent care center with one of my children. On the wall, I noticed a poster. It read: "MAN UP and take care of yourself. People are counting on you." The poster was a deep red with emboldened white print and included a bold white clip art image of a vintage mustache curled at the outer edges. Like a stop sign, it jumped out visually, demanding our attention. My son noticed me noticing it and asked what it meant. I told him it was a poster encouraging men to come to the doctor to make sure they are healthy. He looked puzzled. I shared that sometimes men go to the doctor less than they should and we talked about why that might be the case while waiting to be seen. In this chapter, I summarize why "healthy masculinity" discourses presented in public health campaigns are not the feminist strategy they might appear to be and are unlikely to provoke the sorts of change they seem designed to encourage.

A great deal of scholarship has documented that, compared with cisgender women, cisgender men are much more likely to engage in lifestyles that put them at elevated health risks. For instance, cisgender men are more likely to smoke and drink and less likely to make healthy decisions about eating and lifestyle than are cisgender women (Courtenay 2000a). Partially as a result, cisgender men are also more likely to have life-threatening chronic diseases like diabetes, liver disease, and heart disease (Courtenay 2000b). In addition to these elevated health risks, research has long documented that cisgender men engage with health professionals and pursue health care for themselves at rates far lower than cisgender women do (Clark et al. 2020; Haischer et al. 2020). All of this means that cisgender men are at greater risk of mortality—both from all causes and from specific causes like accidents, suicide, and COVID-19 (e.g., Bridges et al. 2021). Indeed, all of these trends came together during the most recent global pandemic, when research found that cisgender men were more likely to engage in behaviors that put themselves (and anyone interacting with them) at risk of contracting COVID-19 and were more likely to die from it due to their higher rates of comorbidities (National Center for Immunization 2020).

Many scholars studying masculinity attribute cisgender men's health averse behaviors to their adherence to cultural scripts associated with "doing" masculinity in ways that not only hurt others but hurt themselves as well (e.g., Courtenay 2000a). Consider Janani Umamaheswar and Catherine Tan's (2020) longitudinal study with American college students who were sheltering in place during the pandemic. Through a series of interviews, they found that men in their sample were more likely than women to downplay the risks associated with COVID-19. Interestingly, however, they also found that this was not universally true of men. Men with significant caregiving responsibilities professed similar levels of fear and concern as women in their sample. The researchers argued that this demonstrated that different kinds of gendered investments in households (rather than in cisgender men's biology) are a better explanation of health-promoting behaviors. Similarly, in a survey of over six thousand adults in the United States, political scientist Dan Cassino (2021) found that men identifying as "completely masculine" were almost three times more likely than everyone else to report having been diagnosed with COVID-19. This was a powerful demonstration of how specific kinds of commitments to masculinity can be at odds with health—for an individual, a household, a community, and sometimes the general public. For example, during the pandemic, risky health behavior for individuals contributed to community spread of the virus.

Simply put, sometimes masculinity is bad for your health, and in some circumstances, it is also dangerous for the health and well-being of those connected to you. Those who created the Man Up Checkup campaign know this. They sought to address this issue with what I have learned is a common tactic. Rather than coming up with campaigns that encourage men to consider the negative impacts of their commitment to masculinity, the social advertising groups pursued a different tactic: they sought to *masculinize* cisgender men's health-seeking behavior.

The Man Up Checkup poster was part of a major public health campaign produced by American Family Care, a for-profit, urgent care franchise with over three hundred locations across the country aimed at providing better health care for all. In a society marked by stark inequalities with respect to access to health care, urgent care centers offer some of the only options for many people living in the United States to obtain health care at all. Starting in 2017, American Family Care started this particular public health campaign aimed at cisgender men, which featured posters, like the one I saw with my son, in urgent care centers all across the United States alongside a social media campaign complete with videos encouraging men to have regular health screenings and invest in their own preventative health care.

All the posters and videos are directed at cisgender men, encouraging them to "Man Up. Take care of yourself and your family." Posts on social media sites like Twitter, Facebook, and Instagram were accompanied by pictures of mustaches and sports equipment and vintage images of bare-knuckled boxers. Text included hashtags like #ManUp and #Manly, phrases like "You can be too macho," and references to sports imagery and metaphors like "Stay on par" or "Step up to the plate." One of the campaign videos depicts a father playing with his kids while recommending, "Men, don't miss out on life's special moments. Stop by American Family Care for a Man Up Checkup. It's a basic health screening designed specifically for men. So man up and take care of yourself" (AFC Urgentcare Clearwater 2022). Indeed, men in the campaign are often depicted in heterosexual monogamous relationships and as fathers. So, while the ads appear as a call to *all* men, they also seem to particularly center cisgender men in heterosexual relationships with children.

Perhaps motivated by the large and interdisciplinary body of scholarship documenting adverse health outcomes for men, twenty-first century public health campaigns in the United States and other parts of the world commonly target cisgender men with messaging like the Man Up Checkup campaign. I refer to these strategies as "healthy masculinity strategies." And once you learn to identify them, you will notice that they are everywhere.

Similar tactics have been used in a variety of sexual violence prevention campaigns aimed at cisgender men. President Barack Obama's

"1 is 2 many" campaign encouraging men to take part in efforts to curb sexual violence against women, campaigns like "Real Men Don't Rape" and "My Strength is Not for Hurting," and the US Army's "I AM STRONG" campaign work to culturally masculinize cisgender men's roles of preventing sexual violence (e.g., Murphy 2009; Masters 2010; Pascoe and Hollander 2016). I discovered similar issues in a series of "Walk a Mile in Her Shoes" marches I studied, a campaign aimed at providing a structured opportunity for men to come together publicly to take a stand against sexual violence and assault perpetrated by men. At these marches, groups of men walk one mile wearing high heels with the goal of raising awareness about issues of gender-based violence against women. But I found that men routinely mocked femininity alongside advocating for ending gender-based violence. Sadly, participation at the events I studied suggested behavior that shored up women's status as subordinate to men (Bridges 2010).

From campaigns aimed at encouraging cisgender men to get checkups and engage in public health practices like mask wearing or blood donation to those that challenge cisgender men's sexual violence and assault, discourses encouraging men to participate in "healthier masculinities" is a common tactic. But there are problems with this approach. Consider Jill Cermele and Martha McCaughey's (2016) critique of the "Real Men Don't Rape" campaign: "The 'Real Men Don't Rape' campaign trades on how important manhood is to men, and attempts to redefine manhood as respectful, gentlemanly. The 'real men don't rape' strategy hopes to convey that manhood ought to be defined by morality, not muscle. But . . . the campaign . . . winds up essentializing male strength—as if that's the one thing no one can challenge, that at the end of the day (or date), the man is more physically powerful and ultimately dominant over the woman."

In addition to leaving untouched the problematic aspects of masculinity, some of the campaigns are so focused on shoring up masculinity that their primary message is obscured. One example comes from the Movember Foundation's efforts to raise awareness and funds for various issues associated with men's health. Starting in 2003, the charity encouraged men to grow mustaches in the month of November as a public awareness campaign with the goal to "change the face of men's health." But social scientists have cast some doubts as to the effectiveness of the campaign, finding that most men who participate focus primarily on the social aspects of the campaign (growing mustaches "for a cause") rather than the public health aspects. As Jenna Jacobson and Christopher Mascaro's (2016, 1) study of participation in Movember on social media found, "There is limited true conversation taking place although the stated purpose of the campaign is to facilitate conversation" and "participants are more engaged with Movember as a branded movement than engaged in health promotion."

The Movember Foundation claims to be raising awareness of and support for three critical public health issues for men: prostate cancer, testicular cancer, and men's mental health and suicide prevention. But so far, scholarship suggests that men participating in the Movember campaign seem to be more invested in the stubble than the salubrity. That is, the campaign encourages men to grow visible symbols of masculinity for a cause. It appears men embrace the invitation to don symbols of masculinity (whether earnestly or tongue in cheek). But somewhere within this gendered symbolic transaction, the causes seem to consistently take a back seat.

This leads to an important question: are "healthy masculinity" strategies actually successful? Somewhat surprisingly, there is less actual research on this than we should expect. Certainly, a good deal of funding goes into producing these campaigns. And perhaps it is undertaken under the assumption that "something is better than nothing" or, possibly even more problematically, "it might help, but it can't hurt." My sense is that they are much less successful in promoting health than popularly imagined, and possibly not successful at all.

Healthy masculinity strategies proceed from the notion that masculinity is culturally constructed in ways that are at odds with health-seeking and prosocial behavior, healthy living, and more. Indeed, they are premised on this understanding. However, taking into account the insights from social scientific research on masculinity, I believe it is unlikely that such strategies will succeed in changing cisgender men's behaviors related to health. Healthy masculinity strategies implicitly suggest that the solution for obtaining cisgender men's participation and buy-in is that healthy and prosocial behaviors simply need to be *masculinized*. Such campaigns symbolically offer men masculine gender status in exchange for investments in healthy and prosocial behaviors. In short, if we understand that cultural constructions of masculinity are the problem, is it possible to simultaneously present them as the solution?

Fostering feminist change in cisgender men's health is a vitally important issue. But healthy masculinity strategies are unlikely to provoke the sorts of change they are designed to encourage. While these campaigns may help some cisgender men identify as "good men" (to themselves and others), I see the enduring fixation on masculinity as the crucial issue. Rather than purporting to redefine cultural notions of manhood through public health campaigns, we need to rethink how we engage cisgender men to ensure their behaviors are less costly to their own health and well-being and to the health and well-being of everyone around them.

Rather than *masculinizing health*, we should challenge men to consider what investments they have in masculinity and what those investments might cost them, their loved ones, and their communities. Perhaps, in other words, we should not be encouraging men to "man up" in pursuing personal and public health; maybe we should be encouraging them to man down.

REFERENCES

AFC Urgentcare Clearwater. "Best burgers in town can be found at Bob's Diner on Main St!" Facebook, June 21, 2022. https://www.facebook.com/watch/?v=572693407800172.

Bridges, Tristan. 2010. "Men Just Weren't Made to Do This: Performances of Drag at 'Walk a Mile in Her Shoes' Marches." *Gender & Society* 24 (1): 5–30. https://doi.org/10.1177/0891243209356924.

Bridges, Tristan, Kristen Barber, Joseph D. Nelson, and Anna Chatillon. 2021. "COVID-19 and Masculinity: Symposium Introduction." *Men and Masculinities* 24 (1): 163–67. https://psycnet.apa.org/doi/10.1177/1097184X211004325.

Cassino, Dan. 2021. "Masculinity is a Major Risk Factor for COVID-19." *Farleigh Dickinson University News*. Last accessed February 17, 2021. www.fdu.edu.

National Center for Immunization and Respiratory Diseases (US), Division of Viral Diseases. 2020. "Health equity considerations and racial and ethnic minority groups." Centers for Disease Control and Prevention, July 24, 2020. https://stacks.cdc.gov.

Cermele, Jill, and Martha McCaughey. 2016. "Hey Guys, It's Not About Your Manhood!" *Girl W/ Pen* (blog). https://thesocietypages.org.

Clark, Cory, Andrés Davila, Maxime Regis, and Sascha Kraus. 2020. "Predictors of COVID-19 Voluntary Compliance Behaviors." *Global Transitions* 2:76–82. https://doi.org/10.1016/j.glt.2020.06.003.

Courtenay, Will. 2000a. "Constructions of Masculinity and their Influence on Men's Well-being: A Theory of Gender and Health." *Social Science & Medicine* 50 (10): 1,385–401. https://doi.org/10.1016/S0277-9536(99)00390-1.

Courtenay, Will. 2000b. "Behavioral Factors Associated with Disease, Injury, and Death among Men: Evidence and Implications for Prevention." *Journal of Men's Studies* 9 (1): 81–142. https://psycnet.apa.org/doi/10.3149/jms.0901.81.

Haischer, Michael H., Rachel Beilfuss, Meggie Rose Hart, Lauren Opielinski, David Wrucke, Gretchen Zirgaitis, Toni D. Uhrich, and Sandra K. Hunter. 2020. "Who Is Wearing a Mask? Gender-, Age-, and Location-Related Differences during the COVID-19 Pandemic." *PLOS ONE* 15 (10): e0240785. https://doi.org/10.1371/journal.pone.0240785.

Jacobson, Jenna, and Christopher Mascaro. 2016. "Movember: Twitter Conversations of a Hairy Social Movement." *Social Media + Society* 2 (2). https://doi.org/10.1177/2056305116637103.

Masters, N. Tatiana. 2010. "'My Strength is Not for Hurting': Men's Anti-Rape Websites and their Construction of Masculinity and Male Sexuality." *Sexualities* 13 (1): 33–46. https://doi.org/10.1177/1363460709346115.

Murphy, Michael J. 2009. "Can 'Men' Stop Rape?: Visualizing Gender in the 'My Strength is Not for Hurting' Rape Prevention Campaign." *Men and Masculinities* 12 (1): 113–30. https://doi.org/10.1177/1097184X09331752.

Pascoe, C. J. and Jocelyn A. Hollander. 2016. "Good Guys Don't Rape: Gender, Domination, and Mobilizing Rape." *Gender & Society* 30 (1): 67–79. https://doi.org/10.1177/0891243215612707.

Umamaheswar, Janani, and Catherine Tan. 2020. "'Dad, Wash Your Hands': Gender, Care Work, and Attitudes toward Risk during the COVID-19 Pandemic." *Socius* 6:1–14. https://doi.org/10.1177/2378023120964376.

5

Introducing a Stratified Reproductive Justice Framework for Sperm, Health, and Politics

KRYSTALE E. LITTLEJOHN

I want to start with an admittedly provocative but nevertheless important assertion: I am not sure that Reproductive Justice is for everyone. To be clear, that does not mean that reproductive justice is not. Reproductive Justice is a framework and movement with a specific history, meaning, and definition. It is not equivalent to combining *reproductive* and *justice* to signal a general desire for just experiences in reproduction. To truly grapple with and apply Reproductive Justice, I believe that researchers, teachers, health care providers, activists, and all others must think critically about what the Reproductive Justice perspective is, what it is not, and what it must be to maintain its integrity as a radical framework and movement started by women of color to address the reproductive oppression that they face.

This is especially important when considering sperm, health, and politics. Indeed, the notion of extending a reproductive justice lens to people who produce sperm is a radical concept. At its inception, Reproductive Justice provided a vision for meeting the needs of people who can become pregnant, who give birth, and who strive to raise their children in safe and healthy communities as mothers facing multiple structural hardships. Thus, to appropriately extend a reproductive justice lens to sperm, we need a framework that takes up what Reproductive Justice has to offer without sacrificing its commitment to a radical, reproductively just future for women of color, marginalized women, and all people capable of pregnancy, regardless of their gender identity.

In this essay, I develop *stratified reproductive justice* as a flexible framework that offers one way to move forward for people interested in applying Reproductive Justice to other contexts—whether their work focuses on people who produce sperm or on the experiences of people who contribute eggs but are not from multiply marginalized populations.

Reproductive Justice and Stratified Reproduction

Reproductive Justice is a framework and movement that was created by women of color activists who believed that the mainstream reproductive rights movement failed to adequately address the needs of Black and marginalized women. A group of Black women activists coined the term *Reproductive Justice* in 1994 and the SisterSong Women of Color Reproductive Health Collective—a group of sixteen women of color organizations—promoted the use of the term with a human rights framework (Asian Communities for Reproductive Justice 2005). The central tenets of Reproductive Justice are that every person who can become pregnant has the right to (1) have a child, (2) not have a child, and (3) parent the children they have in safe and healthy communities (Ross and Solinger 2017). For several decades now, it has been an incredibly powerful vehicle for articulating and advocating for the rights of women of color and marginalized women. It has been a feature in many media pieces published in the aftermath of the Supreme Court's decision to overturn *Roe v. Wade* in June 2022 (e.g., Boorstein 2022; Henneberg 2023; Zernike 2023).

While I firmly believe that everyone should know about Reproductive Justice and the importance of its centrality in guiding all of our thinking and action about reproductive health and rights, I also believe that we must think critically and strategically about how we take it up and deploy it as a framework to avoid co-opting it and decentering the experiences of the very people that Reproductive Justice emerged to protect. As a Black feminist and scholar of reproductive justice, I believe that it is within an *intersectional context* that we need to think about sperm, health, and politics.

As sociologist Zandria Robinson (2016, 478) describes it, intersectionality "is concerned with how multiple systems of oppression—racism, classism, sexism, heterosexism, cissexism, and ableism in particular—simultaneously reinforce and constitute one another to maintain existing stratification hierarchies across categories." Extending a reproductive justice lens to sperm while bearing intersectionality in mind means paying keen attention to intersectional gendered histories of subjugation and how those histories affect contemporary experiences with oppression for people who produce sperm. It is my view that thinking about reproductive justice, even within a paradigm that rejects an intrinsic link between sex, gender, and gametes, sometimes necessarily requires taking bodies into account to honor the embodied experiences and existence of anti-Black racism and structural gendered racism (Pirtle and Wright 2021) and their interrelationship with reproductive oppression. While disentangling gametes from gendered logics is important work, reproductions are stratified based not only on gender but also on white supremacist and classist logics. Appropriately drawing on Reproductive Justice in sperm, health, and politics requires, for example, that we think about how visions of achieving justice might necessarily look different depending on whom exactly we envision. The requirements for achieving reproductive justice will differ between a low-income cisgender woman of color, a white cisgender man, and a trans person navigating their reproductive future amid a different set of gendered constraints. It is in the spirit of recognizing and honoring these differences that I offer *stratified reproductive justice*.

Stratified reproductive justice is a framework that extends Reproductive Justice by integrating it with *stratified reproduction*, a concept developed by Shellee Colen (1995, 78) to capture the fact that reproduction is experienced, valued, and rewarded differently based on hierarchies organized according to race, gender, class, migration status, and global social position, among other dimensions. Colen's theorizing helped scholars grapple with the way that marginalized people's reproduction is devalued. I deploy it here to call attention to the ways that *people who produce sperm* may simultaneously experience both privilege and oppression depending on the particular intersection of their social identities. Drawing on stratified reproduction acknowledges that struggles to articulate reproductive justice for a broader group of individuals and issues must occur first by situating people's experiences and histories within these respective contexts. As reproductive actors, people have their emotional, physical, and mental labor valued differently based on their social location. Contextualizing people's experiences within the context of stratification when applying a Reproductive Justice lens increases the chances that we will address the needs of a broader group of individuals without encroaching on the often-fragile rights of targeted groups. Uncritically applying Reproductive Justice can lead to harming the very people the framework was created to protect.

Stratified reproductive justice is meant to offer not a specific definition but a way of thinking that helps develop visions of reproductive justice that remain grounded in a rejection of oppression and the multitudinous ways that it affects different communities rather than an obfuscation of power and inequity in service of achieving "reproductive justice for all."

I offer here some ways to extend a reproductive justice lens to sperm by deploying stratified reproductive justice as an analytic frame.

The Human Right to Have a Child

When it comes to sperm, this tenet is perhaps the most obviously susceptible to co-optation and furtherance of harm without a stratified reproductive justice lens. It is not uncommon for people to link sperm to both bodies and gender identities to advocate for the rights of someone other than the pregnant person. In fact, political scientist Anthony DiMaggio (2023) argues that the men's rights ideology that promotes men's control and domination of women plays an important role in motivating antiabortion sentiment. Of course, subordinating the rights of the pregnant person in favor of the person who coconceived the pregnancy violates a core tenet of Reproductive Justice and is a familiar form of reproductive oppression.

In thinking about the human right to have a child using a stratified reproductive justice lens, it becomes clear that applying Reproductive Justice to sperm requires grappling with how articulating rights in this domain affects existing power structures used to regulate and surveil the bodies of those capable of pregnancy. To argue that people who contribute their sperm to create a fetus have the human right to have a child could contribute to the continued entrenchment of horrific violations that occurred before *Dobbs v. Jackson Women's Health Organization* and that can occur even more frequently in its wake as some people who helped conceive a pregnancy fight to control its resolution by blocking abortion (Earley 2023; Gunia 2019).

Instead, stratified reproductive justice suggests the importance of articulating a different set of principles that draw on the Reproductive Justice vision of human rights but apply in the context of people who produce sperm. For example, low-income people who produce sperm have the human right to have their infertility understood. They have the human right to have the etiology of their infertility researched and taken seriously. They have the right to access support for infertility treatments without stigma. If they identify as trans and decide to have a biological child, they have the right to pursue that option without fear of violence or retribution.

Thus, Reproductive Justice offers a vision for people's rights, and stratified reproductive justice offers a framework for thinking about how to envision these basic rights in other contexts. Drawing on a core tenet of Reproductive Justice in this way uplifts its radical potential for advancing justice for people denied rights in and out of court without siphoning power from the disenfranchised. It can center the experiences of the marginalized while remaining applicable to people who have more privilege, just as Reproductive Justice has long done.

The Human Right Not to Have a Child

With this second core tenet of reproductive justice, the framework of stratified reproductive justice calls our attention to the grave importance of rejecting a simplistic application of Reproductive Justice to sperm. People who can produce sperm do not have the right to apply coercive tactics or otherwise compel partners to act in particular ways to fulfill their own desires to avoid pregnancy and births. Instead, upholding reproductive justice means that people have a right to pursue knowledge, access tools, and receive resources to prevent pregnancy. They have a right to access vasectomy affordably and without stigma. They have a right to use and have access to prescription methods designed to target sperm so that they may feel secure in preventing pregnancy at each act of sexual intercourse. They have a right to have access to these methods when and where they need them. They have a right to learn about fertility and all birth control methods, rather than only those considered "male methods" so that they can approach sexual intercourse with the knowledge they need to achieve their reproductive goals. And, though it is often de-emphasized as a contraceptive tool in relation to prescription contraception, they have the human right to wear condoms for the prevention of pregnancy and disease. Of course, this is just a short list of issues that relate to the human right not to have a child. My hope is that stratified reproductive justice serves as a generative framework that can be applied to a whole host of issues under this and the other core Reproductive Justice tenets.

The Human Right to Parent the Children They Have in Safe and Healthy Environments

Last, stratified reproductive justice suggests that thinking through parenting requires grappling with the complex matrices of oppression that entangle caregivers, whether they contribute their sperm or eggs. It means fighting for environmental justice. It means fighting against a carceral system that would see Black and Brown children removed from their fathers, mapas (a gender-neutral parenting term that combines "mama" and "papa"), and caregivers of other identities. It means putting an end to gun violence that robs people of their children. It means eradicating police violence that disproportionately robs Black and Brown children of their parents. It means fighting against laws that would see children removed from homes with parents who support their gender-affirming care. Applying Reproductive Justice to sperm without thinking critically about what it means to decenter birthing people may obfuscate the ways that advocating for the rights of coparents can be used to support everyone involved in raising children in safe and healthy communities.

Rather than offering a myopic and simplistic vision of reproductive justice as "Reproductive Justice for all," stratified reproductive justice calls on us to consider multiple dimensions of privilege and oppression for the targeted group to center a vision that addresses the most marginalized to pull them in from the periphery while also being applicable for people traditionally at the center.

A Brief, Concrete Application of a Stratified Reproductive Justice Approach

Given that stratified reproductive justice is a framework that draws on multiple important concepts, it may be helpful before concluding to provide a concrete example of how researchers interested in applying the perspective might go about doing so. Consider a researcher planning a study on contraceptive use among a diverse population of cisgender men. In applying a stratified reproductive justice lens, such a qualitative study might ask certain questions: How do participants understand the barriers that they face to accessing and using contraceptives to prevent pregnancy? What advantages do they face relative to their less privileged counterparts? Answering the latter question could involve putting findings from the study in conversation with existing research on barriers to accessing and using contraception among less advantaged populations. Next, researchers might discuss the ways that the specific barriers revealed in the study are shaped by the privileges and constraints that cisgender men face in an unequal society. And, finally, researchers could make suggestions for what helping cisgender men achieve reproductive justice might look like based on the challenges that they experience and pay careful attention to the implications of their suggestions for pregnant and birthing partners and people. This is simply one example. The framework is meant to be flexible to allow scholars using all kinds of methodologies to conceive of novel ways to structure their questions and suggested interventions.

Conclusion

In sum, it is my hope that in advancing stratified reproductive justice as a framework for those looking to apply Reproductive Justice to their communities of interest, we can uplift the voices of Reproductive Justice leaders while maintaining the integrity of a radical activist framework created to address the systemic oppression that women of color suffer. Stratified reproductive justice rests on the premise that true reproductive justice requires recognizing the differences in needs and the disproportionate violation of rights faced by targeted and nontargeted groups when advocating for better conditions using a Reproductive Justice frame. I offer stratified reproductive justice as an emergent concept that I hope will generate conversation and new ideas to move forward with crucial transformative and liberatory work.

REFERENCES

Asian Communities for Reproductive Justice. 2005. *A New Vision for Advancing Our Movement for Reproductive Health, Reproductive Rights, and Reproductive Justice*. Oakland, CA: Asian Communities for Reproductive Justice. https://forwardtogether.org.

Boorstein, Michelle. 2022. "Clergy Sue to Halt Florida Abortion Law, Citing Religious Freedom." *Washington Post*, September 1, 2022.

Colen, Shellee. 1995. "'Like A Mother to Them': Stratified Reproduction and West Indian Childcare Workers and Employers in New York." In *Conceiving the New World Order: The Global Politics of Reproduction*, edited by Faye D. Ginsburg and Rayna Rapp, 78–102. Berkeley: University of California Press.

DiMaggio, Anthony. 2023. "War on Women: The Link between White Supremacy, 'Men's Rights' and Anti-Abortion Politics." *Salon*, April 1, 2023. www.salon.com.

Earley, Neal. 2023. "Bill Would Expand Exception to Arkansas' Abortion Ban." *Arkansas Democrat Gazette*, March 23, 2023. www.arkansasonline.com.

Gunia, Amy. 2019. "An Alabama Man Is Suing an Abortion Clinic on Behalf of an Aborted Fetus." *TIME*, March 7, 2019. https://time.com.

Henneberg, Christine. 2023. "Abortion Stories Matter." *New York Times*, July 5, 2023.

Pirtle, Whitney N. Laster, and Tashelle Wright. 2021. "Structural Gendered Racism Revealed in Pandemic Times: Intersectional Approaches to Understanding Race and Gender Health Inequities in COVID-19." *Gender & Society* 35 (2): 168–79.

Robinson, Zandria Felice. 2016. "Intersectionality." In *Handbook of Contemporary Sociological Theory*, edited by Seth Abrutyn, 477–99. Switzerland: Springer International Publishing.

Ross, Loretta, and Rickie Solinger. 2017. *Reproductive Justice: An Introduction*. Berkeley: University of California Press.

Zernike, Kate. 2023. "Abortion Views Shifted in Polls After Roe's End." *New York Times*, June 25, 2023.

PART II

Counting Sperm

6

Male Infertility Is a Public Health Problem

CHRISTOPHER DE JONGE

In 2012, the World Health Organization (WHO) impaneled a group of reproductive health experts to systematically scope the relevant science literature with the goal of developing comprehensive guidelines on infertility based on recommendations from answers to key PICO (Problem/Population, Intervention, Comparison, Outcome) questions (WHO 2014). A subset of the experts was tasked specifically with evaluating the literature on the "diagnosis of male infertility." An overarching and alarming conclusion from the panel was that the global frequency and proportion of infertility attributed to the male could not be determined (Barratt et al. 2017). The reasons contributing to the conclusion were significant knowledge gaps in the literature database, poor quality or no research as a part of the gaps, and low quality in the evidence published. To address the gaps, the male infertility panel made recommendations to substantively increase funding and infrastructure to support basic and clinical research to yield high-quality research data outputs. The paths to address the recommendations may superficially appear simple but upon closer investigation are complex, and quite necessary. To put it simply, deficits in high-quality research inhibit the development of novel diagnostic tests and new treatment strategies, which directly impacts bettering public health. Such is the case for male infertility.

The Male Infertility Problem in the United States

One in six couples who are of reproductive age are afflicted by infertility, meaning they have been unsuccessful in attempts to achieve pregnancy over a twelve-month period in the absence of contraception (WHO 2023). An etiology, or cause, of infertility is found with equal incidence in females and males, with 40 percent for each. However, for the remaining 20 percent of couples, no diagnosis can be made, so the cause of infertility is left as unexplained.

The number of people in the United States seeking help for infertility has been steadily rising, as evidenced by the annual publication of the *Assisted Reproductive Technology Fertility Clinic and National Summary Report* by the Centers for Disease Control and Prevention.[1] Perhaps reflective of how impactful infertility is, the CDC developed an IVF (in vitro fertilization) Success Estimator, in which an individual enters data (e.g., age, weight, height) to calculate the chance of success for pregnancy and live birth after IVF.[2] While the estimator is informative, it is so only for the female; regrettably, male and couple information are not able to be entered into the calculation. This bias is not surprising because since the beginning of human IVF—and even predominant today—the female is frequently considered the primary patient, even though the couple's infertility diagnosis might be due to a male factor. For example, if a male factor, such as abnormal semen parameters—whether attributable to hormonal, structural, or genetic factors—cannot be treated through pharmaceutical, surgical, or lifestyle interventions, then the reproductively healthy female becomes the surrogate patient for the male and must suffer the burden of being "treated" for infertility in the male.

For a couple having difficulty conceiving, the infertility investigation most frequently begins with the obstetrician-gynecologist or reproductive gynecologist, in part because men of reproductive age tend to be absent from health care seeking (e.g., Mahalik, Burns, and Syzdek 2007). If the clinician determines that more advanced diagnostic testing and therapeutic intervention is indicated, then the next step is patient referral to a provider with subspeciality training in reproductive medicine and assisted reproductive technologies. In fact, a recent study presented data that an ob-gyn with subspecialty training in reproductive endocrinology and infertility is also the primary gatekeeper for the *male* infertility investigation (Samplaski et al. 2019).

In addition, the data alarmingly revealed that prior to being referred to a reproductive endocrinologist, only 4.8 percent of the men had a prior male reproductive health evaluation (Samplaski et al. 2019). This is significant for at least two reasons: (1) approximately 17 percent of referred couples had previously undergone a medically assisted reproduction procedure, such as intrauterine insemination or IVF, and (2) an earlier medical evaluation of the male for infertility may have revealed infertility-associated medical problems, such as testicular tumors, metabolic disorders, and cardiovascular disease (see, e.g., Kolettis and Sabanegh 2001; Eisenberg et al. 2015). Furthermore, the study raises questions regarding adequacy of access for males to reproductive health services and male infertility specialists.

Barriers in Access to Male Infertility Care

Infertility is classified as a disease by the American Medical Association and the World Health Organization. However, unlike most other diseases, many insurance companies in the United States do not cover male infertility diagnosis or treatment. In fact, of the fifteen states where infertility coverage is mandated by law, only eight include coverage for the male (Dupree, Dickey, and Lipshultz 2016). Lack of insurance coverage creates a barrier for males to access infertility health care and also results in missed opportunities to diagnose potentially serious infertility-related health conditions or treat diseases, such as testicular cancer, at an earlier stage and places an undue burden on the female partner should the couple progress in IVF treatment (Dupree 2018).

In 2019, 448 US fertility clinics reported over 330,000 IVF cycles to the CDC (CDC 2021). This number of IVF cycles is double the number reported in 2010 and shows no signs of slowing growth. In the CDC report, 27 percent of cases of infertility for which couples used IVF were directly attributed to a male factor. Using this percentage and allowing for the fact that some cycles reported were for egg banking and not for insemination of eggs in a current IVF treatment cycle, it can reasonably be estimated that 300,000 IVF procedures required sperm and that a male factor was the diagnosis for the couple's infertility in over 81,000 cycles.

The American Society for Reproductive Medicine (ASRM) is an organization with over 8,000 members dedicated to advancing the science and practice of reproductive medicine. In 2019, Bobby B. Najari, MD, reported that there were more than 1,300 ob-gyn ASRM members registered from North America. In stark contrast, there were only 185 urologist members registered from North America. These latter data suggest the possibility of a barrier in access to infertility care for the more than 80,000 men with a diagnosis of male infertility due to an inadequate number of urologists (Najari 2019).

The 2021 US census reported almost sixty-seven million people between twenty-five and forty years of age. It is estimated that approximately 16 percent of reproductive-age couples suffers from subfertility. Using the 2021 census data, more than ten million couples in the United States are likely to suffer from subfertility and an estimated four to five million may be the result of a male factor. The American Urological Association (AUA) in their 2021 annual census reported that there were 13,790 practicing urologists in the United States, of which 40 percent (5,547) had advanced fellowship training (AUA 2022). Only 2.2 percent (303) of practicing urologists had a primary subspeciality area in male infertility. Including general urologists with male infertility subspecialists brings the total to 8,546. Thus, there are less than 10,000 urologists in the United States to provide health care for a potential five million male infertility patients. Based on an extrapolation from National Survey of Family Growth data, an estimated 900,000 men in the infertile population did not have a male evaluation when they and their female partner met with an infertility specialist for treatment (Eisenberg et al. 2013). Collectively, these back-of-the-envelope calculations suggest that a formidable barrier exists in access for men in need of a reproductive health evaluation, due in part to inadequate numbers of male reproductive health specialists. What might be contributing to this health care problem?

To help address this question, a survey of aspiring urology medical residents, residency directors, and urology educators was conducted (Kerfoot and Turek 2008). The participants were asked to rank the most important topics in the urology core curriculum at their medical schools. The highest ranked topic related to infertility was impotence (erectile dysfunction), which ranked ninth out of twenty topics. The next highest ranked infertility-related topic was vasectomy, which ranked sixteenth. The data reveal that the importance of male infertility education and training ranks low in the core curricula of future urologists.

In a more recent survey of medical students representing half of accredited medical schools in the United States, the results revealed that 98 percent of respondents did not have a clinical urology rotation required at their school, and male infertility was the least frequent topic experienced by students in either preclinical or clinical teaching (Kreshover et al. 2022). Perhaps more surprising is the lack in education and training regarding male reproductive health to future urologists. Only 6 percent of urologists who identify as an andrologist (male reproductive health specialist) perform male infertility procedures (AUA 2022). Making matters worse is that the number of new urologists is declining (Nam et al. 2021). Collectively, these data demonstrate that a barrier exists for men who desire access to infertility evaluation due, in part, to insufficiency in medical education and training in urology residency programs and declining numbers of new urologists. The increasing frequency of infertility along with associated male ill-health conditions raises an urgent question of whether a redesign of medical training programs is indicated (Mehta et al. 2016). However, on an encouraging note, there are now fifteen andrology-specific fellowship training programs in the United States with the specific mission of training the next generation of clinical andrology specialists.

Additional formidable obstacles exist for males beyond access to reproductive health care, such as provision of infertility insurance, geographic location, race, education, and cultural beliefs (Mehta et al. 2016; Grover 2023).

The Rationale for a Male Reproductive Health Initiative

In 2018, we published an opinion piece with the striking call to action of "Man Up" in the title. In the paper, we advocated for the global need to position male reproductive health prominently in national political and research funding initiatives (Barratt, De Jonge, and Sharpe 2018). The paper expanded on the conclusions of the WHO panel by outlining goals to address other knowledge gaps regarding male reproductive health (Barratt et al. 2017). For example, one critical knowledge gap regards the view of male infertility as a disease state and the impact it has on socioeconomics. For other diseases (e.g., infectious diseases) there are ample high-quality data that help to characterize impacts on society and the economy. For male infertility, those research data are elusive at best and, as such, represent an important goal to be achieved.

In the 2018 paper, we presented a strategy, termed the Male Reproductive Health Ecosystem, that identifies essential components to accomplish the goals outlined (see figure 6.1) (Barratt, De Jonge, and Sharpe 2018). Briefly, the strategy sets forth (1) the identification and prioritization by diverse stakeholders of fundamental research gaps that exist, (2) the development of a "roadmap" that has clear deliverables throughout the process, (3) strategic funding to support essential research, and (4) changes in policies to reinforce strategic funding schemes. The strategic goals in the Male Reproductive Health Ecosystem are dynamic and multidimensional, with the various components in a constant state of interaction, generating results, progress, and paths forward.

One of our first tasks toward accomplishing Male Reproductive Health Ecosystem goals was to conduct a comprehensive examination of the emerging male reproductive health literature, which led to the conclusion that male reproductive health is in a state of crisis (De Jonge and Barratt 2019). Evidence to support use of the term *crisis* to characterize the global state of male reproductive health are (1) reports of globally declining sperm counts (Levine et al. 2023), (2) increasing testicular cancer rates (Znaor et al. 2014), and (3) growing evidence that male infertility is a likely portent of future health problems (Latif et al. 2017; Del Giudice et al. 2020). These health problems include cardiovascular disease (Kasman et al. 2019) and metabolic disorders (Glazer et al. 2017). Equally alarming is emerging evidence that male infertility negatively impacts maternal peripartum wellness and new baby wellness and that some paternally inherited health conditions are being transmitted to offspring (e.g., Pembrey et al. 2006; De Jonge and Barratt 2019; Eisenberg, Barratt, and De Jonge 2022).

The reproductive, somatic (bodily) and transgenerational health issues briefly outlined here should be a significant cause of concern for the whole of society, the US health care system, and the federal government. Further, it reinforces the Male Reproductive Health Ecosystem model that advocates for a broad spectrum of stakeholders be engaged so that more comprehensive and inclusive action can be taken. In an effort to catalyze these actions, we organized the Male Reproductive Health Initiative (MRHI) in 2019.[3] MRHI is a consortium of key opinion leaders representing reproductive medicine and science, economics, and patient

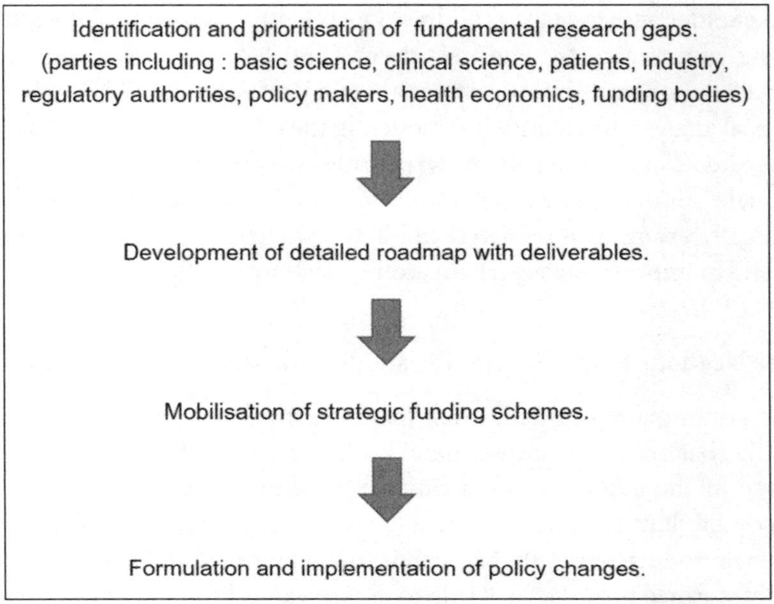

Identification and prioritisation of fundamental research gaps.
(parties including : basic science, clinical science, patients, industry, regulatory authorities, policy makers, health economics, funding bodies)

Development of detailed roadmap with deliverables.

Mobilisation of strategic funding schemes.

Formulation and implementation of policy changes.

Figure 6.1: Male Reproductive Health Ecosystem (Barratt, De Jonge, and Sharpe 2018).

support groups. In just the past few years, MRHI has produced numerous publications that have presented substantive evidence of the critical gaps in scientific knowledge, medical practice, financial and health care resources, policy, and social support systems (e.g., De Jonge, Barratt, and Pacey 2022; Gumerova et al. 2022; De Jonge et al. 2023). Most recently, after a thorough review of MRH literature data, a comprehensive male reproductive health needs assessment was done to address the most significant gaps and formulate an end-to-end strategy to remedy the gaps (Barratt et al. 2021, Kimmins et al. 2023).

The reception of MRHI from scientific, medical, and support group communities has been overwhelmingly positive and encouraging, as reflected by invitations to present plenary lectures at reproductive medicine meetings around the world. In 2022, a globally accessible hybrid workshop on male reproductive health, supported by the European Society of Human Reproduction and Embryology, was convened in Budapest, Hungary. The aims of the workshop were to engage a diverse stakeholder audience to (1) address key scientific and clinical questions along with strategies to address them, (2) delve into current practices for education and training of health care professionals and to provide critical analysis to identify if remodeling the current structure would be more beneficial to the patient, (3) provide background for why the study of male reproductive health is necessary and of global urgency, and (4) critically examine how MRHI can better interact with and inform the public to improve male participation in seeking health care.

The Need for Social Awareness about Male Reproductive Health

The accumulating evidence that male infertility may serve as a canary in the coal mine for future general health issues emphasizes the importance of the evidence being rapidly integrated into medical school curricula. Future clinicians are a lynchpin for social awareness about male reproductive health. Early education of teenage and adult males by well-informed providers will help to mitigate and allow for early detection of disease states (Shand and Marcell 2021; O'Brien et al. 2018). As the adage goes, "An ounce of prevention is worth a pound of cure," and this makes financial sense for payors, i.e., insurance companies, as well. It goes without saying that a loss of a partner/husband/father/worker to acute or chronic disease negatively impacts not only a household but a community and economy.

For progress to occur in the men's health care seeking, there must also be a reorientation of men's health care services to better meet their specific needs, and that starts with identifying how men best communicate. For example, women, in general, tend to volunteer information whereas men are reticent to volunteer information, especially information that might threaten their perceptions of masculinity. Therefore, with feedback from diverse groups of men, new strategies of communication can be developed that will ask men key questions about problems or issues regarding their physical health and mental well-being. Further, reproductive health services from family planning and beyond need to design an environment that is inclusive of and welcoming to men (Mursa, Patterson, and Halcomb 2022).

To demonstrate and prioritize the social and economic importance of male reproductive health, it is necessary that legislation be passed to establish an Office on Men's Health that is analogous to the existing Office on Women's Health.[4] Like the Office of Women's Health, the Office of Men's Health could be embedded in the Department of Health and Human Services and with the vision that all men and boys achieve the best possible health (Miner et al. 2018). Currently, the Men's Health Awareness and Improvement Act (H.R. 5986) is stalled within the US House of Representatives and faces an uncertain future. Finally, the federal government offers a free resource in the form of Public Service Announcements supported by broadcast media, which might be an effective tool to broadcast the social importance of how a healthy lifestyle contributes to overall health, including reproductive health, for men, women, and children.

Conclusion

This brief essay started with a declaration that sperm counts are reportedly declining and male infertility is increasing and *we don't have clear evidence about why these changes are happening* except that they are inexorably related. What we have learned is that these two male reproductive health issues are but the tip of the iceberg of a much bigger problem and that to fully appreciate the full scale of the problem required a thorough analysis of the scientific literature.

The results from our deep dive revealed numerous fundamental knowledge gaps and that to fill those gaps required much more basic research and an increase in strategic funding (Kimmins et al. 2023). High-quality research outputs translate into the development of new and better medical diagnostic tests and therapeutic strategies, both of which are desperately needed for male infertility.

Along with the need for a better understanding of factors that cause infertility, we are also learning that a diagnosis of male infertility appears to serve as a bellwether for overall male wellness. Consequently, with an increasing incidence of infertility there is also an increase in infertility-related illnesses, and this means that men will have an even greater need to access health care.

Access presents a critical problem not only from the patient position but also from the provider side. For the former, it is important for men from all demographics to feel that when they access health care services they are in a welcoming and safe environment that is sensitive to their physical and emotional needs. For the latter, data show that there is an inadequate number of providers with advanced training in male reproductive health, and that serves as a limiting barrier to access.

The acknowledgment and acceptance of male infertility as a disease and a critical public health problem requires much needed socioeconomic data as evidence to demonstrate that infertility and related illnesses have an impact on the family, community, and society. It is important to conclude this piece by stressing that men's health is also women's health, family health, and community health (Miner et al. 2108; De Jonge and Barratt 2019).

NOTES

1 The report can be found at Centers for Disease Control and Prevention, "ART Success Rates," last reviewed January 8, 2024, www.cdc.gov.
2 The tool can be found at Centers for Disease Control and Prevention, "IVF Success Estimator," last reviewed September 13, 2019, www.cdc.gov.
3 More information on the MRHI can be found at https://www.eshre.eu/Specialty-groups/Special-Interest-Groups/Andrology/MRHI.
4 The Office on Women's Health website: www.womenshealth.gov.

REFERENCES

American Urological Association (AUA). 2022. *The State of Urology Workforce and Practice in the United States 2021*. Linthicum, MD: American Urological Association. www.AUAnet.org.

Barratt, Christopher L. R., Lars Björndahl, Christopher J. De Jonge, Dolores J. Lamb, Francisco Osorio Martini, Robert McLachlan, Robert Oates et al. 2017. "The Diagnosis of Male Infertility: An Analysis of the Evidence to Support the Development of Global WHO Guidance Challenges and Future Research Opportunities." *Human Reproduction Update* 23 (6): 660–80.

Barratt, Christopher L. R., Christopher J. De Jonge, and Richard M. Sharpe. 2018. "'Man Up': The Importance and Strategy for Placing Male Reproductive Health Centre Stage in the Political and Research Agenda." *Human Reproduction* 33 (4): 541–45.

Barratt, Christopher L. R., Christopher J. De Jonge, Richard A. Anderson, Michael L. Eisenberg, Nicolàs Garrido, Satu Rautakallio Hokkanen, Csilla Krausz et al. 2021. "A Global Approach to Addressing the Policy, Research and Social Challenges of Male Reproductive Health." *Human Reproduction Open* 2021 (1): hoab009.

Centers for Disease Control and Prevention (CDC). 2021. *2019 Assisted Reproductive Technology Fertility Clinic and National Summary Report*. N.p.: US Dept of Health and Human Services.

De Jonge, Christopher J., and Christopher L. R. Barratt. 2019. "The Present Crisis in Male Reproductive Health: An Urgent Need for a Political, Social, and Research Roadmap." *Andrology* 7:762–68.

De Jonge, Christopher J., Steven A. Gellatly, Mónica H. Vazquez-Levin, Christopher L. R. Barratt, and Satu Rautakallio Hokkanen. 2023. "Male Attitudes Towards Infertility—Results from a Global Questionnaire." *World Journal of Men's Health* 41 (1): 204–14.

De Jonge, Christopher J., Christopher L. R. Barratt, and Allan A. Pacey. 2022. "Counting the Hidden Costs of Male Reproductive Health." *World Journal of Men's Health* 40 (2): 344–45.

Del Giudice, Francesco, Alex M. Kasman, Matteo Ferro, Alessandro Sciarra, Ettore De Berardinis, Federico Belladelli, Andrea Salonia, and Michael L. Eisenberg. 2020. "Clinical Correlation among Male Infertility and Overall Male Health: A Systematic Review of the Literature." *Investigative and Clinical Urology* 61 (4): 355–71.

Dupree, James M. 2018. "Insurance Coverage of Male Infertility: What Should the Standard Be?" Supplement, *Translational Andrology and Urology* 7 (S3): S310–16.

Dupree, James M., Ryan M. Dickey, and Larry I. Lipshultz. 2016. "Inequity Between Male and Female Coverage in State Infertility Laws." *Fertility and Sterility* 105 (6): 1,519–22.

Eisenberg, Michael L., Ruth B. Lathi, Valerie L. Baker, Lynn M. Westphal, Amin A. Milki, and Ajay K. Nangia. 2013. "Frequency of the Male Infertility Evaluation: Data from the National Survey of Family Growth." *Urology* 189:1,030–34.

Eisenberg, Michael L., Shufeng Li, Barry Behr, Renee Reijo Pera, and Mark R. Cullen. 2015. "Relationship Between Semen Production and Medical Comorbidity." *Fertility and Sterility* 103:66–71.

Eisenberg, Michael L., Christopher L.R. Barratt, and Christopher J. De Jonge. 2022. "Don't Forget the Father." *Fertility and Sterility* 117:936–937.

Glazer, Clara H., Jens P. Bonde, Michael L. Eisenberg, Aleksander Giwercman, Katia K. Hærvig, Susie Rimborg, Ditte Vassard, Anja Pinborg, Lone Schmidt, and Elvira V. Bräuner. 2017. "Male Infertility and Risk of Nonmalignant Chronic Diseases: A Systematic Review of the Epidemiological Evidence." *Seminars in Reproductive Medicine* 35:282–90.

Grover, Atul. 2023. "A Physician Crisis in the Rural US May Be About to Get Worse." *JAMA* 330:21–22.

Gumerova, Eva, Christopher J. De Jonge, and Christopher L.R. Barratt. 2022. "Research Funding for Male Reproductive Health and Infertility in the UK and USA (2016–2019)." *Human Fertility* 26:439–49.

Kasman, Alex M., Shufeng Li, Barbara Luke, Alastair G. Sutcliffe, Allan A. Pacey, and Michael L. Eisenberg. 2019. "Male Infertility and Future Cardiometabolic Health: Does the Association Vary by Sociodemographic Factors?" *Urology* 133:121–8.

Kerfoot, B. Price, and Paul J. Turek. 2008. "What Every Graduating Medical Student Should Know about Urology: The Stakeholder Viewpoint." *Urology* 71:549–53.

Kimmins, Sarah, Richard A. Anderson, Christopher L.R. Barratt, Hermann M. Behre, Sarah R. Catford, Christopher J. De Jonge CJ, Geraldine Delbes G et al. 2023. "Frequency, Morbidity and Equity—The Case for Increased Research on Male Infertility." *Nature Reviews Urology* 21:102–124.

Kolettis, Peter N., and Edmund S. Sabanegh. 2001. "Significant Medical Pathology Discovered During a Male Infertility valuation." *Journal of Urology* 166:178–80.

Kreshover, Jessica E., Alex J. Vanni, Kevan M. Sternberg, Naeem Bhojani, and Kathleen C Kobashi. 2022. "Urological Education in United States Medical Schools: Where Are We Now and How Can We Do Better?" *Urology Practice* 9:581–586.

Latif, Tabassam, Tina K. Jensen, Jesper Mehlsen, Stine A. Holmboe, Louise Brinth, Kirsten Pors, Sven O. Skouby, Niels Jørgensen, and Rune Lindahl-Jacobsen. 2017. "Semen Quality as a Predictor of Subsequent Morbidity: A Danish Cohort Study of 4,712 Men With Long-Term Follow-up." *American Journal of Epidemiology* 186:910–917.

Levine, Hagai, Niels Jørgensen, Anderson Martino-Andrade, Jaime Mendiola, Dan Weksler-Derri, Maya Jolles, Rachel Pinotti, and Shanna H. Swan. 2023. "Temporal Trends in Sperm Count: A Systematic Review and Meta-regression Analysis of Samples Collected Globally in the 20th and 21st Centuries." *Human Reproduction Update* 29:157–176.

Mahalik, James R., Shaun M. Burns, and Matthew Syzdek. 2007. "Masculinity and Perceived Normative Health Behaviors as Predictors of Men's Health Behaviors." *Social Science & Medicine* 64:2,201–9.

Mehta, Akanksha, Ajay K. Nangia, James M. Dupree, and James F. Smith. 2016. "Limitations and Barriers in Access to Care for Male Factor Infertility." *Fertility and Sterility* 105:1,128–37.

Miner Martin M., Joel Heidelbaugh, Mark Paulos, Allen D. Seftel, Jason Jameson, and Steven A. Kaplan. 2018. "The Intersection of Medicine and Urology: An Emerging Paradigm of Sexual Function, Cardiometabolic Risk, Bone Health and Men's Health Centers." *Medical Clinics of North America* 102:399–415.

Mursa, Ruth, Christopher Patterson, and Elizabeth Halcomb. 2022. "Men's Help-Seeking and Engagement with General Practice: An Integrative Review." *Journal of Advanced Nursing* 78:1,938–53.

Najari, Bobby B. 2019. "The Demographics of Men Presenting to Male Factor Infertility Specialists: The Impressive First Report from the Andrology Research Consortium." *Fertility and Sterility* 112:642–43.

Nam, Catherine S., Stephanie Daignault-Newton, Kate H. Kraft, and Lindsey A. Herrel. 2021. "Projected US Urology Workforce per Capita, 2020–2060." *JAMA Network Open* 4 (11): e2133864.

O'Brien, Anthony P., John Hurley, Paul Linsley, Karen A. McNeil, Richard Fletcher, and John R. Aitken. 2018. "Men's Preconception Health: A Primary Health-Care Viewpoint." *American Journal of Men's Health* 12:1575–1581.

Pembrey, Marcus E., Lars O. Bygren, Gunnar Kaati, Sören Edvinsson, Kate Northstone, Michael Sjöström, and Jean Golding; ALSPAC Study Team. 2006. "Sex-Specific,

Male-Line Transgenerational Responses in Humans." *European Journal of Human Genetics* 14:159–66.

Samplaski, Mary K., James F. Smith, Kirk C. Lo, James M. Hotaling, Susan Lau, Ethan D. Grober, and J.C. Trussell et al. 2019. "Reproductive Endocrinologists are the Gatekeepers for Male Infertility Care in North America: Results of a North American Survey on the Referral Patterns and Characteristics of Men Presenting to Male Infertility Specialists for Infertility Investigations." *Fertility and Sterility* 112:657–662.

Shand, Tim, and Arik V. Marcell. 2021. "Engaging Men in Sexual and Reproductive Health." *Oxford Research Encyclopedia of Global Public Health*. https://oxfordre.com.

Soubry, Adelheid, Cathrine Hoyo, Randy L. Jirtle, and Susan K. Murphy. 2014. "A Paternal Environmental Legacy: Evidence for Epigenetic Inheritance Through the Male Germ Line." *BioEssays* 36:359–371.

World Health Organization (WHO). 2014. "WHO Handbook for Guideline Development." World Health Organization, www.who.int.

World Health Organization (WHO). 2023. Infertility prevalence estimates, 1990–2021. Geneva: World Health Organization; 2023. www.who.int.

Znaor, Ariana, Joannie Lortet-Tieulent, Ahmedin Jemal, and Freddie Bray. 2014. "International variations and trends in testicular cancer incidence and mortality." *European Urology* 65:1095–106.

7

How Male Infertility Diagnosis and Treatment Evolved over the Last Two Decades

STANTON HONIG

The study and treatment of sperm historically has taken a back seat to the oocyte. This is in contradistinction to historical gender disparities leaning toward male bodies (Epstein 2007). As a provider, patient advocate, and professional society leader, it has been my goal to promulgate appropriate information to health care providers, health care administration, legislative bodies and patients regarding the disparity of knowledge and information regarding the diagnosis and treatment of problems related to sperm.

While we are focused on the word *sperm* in this volume, it is critical to remember that there is a person with medical issues, emotions, and often strong feelings of inadequacy regarding the inability to achieve a pregnancy with a partner. It is clear that 50 percent of fertility problems are related to sperm issues (see De Jonge, this volume).

Historically, and generally speaking, the concept of pregnancy has been driven by the female partner. Male participation has been more limited and, in heterosexual relationships, medical care is often driven by the female partner; much of the time they are gate keepers for medical care in the family. As boys age into adults, they are less likely to engage in regular visits with a primary care doctor until some medical problem exists (see Marcell, this volume). When it comes to producing a semen analysis, there tends to be tremendous fear and embarrassment that a problem may exist. This may delay care in many situations. This is in contradistinction to patients with reproductive organs such as ovaries and uterus, who often develop relationships with their OB-GYN team and generally participate in regular care throughout the years (see Marcell, this volume). (There are direct-to-consumer "home sperm tests" available for screening for male infertility. They are good but not great tests. However, they do give the patient an opportunity to start to be checked on his own without the embarrassment of dropping off a sperm sample in a laboratory.)

When there are problems with sperm, there are significant barriers to the spread of knowledge and care. This occurs because many dollars are being made on direct use of assisted reproductive technologies, as opposed to evaluating the male. Much of this is driven by a health care industry that offers assisted reproductive services, such as intrauterine insemination, in vitro fertilization, intracytoplasmic sperm injection (ICSI), and so on. In addition, support from industry drives the IVF market and tends to neglect the diagnosis and treatment of sperm-related problems. Patient advocacy groups such as Resolve have, in recent years, increased their focus on sperm issues, but most support groups, discussion groups, and chat rooms are driven by medical and emotional issues associated with oocytes and pregnancy.

Likewise, much of the legislative support at federal and state levels has been driven by assisted reproductive technologies. Many states mandate insurance coverage for IVF but do not mandate treatment of the male partner. In addition, the Centers for Disease Control and Prevention (CDC) does not have a division of Men's Health. Rather men's reproductive health is incorporated under the umbrella of Women's Reproductive Care. We convened a CDC meeting about fifteen years ago for the specific discussion of sperm-related issues (CDC 2010). This meeting brought together thought leaders in urology, psychiatry, legislation, and industry. This was in an attempt to clarify how to identify treatable and reversible causes of male infertility and how to spread the word about the importance of this. In fact, one of the important points that was stressed was that some patients with male reproductive issues can present with significant medical pathology such as testis cancer, pituitary brain issues, genetic abnormalities, diabetes, and nerve related issues that need treatment above and beyond treatment of the infertility. But there have been no further discussions at the CDC since. The importance of understanding the link between medical pathology and male factor infertility cannot be emphasized enough.

When I started in this field over thirty years ago, there were two fellowships in male infertility. There are now twenty fellowships in male reproductive medicine and surgery. We have made great progress in learning about the health of patients with male infertility, sperm abnormalities, and genetic abnormalities that may cause these problems. But we still have a long way to go. Basic research and continuing efforts from the CDC are necessary to move this field forward.

So how do we move forward? In my view, recent guidelines on male infertility developed jointly by the American Urological Association and the American Society of Reproductive Medicine are the best way to start (Brannigan et al. 2024). In total, there are fifty-two guidelines, reflecting evidence-based data and expert opinions of leaders in the field. The level of evidence determines whether the recommendation is a strong, moderate, or weak recommendation or based only on "expert opinion." Here are some of the most important guidelines with my explanations:

- *For initial infertility evaluation, both male and female partners should undergo concurrent assessment. (Expert Opinion)*[1]

Historically, the female partner was evaluated first, but now the recommendation is to evaluate both partners at the same time.

- *Men with one or more abnormal semen parameters or presumed male infertility should be evaluated by a male reproductive expert for complete history and physical examination as well as other directed tests when indicated. (Expert Opinion)*

There are now reproductive specialists in large numbers around the country who are available to evaluate the male patient in detail with a history and physical examination.

- *In couples with failed assisted reproductive technology cycles or recurrent pregnancy losses (two or more losses), evaluation of the male should be considered. (Expert Opinion)*

Couples that have unsuccessful in vitro fertilization cycles or recurrent pregnancy loss were thought to always be related to the female. New studies point to the fact that both these situations may involve a male factor and that treatments are available to improve pregnancy likelihood. This includes evaluation of the DNA of the sperm as well as evaluating genetic material, such as chromosome abnormalities.

- *Clinicians should counsel infertile men or men with abnormal semen parameters of the health risks associated with abnormal sperm production. (Moderate Recommendation; Evidence Level: Grade B)*
- *Infertile men with specific, identifiable causes of male infertility should be informed of relevant, associated health conditions. (Moderate Recommendation; Evidence Level: Grade B)*

Patients who have sperm problems are more likely to have health risks such as testicular cancer, other cancers, pituitary abnormalities, diabetes, neurological issues, or genetic issues that may affect the sperm.

- *Clinicians should advise couples with advanced paternal age (≥ 40) that there is an increased risk of adverse health outcomes for their offspring. (Expert Opinion)*

We are aware now that older men have a high risk of both lower fertility potential and a higher risk for birth defects that can affect children.

- *Clinicians may discuss risk factors (i.e., lifestyle, medication usage, environmental exposures) associated with male infertility, and patients should be counseled that the current data on the majority of risk factors are limited. (Conditional Recommendation; Evidence Level: Grade C)*
- *Clinicians should counsel patients that the benefits of supplements (e.g., antioxidants, vitamins) are of questionable clinical utility in treating male infertility. Existing data are inadequate to provide recommendation for specific agents to use for this purpose. (Conditional Recommendation; Evidence Level: Grade B)*

While most patients look toward supplements to improve sperm quality, the published data is mixed regarding their overall benefit. In addition, while it makes sense to change lifestyle behaviors (stop smoking, decrease marijuana and alcohol use, increase exercise), data is limited in terms of positive effects. However, lifestyle improvement in the face of poor sperm quality may make some difference to improve sperm quality.

- *Surgical varicocelectomy should be considered in men attempting to conceive who have palpable varicocele(s), infertility, and abnormal semen parameters, except for azoospermic men. (Moderate Recommendation; Evidence Level: Grade B)*

Enlarged veins around the testes, called varicoceles, can affect fertility. Procedures to repair this can result in improvement in sperm quality.

- *The patient presenting with hypogonadotropic hypogonadism should be evaluated to determine the etiology of the disorder and treated based on diagnosis. (Clinical Principle)*

Patients may present with pituitary abnormalities that need evaluation to determine whether there are brain tumors (benign or malignant) as a cause or something else.

- *For the male interested in current or future fertility, testosterone monotherapy should not be prescribed. (Clinical Principle)*
- *Clinicians may use aromatase inhibitors, human chorionic gonadotropin, selective estrogen receptor modulators, or a combination thereof for infertile men with low serum testosterone. (Conditional Recommendation; Evidence Level: Grade C)*

Use of testosterone shuts off sperm production. There are other medications that can be utilized to increase testosterone without having a negative effect on sperm production.

- *Clinicians should discuss the effects of gonadotoxic therapies and other cancer treatments on sperm production with patients prior to commencement of therapy. (Moderate Recommendation: Evidence Level: Grade C)*
- *Clinicians should inform patients undergoing chemotherapy and/or radiation therapy to avoid pregnancy for a period of at least 12 months after completion of treatment. (Expert Opinion)*

- *Clinicians should encourage men to bank sperm, preferably multiple specimens when possible, prior to commencement of gonadotoxic therapy or other cancer treatment that may affect fertility in men. (Expert Opinion)*

It is important for clinicians to offer sperm freezing in cases where use of medications can affect sperm quality. This is clear with chemotherapy, but it can also be seen in diseases such as autoimmune diseases, kidney disease, and so on. It is our job to make sure patients and health care teams are aware of these effects and the importance of sperm freezing prior to treatment.

* * *

In summary, over the years, we have made significant progress in the diagnosis and treatment of sperm-related issues. However, there is more work to do to ensure that sperm is given equal care to that of the oocyte. Goals should include breaking down barriers to access to care, promulgating important medical information, and including the thoughts and the emotions of the male partner in the decision-making process.

NOTE

1 All guidelines can be found in Brannigan et al. 2024.

REFERENCES

Brannigan, Robert. E, Linnea Hermanson, Janice Kaczmarek, Sennett K. Kim, Erin Kirkby, and Cigdem Tanrikut. 2024. "**Updates to Male Infertility: AUA/ASRM Guidelines.**" *Journal of Urology* 212 (6): 789–99. https://www.auajournals.org/doi/10.1097/JU.0000000000004180.

Centers for Disease Control and Prevention (CDC). 2010. *Advancing Men's Reproductive Health in the United States: Current Status and Future Directions.* Atlanta: Centers for Disease Control and Prevention.

Epstein, Steven. 2007. *Inclusion: The Politics of Difference in Medical Research.* Chicago: University of Chicago Press.

Schlegel, Peter N., Mark Sigman, Barbara Collura, Christopher J. De Jonge, Michael L. Eisenberg, Dolores J. Lamb, John P. Mulhall et al. 2021. "Diagnosis and Treatment of Infertility in Men: AUA/ASRM Guideline Part I." *Fertility and Sterility* 115 (1): 54–61. https://doi.org/10.1097/ju.0000000000001521.

8

Sperm Counts in Crises

MARION BOULICAULT

We are in the midst of a crisis. For decades, scientists have been warning the world about declines in sperm counts, with a recent high-profile study finding that average counts among men from countries categorized by the authors as "Western" (the United States, Canada, Australia, New Zealand, and countries in Europe) have decreased by 59.3 percent between 1973 and 2011 (Levine et al. 2017). A follow-up study by the same group found this already alarming rate of decline to be accelerating (Levine et al. 2023).

The stakes are high. The study's lead author, Dr. Hagai Levine, does not mince his words: "We are facing possible extinction. This is very clear to me" (quoted in Engber 2018). Other fertility experts such as Niels Skakkebaek concur: "It is a matter of whether we can sustain ourselves" (quoted in Kristof 2018). Shanna Swan, coauthor of the aforementioned 2017 study and the book *Count Down: How Our Modern World Is Threatening Sperm Counts, Altering Male and Female Reproductive Development, and Imperiling the Future of the Human Race*, compares our current sperm count moment to "where global warming was forty years ago—reported upon but denied or ignored. . . . We need the public to take this issue seriously" (Swan and Colino 2021, 3). She underscores the urgency of the crisis through comparisons to popular science fiction narratives: "Some of what we've been thinking of as fiction from stories such as *The Handmaid's Tale* and *Children of Men* is rapidly becoming a reality" (8).

In this essay, I examine the crisis rhetoric used in accounts of and research about sperm count trends. I show that there is no single sperm count decline crisis, but rather a set of interconnected crises. Drawing on work in political science, history, and gender studies, I argue that we can make sense of this array of crises only if we consider the intertwined biological, cultural, social, and political power of sperm counts.

On Crises

What is a crisis? The following useful working definition is offered by communication scholars Matthew W. Seeger, Timothy L. Sellnow, and Robert R. Ulmer (2003, 7): an event or state of affairs that is (a) unexpected; (b) creates high levels of uncertainty; and (c) is a significant threat (or perceived threat) to high priority goals or values. In other words, a crisis is a sudden, uncertain, high-stakes threat to something that matters to us. As such, crises call for action.

Which actions are called for depends on two questions: whether we deem something to be a crisis, and, if we do, what we determine it to be a crisis *of*. Answering these questions is rarely straightforward; they cannot be resolved by empirical investigation alone, since the nature of a crisis is entangled with what matters to us—with a society's (always complex, evolving, and often conflicting) goals and values. A crisis designation is, as political scientist Dara Z. Strolovitch (2023) argues, itself an operation of politics.

The implications of deeming something a crisis are nicely illustrated by the COVID-19 pandemic. The deployment of the first COVID-19 vaccines without standard testing protocols was justified by the massive threat of infection to public health. Designating a state or event as a crisis, then, can do critical work: it can serve as a rallying cry, bringing people together in the face of a common threat, and it can compel extraordinary attention, investment, and action. But there are risks and trade-offs. In some contexts, a crisis designation can generate excessive fear and anxiety, draw attention and resources away from other goals (including other perhaps more urgent crises), and threaten public trust if actions are seen to be overly rash, unjust, or unnecessary.

The 2008 financial crisis offers a case study of the consequences of classifying a crisis as being of one thing rather than another. Political scientist Colin Hay argues that that in the United Kingdom, a choice was made to construe the crisis as a *crisis of debt*, "to which, of course, austerity and deficit reduction are the solution" (2013, 23–24). But the crisis could justifiably also have been interpreted as a *crisis of growth*, in which case "austerity and deficit reduction would be no solution at all." He summarizes, "A politics based on construing the crisis as one of public debt will have very different redistributive consequences from a politics based on construing the crisis as one of growth" (Hay 2016, 528).

All of this is well encapsulated by Hay's observation that "crises are, in effect, what we make of them; and what we make of them determines how we respond" (Hay 2013, 23). With this in mind, I now turn to investigating what exactly the sperm crisis is a crisis of and, indeed, whether it should be considered a crisis at all.

The Sperm Count Decline Crises

Scientific findings of a reduction in average sperm counts among certain populations over the last fifty years are overwhelmingly framed as a crisis. But what exactly is it a crisis of? What do declining sperm counts mean? Is the decline in sperm cells a crisis in and of itself, or because of what it signifies? What—and whose—values and goals are under threat? In examining the scientific literature and media response regarding sperm count declines, one finds that there is in fact no single crisis; instead, there are many distinct (but interconnected and not mutually exclusive) crises. Further, the scientific evidence for each of these crises is complex and contested to varying degrees. Setting aside these contestations for now, I briefly summarize some of the key crises below. In the following section I will analyze how we might explain, and what we might learn from, this cornucopia of sperm count crises.

A Fertility Crisis

Perhaps first and foremost, sperm count trend findings are interpreted by scientists and media as evidence of a fertility crisis, where what is under threat is the continued survival of the human species. As noted above, following the publication of his 2017 study, scientist Levine warned that "we are facing possible extinction" (quoted in Engber 2018), a warning that he frequently repeated; "We have a serious problem on our hands that, if not mitigated, could threaten mankind's survival" (quoted in Hurst 2023). Mainstream media publications followed suit, with the BBC suggesting that declining sperm count "could make humans extinct" and the men's interest magazine *GQ* cautioning, "We're on track . . . to void the species entirely" (Ghosh 2017; Halpern 2018). Some journalists have intensified the stakes and urgency of the fertility crisis by linearly extrapolating the 2017 paper trends: "At this rate, sperm counts will likely reach zero by as soon as 2045. Zero" (Ho 2021).

A Crisis of Male Health

Sperm count decline is also interpreted as a sign of a much broader crisis of male health. As Levine et al. (2017, 654) put it, dropping sperm counts represent "a canary in the coal mine for male health across the lifespan." A recent study found that "men with low sperm counts are more likely than those with normal sperm counts to have greater body fat, higher blood pressure, higher 'bad' (low-density lipoprotein) cholesterol and triglycerides, and lower 'good' (high-density lipoprotein) cholesterol" (Ferlin et al. 2021, 206). Noting correlations between sperm count decline, changes in average circulating testosterone levels, and incidences of testicular cancer, some scientists have postulated that sperm count declines are one symptom of "testicular dysgenesis syndrome," a hypothesized (but contested) syndrome purported to be threatening the future of male health (Aitken 2022; Wohlfahrt-Veje, Main, and Skakkebaek 2009; Fénichel and Chevalier 2019). Prominent andrologist Richard Sharpe encapsulates this crisis interpretation well when he writes, "We think of sperm counts as a fairly crude barometer of overall male health. It's a warning shot across our bows" (quoted in Kleeman 2017).

A Modern Lifestyle Crisis

Another prevalent interpretation takes sperm count decline to be the result of a more general crisis of "modern living" (Kelland 2017). As Levine puts it, declining sperm counts are an "indicator that there is something very wrong in our modern environment or lifestyle" (Carr 2019). Scientists hypothesize that diet (Afeiche et al. 2013; Jensen et al. 2013), body mass index (Sermondade et al. 2013; Eisenberg et al. 2014), smoking habits (Sharma et al. 2016), and stress levels (Gollenberg et al. 2010; Nordkap et al. 2016) are just some of the modern lifestyle factors contributing to sperm count decline. Furthermore, this crisis is not positioned solely as a crisis of men's lifestyle choices, but also of women's, and particularly of pregnant women's. In media interviews, Swan emphasizes the outsized influence of pregnant women's decisions on their male offspring, reporting that when a man smokes, "he lowers his sperm count by about 20%. When a male is born to a woman who smokes, his sperm count is reduced by about 50%" (quoted in van Deelen 2022). A recent article in a top reproductive science journal, *Human Reproduction*, warns of the dangers of modern lifestyles and "increasing prosperity" on sperm quantity and quality (Aitken 2022, 629). Further, the author suggests that modern technological changes, such as increased use of assisted reproductive technologies (ART), could have longer-term genetic implications for sperm counts: "The retention of poor fertility genes within the human population is also being exacerbated by the increased uptake of ART" (Aitken 2022, 629). All these modern lifestyle factors risk driving "our species into an *infertility trap*" (Aitken 2022, 629, emphasis added).

An Environmental Crisis

Declining sperm counts are also hypothesized as evidence of an environmental crisis, in particular, a crisis resulting from exposure to endocrine-disrupting chemicals, synthetic chemicals with "estrogen-like activity" that can interfere with the body's hormones (Aitken 2022; Swan and Colino 2021). Found in many everyday products, such as plastics, fragrances, and pesticides, environmental exposure to endocrine-disrupting chemicals is widespread (Kumar et al. 2020). Endocrine-disrupting chemicals have been found to negatively affect health across multiple species, with most research focusing on the impacts on reproductive health and fertility, including sperm quantity and quality (Vos et al. 2000; Swan and Colino 2021). This has resulted in urgent calls for more research and regulations. In a *Guardian* newspaper op-ed entitled "Plummeting Sperm Counts, Shrinking Penises: Toxic Chemicals Threaten Humanity," renowned environmental activist Erin Brockovich (2021) even called for international political intervention:

"Forgive me for asking: why isn't the UN calling an emergency meeting on this right now?"

A (White) Masculinity Crisis

The interpretation of sperm count decline as a sign of an environmental crisis caused by endocrine-disrupting chemicals is sometimes entangled with another crisis narrative: sperm count decline as a crisis of masculinity. In analyzing some of the rhetoric surrounding endocrine-disrupting chemicals, political scientist Cynthia Daniels has observed a tendency to describe their threat to sperm counts (and male health in general) as a kind of feminization or "chemical castration" of men (Daniels 2006, 58). Daniels goes on, "The most disturbing effect of exposure to estrogens was often said to be . . . [that] as men became 'more like women,' the dissolution of the boundaries between them produced disease and 'weakness.' It was this presumed feminization of men that had produced testicular cancer, lower sperm counts, and increased rates of 'abnormal' development in men" (Daniels 2006, 56).

We can see examples of similar rhetoric applied to sperm count decline in more recent publications. In their book *Count Down*, Shanna Swan and Stacey Colino (2021) claim that men face "environmental emasculation" (2) from endocrine-disrupting chemicals and these not only reduce sperm count but "blur" gender differences in "language-development . . . and many other qualities," resulting in possible "gender dysphoria" (59–60). Media reports bolster this crisis interpretation (Clancy and Davis 2019; Halpern 2018), using headlines such as "Common Pollutants Undermine Masculinity" (Daniels 2006, 57).

Further, the interpretation of sperm count decline as a masculinity crisis is often implicitly or explicitly racialized, reflecting anxieties about the decline of white, Western norms of masculinity (Borsa et al. 2021; Boulicault et al. 2021; Boulicault and Reiches 2021; Perret 2021). Levine et al.'s 2017 study disaggregated sperm count data into the categories of "Western" (i.e., whiter) and "Other" countries, only finding a statistically significant decline in sperm counts in "Western" countries. This finding was taken up by white supremacist, misogynist groups as evidence in support of a "white-genocide conspiracy theory"—a belief that immigration, low fertility rates, abortion, and miscegenation are causing the decline or even "extinction" of white people (Perret 2021).

Making Sense of and Learning from the Cornucopia of Sperm Count Decline Crises

In her essay in this volume, Janelle Lamoreaux argues that sperm cells play the role of a "biological sentinel," or what Frédéric Keck and Andrew Lakoff (2013) term a "sentinel device": a living being or a technical device that warns of crisis. Above, I argued that sperm counts are not just any old sentinel devices, they are particularly potent devices capable of warning us of many crises all at once. What makes sperm cells such loud and powerful canaries in the proverbial coal mine? How and why are sperm counts taken to be signals of threats to so many different goals and values? One reason, of course, is that sperm cells are biologically significant cells connected to important biological processes and mechanisms, most obviously to reproduction. But their impressive signaling power is due to more than their biological properties; it is also due to their deeply held symbolic and cultural properties.

Anthropologist Emily Martin's groundbreaking classic "The Egg and the Sperm" (1991) provides a vivid illustration of how sperm serves as a potent symbol of Western masculinity. Martin analyzes the use of gendered metaphors in biology textbooks that portray sperm cells in the stereotypically masculine role of a strong, aggressive, competitive pursuer that embarks on a "perilous journey" to penetrate the passive, feminine egg cell, thereby perpetuating "some of the hoariest old stereotypes about weak damsels in distress and their strong male rescuers" (Martin 1991, 490, 500). Daniels (2006) brings Martin's work to the realm of sperm count decline science, describing how media accounts describe sperm cells as "'little men' weathering an assault of social, technological, and environmental forces" (52). According to Daniels, sperm counts symbolize "not only a measure of one's manhood but also the symbolic measure of a nation's strength and well-being" (52). Meredith P. Field's essay in this volume summarizes Daniels's arguments, explaining how sperm are "culturally constructed as the main symbol of virility, an essential trait of 'Western' hegemonic masculinity."

The symbolic power of sperm is perhaps most starkly illustrated by the move to declare a sperm count crisis in the first place. Evidence suggests that this declaration of crisis—and the calls to urgent action that it brings—may be premature: there is much we actually still do not know about the relationships between sperm counts, fertility, male health, endocrine-disrupting chemicals, and modern lifestyles (Boulicault et al. 2021).

Some doubt whether sperm is declining at all. For instance, andrologist Allan Pacey has hypothesized that findings of sperm count decline may actually be findings of changing measurement procedures. As Pacey writes, "Counting sperm, even with the gold standard technique of haemocytometry, is really difficult. I believe that over time we have simply got better at it because of the development of training and quality control programmes around the world. I still think this is much of what we are seeing in the data" (Science Media Centre 2022).

This doubt about sperm count decline is also fueled by the fact that sperm count measurement—that is, the technologies and practices used to generate data and test hypotheses about sperm count decline—is a site of deep consternation. As journalist Gina Kolata (1996) eloquently puts it in a *New York Times* article on sperm count decline, "The question sounds so simple: Do men today have fewer sperm than their forebears? And the answer seems easy to get: Just look at sperm counts at different time periods. But such an exercise is fraught with peril." In 2016, the journal *Andrology* published a special issue on the "troubling state of the semen analysis," arguing that semen measurement standards are profoundly uncertain and ambiguous (Tomlinson 2016, 763). A 2011 editorial in *Epidemiology* lays the issues out clearly: "Measurements of semen parameters are fraught with problems at every level: wide variations within a given man, incomplete and selective participation among groups of men, difficult-to-control confounding factors (such as abstinence time), and vagaries of laboratory methods" (Wilcox 2011, 615).

None of this is to suggest that sperm counts do not deserve our urgent attention; they do. Rather, my message is one of caution: as we have seen, designations of crises are powerful and so should be treated with great care. In the case of sperm count decline, the form this care must take is, on the one hand, political and social care that critically takes into account the potent and dangerous symbolic ties between sperm cells and Western hegemonic norms of racialized masculinity and virility. On the other hand, the form of care needed is also scientific: we need more research involving robust, valid, reliable, and effective measurement practices for sperm counts.

Researchers have long called (and continue to call) for prospective studies on sperm counts, as opposed to retrospective meta-analyses, which was the methodology used in both the 2017 and 2022 Levine et al. papers. "What is needed are new, unbiased data. Repeated prospective semen studies randomly sampled from a truly global frame," write Raywat Deonandan and Marya Jaleel (2012, 305). Eberhard Nieschlag and Alexander Lerchl (2013, 185) suggest that the question of sperm count decline can "not be resolved by retrospective or short-lived studies, but only by a prospective monitoring system encompassing longer time periods and including semen quality." Indeed, some of the top andrologists today, led by Levine and colleagues, have added their voices to this call for research. At the 2018 International Symposium on Spermatology, they jointly published a statement: "We, scientists, public health professionals and clinicians working in spermatology, are calling on governments, organizations, the scientific and medical communities, and individuals to acknowledge the importance of male reproductive health for the survival of the human and other species, to increase efforts and resources allocated to studying the causes of disruption of male reproductive health, and to implement policies to remove hazards to, and promote optimal environments for, male health and reproduction" (Levine et al. 2018).

I close with a reflection on the relationship between the current state of sperm count research and the many sperm count crises. As Rene Almeling (2020) convincingly argues, gender norms that associate women's, but not men's, bodies with reproduction may partially explain why we know disproportionately little about men's reproductive health and capacities. That is, ironically, some of the very norms and standards of masculinity that fuel the sperm count crisis rhetoric also contribute to our lack of knowledge about sperm counts. I want to suggest that the use of crisis rhetoric—and particularly the number and magnitude of the proposed intertwined crises—risks further compounding the barriers to our scientific understanding of sperm count trends. While critical in certain contexts, crisis designations demand urgent action, condensing the time and space allocated for scientific debate and consideration of alternative hypotheses and methods, and creating impediments for the kind of robust, slow, prospective studies needed to truly understand—and act upon if necessary—the nature and meaning of sperm count trends.

REFERENCES

Afeiche, M., P. L. Williams, J. Mendiola, A. J. Gaskins, N. Jørgensen, S. H. Swan, and J. E. Chavarro. 2013. "Dairy Food Intake in Relation to Semen Quality and Reproductive Hormone Levels among Physically Active Young Men." *Human Reproduction* 28 (8): 2265–75. https://doi.org/10.1093/humrep/det133.

Aitken, R. John. 2022. "The Changing Tide of Human Fertility." *Human* 37 (4): 629–38. https://doi.org/10.1093/humrep/deac011.

Almeling, Rene. 2020. *GUYnecology: The Missing Science of Men's Reproductive Health*. Oakland: University of California Press.

Borsa, Alexander, Marion Boulicault, Meredith Reiches, and Sarah S. Richardson. 2021. "The Doomsday Sperm Theory Embraced by the Far Right." *Slate*, May 14, 2021. https://slate.com.

Boulicault, Marion, Meg Perret, Jonathan Galka, Alex Borsa, Annika Gompers, Meredith Reiches, and Sarah Richardson. 2021. "The Future of Sperm: A Biovariability Framework for Understanding Global Sperm Count Trends." *Human Fertility* 25 (5): 888–902. https://doi.org/10.1080/14647273.2021.1917778.

Boulicault, Marion, and Meredith Reiches. 2021. "Falling Sperm Counts Aren't as Alarming as They Sound." *The Guardian*, June 7, 2021, sec. Opinion. www.theguardian.com.

Brockovich, Erin. 2021. "Plummeting Sperm Counts, Shrinking Penises: Toxic Chemicals Threaten Humanity." *The Guardian*, March 18, 2021, sec. Opinion. www.theguardian.com.

Carr, Teresa. 2019. "Sperm Counts Are on the Decline—Could Plastics Be to Blame?" *The Guardian*, May 24, 2019, sec. US news. www.theguardian.com.

Clancy, Kathryn B. H., and Jenny L. Davis. 2019. "Soylent Is People, and WEIRD Is White: Biological Anthropology, Whiteness, and the Limits of the WEIRD." *Annual Review of Anthropology* 48 (1): 169–86. https://doi.org/10.1146/annurev-anthro-102218-011133.

Daniels, Cynthia R. 2006. *Exposing Men: The Science and Politics of Male Reproduction*. New York: Oxford University Press.

Deonandan, Raywat, and Marya Jaleel. 2012. "Global Decline in Semen Quality: Ignoring the Developing World Introduces Selection Bias." *International Journal of General Medicine* 5:303–6. https://doi.org/10.2147/IJGM.S30673.

Eisenberg, Michael L., Sungduk Kim, Zhen Chen, Rajeshwari Sundaram, Enrique F. Schisterman, and Germaine M. Buck Louis. 2014. "The Relationship between Male

BMI and Waist Circumference on Semen Quality: Data from the LIFE Study." *Human Reproduction* 29 (2): 193–200. https://doi.org/10.1093/humrep/det428.

Engber, Daniel. 2018. "Why Is Everybody Freaking Out About Sperm Counts?" *The Cut*, October 2, 2018. www.thecut.com.

Fénichel, Patrick, and Nicolas Chevalier. 2019. "Is Testicular Germ Cell Cancer Estrogen Dependent? The Role of Endocrine Disrupting Chemicals." *Endocrinology* 160 (12): 2981–89. https://doi.org/10.1210/en.2019-00486.

Ferlin, Alberto, Andrea Garolla, Marco Ghezzi, Riccardo Selice, Pierfrancesco Palego, Nicola Caretta, Antonella Di Mambro et al. 2021. "Sperm Count and Hypogonadism as Markers of General Male Health." *European Urology Focus* 7 (1): 205–13. https://doi.org/10.1016/j.euf.2019.08.001.

Ghosh, Pallab. 2017. "Sperm Count Drop 'Could Make Humans Extinct.'" *BBC News*, July 25, 2017. www.bbc.com.

Gollenberg, Audra L., Fan Liu, Charlene Brazil, Erma Z. Drobnis, David Guzick, James W. Overstreet, James B. Redmon, Amy Sparks, Christina Wang, and Shanna H. Swan. 2010. "Semen Quality in Fertile Men in Relation to Psychosocial Stress." *Fertility and Sterility* 93 (4): 1104–11. https://doi.org/10.1016/j.fertnstert.2008.12.018.

Halpern, Daniel Noah. 2018. "What Happens If We Hit Sperm Count Zero?" *GQ*, September 4, 2018. www.gq.com.

Hay, Colin. 2013. "Treating the Symptom Not the Condition: Crisis Definition, Deficit Reduction and the Search for a New British Growth Model." *British Journal of Politics and International Relations* 15 (1): 23–37. https://doi.org/10.1111/j.1467-856X.2012.00515.x.

Hay, Colin. 2016. "Good in a Crisis: The Ontological Institutionalism of Social Constructivism." *New Political Economy* 21 (6): 520–35. https://doi.org/10.1080/13563467.2016.1158800.

Ho, Sally. 2021. "'Sperm Counts Could Reach Zero By 2045': 'Everywhere' Plastic Toxins Behind Fertility Crisis That Threatens Human Survival." *Green Queen*, March 23, 2021. www.greenqueen.com.

Hurst, Luke. 2023. "Sperm Counts Are Declining Globally. Scientists Believe They Have Pinpointed the Main Causes Why." *Yahoo News*, June 15, 2023. www.uk.news.yahoo.com.

Jensen, Tina K., Berit L. Heitmann, Martin Blomberg Jensen, Thorhallur I. Halldorsson, Anna-Maria Andersson, Niels Erik Skakkebaek, Ulla N. Joensen et al. 2013. "High Dietary Intake of Saturated Fat Is Associated with Reduced Semen Quality among 701 Young Danish Men from the General Population." *American Journal of Clinical Nutrition* 97 (2): 411–18. https://doi.org/10.3945/ajcn.112.042432.

Keck, Frédéric, and Andrew Lakoff. 2013. "Preface: Sentinel Devices." *Limn* 1 (3). https://escholarship.org/uc/item/0xq1t67m.

Kelland, Kate. 2017. "Sperm Count Dropping in Western World." *Scientific American*, July 26, 2017. www.scientificamerican.com.

Kleeman, Jenny. 2017. "'It Tears Every Part of Your Life Away': The Truth about Male Infertility." *The Guardian*, November 18, 2017, sec. Life and Style. www.theguardian.com.

Kolata, Gina. 1996. "Ideas & Trends; How Men Measure Up, Sperm for Sperm." *New York Times*, May 5, 1996, sec. Week in Review. www.nytimes.com.

Kristof, Nicholas. 2018. "Are Your Sperm in Trouble?" *New York Times*, January 20, 2018, sec. Opinion. www.nytimes.com.

Kumar, Manoj, Devojit Kumar Sarma, Swasti Shubham, Manoj Kumawat, Vinod Verma, Anil Prakash, and Rajnarayan Tiwari. 2020. "Environmental Endocrine-Disrupting Chemical Exposure: Role in Non-Communicable Diseases." *Frontiers in Public Health* 8. www.frontiersin.org.

Levine, Hagai, Niels Jørgensen, Anderson Martino-Andrade, Jaime Mendiola, Dan Weksler-Derri, Irina Mindlis, Rachel Pinotti, and Shanna H Swan. 2017. "Temporal Trends in Sperm Count: A Systematic Review and Meta-Regression Analysis." *Human Reproduction Update* 23 (6): 646–59. https://doi.org/10.1093/humupd/dmx022.

Levine, Hagai, Hideo Mohri, Anders Ekbom, Liliana Ramos, Geoff Parker, Eduardo Roldan, Luca Jovine et al. 2018. "Male Reproductive Health Statement (XIIIth International Symposium on Spermatology, May 9th–12th 2018, Stockholm, Sweden." *Basic and Clinical Andrology* 28 (2018). https://doi.org/10.1186/s12610-018-0077-z.

Levine, Hagai, Niels Jørgensen, Anderson Martino-Andrade, Jaime Mendiola, Dan Weksler-Derri, Maya Jolles, Rachel Pinotti, and Shanna H. Swan. 2023. "Temporal Trends in Sperm Count: A Systematic Review and Meta-Regression Analysis of Samples Collected Globally in the 20th and 21st Centuries." *Human Reproduction Update* 29 (2): 157–76. https://doi.org/10.1093/humupd/dmac035.

Martin, Emily. 1991. "The Egg and the Sperm: How Science Has Constructed a Romance Based on Stereotypical Male-Female Roles." *Signs* 16 (3): 485–501.

Nieschlag, Eberhard, and Alexander Lerchl. 2013. "Sperm Crisis: What Crisis?" *Asian Journal of Andrology* 15 (2): 184–86. https://doi.org/10.1038/aja.2012.90.

Nordkap, Loa, Tina Kold Jensen, Åse Marie Hansen, Tina Harmer Lassen, Anne Kirstine Bang, Ulla Nordström Joensen, Martin Blomberg Jensen, Niels Erik Skakkebaek, and Niels Jørgensen. 2016. "Psychological Stress and Testicular Function: A Cross-Sectional Study of 1,215 Danish Men." *Fertility and Sterility* 105 (1): 174–87. e2. https://doi.org/10.1016/j.fertnstert.2015.09.016.

Perret, Meg. 2021. "Alt-Right Uptake of Sperm Decline Science." *GenderSci Lab* (blog). May 4, 2021. www.genderscilab.org.

Science Media Centre. 2022. "Expert Reaction to Study of Sperm Counts over Time." *Science Media Centre*, November 15, 2022. www.sciencemediacentre.org.

Seeger, Mathew W., Timothy L. Sellnow, and Robert R. Ulmer. 2003. *Communication and Organizational Crisis*. Westport, CT: Greenwood Publishing Group.

Sermondade, N., C. Faure, L. Fezeu, A.G. Shayeb, J.P. Bonde, T.K. Jensen, M. Van Wely, et al. 2013. "BMI in Relation to Sperm Count: An Updated Systematic Review and Collaborative Meta-Analysis." *Human Reproduction Update* 19 (3): 221–31. https://doi.org/10.1093/humupd/dms050.

Sharma, Reecha, Avi Harlev, Ashok Agarwal, and Sandro C. Esteves. 2016. "Cigarette Smoking and Semen Quality: A New Meta-Analysis Examining the Effect of the 2010 World Health Organization Laboratory Methods for the Examination of

Human Semen." *European Urology* 70 (4): 635–45. https://doi.org/10.1016/j.eururo.2016.04.010.

Strolovitch, Dara Z. 2023. *When Bad Things Happen to Privileged People: Race, Gender, and What Makes a Crisis in America.* Chicago, IL: University of Chicago Press.

Swan, Shanna H., and Stacey Colino. 2021. *Count Down: How Our Modern World Is Threatening Sperm Counts, Altering Male and Female Reproductive Development, and Imperiling the Future of the Human Race.* New York: Scribner.

Tomlinson, M. J. 2016. "Uncertainty of Measurement and Clinical Value of Semen Analysis: Has Standardisation through Professional Guidelines Helped or Hindered Progress?" *Andrology* 4 (5): 763–70. https://doi.org/10.1111/andr.12209.

van Deelen, Grace. 2022. "A New Analysis Shows a 'Crisis' of Male Reproductive Health—EHN." *Environmental Health News*, November 17, 2022. www.ehn.org.

Vos, Joseph G., Erik Dybing, Helmut A. Greim, Ole Ladefoged, Claude Lambré, Jose V. Tarazona, Ingvar Brandt, and A. Dick Vethaak. 2000. "Health Effects of Endocrine-Disrupting Chemicals on Wildlife, with Special Reference to the European Situation." *Critical Reviews in Toxicology* 30 (1): 71–133. https://doi.org/10.1080/10408440091159176.

Wilcox, Allen J. 2011. "Editorial: On Sperm Counts and Data Responsibility:" *Epidemiology* 22 (5): 615–16. https://doi.org/10.1097/ede.0b013e318225036d.

Wohlfahrt-Veje, Christine, Katharina M. Main, and Niels Erik Skakkebaek. 2009. "Testicular Dysgenesis Syndrome: Foetal Origin of Adult Reproductive Problems." *Clinical Endocrinology* 71 (4): 459–65. https://doi.org/10.1111/j.1365-2265.2009.03545.x.

9

Sperm as Sentinel

JANELLE LAMOREAUX

Postgenomic perspectives, which center an understanding of health and the body as influenced by more than genes, are increasingly common in scientific studies, leading to research on bodily entities and processes as influenced by environments (Richardson and Stevens 2015). At the same time, increasing environmental activism has focused on how climate change, toxic exposures, and water and air pollution are making future life untenable. Has this growing attention to the environment—both in an anthropocenic sense (A. Moore 2016), where humans have fundamentally altered the environment, and in a postgenomic sense, where the environment is interpreted as increasingly influential to human health—changed the way people think about sperm and its decline?

Since the early 1990s, the apparent decline of sperm counts has been at the center of reoccurring reports of men's reproductive health in both scientific and popular publications (Daniels 2006). For example, a Smithsonian article titled "Human Sperm Counts Declining Worldwide, Study Finds" not only echoes previous publications making similar factual claims, it also makes similar rhetorical moves (Sullivan 2022). The article draws attention to sperm decline as a seemingly global or universal issue; it raises multiple possible causal factors but presents no claims to clear correlations or explanations; and, more implicitly, the article asserts a vision of virility as an ever-present masculine attribute with no expectation of change (as discussed by Daniels [2006]). The article, like many publications before it, interprets sperm decline as a foreboding signal, ending with a quote from Stanford urologist Michael Eisenberg: "We don't understand why we're seeing this pattern, so I think it's hard to be alarmist for an individual. . . . But at a policy level, this should be a wake-up call to try and understand" (quoted in Sullivan 2022).

For the last forty years, falling sperm counts have served as "a wake-up call," both in scientific and media portrayals of male fertility. Sperm are what Frédéric Keck and Andrew Lakoff (2013) describe as a biological sentinel or "sentinel device": a living being or a technical device that warns of catastrophe to come. Similar to melting glaciers, endangered species, and disappearing rainforests, declining sperm counts serve as a warning signal of environmental damage wrought by humans (Lamoreaux and Wahlberg 2022). But what these falling sperm counts mean in terms of the health of men and their children is a more complicated story. This is because the potential influence of falling global and national sperm counts on male fertility remains unclear. In the Smithsonian article, author Will Sullivan veers from media's often-sensationalist sperm narrative by trying to account for the nuance of sperm science. He writes, "It's unclear what lower sperm counts would really mean for human fertility," although he also suggests that declining sperm counts may be indicative of other health problems at the individual level (Sullivan 2022).

I am a medical anthropologist who spent over a year conducting research in China on how reproductive toxicologists, physicians, and environmental activists understand and study the problem of male infertility through scientific practice. In my book *Infertile Environments* (Lamoreaux 2023), I describe a similar sentiment to Sullivan's among the reproductive toxicologists I interviewed and observed. Many of these professionals that I spent time with critiqued typical semen analyses, which rely on fairly simple counts and observations of sperm cells. What mattered more to these toxicologists were the ways that environments can potentially damage sperm beyond simple quantitative decline. At the forefront of their research was a focus on epigenetic changes, or transformations to the way genes work that do not change DNA sequence. To the toxicologists I studied, it was these potential epigenetic changes that caused great concern, not counts themselves. They stressed that even when sperm counts are "normal" and male fertility remains intact, important kinds of epigenetic transformation can occur within sperm and potentially be transmitted to future offspring. We are now learning more and more about how these transformations can potentially affect reproductive and developmental health within and across generations.

By comparison, concern about falling sperm counts may be more akin to worries about endangerment and extinction, where numbers in and of themselves are meant to signal demise. Other parts of men's bodies are also approached through such a numerical lens. For instance, consider Greta Thunberg's March 24, 2021, retweet of the *Sky News* article headline, "Human Penises Are Shrinking because of Pollution." Her response read: "See you all at the next climate strike :)" (Thunberg 2021). Another response to this 2021 shrinking penis research was published in *Men's Health* magazine with the subheading: "If that doesn't make you consider your environmental impact, what will?" Such framing of this research suggests that in order for men to care about the environment they need to have their masculinity threatened through the quantitative depletion of their gendered body. Meanwhile, environmentally related epigenetic transformations receive less media attention as potential instigators for men's environmental activism. When epigenetics is discussed as a motivator for change, it is often through a focus on women's prenatal behavior as having the potential to affect future generations (Lappé, Jeffries Hein, and Landecker 2019; Warin et al. 2012).

With men's falling sperm counts and shrinking penises holding the most media traction, epigenetic influences have yet to mobilize much social action. Still, there are some examples. Scott Frickel's historical study of the science of DNA damage demonstrates how research on the genotoxic threats of synthetic chemicals to sperm galvanized public policy change to environmental regulations through fears of compromised genetic integrity (Frickel 2004). Ayo Wahlberg reveals how a growing perception of sperm as an "exposed biology" in need of protection from a wide variety of exposures in China led to the routinization of cryopreservation and an industry offering "fertility insurance" (Wahlberg 2018). In my book, I describe how studies of sperm-environment interaction based in Nanjing serve as an entry point to formulate critiques of economic and environmental policies, as well as to elucidate transnational hierarchies in toxic exposure levels and scientific infrastructure. Studying sperm and its transformation through environments is, then, often about studying much more than fertility. Epigenetic sperm-environment interaction studies are increasingly a means through which attention to a variety of environmental, social, and political issues might be generated.

In this moment of thinking about male infertility environmentally, sperm might become a different kind of sentinel. Concern about sperm may not be just about the numbers, where *more* and *bigger* signal fertility and virility (L. Moore 2007), but also about the more subtle and potentially intergenerational effects of humans living in toxic environments.

REFERENCES

Daniels, Cynthia R. 2006. *Exposing Men: The Science and Politics of Male Reproduction.* Oxford: Oxford University Press.

Frickel, Scott. 2004. *Chemical Consequences: Environmental Mutagens, Scientist Activism, and the Rise of Genetic Toxicology.* New Brunswick, NJ: Rutgers University Press.

Keck, Frédéric, and Andrew Lakoff. 2013. "Preface: Sentinel Devices." *Limn* (3). http://limn.it/preface-sentinel-devices-2/.

Lamoreaux, Janelle. 2023. *Infertile Environments: Epigenetic Toxicology and Chinese Men's Reproductive Health.* Durham, NC: Duke University Press.

Lamoreaux, Janelle, and Ayo Wahlberg. 2022. "Sperm." In *An Anthropogenic Table of Elements*, edited by Courtney Addison, Timothy Neale, and Thao Phan, 158–67. Toronto: University of Toronto Press.

Lappé, Martine, Robbin Jeffries Hein, and Hannah Landecker. 2019. "Environmental Politics of Reproduction." *Annual Review of Anthropology* 48 (1): 133–50. https://doi.org/10.1146/annurev-anthro-102218-011346.

Moore, Amelia. 2016. "Anthropocene Anthropology: Reconceptualizing Contemporary Global Change." *Journal of the Royal Anthropology Institute*, 22 (1): 27–46. https://doi.org/10.1111/1467-9655.12332.

Moore, Lisa Jean. 2007. *Sperm Counts: Overcome by Man's Most Precious Fluid.* New York: New York University Press.

Richardson, Sarah S., and Hallam Stevens. 2015. *Postgenomics: Perspectives on Biology after the Genome.* Durham, NC: Duke University Press.

Sullivan, Will. 2022. "Human Sperm Counts Declining Worldwide, Study Finds." *Smithsonian Magazine*, November 22, 2022. www.smithsonianmag.com.

Thunberg, Greta (@GretaThunberg). "See you all at the next climate strike :)." Twitter, March 25, 2021, 2:11 p.m. https://twitter.com/GretaThunberg/status/1375148442176131073.

Wahlberg, Ayo. 2018. *Good Quality: The Routinization of Sperm Banking in China.* Berkeley: University of California Press.

Warin, Megan, Tanya Zivkovic, Vivienne Moore, and Michael Davies. 2012. "Mothers as Smoking Guns: Fetal Overnutrition and the Reproduction of Obesity." *Feminism & Psychology* 22 (3): 360–75. https://doi.org/10.1177/0959353512445359.

10

Sperm Banks and the Shortage of Black Sperm Donors

ALYSSA M. NEWMAN

The first part of an October 2022 *Washington Post* headline declared, "America Has a Black Sperm Donor Shortage" (Ferguson 2022). While there has been a decline in the availability of donor sperm from all racial groups due to the COVID-19 pandemic, the shortage among Black donors is particularly acute. Although supply constantly fluctuates, a snapshot of donor availability on October 11, 2022, from the four largest sperm banks in the United States found a total of only 12 Black donors; in contrast, the number of white donors available at that moment was 391 (Ferguson 2022). Likewise, a recent systematic search of donor sperm banks in the United States revealed that 70 percent of donors were white, while only 4 percent were Black—a far cry from the representation of Black men on the latest US Census, which stood at 13 percent (Moreta et al. 2022).

Traditional explanations for Black donor underrepresentation in sperm banks include mistrust of the medical profession, lack of Black representation within clinic staff, lack of awareness about donating options, and the rigor of the donor screening process—all reasons offered by the spokespersons from various sperm banks (Dockser Marcus 2022; Hatem 2020). Scholarship on the topic largely fails to interrogate these explanations (Walther 2014; Whittaker and Spier 2010). Much of our knowledge about the experiences, motivations, and preferences of sperm donors is based on overwhelmingly white samples—including in studies of online sperm donation, where most of these explanations for Black underrepresentation do not apply (Freeman et al. 2016). What are the roots of this perceived shortage, and what should be done about it?

The second part of the headline lamented, "Black Women Are Paying the Price" (Ferguson 2022). Black women, already impacted by exceptionally high and worsening maternal mortality rates (Gunja, Gumas, and Williams 2022), are forced into even more vulnerable positions when seeking Black donor sperm. When they choose to wait for sperm bank supplies of Black donors to become available, they delay their childbearing, placing them at increased risk for complications with conceiving, pregnancy, and childbirth associated with advancing maternal age. Waitlists for Black donors can sometimes stretch as long as eighteen months; in contrast, waitlists for the most in-demand white donors are generally three months. Black women may choose to pivot their donor preference, often choosing between donors with lighter skin tones, exposing them to potential criticisms and accusations of colorism within the Black community (Ferguson 2022). They may also turn to other potential sources of sperm from Black donors, such as online social media groups or websites, where they face the challenges, ambiguities, and risks associated with unregulated sperm donation (Pennings 2023). Access to same-race sperm donors raises questions I have explored in my past research (Newman 2019) about what a family "should" look like and invites broader discussions about whether our conceptions of reproductive justice also include a right to find gamete donors who look like us (for more on reproductive justice, see Littlejohn's essay in this volume).

Beyond these questions, though, there is also the matter of what concrete harms are being perpetuated through unevenness in sperm bank donor supply across racial groups. The lack of availability of Black donor sperm is hardly new; it is a feature, rather than an anomaly, of sperm banks, as scholars have pointed out for well over a decade the unevenness in standards and practices of donor matching for recipients of color (Fox 2011; Quiroga 2007). At issue is the *reproduction of racial inequality through donor sperm markets,* which the COVID-19 pandemic has only exacerbated. The impact of this inequality distributes both burden and blame to marginalized populations: Black women as recipients are forced to turn to less-than-ideal options for obtaining donor sperm, which often involve additional health risks or legal vulnerabilities, and Black men are blamed for not participating in sperm banks, as their mistrust of medicine leads them to rebuff the outreach efforts of sperm banks to recruit them.[1] If these sperm banks are not serving the needs of Black sperm recipients, do unregulated, informal markets or online platforms address them?

Online sperm donation includes the use of social media groups, smartphone applications, and connection websites that allow recipients and donors to locate one another. While there have been extensive studies of online sperm donors and their motivations, these studies focus on platforms where donors are predominately white and do not shed light on the motivations of Black donors (Freeman et al. 2016; Graham, Freedman, and Jadva 2019). Are Black men simply less altruistic or procreative than other groups, and hence do not become donors?[2] Are their reasons for not participating in some of these online platforms similar to their motivations for avoiding sperm banks? We do not have the answers to these questions because of the collective failure to address or engage the lack of Black sperm donor representation among these samples.

Resolving the Black sperm donor shortage requires better explanations than the literature currently provides. Are Black men simply not interested in sperm donation? A cursory review of Facebook groups centered around connecting Black sperm donors with recipients seems to suggest that is not the case. The largest of these dedicated groups appears to have over twenty thousand members, including both interested donors and recipients. If lack of interest fails to explain the shortage among sperm banks, perhaps some scrutiny should be turned on the banks themselves—not just their recruitment practices, but the logics behind who they include and exclude, and who they perceive to be a desirable donor to recipients.

This also raises a larger set of questions: What type of arrangements and connections would potential Black donors feel comfortable with? What kind of scrutiny and interaction would they find acceptable? What motivates the Black sperm donors who *do* participate in these online connection platforms or with these larger sperm banks, and what models of sperm donation would encourage others to participate? Identifying answers to these questions, rather than accepting the explanations offered by sperm bank spokespersons, would help clarify whether there is an actual shortage of Black sperm donors, or simply a failure to offer them desirable options for contributing their sperm to wanting recipients.

NOTES

1 Elsewhere I have written about medical mistrust and critiqued the mistrust framework as inherently approaching the mistrustful as deviant and in need of correction (Newman 2022).

2   Top motivations of online sperm donors can be found in Freeman et al. 2016.

REFERENCES

Dockser Marcus, Amy. 2022. "Sperm Banks Struggle to Recruit Black Donors and Other Donors of Color." *Wall Street Journal*, February 26, 2022. www.wsj.com.

Ferguson, Amber. 2022. "The Severe Black Sperm Donor Shortage and its Impact on Black Women." *Washington Post*, October 20, 2022. www.washingtonpost.com.

Fox, Dov. 2011. "Choosing Your Child's Race." *Hastings Women's Law Journal* 22 (1): 3–16.

Freeman, T., V. Jadva, E. Tranfield, and S. Golombok. 2016. "Online Sperm Donation: A Survey of the Demographic Characteristics, Motivations, Preferences and Experiences of Sperm Donors on a Connection Website." *Human Reproduction* 31 (9): 2,082–89.

Graham, S., T. Freeman, and V. Jadva. 2019. "A Comparison of the Characteristics, Motivations, Preferences and Expectations of Men Donating Sperm Online or Through a Sperm Bank." *Human Reproduction* 34 (11): 2,208–18.

Gunja, Munira, Evan Gumas, and Reginald Williams II. 2022. "The U.S. Maternal Mortality Crisis Continues to Worsen: An International Comparison." *To the Point* (blog), Commonwealth Fund, December 1, 2022. www.commonwealthfund.org.

Hatem, Angela. 2020. "Sperm Donors Are Almost Always White, and It's Pushing Black Parents Using IVF to Start Families That Don't Look Like Them." *Insider*, September 17, 2020. www.insider.com.

Moreta, Latisa, Arren Simpson, Luwan Ghide, and Ashley Wiltshire. 2022. "Sperm Donor Availability and Selection Based on Race and Ethnicity." *Fertility and Sterility* 118 (4): e383–84. https://doi.org/10.1016/j.fertnstert.2022.09.358.

Newman, Alyssa. 2019. "Mixing and Matching: Sperm Donor Selection for Interracial Lesbian Couples." *Medical Anthropology* 38 (8): 710–24.

Newman, Alyssa. 2022. "Moving Beyond Mistrust: Centering Institutional Change by Decentering the White Analytical Lens." *Bioethics* 36 (3): 267–73.

Pennings, Guido. 2023. "A SWOT Analysis of Unregulated Sperm Donation." *Reproductive Biomedicine Online* 46 (1): 204–9. https://doi.org/10.1016/j.rbmo.2022.09.013.

Quiroga, Seline. 2007. "Blood is Thicker than Water: Policing Donor Insemination and the Reproduction of Whiteness." *Hypatia* 22 (2): 143–61.

Walther, Carol. 2014. "Skin Tone, Biracial Stratification and Tri-Racial Stratification Among Sperm Donors." *Ethnic and Racial Studies* 37 (3): 517–36.

Whittaker, Andrea, and Amy Spier. 2010. "Cycling Overseas: Care, Commodification, and Stratification in Cross Border Reproductive Travel." *Medical Anthropology* 29 (4): 363–83.

PART III

Making Sperm

11

State Surveillance and the Politics of Paternity

LYNNE HANEY

When we think about reproductive politics, rarely do we consider disadvantaged fathers or fathers of color. This is not out of some conscious act of exclusion. Rather, it is more of a reflection of the institutional spaces we have tended to prioritize when studying reproductive life: health care, science, policy and law, education, social movements, and so on. Yet if we think even more broadly about all the different spaces through which people come into reproductive life, new institutions emerge as shaping and regulating those lives. As I argue in this think piece, millions of fathers become procreative beings and parents while living in the most punitive of state institutions—and under enormous state surveillance and control. Paternity, poverty, and punishment can thus become entangled in extremely complex ways. And those entanglements end up being quite consequential for fathers, for families, and for reproductive politics in general.

Punishing Fatherhood

Even though James had not seen his daughter in almost thirty years, he still beams with pride when he talks about her. His memories of the few years they spent together when Renee was a baby continue to sustain him, as do the videos he regularly watches of her doing media interviews now as a global health expert. The walls separating them over the years have been both physical and emotional. Prison walls created the first barriers, as James served a life sentence in penal facilities across New York. Those prison walls soon became emotional ones as James found it impossible to connect to Renee, much less to help parent her, while incarcerated. "She was so angry with me cause of everything," he explained to me. "It was so hard for us to communicate . . . when she was little, she was too young to understand why I was in there [prison]. ... There was a lot of pain." No one spoke to James about that pain. Since he never imagined he would experience life outside of prison, he repressed it and eventually stopped contacting Renee. Relieved that she was being cared for by his own mother, he resigned himself to fathering through an intermediary—and to parenthood through memory.

Then, in 2022, after over twenty-five years in prison, James was released; a state parole board unexpectedly granted him early release during the COVID-19 pandemic. When I interviewed him a year later, his life was still full of adjustments—from cell phones to the internet to pandemic protocols, the world that he had reentered was unrecognizable. Amid all these adjustments, one of the hardest was coming to terms with his estrangement from Renee. Since a reunion with her was out of the question, he tried to redeem himself as a parent by helping his mother, who had been Renee's sole caretaker for most of her life. Like so many other reentering fathers, James hoped to repay at least this part of his familial debt. "My mother raised her . . . did such a great job . . . my parenting was through her. I owe her."

But even those hopes were dashed when James hit another wall upon his release: the financial wall of child support debt. Within months of getting out, he discovered he owed over $85,000 in back child support. How was this possible, he asked, since Renee's mother had passed away decades earlier? As with so many incarcerated fathers, James did not owe an actual person, but rather the state of New York. During his long prison sentence, New York State charged him "child support" for all public benefits Renee received. They included the two years that Renee spent in foster care before James's mother could formally adopt her, as well as the three years she received Medicaid. Those costs then accrued 9 percent interest during his time in prison, spiraling into a huge debt. Now debt was foiling his plan to repay his mother and overlaying feelings of shame, guilt, and remorse onto an already fraught familial relationship.

The State Politics of Paternity

The experiences of parents like James are rarely thought of as reproductive struggles. In fact, we often do not think about men's reproductive experiences at all—or, if we do, we tend to center those of middle-class men and definitely not those of men with the intersecting disadvantages that marked James's life as a parent, including race, class, gender, and system involvement (hooks 2004; McCall 2005). In part, this is because we rarely include institutional contexts like the criminal justice and child support systems as forces shaping reproductive life. Yet these systems do exactly that: they leave a deep imprint on procreative and reproductive life. For fathers like James, issues of reproductive justice take specific forms and are inexorably linked to the inequities of class and race. For disadvantaged men, reproductive life is intricately linked to state politics, policies, and practices.

It took me decades to acknowledge this link between paternity and the state. For most of my career, I have studied gender and the state, through research on welfare, punishment, or combinations of the two. Like other feminist scholars, I did so by centering women. Initially, this focus on women and the state seemed new and exciting. As Catherine MacKinnon (1989) famously proclaimed decades ago, feminism seemed to have no theory of the state. The reverse was also true: state theory seemed to have no conception of gender. So, many of us set out to change this, conceptualizing the "gender regime" of a variety of state systems, public institutions, and policy arenas (Pateman 1988; Orloff 1993; Sainsbury 1996). We now know an enormous amount about how women become legible, or recognizable, to the state and how they are brought into being by the state as mothers, workers, victims, pregnant bodies, and so on (Roberts 1998; Haney 2008; Suffrin 2017; Sweet 2021). We have many exceptional theorizations of how those positions have shaped reproductive culture and state politics across time and place (O'Connor, Orloff, and Shaver 1999; Ross and Solinger 2017; Briggs 2018).

Implicit in much of our scholarship was the idea that men need not become legible to the state—at least, not *as men*. Men were understood as the inherent norm, so their legibility was assumed. Indeed, states seemed to ignore them as gendered beings. Whenever I was asked about men and the state in my previous work, I responded with elaborate claims about how men fell outside the state's radar screen. With few criminal justice or welfare policies directed explicitly at men as parents, I assumed that men enjoyed the reproductive choice and autonomy denied to women. I saw paternity, to the extent that it was shaped by larger forces, as constrained by economic displacement and dislocation but certainly not by state politics.

Over the past decade, I began questioning each and every one of these assumptions. In researching my most recent book, *Prisons of Debt: The Afterlives of Incarcerated Fathers*, I worked with hundreds of disadvantaged fathers like James (Haney 2022). I learned about their lives in two of the largest, most punitive state systems in the United States: the criminal justice and child support systems. To do this, I spent over three years in child support courts across the country, observing 1,200 distinct child support cases in New York, California, and Florida. I interviewed 145 formerly incarcerated fathers from these same states about their experiences as parents. And I reviewed a vast array of federal and state policies and laws. All of these data pointed to a clear conclusion: men's reproductive lives were in fact deeply entangled with state policies and practices.

How could I have missed this? Millions of men come of age and into reproductive life while living in punitive state institutions. The majority of them also become fathers under the heavy weight of these punitive systems. There are seven million people under correctional supervision in the United States; half of them are fathers with minor children (Carson 2020). Another six million parents live with child support debt; 90 percent of them are fathers (Turetsky and Waller 2020; OCSE 2021). These fathers overlap in other predictable ways: all of them are poor, most have never been married, and the majority are men of color (Haney 2018; Brito 2019).

Mandating Paternity, Undermining Parenthood

Punitive state institutions constitute men as procreative beings in particular ways using methods and models of fatherhood that I am only now coming to understand and theorize. When I reflect on the hundreds of fathers I have met who parent at the intersection of these punitive systems, a few commonalities mark their procreative lives. While not all of these fathers are the same, they do face a similar set of constraints on their reproductive lives. And these constraints are intertwined with state imperatives and mandates.

First, for so many men, *parenthood, poverty, and punishment are conflated*. Complex institutional cycles trap fathers like James in seemingly inescapable processes of confinement and debt. For many, the cycle starts with imprisonment and then cascades into indebted parenthood—a dynamic I call the "debt of imprisonment." This is what happened to James as his time in prison led to massive support debt. While his debt was especially large, the support debt of the other fathers I worked with averaged over $36,000. The majority of it was owed to the state and *not* to mothers or families. For other fathers, the cycle starts with child support debt and cascades into penal confinement—a dynamic I call the "imprisonment of debt." Here, men's debt as fathers led to new criminal justice involvement and reimprisonment as indebted fathers. No matter how the cycles began, the consequences were similar: reproductive life was interwoven with debt and confinement.

Connected to this, *paternity is compelled and mandated* for these men. Too often, we continue to assume that men can simply opt out of their reproductive responsibilities. In a post-*Dobbs v. Jackson Women's Health Organization* world, men are frequently portrayed as able to walk away from the effects of their sperm if and when they choose. Their reproduction is not policed in the same way as women's; it is not constrained by restrictive reproductive policies and abortion laws. Instead, it is compelled by other state-mandated enforcements. These include federal requirements on paternity establishment and mandatory wage garnishment for child support. They also include the state-mandated punishments of drivers' license revocation and passport suspension for child support debt. Then there is "public assistance payback," whereby all public aid received by their offspring is billed to fathers as child support. This state regulatory practice is partly what caused national child support debt to surge to $116 billion in 2021, with 70 percent of it owed by the poorest of fathers who earn less than $15,000 per year (Haney 2018; Turetsky and Waller 2020; OCSE 2021).

This leads to a third commonality: for many disadvantaged men, *paternity is monetarized and financialized*. This dynamic shapes almost every aspect of the child support system and thus the lives of men connected to it. Its policies are guided by a stale, outdated breadwinner model of masculinity and the nuclear family, which reduces paternal responsibility to financial obligation. Its court practices reduce men to money and negate other contributions they make to their offspring's lives. Here, I am reminded of all the child support judges who told fathers to "man up and pay," thus conflating parental debt with parental failure and questioning fathers' masculinity in one fell swoop. I recall all the men who desperately tried to be recognized as caring parents, even when unable to pay what they owed. I remember all the times fathers begged state officials to stop holding them up to the one parental standard they were least able to meet. And I return to all the fathers who struggled to get judges to acknowledge the lack of jobs with livable wages, racial discrimination in hiring, and the long-term economic effects of the mark of a criminal record—usually to no avail.

Fourth, for many disadvantaged fathers, *parenthood is denied*. While their paternity might be mandated and monetarized, their parenting is often negated. Or, more precisely, their caregiving is unrecognized, disrespected, and undervalued, even as their paternity is policed. Child support does this through its monetarization of paternity. But the penal system does it as well: through laws that forcibly separate fathers and children without taking into account men's parental responsibilities during sentencing. Prison policies essentially determine who can father, when they can father, and what their fathering must look like—may it be through the rules and regulations structuring family visits to the constraints on prison communications. Moreover, prisons rarely address the pain and loss men suffer as parents during incarceration. While some penal institutions do offer "responsible fatherhood" programming as part of their reentry services, the scope and focus of those programs remains limited, particularly when compared to the resources channeled into postprison state supervision and child support enforcement.

* * *

Instead of seeing the state as ignoring men's procreative lives, I now see it as overregulating them. Or surveilling them with what Ronald Mincy once described as a "heat-seeking missile" (Mincy, Jethwani, and Klempin 2015)—a state apparatus with a stunning ability to track and destroy its targets. Like anyone under such threat, fathers lived in fear of making a wrong move: of outing themselves, of exposing themselves, and of speaking to the wrong person. So reproduction and fear became entangled for many men. Here, I am reminded of all the men too fearful to talk with me and concerned I was an enforcement officer in disguise. Or all the men I watched become paralyzed in court as they observed judges humiliate and berate other fathers, proudly claiming to "give the deadbeats hell." Or all the men taken off the streets by police on "dead beat raids"—even with their children and families watching. So these fathers often went underground and off the grid. Once in hiding, it's hard for the state to track them—but it is also hard for the rest of us to see how this surveillance affects them and their families.

It will take a lot more research from a lot more people to untangle the causes and effects of these state systems of sperm regulation. My goal here was more modest: to encourage us to be attentive to how reproductive life is regulated in difficult and painful ways for many disadvantaged men. And how that regulation occurs in spaces we do not usually consider sites of reproductive politics. When we start from a place of state surveillance and control, a series of new questions emerge: What is the state's interest in sperm surveillance? In what ways does its control cascade out to affect kin and community life? How does this control differ from the state's regulation of women's reproduction? And how can we integrate these reproductive struggles so that addressing one set no longer appears to negate the others?

REFERENCES

Briggs, Laura. 2018. *How All Politics Became Reproductive Politics*. Oakland, CA: University of California Press.
Brito, Tonya. 2019. "The Child Support Bubble." *UC Irvine Law Review* 953 (9): 953–88.
Carson, E. Ann. 2020. *Prisoners in 2019*. Washington, DC: US Department of Justice, Bureau of Justice Statistics.
Collins, Patricia Hill.1991. *Black Feminist Thought*. New York: Routledge.
Haney, Lynne. 2008. *Offending Women*. Berkeley: University of California Press.
Haney, Lynne. 2018. "Incarcerated Fatherhood: The Entanglements of Child Support Debt and Mass Imprisonment." *American Journal of Sociology* 124 (1): 1–48. https://doi.org/10.1086/697580
Haney, Lynne. 2022. *Prisons of Debt: The Afterlives of Incarcerated Fathers*. Berkeley: University of California Press.
hooks, bell. 2004. *The Will to Change: Men, Masculinity and Love*. New York: Washington Square Press.
MacKinnon, Catherine. 1989. *Toward a Feminist Theory of the State*. Cambridge, MA: Harvard University Press.

McCall, Leslie. 2005. "The Complexity of Intersectionality." *Signs* 30 (1): 771–800. https://doi.org/10.1086/426800.

Mincy, Ronald, Monique Jethwani, and Serena Klempin. 2015. *Failing Our Fathers: Confronting the Crisis of Economically Vulnerable Nonresident Fathers*. New York: Oxford.

O'Connor, Julia, Ann Orloff, and Sheila Shaver. 1999. *States, Markets, and Families: Gender, Liberalism and Social Policy in Australia, Canada, Great Britain and the United States*. New York: Oxford University Press.

Office of Child Support Enforcement (OCSE). 2021. *Preliminary Report 2021*. Washington, DC: Department of Health and Human Services, Administration of Children and Families.

Orloff, Ann. 1993. "Gender and the Social Rights of Citizenship: The Comparative Analysis of Gender Relations and Welfare States." *American Sociological Review* 58: 303–28. http://www.jstor.org/stable/2095903.

Pateman, Carole. 1988. *The Sexual Contract*. Stanford, CA: Stanford University Press.

Roberts, Dorothy. 1998. *Killing the Black Body: Race, Reproduction, and the Meaning of Liberty*. New York: Vintage.

Ross, Loretta, and Rickie Solinger. 2017. *Reproductive Justice*. Oakland, CA: University of California Press.

Sainsbury, Diane. 1996. *Gender, Equality, and Welfare States*. Cambridge: Cambridge University Press.

Suffrin, Carolyn. 2017. *Jailcare: Finding a Safety Net for Women Behind Bars*. Oakland, CA: University of California Press.

Sweet, Paige. 2021. *The Politics of Surviving*. Oakland, CA: University of California Press.

Turetsky, Vicki, and Maureen Waller 2020. "Piling on Debt: The Intersections between Child Support Arrears and Legal Financial Obligations." *UCLA Criminal Justice Law Review* 4 (1): 117–41.

12

Caught Between Sperm and Transition Care

JEREMY A. GOTTLIEB

Transgender children lie at the intersection of cutting-edge medical care, politics, and the culture wars. Trans youth's challenges accessing hormones and puberty blockers,[1] gender-affirming bathrooms, and youth sports are well documented in academic literature and the media. At the time of writing, 589 anti-Trans bills were proposed across forty-nine states of the United States during 2023 (Trans Legislation Tracker, n.d.). These bills, some of which have been ratified, range from bans on gender-affirming health care for Trans youth (some naming it as child abuse) to book bans for works that describe gender fluidity to the prohibited use of Trans youth's pronouns and names in schools.

Laws such as these—passed or not—add to Trans youth's inflated suicide rate. One recent survey in the United States found that 80 percent of Trans people have considered suicide and 40 percent have attempted it (James et al. 2016). The percentage of Trans youth who have attempted suicide in the United States ranges from 25 to 33 percent (Grossman and D'Augelli 2007; Peterson et al. 2017; Perez-Brumer et al. 2017). In contrast, the Centers for Disease Control and Prevention (2015) found that 8 percent of US high school students have attempted suicide.

Despite these grim statistics, gender-affirming health care dramatically decreases Trans children's risk of suicide (Tordoff et al. 2022; Turban et al. 2020). Similarly, Trans youth supported by their families and medical teams through their transitions have no increases in depression and only minor increases in anxiety when compared to their cisgender peers (Olson et al. 2016). Yet, disparities still exist for Trans youth who pursue gender-affirming care.

In this essay, I focus specifically on Trans children's access to fertility treatment and preservation (i.e., "freezing" sperm or eggs) and its Reproductive Justice implications. Reproductive Justice is the right not only to choose to have children or not but also to have access to those medical and social services necessary for raising a healthy child (Sister-Song, n.d.). According to a 2017 study, less than 5 percent of Trans and gender diverse children in the United States pursue fertility preservation (Nahata et al. 2017). Similar results were repeated in a 2022 study (Cooper, Long, and Aye 2022). This is compared to 25 percent of youth with cancer (National Cancer Policy Forum et al. 2014), which can be viewed as a primarily cisgender "control group" for young people engaging in fertility preservation. The reasons behind such low utilization of fertility preservation in Trans youth and its consequences are numerous and reveal a complicated and culturally rich terrain.

The World Professional Association for Transgender Health and the US Endocrine Society both recommend that providers of gender-affirming care to Trans and gender diverse youth, including physicians, mental health providers, and social workers, assess their patients' desires for "biological children"[2]—meaning children produced from a patient's sperm or eggs—and counsel them on the possibly permanent effects that medical treatment can have on their ability to have "biological children" (Coleman et al. 2022; Hembree et al. 2017). In states and cases where insurance coverage provides fertility preservation, both organizations recommend a referral to a reproductive endocrinologist or specialist for fertility preservation.

Medical Interventions for Trans and Gender Diverse Children

It is important to note that the medical interventions available to Trans and gender diverse children, namely puberty blockers (gonadotropin-releasing hormone agonists) and gender-affirming hormones (i.e., estrogen and testosterone), can be antithetical to fertility preservation. This is especially true for pre- and early-pubescent youth who begin such medical treatment.[3] On the whole, puberty blockers inhibit the spermatogenesis (sperm production) and oogenesis (egg production) that is requisite for fertility preservation (Hembree et al. 2017). There are no prospective studies to date that evaluate the effects on fertility in those treated with puberty blockers in early puberty followed by long-term hormone therapy (Coleman et al. 2022).

That is to say, Trans mascs and femmes (I use this terminology to be inclusive of nonbinary Trans individuals, who may not identify as a Trans boy/man or Trans girl/woman) who begin puberty blockers at the beginning of puberty and then begin exogenous (coming from outside the body) hormone therapy will not have the endogenous hormones (meaning produced from inside the body; in this case, estrogen or testosterone) necessary to develop viable sperm or eggs for reproduction. All possible treatments, including cryopreservation (freezing) of ovarian or testicular tissue, for these children who seek care at or before puberty are experimental or have very few case reports of success.[4]

I will review the possibilities for fertility preservation that include delay or cessation of puberty blockers or hormone therapy, or both. Yet, for both Trans femmes and mascs, delaying puberty blockers can have permanent (and, for many, negative) effects. Trans youth's endogenous testosterone or estrogen has irreversible effects on the body, including changes to bone structure (wider hips and shoulders or a more prominent brow bone), depth of voice, height, and hair distribution. It is between these two choices—(1) delaying or suspending puberty blockers to allow for fertility preservation and risking permanent bodily changes and (2) beginning puberty blockers, thus foreclosing fertility preservation options—that Trans youth, their families, and the clinicians that care for them must choose.

Trans boys and Trans-masculine nonbinary children (those assigned female at birth) who begin puberty blockers at the beginning of puberty and go on to use exogenous testosterone will not have had the endogenous estrogen necessary to develop viable oocytes (eggs). Prospective studies on the effects of puberty blockers and hormone therapy started in a person's youth on adult fertility have not yet been conducted (Coleman et al. 2022). Thus, the question remains if fertility preservation is viable for Trans-masc *adults* who began puberty blockers early in their youth and want to attempt fertility preservation in adulthood. However, at any age, the possible gender dysphoria associated with the hormonal medications and procedures (including pelvic exams, vaginal ultrasounds, and oocyte retrieval) necessary for fertility preservation and treatment may serve as a (insurmountable) barrier (Armuand et al. 2020). Testosterone or puberty blockers, or both, would also need to be halted, potentially leading to dysphoria and, especially for youth, unwanted changes to Trans-masc people's bodies.

A parallel situation is present for Trans girls and Trans-feminine nonbinary children (those assigned male at birth) who employ puberty blockers at the beginning of puberty, followed by estrogen treatment. Spermatogenesis is halted when gonadotropin-releasing hormone agonists are initiated (Coleman et al. 2022; Hembree et al. 2017; Rodriguez-Wallberg et al. 2021). Estrogen treatment, similarly, results in impaired sperm production (de Nie et al. 2020; Jindarak et al. 2018; Kent, Winoker, and Grotas 2018). Iris de Nie et al. (2023) note that most studies have found that Trans women on hormone treatment are not producing sperm, although there is a small, variable minority who do produce sperm. Another study, Gertjan Vereecke et al. (2021), found no complete spermatogenesis in any of the testes removed during bottom surgery (gender-affirming surgeries attending to the genitals). Discontinuing estrogen can lead to viable sperm production, but data are limited and do not include Trans femmes who began puberty blockers at or before puberty (Adeleye et al. 2019; Alford et al. 2020; de Nie et al. 2023; Schneider et al. 2017). Moreover, again, the negative psychological effects of (re)exposure to testosterone is likely a barrier to ceasing these medications. For adolescent Trans girls and femmes who initiate care after spermatogenesis (i.e., puberty) has begun, there is also the hesitation some may have with having to masturbate to collect sperm.

In the Clinic with Trans Children

In my ethnographic research observing and interviewing over one hundred children, parents, and clinicians in pediatric care clinics, I have witnessed the care physicians, mental health professionals, and social workers take in guiding their patients (and patients' families) through gender transitions (Gottlieb 2022). Guided by recommendations from the World Professional Association for Transgender Health and the Endocrine Society—and, moreover, their tender consideration—these clinicians take personalized approaches to assessing and meeting their patients' desires for future family planning. This is extremely challenging, though.

Children as young as nine are starting on puberty blockers (they can start puberty blockers when puberty begins), and while these medications provide more time for gender diverse children and their families to think about future treatments—including all their benefits and risks—often these children *are* making a decision about their future fertility. The medical system already poses roadblocks to treatment, including mental health and physical assessments, for children, not to mention the social challenges of transitioning (often in states hostile to these children's flourishing). As such, many gender diverse children may feel expressing a desire for future fertility will jeopardize their "chances" of receiving the medical care they are seeking and deeply desire. We know this is true of Trans adults (Spade 2006). Why would it not also be true for Trans and gender diverse children?

Of course, it is our duty as the adult clinicians, family members, and advocates of these children to make space for them to explore their desires around future family planning. Moreover, we must make space for them to express—and if desired, tolerate—the gender dysphoria that they may anticipate or experience with fertility preservation. We must not forget that what is "preserved" in these procedures—sperm or ova—are not just cells but culturally rich symbols of gender, symbols that many gender diverse children may not want to invest any further energy into (Gottlieb 2022; Hoffkling, Obedin-Maliver, and Sevelius 2017; Martin 1991).

Ensuring Trans Children Receive the Care They Desire

A variety of interventions, both material and philosophical, will help to ensure all Trans and gender diverse youth receive the fertility preservation care they desire. First and most importantly, there must be guaranteed access to high-quality pediatric transgender health care. State Medicaid programs have been one of the most effective avenues for ensuring the availability of Trans health care, including for children. Now that twenty states have banned gender-affirming health care for Trans youth, and seven more states are considering similar policies, these protections to ensure gender-affirming care are essential (Human Rights Campaign, n.d.). Similarly, insurance coverage for such care, as well as fertility preservation—which could potentially last for years, given these patients' young age—must be guaranteed. Currently, only fourteen states require insurers to cover fertility preservation (Alliance for Fertility Preservation, n.d.).

Second, more research is also necessary, both into in vitro maturation techniques for gonadal tissue and into how Trans adults who began puberty blocker and hormone therapy at young ages experienced their treatment in relation to family planning. At present, there are experiments being conducted with testicular or ovarian tissue cryopreservation ("freezing") with subsequent in vitro maturation for pre- or early-pubescent youth. E. Coleman et al. (2022) highlight a few cases of this occurring for cisgender girls, who then later conceived through in vitro fertilization; however, this has not been studied with Trans and gender diverse youth.

Finally, given the realities of our current medical system, treatments, and technologies, we must expand the conception of "family" and "family planning." Queer individuals have long challenged normative conceptions of the family, that is, a traditional cis-hetero-monogamous couple's nuclear family, and made varied and diverse families of their own. In the news media, this is most often seen in activist work around the availability of adoption and marriage as forms of family making. But even more significantly, queer and Trans people have pushed the definition of family beyond a medical definition of "blood-ties." "Chosen family" denotes the intimate relations of mutual-reliance one makes in community, especially when one has been rejected by one's "traditional family." This is eminently pertinent for queer and Trans people, especially Trans youth, who experience youth homelessness and family rejection at a higher rate than any other population (Morton et al. 2018).

In essence, the bonds of chosen family challenge heteronormative and medical standards of "biological family." While all Trans children should have access to fertility preservation as part of their care, this must not reinforce the privileging of "biology" in defining family or the prioritization of "biological" offspring. All children are biological! No matter how they are conceived, they all begin as a collection of cells, the basis of biology. The value of queer family practices, including adoption, chosen family, coparenting, and surrogacy, should be shared with Trans youth, while also making space for them to desire "biological" children and receive the medical care necessary to fulfill these desires.

Reproductive Justice for Trans and Gender Diverse Children

Balancing the virtue of access to fertility preservation with the value of nonnormative family relations and (re)production is a central tenet of Reproductive Justice. *Reproductive Justice* is defined as the human right to maintain bodily autonomy, to have or not have children, and to be safe and supported in community when one raises a child (Sister-Song, n.d.). It posits that abortion, while critical, is not the sole arena for furthering reproductive rights, and that *access*, rather than only *choice*, must be a focus of our work toward a more reproductively just society.

Expanding the definition of what it means to be a family, and how one might choose to bring children into a family and raise them, helps not only the queer and Trans community but also everyone who is considering having—or not having—children. The principles of Reproductive Justice apply not only to Trans youth presently, with the availability of fertility preservation, but also to their future. It is a Reproductive Justice issue to make it safe for Trans adults to gestate and carry children, as well as to raise them.

Likewise, we must ensure the children of Trans adults exist in a world where they are safe from discrimination. In this way, reproductive justice pushes us to think of the reproductive health of Trans youth not just as a medicolegal matter but also as a community concern. Said differently, Trans reproductive care is inherently an intersectional issue. *Intersectionality* is an activist lens coined by Kimberlé Crenshaw (1989) that focuses on how power imbalances overlap and intersect in people's multiple identities. The intersecting identities Trans people and their families may carry, as well as the many arenas in which Trans people experience discrimination—such as housing, job protections, insurance coverage—will and do affect their choices to form families. A perception that their children might face discrimination for their identity as a Trans parent may deter potential Trans parents from considering having children and seeking fertility preservation.

Furthermore, fertility preservation itself is an instrument of stratification; race and class heavily influence who is able to access fertility preservation technologies and forms of care (Galic et al. 2020). In counseling Trans children and their families around fertility preservation, clinicians must, therefore, consider that adult people of color are less likely to go to a medical provider for help getting pregnant (Chandra, Copen, and Stephen 2014). They must be cognizant of and anticipate the barriers to access that often exist for their patients of color.

Similarly, for the parents of Trans youth, racial imaginaries—in this case, the imagined race of their grandchild—can come into play. Fertility preservation is a commercialized (racial) imaginary of futurity (Rankine, Loffreda, and King 2015). That is, fertility preservation acts as an embodiment of futurity that can be leveraged for commercial interests. It brings to light questions of what the ideal grandchild looks like—especially along lines of race—for a parent and how much they might be willing to pay to ensure a specific future, both for themself and for their child. As fertility preservation is not directly linked to the choice to have a "biological" child, such a future is in fact not assured. Instead, the payment to maintain frozen ova or sperm can be understood as *insurance against the loss of*—rather than assurance of—a specific (racial) idea of family and future.

In the ethics literature, this might be considered the right to "an open future," meaning a right to not have future choices curtailed (Davis 2009; Feinberg 1992). Thus, the right to an open future would direct medical providers and parents to pursue fertility preservation for Trans children. The child would then be able to decide whether they want to have children when they are of age. Yet, this open future can obscure racialized logics. Fertility preservation is an insurance toward a particularly raced grandchild, one that is (more) likely the same as the grandparent's. This is especially salient when one considers that LGBTQ+ people are more likely to adopt cross-racially than cis, heterosexual adopting couples (Gates 2013). As such, race can be operationalized as a justification for or against reproductive preservation, although it may not appear to on the surface.

Conclusion

On the whole, reproductive health care for Trans youth remains underutilized compared to their cisgender peers. The reasons behind this are nuanced and, at times, culturally contentious. They bring into conversation the expertise of clinicians, the policies of state houses, and the commercial interests of health insurers and fertility preservation services and are a part of ongoing conversations on race, reproductive justice, and diverse definitions of family. However, it is within, not despite, the challenges of such complexity that we will be able to do right by Trans children and to best serve their care and allow them to flourish.

NOTES

1 Following a similar move to those in the Deaf community, I capitalize the word *Trans* to name and honor the Trans community and identity, beyond its simple adjectival description.
2 The term "biological children" does not appear in the Wylie C. Hembree et al. 2017 report. Furthermore, it is a stratifying term in-and-of-itself, indexing kinship relations and adoption status. For, are not all children "biological"? No child is created without a sperm and an egg—although how this occurs may be changing, as discussed by Anne Le Goff in this volume.
3 In my previous ethnographic research (Gottlieb 2022), I found that many Trans youth present to care at the beginning of puberty because of the unwanted changes to their bodies. Others present younger (age nine) or older (up to eighteen).
4 Eli Coleman et al. 2022 write this about ovarian cryopreservation in prepubertal people assigned female at birth:
> "Although the recent American Society for Reproductive Medicine guideline has lifted the experimental label from ovarian tissue cryopreservation (Practice Committee of the ASRM, 2019), there are very few case reports describing a successful pregnancy in a woman following the transplantation of ovarian tissue cryopreserved before puberty. Demeestere et al. (2015) and Rodriguez-Wallberg, Milenkovic et al. (2021) described cases of successful pregnancies following transplantation of tissue procured at the age of 14, and recently Matthews et al. (2018) described the case of a girl diagnosed with thalassemia who had ovarian tissue stored at the age of 9 and transplantation 14 years later. She subsequently conceived through IVF and delivered a healthy baby" (S160).

REFERENCES

Adeleye, Amanda J., Marcelle I. Cedars, James Smith, and Evelyn Mok-Lin. 2019. "Ovarian Stimulation for Fertility Preservation or Family Building in a Cohort of Transgender Men." *Journal of Assisted Reproduction and Genetics* 36 (10): 2,155–61. https://doi.org/10.1007/s10815-019-01558-y.

Alford, Ashley V., Katherine M. Theisen, Nicholas Kim, Joshua A. Bodie, and Joseph J. Pariser. 2020. "Successful Ejaculatory Sperm Cryopreservation After Cessation of Long-Term Estrogen Therapy in a Transgender Female." *Urology* 136 (February): e48–50. https://doi.org/10.1016/j.urology.2019.08.021.

Alliance for Fertility Preservation. n.d. "State Laws & Legislation." Accessed June 15, 2023. https://www.allianceforfertilitypreservation.org.

Armuand, Gabriela, Cecilia Dhejne, Jan I. Olofsson, Margareta Stefenson, and Kenny A. Rodriguez-Wallberg. 2020. "Attitudes and Experiences of Health Care Professionals When Caring for Transgender Men Undergoing Fertility Preservation by Egg Freezing: A Qualitative Study." *Therapeutic Advances in Reproductive Health* 14. https://doi.org/10.1177/2633494120911036.

Austin, Ashley, Shelley L. Craig, Sandra D'Souza, and Lauren B. McInroy. 2022. "Suicidality Among Transgender Youth: Elucidating the Role of Interpersonal Risk Factors." *Journal of Interpersonal Violence* 37 (5–6): NP2696–718. https://doi.org/10.1177/0886260520915554.

Bertelloni, Silvano, Giampiero I. Baroncelli, Marco Ferdeghini, Fabrizio Menchini-Fabris, and Giuseppe Saggese. 2000. "Final Height, Gonadal Function and Bone Mineral Density of Adolescent Males with Central Precocious Puberty after Therapy with Gonadotropin-Releasing Hormone Analogues." *European Journal of Pediatrics* 159 (5): 369–74. https://doi.org/10.1007/s004310051289.

Center for Disease Control. 2015. "Suicide: Facts at a Glance, 2015." Center for Disease Control. https://www.cdc.gov.

Chandra, Anjani, Casey E. Copen, and Elizabeth Hervey Stephen. 2014. "Infertility Service Use in the United States: Data from the National Survey of Family Growth, 1982–2010." *National Health Statistics Reports*, no. 73, 1–21.

Coleman, Eli, Asa Radix, Walter P. Bouman, Gillian R. Brown, Annelou L. C. De Vries, Madeline B. Deutsch, Randi Ettner et al. 2022. "Standards of Care for the Health of Transgender and Gender Diverse People, Version 8." *International Journal of Transgender Health* 23 (S1): S1–259. https://doi.org/10.1080/26895269.2022.2100644.

Cooper, Holly C., Jin Long, and Tandy Aye. 2022. "Fertility Preservation in Transgender and Non-Binary Adolescents and Young Adults." *PLOS ONE* 17 (3): e0265043. https://doi.org/10.1371/journal.pone.0265043.

Crenshaw, Kimberlé. 1989. "Demarginalizing the Intersection of Race and Sex: A Black Feminist Critique of Antidiscrimination Doctrine, Feminist Theory and Antiracist Politics." *University of Chicago Legal Forum* 1989 (1): 139–67. https://scholarship.law.columbia.edu/faculty_scholarship/3007.

Davis, Dena. 2009. *Genetic Dilemmas: Reproductive Technology, Parental Choices, and Children's Futures*. 2nd ed. New York: Oxford University Press.

de Nie, I., A. Meißner, E. H. Kostelijk, A. T. Soufan, I. a. C. Voorn-de Warem, M. den Heijer, J. Huirne, and N. M. van Mello. 2020. "Impaired Semen Quality in Trans Women: Prevalence and Determinants." *Human Reproduction* 35 (7): 1,529–36. https://doi.org/10.1093/humrep/deaa133.

de Nie, Iris, Norah M. van Mello, Emanuel Vlahakis, Charlie Cooper, Angus Peri, Martin den Heijer, Andreas Meißner, Judith Huirne, and Ken C. Pang. 2023. "Successful

Restoration of Spermatogenesis Following Gender-Affirming Hormone Therapy in Transgender Women." *Cell Reports Medicine* 4 (1): 100858. https://doi.org/10.1016/j.xcrm.2022.100858.

Feinberg, Joel. 1992. "Chapter 3: The Child's Right to an Open Future (1980)." In *Freedom and Fulfillment: Philosophical Essays*, 76–97. Princeton, NJ: Princeton University Press. https://doi.org/10.1515/9780691218144-005.

Galic, Isabel, Olivia Negris, Christopher Warren, Dannielle Brown, Alexandra Bozen, and Tarun Jain. 2020. "Disparities in Access to Fertility Care: Who's in and Who's out." *F&S Reports* 2 (1): 109–17. https://doi.org/10.1016/j.xfre.2020.11.001.

Gates, Gary J. 2013. *LGBT Parenting in the United States*. Los Angeles: Williams Institute, UCLA School of Law. https://escholarship.org/uc/item/9xs6g8xx.

Gottlieb, Jeremy. 2022. "Trans in Practice, Transition in Sequence: Providing Medical Assistance for Gender Transitions in Trans and Gender Non-Conforming Youth." In *Trans Health: International Perspectives on Care for Trans Communities*, edited by Max Nicolai Appenroth and María do Mar Castro Varela, 157–80. Bielefeld, Germany: transcript Verlag. https://doi.org/10.14361/9783839450826-012.

Grossman, Arnold H., and Anthony R. D'Augelli. 2007. "Transgender Youth and Life-Threatening Behaviors." *Suicide and Life-Threatening Behavior* 37 (5): 527–37. https://doi.org/10.1521/suli.2007.37.5.527.

Hembree, Wylie C., Peggy T. Cohen-Kettenis, Louis Gooren, Sabine E. Hannema, Walter J. Meyer, M. Hassan Murad, Stephen M. Rosenthal, Joshua D. Safer, Vin Tangpricha, and Guy G. T'Sjoen. 2017. "Endocrine Treatment of Gender-Dysphoric/Gender-Incongruent Persons: An Endocrine Society Clinical Practice Guideline." *Journal of Clinical Endocrinology and Metabolism* 102 (1): 3869–903. https://doi.org/10.1210/jc.2017-01658.

Hoffkling, Alexis, Juno Obedin-Maliver, and Jae Sevelius. 2017. "From Erasure to Opportunity: A Qualitative Study of the Experiences of Transgender Men around Pregnancy and Recommendations for Providers." *BMC Pregnancy and Childbirth* 17 (2): 332. https://doi.org/10.1186/s12884-017-1491-5.

Human Rights Campaign. n.d. "Map: Attacks on Gender Affirming Care by State." Accessed June 15, 2023. www.hrc.org.

James, Sandy E., Jody L. Herman, Susan Rankin, Mara Keisling, Lisa Mottet, and Ma'ayan Anafi. 2016. *The Report of the 2015 U.S. Transgender Survey*. Washington, DC: National Center for Transgender Equality.

Jindarak, Sirachai, Kasama Nilprapha, Taywin Atikankul, Apichai Angspatt, Pornthep Pungrasmi, Seree Iamphongsai, Pasu Promniyom, Poonpissamai Suwajo, Gennaro Selvaggi, and Preecha Tiewtranon. 2018. "Spermatogenesis Abnormalities Following Hormonal Therapy in Transwomen." *BioMed Research International* 2018:7919481. https://doi.org/10.1155/2018/7919481.

Kent, Marissa A., Jared S. Winoker, and Aaron B. Grotas. 2018. "Effects of Feminizing Hormones on Sperm Production and Malignant Changes: Microscopic Examination of Post Orchiectomy Specimens in Transwomen." *Urology* 121 (November): 93–96. https://doi.org/10.1016/j.urology.2018.07.023.

Martin, Emily. 1991. "The Egg and the Sperm: How Science Has Constructed a Romance Based on Stereotypical Male-Female Roles." *Signs: Journal of Women in Culture and Society* 16 (3): 485–501. https://doi.org/10.1086/494680.
Morton, Matthew H., Amy Dworsky, Jennifer L. Matjasko, Susanna R. Curry, David Schlueter, Raúl Chávez, and Anne F. Farrell. 2018. "Prevalence and Correlates of Youth Homelessness in the United States." *Journal of Adolescent Health: Official Publication of the Society for Adolescent Medicine* 62 (1): 14–21. https://doi.org/10.1016/j.jadohealth.2017.10.006.
Nahata, Leena, Amy C. Tishelman, Nicole M. Caltabellotta, and Gwendolyn P. Quinn. 2017. "Low Fertility Preservation Utilization Among Transgender Youth." *Journal of Adolescent Health: Official Publication of the Society for Adolescent Medicine* 61 (1): 40–44. https://doi.org/10.1016/j.jadohealth.2016.12.012.
National Cancer Policy Forum, Board on Health Care Services, A Livestrong and Institute of Medicine Workshop, and Institute of Medicine. 2014. *Identifying and Addressing the Needs of Adolescents and Young Adults with Cancer: Workshop Summary*. Washington, DC: National Academies Press.
Olson, Kristina R., Lily Durwood, Madeleine DeMeules, and Katie A. McLaughlin. 2016. "Mental Health of Transgender Children Who Are Supported in Their Identities." *Pediatrics* 137 (3): e20153223. https://doi.org/10.1542/peds.2015-3223.
Perez-Brumer, Amaya, Jack K. Day, Stephen T. Russell, and Mark L. Hatzenbuehler. 2017. "Prevalence and Correlates of Suicidal Ideation among Transgender Youth in California: Findings from a Representative, Population-Based Sample of High School Students." *Journal of the American Academy of Child & Adolescent Psychiatry* 56 (9): 739–46.
Peterson, Claire M., Abigail Matthews, Emily Copps-Smith, and Lee Ann Conard. 2017. "Suicidality, Self-Harm, and Body Dissatisfaction in Transgender Adolescents and Emerging Adults with Gender Dysphoria." *Suicide and Life-Threatening Behavior* 47 (4): 475–82. https://doi.org/10.1111/sltb.12289.
Rankine, Claudia, Beth Loffreda, and Cap Max King. 2015. *The Racial Imaginary: Writers on Race in the Life of the Mind*. Albany, NY: Fence Books.
Rodriguez-Wallberg, Kenny A., Jakob Häljestig, Stefan Arver, Anna L. V. Johansson, and Frida E. Lundberg. 2021. "Sperm Quality in Transgender Women before or after Gender Affirming Hormone Therapy-A Prospective Cohort Study." *Andrology* 9 (6): 1,773–80. https://doi.org/10.1111/andr.12999.
Schneider, F., S. Kliesch, S. Schlatt, and N. Neuhaus. 2017. "Andrology of Male-to-Female Transsexuals: Influence of Cross-Sex Hormone Therapy on Testicular Function." *Andrology* 5 (5): 873–80. https://doi.org/10.1111/andr.12405.
SisterSong. n.d. "Reproductive Justice." Accessed June 15, 2023. https://www.sistersong.net/reproductive-justice.
Spade, Dean. 2006. "Mutilating Gender." In *The Transgender Studies Reader*, 315–32. New York: Routledge.
Tordoff, Diana M., Jonathon W. Wanta, Arin Collin, Cesalie Stepney, David J. Inwards-Breland, and Kym Ahrens. 2022. "Mental Health Outcomes in Transgender and

Nonbinary Youths Receiving Gender-Affirming Care." *JAMA Network Open* 5 (2): e220978. https://doi.org/10.1001/jamanetworkopen.2022.0978.

Trans Legislation Tracker. n.d. "2023 Anti-Trans Bills: Trans Legislation Tracker." Accessed December 11, 2023. https://translegislation.com.

Turban, Jack L., Dana King, Jeremi M. Carswell, and Alex S. Keuroghlian. 2020 "Pubertal Suppression for Transgender Youth and Risk of Suicidal Ideation." *Pediatrics* 145 (2): e20191725. https://doi.org/10.1542/peds.2019-1725.

Vereecke, Gertjan, Justine Defreyne, Dorien Van Saen, Sarah Collet, Jo Van Dorpe, Guy T'Sjoen, and Ellen Goossens. 2021. "Characterisation of Testicular Function and Spermatogenesis in Transgender Women." *Human Reproduction* 36 (1): 5–15. https://doi.org/10.1093/humrep/deaa254.

13

Whose Sperm Is Worthy? How Eugenics Promotes the Control of Transgender People's Reproduction

STEF M. SHUSTER

It was not until the last few decades that the medical community has begun to address fertility options for transgender people. In 2001, the World Professional Association for Transgender Health (WPATH) released version six of their standards of care for trans and nonbinary health, and a few sentences appeared which encouraged clinicians to speak with their patients about sperm and egg preservation (Meyer et al. 2001). In version eight, released in 2022, there is now an entire chapter devoted to reproductive health (Coleman et al. 2022). The current guidelines advise that all trans and nonbinary people considering hormonal interventions should be counseled about fertility preservation. For trans and nonbinary youths, as Jeremy A. Gottlieb astutely observes in this volume, the guidance is less clear because of the timing of developmental stages and multiple options for youths considering hormone therapy. Some may desire to take puberty pausers to delay puberty or begin hormones before undergoing puberty while others may wait until later adolescence to decide. Fertility preservation options for youths will thus shift depending on if and when they opt into gender-affirming hormone therapy, such as testosterone for masculinizing effects or estrogen for femininizing effects.

While many may applaud the efforts of the WPATH to recognize and affirm the reproductive autonomy of trans people, looking beneath the surface of these guidelines reveals outdated beliefs about who can and should access such technologies, echoing well-worn tropes established by medical professionals in the 1950s. In the research I conducted for my book, *Trans Medicine*, I examined archives from the mid-twentieth century and found that scientific and medical communities created a hierarchy of valued trans people. The most prized patients were those who were white, affluent, able-bodied, and willing to leave behind their families and children. Moreover, patients were expected to disavow masturbation and any other sexual behaviors regarded as "abnormal." Trans people deemed "worthy" of accessing hormonal or surgical interventions were also expected to demonstrate their ability to be productive citizens by holding respectable jobs and moving through social life undetected as transgender (Shuster 2021). During this time, the advancement of medical and surgical knowledge came at the expense of trans people's ability to produce children through physician-mandated surgical or hormonal sterilization, which was an unproblematized consequence for those seeking gender-affirming care.

How trans people were evaluated as "worthy" in the 1950s aligned with the US scientific and medical communities' criteria for ensuring the health of future generations in what is commonly understood as the eugenics movement. Over the nineteenth and twentieth centuries, a broad swath of people in the United States—people of color, poor people, disabled people, people with mental illnesses, sexually active women, "feeble minded" people, homosexual people, and many other groups—were subject to coercive measures such as imprisonment and sterilization (Kline 2001; Schoen 2005; Stern 2016). Such measures were undertaken by physicians and scientists with the broader goal of controlling marginalized groups' reproductive capacities and bodily autonomy in the effort to "improve" future generations by limiting the reproductive autonomy of those deemed "unworthy" to have or raise children (Irvine 2005; Ordover 2003).

But what is the relationship between controlled reproduction in the nineteenth and twentieth centuries and fertility options available to trans people in contemporary society? The links are subtle, but a modified version of the "worthy" trans person that developed in the 1950s has been repurposed and carried forward today. In the present day, notions of worthiness continue to be applied in trans medicine by *individualizing* whose responsibility it is to ensure that trans people can have children. Families with trans youth or trans adults are moderately supported to consider fertility options by medical guidance from WPATH, but they are often on their own when it comes to financing, managing, and planning fertility preservation.

For trans women, cryopreservation is the primary way to preserve their sperm before beginning hormones. The best estimates suggest that cryopreservation of sperm, including testing, collection, and storage, costs around $750 a year *if* an individual has health insurance. For many trans women, especially trans women of color, this is an insurmountable amount of money, as they experience a disproportionate burden of poverty, homelessness, incarceration, and other forms of structural violence (Robinson 2020).

And yet, the cost of cryopreservation services is not the only issue facing trans women. There remains a lack of evidence on fertility preservation options for trans women (De Roo et al. 2018; Lai et al. 2020; Nahata et al. 2019) The paucity of scientific studies about efficacious fertility preservation should be unsurprising because there is a persistent gender bias in the reproductive sciences, which consistently gloss over the challenges of infertility and the possibilities for fertility among cisgender men and trans women. Simply put, we need better scientific data to ensure that those who want to begin hormones and want to keep the door open for using their sperm (or eggs, for trans men) to conceive can access better information to make informed decisions.

Moreover, given the fractured structure of health insurance in the United States and how quickly it is changing—with recent legislative efforts to ban gender-affirming care for trans people, especially youth—many insurance companies do not cover most or any of the costs associated with cryopreservation. A quick skim of the Transgender Legal Defense & Education Fund's website documenting which insurance companies cover cryopreservation suggests that who, when, why, and where coverage is offered is subjective. For example, many insurers use the language of "medically necessary" to define when gender-affirming care will be covered by the insurer. This phrase may seem self-evident. But there is a lot of interpretive work by insurers in what they mean by necessity. Some understand all gender-affirming care as a necessity, other companies interpret hormones as a necessity but not surgery or cryopreservation. Others refuse to cover any gender-affirming care because it is deemed "elective." This situation creates uncertainty for trans people navigating these systems and trying to figure out whether and when they will be denied or approved coverage (Kirkland, Talesh, and Perone 2021).

There are also hidden barriers within insurance coverage. Some insurance companies with clearly worded policies state they will cover the costs associated with cryopreservation, but then stipulate they will only store sperm for one to two years. This insurance-based precarity leaves trans women who desire to start hormones and have future fertility options, but do not have access to financial resources, in quite the bind. For trans women enrolled in Medicaid, fertility-related coverage is also murky. Some state programs cover cryopreservation for trans women or in vitro fertilization for cisgender women who are partners of trans women desiring to bear children, while other states restrict any coverage (Kyweluk, Reinecke, and Chen 2019; Peipert et al. 2022).

Within this complex web of finances, insurance, and the medical establishment, there is an implicit valuation of some trans women's anticipated progeny as more worthy of protection and care than others, especially when considering who has the financial, social (Chapman, Verdery, and Moody 2022), and cultural health capital to access fertility options (Shim 2010). By creating significant economic, health access, and knowledge barriers for poor and working-class trans women, who are disproportionately women of color (Hsieh and Shuster 2021), to preserving their sperm or having children, insurance companies and the medical establishment are recycling early twentieth-century eugenics ideas in prohibiting those deemed "unworthy" from having children.

Rather than reinforcing structural oppression and leaning on eugenics to frame—intentionally or not—which trans people are considered "worthy" of having children and making informed decisions about their anticipated future fertility options, I offer the following recommendations for how to move beyond reproducing inequalities in fertility options:

1. The WPATH should work more closely with other medical professional associations to enshrine Reproductive Justice in the health care landscape of trans medicine. By building intersectional alliances, they could work together to close the loopholes that insurance companies use to deny trans people access to care.
2. Federal agencies must devote funding to studying the long-term effects of hormones on trans people's reproductive health.

3. Insurance companies should remove time limits on cryopreservation.
4. State-based variation in Medicaid fertility coverage needs to be eliminated. All Medicaid programs should offer assistance for trans women to use cryopreservation and in vitro fertilization.
5. To ensure that trans women have better access to fertility options regardless of their ability to pay, LGBTQ+ organizations that purport to work on behalf of trans people should dedicate tangible resources to help trans and nonbinary youth and women with the financial difficulties of accessing care.

As Krystale E. Littlejohn suggests in her essay in this volume, reproductive justice means taking account of the multiple and intersecting axes of oppression that people experience in matters related to reproductive health. While all trans people have experienced the effects of eugenics by the medical community restricting access to future fertility possibilities, poor or working-class trans women of color have faced insurmountable barriers in their efforts to have or raise children because they are perceived as unworthy of having children. By grappling with the long reach of eugenics and restructuring federal programs, insurance coverage, and social support to respond to such a legacy, we can begin to reimagine futures where trans women's efforts to have or raise children is not met with such profound obstruction.

REFERENCES

Chapman, Alexander, Ashton M. Verdery, and James Moody. 2022. "Analytic Advances in Social Networks and Health in the Twenty-first Century." *Journal of Health and Social Behavior* 63 (2): 191–209. https://doi.org/10.1177/00221465221086532.

Coleman, Eli, Asa Radix, Walter P. Bouman, Gillian R. Brown, Annelou L. C. De Vries, Madeline B. Deutsch, Randi Ettner et al. 2022. "Standards of Care for the Health of Transgender and Gender Diverse People, Version 8." Supplement, *International Journal of Transgender Health* 23 (S1): S1–259. https://doi.org/10.1080/26895269.2022.2100644.

De Roo, Chloë, Kelly Tilleman, Guy T'Sjoen, and Petra De Sutter. 2018. "Fertility Options in Transgender People." In *Gender Dysphoria and Gender Incongruence*, edited by Walter Bouman, Annelou de Vries, and Guy T'Sjoen, 124–31. New York: Routledge.

Hsieh, Ning, and Stef M. Shuster. 2021. "Health and Health Care of Sexual and Gender Minorities." *Journal of Health and Social Behavior* 62 (3): 318–33. https://doi.org/10.1177/00221465211016436.

Irvine, Janice R. 2005. *Disorders of Desire: Sexuality and Gender in Modern American Sexology*. Philadelphia: Temple University Press.

Kirkland, Anna, Shauhin Talesh, and Angela K. Perone. 2021. "Health Insurance Rights and Access to Health Care for Trans People: The Social Construction of Medical Necessity." *Law & Society Review* 55 (4): 539–62. https://doi.org/10.1111/lasr.12575.

Kline, Wendy. 2001. *Building a Better Race: Gender, Sexuality, and Eugenics from the Turn of the Century to the Baby Boom*. Berkeley: University of California Press.

Kyweluk, Moira A., Joyce Reinecke, and Diane Chen. 2019. "Fertility Preservation Legislation in the United States: Potential Implications for Transgender Individuals." *LGBT Health* 6 (7): 331–34. https://doi.org/10.1089/lgbt.2019.001.

Lai, Timothy C., Rosalind McDougall, Debi Feldman, Charlotte V. Elder, and Ken C. Pang. 2020. "Fertility Counseling for Transgender Adolescents: A Review." *Journal of Adolescent Health* 66 (6): 658–65. https://doi.org/10.1016/j.jadohealth.2020.01.007.

Meyer, Walter, III, Walter Bockting, Peggy Cohen-Kettenis, Eli Coleman, Domenico DiCeglie, Holly Devor, Louis Gooren, J. Joris Hage, Sheila Kirk, Bram Kuiper. 2001. "The Harry Benjamin International Gender Dysphoria Association: Standards of Care for Gender Identity Disorders, Sixth Version." *Journal of Psychology & Human Sexuality* 13 (1): 1–30. https://doi.org/10.1300/J056v13n01_01.

Nahata, Leena, Diane Chen, Molly B. Moravek, Gwendolyn P. Quinn, Megan E. Sutter, Julia Taylor, Amy C. Tishelman, and Veronica Gomez-Lobo. 2019. "Understudied and Under-reported: Fertility Issues in Transgender Youth—A Narrative Review." *Journal of Pediatrics* 205:265–71. https://doi.org/10.1016/j.jpeds.2018.09.009.

Ordover, Nancy. 2003. *American Eugenics: Race, Queer Anatomy, and the Science of Nationalism*. Minneapolis: University of Minnesota Press.

Peipert, Benjamin J., Melissa N. Montoya, Bronwyn S. Bedrick, David B. Seifer, and Tarun Jain. 2022. "Impact of In Vitro Fertilization State Mandates for Third Party Insurance Coverage in the United States: A Review and Critical Assessment." *Reproductive Biology and Endocrinology* 20 (1): 1–12. https://doi.org/10.1186/s12958-022-00984-5.

Schoen, Johanna. 2005. *Choice & Coercion: Birth Control, Sterilization, and Abortion in Public Health and Welfare*. Chapel Hill: University of North Carolina Press.

Shim, Janet K. 2010. "Cultural Health Capital: A Theoretical Approach to Understanding Health Care Interactions and the Dynamics of Unequal Treatment." *Journal of Health and Social Behavior* 51 (1): 1–15. https://doi.org/10.1177/0022146509361118.

Shuster, Stef M. 2021. *Trans Medicine: The Emergence and Practice of Treating Gender*. New York: New York University Press.

Stern, Alexander. 2016. *Eugenic Nation: Faults and Frontiers of Better Breeding in Modern America*. Berkeley: University of California Press.

Robinson, Brandon Andrew. 2020. *Coming Out to the Streets: LGBTQ Youth Experiencing Homelessness*. Oakland: University of California Press.

Transgender Legal Defense and Education Fund. "Health Insurance Medical Policies: Fertility Preservation." Accessed June 1, 2023. https://transhealthproject.org.

14

Do Young Men Care about Their Fertility?

DAVID L. BELL

Downward trends in semen quality among young men globally have been observed, including total sperm count, sperm concentration, and progressive motile sperm. But total motile sperm do not appear to be trending down or even leveling off. However, the results of overall studies are mixed (Luo et al. 2023; Tong et al. 2022).[1]

Sperm health is not a subject in our medical school curriculums and is seldomly discussed in primary care. As a physician who cares for young males in New York City, usually between the ages of fourteen and thirty-five, it has become quite clear that many cultures pay more attention to adolescent and young adult females' issues than those of adolescent and young adult males, both in general and specifically around sexual and reproductive health. Attention to the health and viability of one's sperm or the politics of one's sperm is seldom discussed with our young males. Are young men concerned about the health of their sperm? Do they care? From the perspective of an adolescent and young adult physician and advocate who focuses on the primary care of males, this think piece will discuss an understanding based on two decades of experiences.

During my fellowship in adolescent medicine, the head nurse in our clinic told me one day that "my guys" were here to see me. Responding to my perplexed look, she said she has observed that the clinic has had more male patients connecting to care through me than she had seen at any point in her thirty years there. I reflected on that conversation over the years and realized that adolescent medicine was somewhat synonymous with adolescent female health and a primary focus on gynecological conditions, pregnancy prevention (i.e., hormonal contraception), and eating disorders. Although males play a role in pregnancy, condoms do not require a medical visit or prescription. Males also can be diagnosed with eating disorders, but the percentages are lower in comparison to females. With that understanding, my personal charge was to bring more attention to the health needs of young men. As circumstances developed, a couple of years later, I became the medical director of the Young Men's Clinic, a focused service within a Title X–funded (state and federal) program. The services focused on primary care with special attention to the sexual and reproductive health needs of young men, including pregnancy prevention.

Adolescence is a time of dynamic changes physically, mentally, and socially. Physically, their bodies are changing. Specifically related to sexual maturation, unlike females born with all the eggs in their ovaries, males start producing sperm for the first time during puberty. In fact, compared to menarche, the first menstrual cycle for females, we know very little about spermarche—the time at which a male experiences their first ejaculation (Laron 2010). We know even less about the time at which sperm starts being produced as a prior step to ejaculation. Mentally, adolescents progress from concrete thinking to abstract thinking. The humorous and traditional sexual-and-reproductive-health example of concrete thinking is the adolescent's response to the question "Are you sexually active?" "No . . . I just lie there." Socially, they start engaging and exploring adult behaviors, such as romantic and sexual relationships. In the field of adolescent medicine, sex has been termed one of the risk behaviors of adolescence, though pregnancy and sexually transmitted diseases are risks of adult sex as well.

There have been significant delays among youth experiencing their sexual debut over the past decades—from 70 percent of youth by age eighteen to 57 percent of twelfth graders recently. Traditionally, the youth who experience their sexual debut early are at risk for early pregnancy due to many factors. For the younger set of sexually active males, concerns about fertility sometimes start due to the limitations of concrete thinking. Our pregnancy prevention mantra is "With even one unprotected sexual encounter, you can get someone pregnant. Use a condom." But the reality is much more complicated. From a concrete thinker's perspective, "I have had one, two, or more unprotected episodes without a pregnancy. I can't get anyone pregnant. I will keep trying to prove my fertility."

Among the minority of adolescent and young adult males who are brave enough or feel secure or safe enough to ask, many do have concerns about their sperm health. Primarily, it is about their desire to know if their sperm is healthy. Sometimes this is due to past or present use of drugs—marijuana, alcohol, or steroids—or just anxiety that they have not gotten anyone pregnant despite having unprotected sex.

"Hold on," I say, "for men, there is a simpler, efficient, less life-changing way to evaluate your fertility." Enter the 40x microscope view: a circle of minute tadpoles with tails whirling—traveling with independent agendas between two plates of glass. The details of sperm count, volume, motility, viscosity, liquefaction, pH, shape, and appearance are reserved for an official lab. Per hospital protocol, I can only say "Sperm is present (or absent)." As the teenaged or twenty-something male is oriented to the view of his sperm sample, he beams at the biological marvel of his body and the genius of nature. I always marvel that this is the best science lesson ever.

To broaden the discussion to some of the politics of sperm and the sexual and reproductive health of young males, I want to restate: we have paid little attention to the sexual and reproductive health of adolescent and young adult males, a point also made by Arik V. Marcell in this volume. Yet, we blame males for thoughts and behaviors that align with a traditional patriarchal society without giving them practical counterpoints and behavioral alternatives in their lived environments. In 1994, one of the outcomes of the International Conference on Population and Development in Cairo, Egypt, was a consensus that women's sexual and reproductive health would not make any further progress without involving men (Roseman and Reichenbach 2010). The terms "male involvement" and "male responsibility" were introduced as concepts for all sexual and reproductive health programs to embrace. These terms encompassed the beliefs that we should help men be supportive of women's sexual and reproductive health by supporting their female partners' use of contraception and getting tested routinely for sexually transmitted infections (as appropriate). Further, they encompass the belief that the pharmaceutical industry should develop new male contraceptive methods. A few years later, there was an understanding and acceptance that attention to men's sexual and reproductive health was appropriate "in their own right," with the secondary benefits of improved women's sexual and reproductive health, as well as the improved health of children and families.

To date, if a young man discloses "I don't want to have kids for the next five or six years," his options are still limited to condoms and support of his female partner to use effective birth control methods. Vasectomies are generally only an option later in life. In my role as an advocate for male sexual and reproductive health and in promoting male responsibility, I discuss with my patients early access to female emergency contraception—a method of birth control one can use if there was sex without using birth control or if a birth control method did not work correctly. According to the original ruling by the Food and Drug Administration (FDA), males can buy emergency contraception over the counter for their partners. Years ago, a few too many males would come to me saying that their pharmacy would not sell them emergency contraception. To understand what was happening, I engaged three young men—nineteen, twenty-five, and twenty-eight years old—to do a mystery shopper survey (Bell, Camacho, and Velasquez 2014). Over a span of four weeks, these three males visited 158 pharmacies in three distinct neighborhoods in New York City. One of the findings of that study was that one in five pharmacies would not sell emergency contraception to males despite the FDA regulation. In presenting the findings of this study at conferences, I was surprised to learn that despite clinician support of the concept of "male involvement," clinicians were often conflicted about involving men. Overall, there was significant push-back and opposition. Male access to emergency contraception was equated with use of a date rape drug. These links are and were phenomenally illogical!

Are young men concerned about the health of their sperm? Yes. Do they care? Yes, in many ways. Do our systems embrace and support young men to understand the health of their sperm or their overall sexual and reproductive health? I would argue no. We have strides to make for the future still.

NOTE

1 A more detailed discussion of these studies can be found in essays by Christopher J. De Jonge and Marion Boulicault in this volume.

REFERENCES

Bell, David L., Elvis J. Camacho, and Andrew B. Velasquez. 2014. "Male Access to Emergency Contraception in Pharmacies: A Mystery Shopper Survey." *Contraception* 90 (4): 413–15. https://doi.org/10.1016/j.contraception.2014.06.032.

Laron, Zvi. 2010. "Age at First Ejaculation (Spermarche)—The Overlooked Milestone in Male Development." *Pediatric Endocrinology Reviews: PER* 7 (3): 256–57.

Luo, Xuefeng, Chongyang Yin, Yuqing Shi, Chengchao Du, and Xiangcheng Pan. 2023. "Global Trends in Semen Quality of Young Men: A Systematic Review and Regression Analysis." *Journal of Assisted Reproduction and Genetics* 40 (8): 1807–16. https://doi.org/10.1007/s10815-023-02859-z.

Roseman, Mindy Jane, and Laura Reichenbach. 2010. "International Conference on Population and Development at 15 Years: Achieving Sexual and Reproductive Health and Rights for All?" *American Journal of Public Health* 100 (3): 403–6. https://doi.org/10.2105/AJPH.2009.177873.

Tong, Nora, Luke Witherspoon, Caitlin Dunne, and Ryan Flannigan. 2022. "Global Decline of Male Fertility: Fact or Fiction? A Broad Summary of the Published Evidence on Sperm-Count and Fertility Trends." *British Columbia Medical Journal* 64 (3).

15

In Vitro Gametogenesis as a Window into Sperm Health and Politics

ANNE LE GOFF

Today, in vitro fertilization or insemination requires that sperm be extracted from a man's body, either the intended father's or a donor's. What if sperm could be produced in the laboratory instead? This is the promise of stem cell research, which aims to enable the production of sperm in a dish, or in vitro. In vitro gametogenesis (IVG) research aims to recreate the generation of sperm (also known as gametes) outside of the body, from an individual's other cells.

With high rates of infertility worldwide and few options for those who, for a variety of reasons, cannot use their own sperm to reproduce, this emerging technology offers new hope for many people. If IVG can produce safe and functional human sperm in the future, it could help cis men whose bodies cannot produce functional sperm, as well as transgender men, lesbian couples, and nonpartnered individuals, to have a biological child. Media and academic commentary on IVG have focused overwhelmingly on the opportunities and issues raised by hypothetical uses of IVG for human reproduction. Yet, this ignores the questions that IVG research raises even before it produces functional human sperm: what does this process of making sperm in vitro teach us about sperm? In this essay, building on my ethnographic study of the field of IVG research in the United States between 2019 and 2023, I propose to take a step back and observe the process of IVG research as it occurs today. After giving a brief overview of the science of IVG, I will present the dominant narrative of IVG as the promise of producing an artificial substitute for sperm. I will then contrast it with another way of looking at IVG through its concrete results, which involves producing knowledge about the stages of sperm development and highlighting specific windows of vulnerability. This leads to further insights into how IVG research can reshape our understanding of what sperm is, with direct implications for health and policy.

What Is In Vitro Gametogenesis?

In the male body, sperm are produced by spermatogonial stem cells. Beginning at puberty, these cells continuously undergo a complex process of differentiation that leads to the formation of mature spermatozoa capable of fertilizing with an oocyte and producing an embryo. While this process occurs later in life, the development of spermatogonial stem cells begins early in embryonic development when embryonic pluripotent stem cells differentiate into primordial germ cells, which in turn become spermatogonial stem cells.

IVG aims to mimic this entire developmental process—from pluripotent stem cells all the way to fertile sperm—outside of the body, in a petri dish. While in the body pluripotent stem cells are found only in the embryo, recent techniques have made it possible to artificially create "induced pluripotent stem cells" (iPSCs) from other cell types (Yamanaka 2012). Through a process known as "reprogramming," specialized body cells, such as skin or blood cells, are made to become pluripotent, capable of giving rise to any cell type. Thus, to complete IVG from an individual animal's own cells, scientists start with skin cells taken from a biopsy; they then reprogram the cells to become iPSCs; and they "coax" (in their own terms) these pluripotent stem cells through appropriate developmental steps for them to become sperm (Saitou and Hayashi 2021).

While, to date, no human sperm has been produced using IVG, complete in vitro spermatogenesis has been performed in mice (Ishikura et al. 2021). Sperm were generated from mouse skin cells using IVG and fertilized with oocytes, resulting in the birth of pups that were themselves fertile. These experiments demonstrated that sperm capable of fulfilling their reproductive function had indeed been produced. Transferring this methodology to human cells has proven to be an arduous task because our knowledge of human sperm development is much more limited than that of mice, with experimentation in humans ethically and practically constrained. To date, scientists have generated the precursor stage of human spermatogonial stem cells in vitro (Hwang et al. 2020), and are exploring ways to support germ cell development in several species by transplanting them into the testes of animal models or by reconstituting testes in vitro (Sosa et al. 2018).

IVG, or the Promise of Regenerative Reproductive Medicine

Although no human sperm has been produced using IVG yet, the birth of mouse pups via IVG has captured the attention of many. These achievements conjure up a future in which sperm and eggs could be produced in the laboratory for those who need them in order to have a baby: a "reproduction revolution" (Ball 2018). Remarkably, IVG would allow the production not only of gametes but of *genetically related* gametes. If the starting cells for making iPSCs were *an individual's own* cells, such as their skin cells, as is the case with mouse experiments today, then the sperm generated from them would have that individual's genome. Therefore, IVG would maintain a biological and genetic link between the individual using it and their child. In this respect, IVG-generated sperm would be just like sperm produced by the testes, albeit produced by a different, artificial process. Therefore, it appears to be a possible *substitute* for in vivo–generated sperm for men.

Today, men who want a biological child but are unable to conceive through traditional in vitro fertilization can use a surgical procedure known as testicular sperm extraction. IVG would be a less invasive alternative and potentially would provide higher quality sperm. For men who do not want to undergo this procedure, or who do not produce sperm at all, the only way to have a baby with in vitro fertilization is to use a donor, and IVG would be the first technology to offer them the option of having a biological child. Similarly, IVG could allow transgender men to have biologically related children and lesbian couples to have children who are related to both parents (Murphy 2018). Even for people who do not attach a specific value to genetic relatedness, IVG could avoid the ethical and legal difficulties associated with sperm donation. The fertility industry has already identified IVG as a significant emerging innovation in assisted reproductive technology (Witt 2023). At the same time, bioethicists have highlighted ethical issues, from nontraditional forms of biological parenthood, to unethical or questionable practices such as gamete creation without an individual's consent or heritable genome editing (Smajdor and Cutas 2015; Suter 2016).

The focus on IVG's future applications for human reproduction comes not only from the media and assisted reproductive technology stakeholders but also from the scientific community itself. IVG scientists describe their work to their nonscientific audiences, namely funders, clinicians, and the public, within the horizon of infertility medicine. In doing so, they enact an "ethos of translation" that has become the norm in biomedicine over the past twenty years, especially in North America as the ability of basic researchers to attract not only private but also public funding depends on their ability to demonstrate the potential of their research to lead to medical tools and treatments (Maienschein et al. 2008). This ethos is particularly evident in the field of stem cells, also known as "regenerative medicine," which seeks to harness the ability of stem cells to regenerate and produce different cell types to replace cells, tissues, or organs in the body (Gardner and Webster 2016). IVG, as a means of replacing a missing gamete, is a prime example of what regenerative medicine would be. However, the narrative of IVG as a regenerative technology that would produce a direct replacement for missing gametes obscures other outcomes of IVG research that add complexity to our understanding of sperm and are important in their own right for reproductive health.

IVG as a Tool for Understanding Spermatogenesis and Infertility

To an observer of the making of IVG science in the laboratory setting and at academic conferences in the United States, the discrepancy between public discussions of IVG, which focus on the imagined IVG gamete, and the reality of IVG research today is striking (see also, in the context of the UK, Merleau-Ponty 2021). Here, I would like to shift the gaze away from the anticipated product of IVG to the "craft" of making sperm in IVG laboratories and ask what we can learn about sperm from it (Meskus 2018).

The reproductive cells that mature to become sperm are unique in many respects: they are the only cells that develop differently according to sex. They also undergo meiosis, the division of their genome in two, to become cells with a uniquely compacted genome and motility.

Our understanding of sperm development is currently limited, in part because early and crucial steps in this development occur in embryos. While embryos cannot be studied in vivo, their culture and study in vitro has to date been technologically and ethically limited to fourteen days (Hyun, Wilkerson, and Johnston 2016). In an oft-repeated metaphor, scientists point to a "black box" in our understanding of sperm formation and its specificity compared to mammalian models.

IVG is an experimental system that models the process of human spermatogenesis in vitro. In particular, it brings into focus the entire process that precedes and leads to the formation of spermatozoa. It thus invites us to move beyond a snapshot understanding of sperm health as the ability to fertilize an oocyte to an understanding of sperm health as a process that extends over time, both before and after fertilization. The attempt to reconstitute functional sperm in vitro also raises the question of what constitutes normal sperm, beyond the criteria used in everyday fertility care of morphology, motility, and count of mature sperm in the ejaculate and the general assessment of infertility rates by sperm count. By opening up the possibility of studying the molecular makeup and developmental trajectory of sperm, the IVG model allows us to ask in more detail what sperm need to be in order to participate in reproduction.

As IVG scientists try to coax pluripotent stem cells to complete sperm development, they are learning about its precise steps and complexity. One area where the IVG model has provided significant insight is the early stage of primordial germ cells, with the discovery that these cells undergo extensive and unique changes in their epigenome. The epigenome refers to a set of molecules that collectively regulate gene expression and is key to genome stability. It is now understood that primordial germ cells undergo a process of "resetting," in which parental epigenetic marks on the cells are almost entirely erased and new epigenetic marks are reinstated, and that successful reinstatement of epigenetic marks at this early stage is key to the formation of viable and healthy sperm (Gruhn et al. 2023). Yet, primordial germ cells are vulnerable to environmental perturbations. For instance, a study examining the effect of bisphenol A (BPA) exposure on primordial germ cells using the IVG model showed that while such exposure did not kill the cells, it altered cell behavior and molecular processes that are important for the cells' future development (Ooi et al. 2021).

The fact that sperm integrity can be affected by environmental toxicants at different stages of its development suggests the need to reconceptualize the health of mature sperm as being partly a result of its environment and its history. It also raises questions about the consequences of these changes for sperm health and future offspring. Molecular changes in reproductive cells that do not kill them or prevent them from fertilizing can be passed on to the offspring and affect health. For example, failure to correctly add epigenetic marks in certain areas of the genome known as imprinted genes can cause severe disorders in offspring (Barlow and Bartolomei 2014). In this perspective, sperm health should be understood not only as its ability to fertilize an oocyte but as the "ability to program a normal pattern of embryonic development" (Aitken et al. 2016).

This ability of sperm to carry subtle but potentially impactful changes also has important implications for how sperm health is assessed in the context of assisted reproduction, raising the question of what sperm needs to be beyond its ability to fertilize. It is particularly relevant in light of the increasingly common procedure of intracytoplasmic sperm injection (ICSI). ICSI involves extracting a single sperm and injecting it into an oocyte in order to ensure fertilization. ICSI effectively bypasses sperm's inability to fertilize on its own. While successful at promoting reproduction, this procedure begs the question of the potential health effects that can be carried through subtle changes in sperm's health.

Shifting the Focus from Fertilization to Sperm Health

Although it may seem that IVG simply fits into the landscape of reproductive medicine as another way to provide the gametes needed for reproduction, its practice disrupts the overwhelming focus on the gametes themselves. Just as in vitro fertilization has proven to be a powerful scientific tool as well as an assisted reproductive technology (Franklin 2013), the importance of IVG lies as much in the knowledge it can produce *about* sperm as much as in its potential to produce sperm. Rather than simply "recapitulating" spermatogenesis in an artificial technological environment, the in vitro model functions as a discovery tool, opening up new questions about sperm and sperm health.

Thus, the implications of IVG research for reproductive health and policy go far beyond those that have been underlined so far, namely in terms of the fertility market in which it would be a new product (National Academies of Sciences, Engineering, and Medicine 2023). Focusing on the process of sperm development, as IVG allows, rather than on the gamete itself, allows us to take a long view of male infertility as a pathology that can arise at any step in this development that begins in embryonic life and ends with the formation of mature sperm in adult life (Lamoreaux 2022). It calls for further basic biological research into the etiology and diagnosis of male infertility, beyond strategies to induce fertilization. It also raises the question of reassessing the role of the male body in aspects of infertility and offspring's health that have been primarily attributed to women, such as the inability to sustain a pregnancy and the so-called maternal effects on child's health (Ravitsky and Kimmins 2019). Finally, the susceptibility of certain stages of sperm development to toxic disruption calls for increased protection of male fertility from environmental toxicants, regardless of any intent to reproduce, and for consideration of how unequal exposure to toxicants may shape the biological process of spermatogenesis itself (Lappé, Hein, and Landecker 2019).

ACKNOWLEDGMENTS

This research is part of a project on the social and ethical implications of in vitro gametogenesis for which Hannah Landecker (UCLA) is the principal investigator and that is funded by the US National Institute of Health, grant #R21HG012248. The content is solely the responsibility of the author and does not necessarily represent the official views of the National Institutes of Health. I thank the workshop participants and editors for their thoughtful comments.

REFERENCES

Aitken, Robert John, Zamira Gibb, Mark A. Baker, Joel Drevet, and Parviz Gharagozloo. 2016. "Causes and Consequences of Oxidative Stress in Spermatozoa." *Reproduction, Fertility and Development* 28 (2): 1–10. https://doi.org/10.1071/RD15325.

Ball, Philip. 2018. "Reproduction Revolution: How Our Skin Cells Might Be Turned into Sperm and Eggs." *The Guardian*, October 14, 2018. www.theguardian.com.

Barlow, Denise P., and Marisa S. Bartolomei. 2014. "Genomic Imprinting in Mammals." *Cold Spring Harbor Perspectives in Biology* 6 (2): a018382. https://doi.org/10.1101/cshperspect.a018382.

Franklin, Sarah. 2013. *Biological Relatives: IVF, Stem Cells, and the Future of Kinship.* Experimental Futures. Durham, NC: Duke University Press.

Gardner, John, and Andrew Webster. 2016. "The Social Management of Biomedical Novelty: Facilitating Translation in Regenerative Medicine." *Social Science & Medicine* 156:90–97. https://doi.org/10.1016/j.socscimed.2016.03.025.

Gruhn, Wolfram H., Walfred W.C. Tang, Sabine Dietmann, João P. Alves-Lopes, Christopher A. Penfold, Frederick C. K. Wong, Navin B. Ramakrishna, and M. Azim Surani. 2023. "Epigenetic Resetting in the Human Germ Line Entails Histone Modification Remodeling." *Science Advances* 9 (3): eade1257. https://doi.org/10.1126/sciadv.ade1257.

Hwang, Young Sun, Shinnosuke Suzuki, Yasunari Seita, Jumpei Ito, Yuka Sakata, Hirofumi Aso, Kei Sato, Brian P. Hermann, and Kotaro Sasaki. 2020. "Reconstitution of Prospermatogonial Specification in Vitro from Human Induced Pluripotent Stem Cells." *Nature Communications* 11 (1): 5656. https://doi.org/10.1038/s41467-020-19350-3.

Hyun, Insoo, Amy Wilkerson, and Josephine Johnston. 2016. "Embryology Policy: Revisit the 14-Day Rule." *Nature* 533 (7602): 169–71. https://doi.org/10.1038/533169a.

Ishikura, Yukiko, Hiroshi Ohta, Takuya Sato, Yusuke Murase, Yukihiro Yabuta, Yoji Kojima, Chika Yamashiro et al. 2021. "In Vitro Reconstitution of the Whole Male Germ-Cell Development from Mouse Pluripotent Stem Cells." *Cell Stem Cell* 28 (12): 2,167–79.e9. https://doi.org/10.1016/j.stem.2021.08.005.

Lamoreaux, Janelle. 2022. *Infertile Environments: Epigenetic Toxicology and the Reproductive Health of Chinese Men.* Durham, NC: Duke University Press.

Lappé, Martine, Robbin Jeffries Hein, and Hannah Landecker. 2019. "Environmental Politics of Reproduction." *Annual Review of Anthropology* 48 (1): 133–50. https://doi.org/10.1146/annurev-anthro-102218-011346.

Maienschein, Jane, Mary Sunderland, Rachel A. Ankeny, and Jason Scott Robert. 2008. "The Ethos and Ethics of Translational Research." *American Journal of Bioethics* 8 (3): 43–51. https://doi.org/10.1080/15265160802109314.

Merleau-Ponty, Noémie. 2021. "Sociology as Technology: A Toolkit for Studying In Vitro Gametogenesis." In *Birthing Techno-Sapiens*, edited by Robbie Davis-Floyd, 77–89. New York: Routledge.

Meskus, Mianna. 2018. *Craft in Biomedical Research: The iPS Cell Technology and the Future of Stem Cell Science.* New York: Palgrave Macmillan. https://doi.org/10.1057/978-1-137-46910-6.

Murphy, Timothy F. 2018. "Pathways to Genetic Parenthood for Same-Sex Couples." *Journal of Medical Ethics* 44 (12): 823–24. https://doi.org/10.1136/medethics-2017-104291.

National Academies of Sciences, Engineering, and Medicine. 2023. *In Vitro-Derived Human Gametes: Scientific, Ethical, and Regulatory Implications: Proceedings of a Workshop.* Edited by Emily Packard Dawson, Chanel Matney, and Katherine Bowman. Washington, DC: National Academies Press. https://doi.org/10.17226/27259.

Ooi, Steen K.T., Hui Jiang, Yanyuan Kang, and Patrick Allard. 2021. "Examining the Developmental Trajectory of an in Vitro Model of Mouse Primordial Germ Cells Following Exposure to Environmentally Relevant Bisphenol A Levels." *Environmental Health Perspectives* 129 (9): 097013. https://doi.org/10.1289/EHP8196.

Ravitsky, Vardit, and Sarah Kimmins. 2019. "The Forgotten Men: Rising Rates of Male Infertility Urgently Require New Approaches for Its Prevention, Diagnosis and Treatment." *Biology of Reproduction* 101 (5): 872–74. https://doi.org/10.1093/biolre/ioz161.

Saitou, Mitinori, and Katsuhiko Hayashi. 2021. "Mammalian in Vitro Gametogenesis." *Science* 374 (6563): eaaz6830. https://doi.org/10.1126/science.aaz6830.

Smajdor, A. C., and Daniela Cutas. 2015. "Artificial Gametes." Nuffield Council on Bioethics, January 12, 2015. www.nuffieldbioethics.org.

Sosa, Enrique, Di Chen, Ernesto J. Rojas, Jon D. Hennebold, Karen A. Peters, Zhuang Wu, Truong N. Lam et al. 2018. "Differentiation of Primate Primordial Germ Cell–like Cells Following Transplantation into the Adult Gonadal Niche." *Nature Communications* 9 (1): 5339. https://doi.org/10.1038/s41467-018-07740-7.

Suter, Sonia M. 2016. "In Vitro Gametogenesis: Just Another Way to Have a Baby?" *Journal of Law and the Biosciences* 3 (1): 87–119. https://doi.org/10.1093/jlb/lsv057.

Witt, Emily. 2023. "The Future of Fertility." *New Yorker*, April 17, 2023. www.newyorker.com.

Yamanaka, Shinya. 2012. "Induced Pluripotent Stem Cells: Past, Present, and Future." *Cell Stem Cell* 10 (6): 678–84. https://doi.org/10.1016/j.stem.2012.05.005.

PART IV

Stopping Sperm

16

Biological Fables, Vasectomies, and the Future of Sperm after *Roe*

ANDRÉA BECKER

Any attempt to parse the biological from the social is ultimately futile, as even "biological facts" are stories we tell—stories with major consequences, that is. Take the biological fable of human reproduction, for instance—how egg and sperm meet. In sexual health classes, most of us likely learned that during sexual intercourse, millions of tiny sperm are released, sparking a ruthless seminal battle to reach the egg. The sole victorious sperm then penetrates the egg wall, capturing and claiming the egg, and thus beginning the process of creating a human baby. This story evokes an image of a passive—feminine—egg, waiting to be chosen and taken by the active, agentic—masculine—sperm. In "reality," the egg is not only selective, but an active participant in the process, and can attract the sperm it likes and reject the sperm it does not via chemokinesis. The egg's release of chemoattractants causes some sperm to swim faster and others to slow down (Fitzpatrick et al. 2020). Telling the "true" story of the sperm and the egg is not simply semantics, however, but rather a demonstration of how cultural narratives—in this case, sexual scripts about active male suitors and passive female objects of affection (Martin 1991)—are woven into our understandings of even the most basic building blocks of biology.

The biological fables we tell and accept have public health consequences. They affect our behaviors and our perceptions, and they even direct education, law, and policy. Perhaps most insidiously, we tend to accept these fables as undisputable truths. Another major biological fable that has gone uncontested for millennia: that human reproduction is a (cis) woman's issue, and a woman's responsibility alone. Of course, the person with the uterus and capacity for pregnancy takes on the physical brunt of reproduction, but as sociologist Rene Almeling (2020) demonstrates, the existence of gynecology for women, without a substantial andrological counterpart, has symbolically construed men as detached from reproduction. In other words, the fable of reproduction as a woman's issue has influenced our construction of reality—resulting in men excluding themselves, or being excluded, from direct participation in reproductive health. Within this constructed world, women are the ones who take birth control and who undergo permanent sterilization to prevent pregnancies. Accordingly, biomedical and social scientific research on men's contraceptive options is sparse and insufficient. This leaves even those men who are interested in being active participants in reproductive health care as willing but unable.

It is no wonder, then, that the vasectomy has gone under the radar for so long, while millions of dollars in policy and biomedical research are poured into "women's birth control" and girl-centric missions like "ending teen pregnancy." Yet when it comes to preventing pregnancy, vasectomy is the contraceptive gold standard (Olson 2019). Vasectomy is a very safe, cost-effective outpatient procedure that can be performed in under ten minutes—sometimes without a scalpel, and sometimes without a needle (Majzoub et al. 2017).

Now compare vasectomy to permanent "female sterilization" like tubal ligation or hysterectomy. While major medical advances have transformed these procedures, they both require general anesthesia and one or more abdominal incisions, and they carry more short and long-term health risks than the vasectomy does. Moreover, all "female birth control" carries a slew of culturally accepted side effects—from weight gain, and acne, to mood changes, painful insertions, and diminished libido.

The risk-benefit ratio should make vasectomy a clear choice for any couple desiring permanent contraception, yet vasectomies are surprisingly rare. National estimates from 2015 show that 22 percent of women undergo surgical sterilization, compared to only 5 percent of men (Kaiser Family Foundation 2018). Meanwhile, the majority of women use contraception (61.7 percent), most commonly the pill (16 percent), and on average, spend thirty years of their lives actively avoiding pregnancy while men are left out of the conversation (Littlejohn 2021).

The gendered discrepancy in preventing pregnancy—particularly in sterilization rates—is not only cultural but rooted in policy failures as well. First, offering postpartum tubal ligation is an expected practice from the American College of Obstetrics and Gynecology, which recognizes the immediate postpartum period as an ideal time to perform the surgery ("Access to Postpartum Sterilization ACOG Committee Opinion," 2021). These guidelines for physicians lead them to preferentially counsel couples—many of whom likely do not think to ask about vasectomy—toward tubal ligation. If a couple who can get pregnant does not want another pregnancy and is considering permanent sterilization, then the onus will fall on the one giving birth, at the very least because of the all-in-one convenience with which a birth-plus-tubal-ligation is often presented by providers. The fable of women as reproductive agents and men as invisible contributors is thus perpetuated in these individual clinical encounters.

On a more macro health policy level, while the Affordable Care Act (aka "Obamacare") deemed no-cost birth control—including female sterilization—a mandatory part of insurance plans, vasectomy is conspicuously omitted from this list. In fact, in 2021, the original list of eighteen types of covered birth control was updated to include male condoms, and yet vasectomy remains markedly absent. Even though vasectomy can benefit women, it is not regarded as a contraceptive *used* by women, and thus is not categorized a "preventative service for women" (Mirk 2016; Torrella 2022).

Without mandated coverage, vasectomy is expensive, particularly for low-income folks. The cost of a vasectomy ranges from $300 to $3,500, and few publicly funded family planning clinics offer it (Nguyen et al. 2021; White et al. 2017). Not to mention, the number of providers trained in vasectomy are far and few between—less than 10 percent of family medicine residency programs offer adequate vasectomy training (Patel et al. 2022). The structure of health care itself is therefore organized to continue placing all reproductive responsibility on the people who can get pregnant.

As a result, vasectomy is not only culturally exceptional but also financially inaccessible. It makes sense, then, that the racial and socioeconomic trends of male versus female sterilization procedures are flipped.

While low-income women of color are more likely to be sterilized, low-income men of color are *less* likely (Kaiser Family Foundation 2018; Shih, Turok, and Parker 2011). Socially constructed narratives regarding reproduction, race, and gender have led to long-acting reversible contraceptives and permanent sterilizations being deemed a societal imperative for swaths of women, while vasectomy remains a contraceptive option of the privileged.

In the quest to prevent unintended pregnancy, women engage in behaviors like taking a pill every day to significantly alter one's endocrine system or having metal instruments inserted into the cervix without anesthesia to have an intrauterine device placed, yet absent is the narrative of a partner removing sperm from the equation. While efforts to introduce "male birth control" have largely stalled or failed (Campo-Engelstein 2019), the vasectomy lacks the side effects that trial monitors found intolerable for men during clinical trials for injectable male contraception. It must be noted that around 80 percent of men and their female partners in these trials found the birth control option satisfactory (Behre et al. 2016).

The discordance between how men in the trials viewed their own side effects versus how the institutions in place to protect them see the side effects is puzzling, yet once more indicative of the deep-rooted notion that reproductive labor is women's to bear. In reality, many cis men would be willing to take hormonal birth control—particularly those who hold gender-equitable attitudes—yet that option remains out of reach (Hill et al. 2022). While the prospect of hormonal birth control for men is highly exciting and overdue, vasectomy—which is presently available while we wait for that fateful day—removes the need for daily upkeep, requiring just the one simple ten-minute outpatient procedure.

At the same time, all reproductive health practices have the capacity to be used coercively, given long-standing reproductive stratification in the United States and abroad (Colen 1986; Ginsburg and Rapp 1991). Reproductive stratification refers to unequal structures, policies, and practices that affect the degree of reproductive freedoms one has, particularly by race and class. For instance, white middle-class women continue to have increased access to fertility enhancing technologies like egg freezing and in vitro fertilization, while women of color are disproportionately encouraged toward long-acting reversible contraceptive methods like IUDs and implants, as well as toward permanent sterilization (Bower et al. 2009; Inhorn et al. 2018; Mann and Grzanka 2018). Unsurprisingly, men are often left out of discussions of stratified reproduction; however, access—or lack thereof—to vasectomy and other types of contraception fits squarely within this literature, and attention toward men's ability to choose reproductive health care, particularly by race and class, is direly needed. After all, men's participation directly impacts the women they partner with, thereby coconstructing women's reproductive freedoms.

Any discussion of a sterilizing procedure such as vasectomy must also contend with the legacy of forced sterilization via state-sanctioned eugenics campaigns in the twentieth-century United States, during which poor, Black, Latine and Chicane, and Indigenous people were disproportionately sterilized (Klein 2012; Lira and Stern 2014; Stern 2005). While the focus of reproductive stratification tends to be on cis women—and indeed, the women who were sterilized far outnumbered men, even across race (Schoen 2005)—these campaigns impacted cis men as well. And in fact, the technology employed during these campaigns was none other than the vasectomy, a dark history that continues to haunt the present day. In Tennessee, incarcerated men were offered thirty days off their sentence if they agreed to a vasectomy, a practice that lasted for years until a federal lawsuit finally shut it down in 2019 (Tamburin 2019).

Moreover, the notion of forced vasectomies is employed as a rhetorical tactic to point out the injustices of abortion bans. For instance, Alabama state representative Rolanda Hollis proposed a law in 2020 to require that all men get a vasectomy after the age of fifty or after the birth of their third child, in order to "give perspective" to the state's abortion ban (Lam 2020). After the fall of *Roe v. Wade* in the summer of 2022, discourse around mandatory vasectomies once more ramped up, as a way of pointing out the cruelty of abortion bans, which likewise remove one's reproductive agency. In the dozens of protests across the country after the *Dobbs v. Jackson Women's Health Organization* decision, some protestors held signs urging men to have vasectomies, and op-ed writers occasionally encouraged "male allies" to have vasectomies (Filipovic 2021; Plank 2022). While this rhetorical tactic can be effective in spurring questions about why the notion of a forced vasectomy is so uncomfortable while abortion bans proliferate, it is also insidious when contextualized amid the backdrop of forced vasectomies from the twentieth century to the present day. Any policy that encourages or incentivizes vasectomy must therefore contend with this history and grapple with its impact on low-income men, incarcerated men, and men of color—particularly Black men. It is also unclear how stigma factors into perceptions of vasectomy—and whether these publicity stunts further perpetuate antivasectomy stigmas.

Despite the dark history of vasectomies, we must remember that reproductive technologies are not inherently good or bad, and minoritized groups regularly reclaim such practices. Take hysterectomies for instance, which, rather than a ruinous experience being forced upon them, some women now reclaim as something they actively *want* (Becker 2023). Accordingly, while all reproductive health policies and practices require an intersectional critical analysis that accounts for historical and contemporary injustices, that should not discourage the benefits and progress that using them could bring.

It is long overdue to recognize (cis) men's role in reproduction and engage men's participation in contraception and abortion—not to mention the need to simply recognize men as beneficiaries of women's fertility limiting efforts. But with the fall of *Roe*, pregnancy has taken on new (and, for many, more terrifying) meanings, especially for those living in places where abortion has become even less accessible. Even women carrying wanted pregnancies have reported receiving subpar care in abortion-hostile states when experiencing pregnancy loss (Belluck 2022). In this climate, the moment is ripe for vasectomy rates to increase, but only if wanted, culturally acceptable, and financially accessible. And indeed, there is early evidence (from clinical chart data and Google search trends) showing a potential uptick in vasectomies after the *Dobbs* court ruling (Bole et al. 2023; Sax 2022; Zhang et al. 2023).

While we wade through the ongoing public health crisis spurred by *Dobbs*, there is an opportunity to acknowledge that what we thought was biological fact was a fable all along. Just like the egg does not sit around waiting for the sperm, men do not need to—and in fact, must not—be excluded from cultural, biomedical, and social scientific discussions of reproduction. We can reintroduce the vasectomy and male contraceptives as not only a public good but also a simple act that men who care about women's well-being can undergo. All in all, this bares the question: could vasectomy be the tipping point for finally increasing men's participation and highlighting the role of sperm in reproduction?

REFERENCES

"Access to Postpartum Sterilization: ACOG Committee Opinion, Number 827." 2021. *Obstetrics & Gynecology* 137 (6): e169–76. https://doi.org/10.1097/aog .0000000000004381.

Almeling, Rene. 2020. *GUYnecology: The Missing Science of Men's Reproductive Health*. Oakland: University of California Press.

Becker, Andréa. 2023. "Stratified Reproduction, Hysterectomy, and the Social Process of Opting into Infertility." *Gender & Society* 37 (4): 614–39.

Behre, Hermann M., Michael Zitzmann, Richard A. Anderson, David J. Handelsman, Silvia W. Lestari, Robert I. McLachlan, M. Cristina Meriggiola et al. 2016. "Efficacy and Safety of an Injectable Combination Hormonal Contraceptive for Men." *Journal of Clinical Endocrinology & Metabolism* 101 (12): 4779–88. https://doi.org/10.1210/jc .2016-2141.

Belluck, Pam. 2022. "They Had Miscarriages, and New Abortion Laws Obstructed Treatment." *New York Times*, July 17, 2022.

Bole, Raevti, Scott D. Lundy, Evonne Pei, Petar Bajic, Neel Parekh, and Sarah C. Vij. 2023. "Rising Vasectomy Volume Following Reversal of Federal Protections for Abortion Rights in the United States." *International Journal of Impotence Research* 36:265–68. https://doi.org/10.1038/s41443-023-00672-x.

Bower, Julie K., Pamela J. Schreiner, Barbara Sternfeld, and Cora E. Lewis. 2009. "Black–White Differences in Hysterectomy Prevalence: The CARDIA Study." *American Journal of Public Health* 99 (2): 300–307. https://doi.org/10.2105/AJPH .2008.133702.

Campo-Engelstein, Lisa. 2019. "Are We Ready for Men to Take the Pill?" *BBC News*, October 21, 2019.

Colen, Shellee. 1986. "Stratified Reproduction: The Case of Domestic Workers in New York City." In *American Ethnological Society Meeting, Wrightsville Beach, North Carolina*.

Filipovic, Jill. 2021. "Hey Fellas, Think You're an Ally to Women? Consider a Vasectomy." *The Guardian*, August 10, 2021.

Fitzpatrick, John L., Charlotte Willis, Alessandro Devigili, Amy Young, Michael Carroll, Helen R. Hunter, and Daniel R. Brison. 2020. "Chemical Signals from Eggs Facilitate Cryptic Female Choice in Humans." *Proceedings of the Royal Society B* 287 (1928): 20200805. https://doi.org/10.1098/rspb.2020.0805.

Ginsburg, Faye, and Rayna Rapp. 1991. "The Politics of Reproduction." *Annual Review of Anthropology* 20 (1): 311–43. https://doi.org/10.1146/annurev.an.20.100191.001523.

Hill, Amber L., Elizabeth Miller, Galen E. Switzer, Kaleab Z. Abebe, Judy C. Chang, Julie Pulerwitz, Lisa D. Brush, and Ashley V. Hill. 2022. "Gender Equitable Attitudes

Among Adolescents: A Validation Study and Associations with Sexual Health Behaviors." *Adolescent Research Review* 7 (4): 523–36. https://doi.org/10.1007/s40894-021-00171-4.

Inhorn, Marcia C., Daphna Birenbaum-Carmeli, Lynn M. Westphal, Joseph Doyle, Norbert Gleicher, Dror Meirow, Hila Raanani, Martha Dirnfeld, and Pasquale Patrizio. 2018. "Medical Egg Freezing: How Cost and Lack of Insurance Cover Impact Women and Their Families." *Reproductive Biomedicine & Society Online* 5:82–92. https://doi.org/10.1016/j.rbms.2017.12.001.

Kaiser Family Foundation. 2018. "Sterilization as a Family Planning Method." December 14, 2018. www.kff.org.

Klein, Jennifer M. 2012. "Compensating Victims of Forced Sterilization: Lessons from North Carolina." *Journal of Law, Medicine & Ethics* 40 (2): 422–27.

Lam, Kristin. 2020. "Mandatory Vasectomy at Age 50? Alabama Lawmaker Proposes Response to Abortion Ban." *USA TODAY*, February 17, 2020.

Lira, Natalie, and Alexandra Minna Stern. 2014. "Mexican Americans and Eugenic Sterilization: Resisting Reproductive Injustice in California, 1920–1950." *Aztlan: A Journal of Chicano Studies* 39 (2): 9–34. https://doi.org/10.1525/azt.2014.39.2.9.

Littlejohn, Krystale E. 2021. *Just Get on the Pill: The Uneven Burden of Reproductive Politics*. Oakland, CA: University of California Press.

Majzoub, Ahmad, Nicholas N. Tadros, A. Scott Polackwich, Rakesh Sharma, Ashok Agarwal, and Edmund Sabanegh. 2017. "Vasectomy Reversal Semen Analysis: New Reference Ranges Predict Pregnancy." *Fertility and Sterility* 107 (4): 911–15. https://doi.org/10.1016/j.fertnstert.2017.01.018.

Mann, Emily S., and Patrick R. Grzanka. 2018. "Agency-Without-Choice: The Visual Rhetorics of Long-Acting Reversible Contraception Promotion." *Symbolic Interaction* 41 (3): 334–56. https://doi.org/10.1002/symb.349.

Martin, Emily. 1991. "The Egg and the Sperm: How Science Has Constructed a Romance Based on Stereotypical Male-Female Roles." *Signs: Journal of Women in Culture and Society* 16 (3): 485–501. http://dx.doi.org/10.1086/494680.

Mirk, Sarah. 2016. "Vasectomies Should Be Covered by Obamacare—But They're Not." *Bitch Media*. Accessed March 21, 2023. www.bitchmedia.org.

Nguyen, Brian T., Minica Long, Nina Petrosyan, Dayna Grundy, Brisa Mahoney, and Katrina J. Heyrana. 2021. "Access to Male Sexual and Reproductive Health Services in Publicly Funded California Clinics in 2018." *Contraception* 104 (2): 165–69. https://doi.org/10.1016/j.contraception.2021.04.004.

Patel, Jasmine, Brian Nguyen, Grace Shih, Maya Or, and Diane Harper. 2022. "Vasectomy Training in Family Medicine Residency Programs: A National Survey of Residency Program Directors." *Family Medicine* 54 (6): 438–43. https://doi.org/10.22454/fammed.2022.649054.

Plank, Liz. 2022. "Opinion: Why 'Where Do I Get a Vasectomy' Is Now a Popular Google Search." *MSNBC*, May 17, 2022.

Sax, Megan R. 2022. "Seeking Vasectomy in Post-Dobbs America: The Male Counterpart Response to the Reversal of *Roe v. Wade* as Evidenced by Google Search Trends." *Fertility and Sterility* 118 (6): 1189.

Schoen, Johanna. 2005. *Choice & Coercion: Birth Control, Sterilization, and Abortion in Public Health and Welfare*. Chapel Hill: University of North Carolina Press.

Shih, Grace, David K. Turok, and Willie J. Parker. 2011. "Vasectomy: The Other (Better) Form of Sterilization." *Contraception* 83 (4): 310–15. https://doi.org/10.1016/j.contraception.2010.08.019.

Stern, Alexandra Minna. 2005. "Sterilized in the Name of Public Health: Race, Immigration, and Reproductive Control in Modern California." *American Journal of Public Health* 95 (7): 1128–38. https://doi.org/10.2105/ajph.2004.041608.

Tamburin, Adam. 2019. "Federal Court Order Officially Ends Tennessee 'Inmate Sterilization' Program." *The Tennessean*. May 20, 2019. www.tennessean.com.

Torrella, Kenny. 2022. "Under Obamacare, Birth Control Pills Are Free. Why Aren't Vasectomies?" *Vox*. July 1, 2022. www.vox.com.

White, Kari, Anthony Campbell, Kristine Hopkins, Daniel Grossman, and Joseph E. Potter. 2017. "Barriers to Offering Vasectomy at Publicly Funded Family Planning Organizations in Texas." *American Journal of Men's Health* 11 (3): 757–66. https://doi.org/10.1177/1557988317694296.

Zhang, Tenny R., Corey Able, Ranjith Ramasamy, and Taylor P. Kohn. 2023. "United States Vasectomy Incidence Rises after the Reversal of *Roe v. Wade* in a National Clinical and Claims Database." *Fertility and Sterility* 121 (1): 196–97.

17

Contraception, Male Engagement, and Reproductive Identity

LOGAN NICKELS

At the intersection of sperm, health, and politics, we find men. Of course, not all who consider themselves men produce sperm, and not all who produce sperm consider themselves men, but for the purposes of this essay, there are generally just under four billion persons around the world who produce sperm, many of whom identify as cisgender men. Beyond identifying as men, they share a number of other identities (in terms of sexuality, race, etc.), which can include a reproductive identity.

Men's reproductive identity, which refers to their sense of self in relation to their reproductive capacity and potential, comes with a range of emotions, thoughts, and behaviors related to their reproductive experiences and desires (Athan 2020). For example, men may experience feelings of pride or disappointment related to their ability to father a child, and they may have concerns about their fertility and reproductive health. Men may also have preferences and values related to family planning and parenting, and they may seek out information and resources to support their reproductive goals. However, men and boys may have limited tools to construct their own reproductive identity as compared to their pregnancy-capable counterparts (Almeling 2020; Grandahl, Bodin, and Stern 2019; Marsiglio 2003; Mohr and Almeling, 2020).

For example, the federal funding of reproductive health care for men is not mandated in the Affordable Care Act, though it is for women in the form of an annual exam. Beyond specific legislation, women exist in a health care system that reinforces gender norms and maintains the status quo regarding reproductive responsibility (Granzow 2007; Hay et al. 2019; van Wijk, van Vliet, and Kolk 1996). These influences also contribute to a health care system in which men do not seek preventive care and are not especially well catered to from a reproductive standpoint (Baroudi et al. 2021; El Ansari et al. 2023; Hardee, Croce-Galis, and Gay 2017; Pazol et al. 2017). Services such as contraception and prenatal care have also been designed and marketed primarily for women, making male engagement in these spaces lacking. When it comes to infertility and assisted reproductive technologies, significantly fewer men undergo infertility evaluations and treatments than their female partners despite male factors being the cause of approximately half of infertility cases (Kumar and Singh 2015). Other areas of sexual health, such as treatment of sexually transmitted infections and research into microbicides and multipurpose prevention technologies, also generally focus on female users.

Yet, men can be effective and productive health care advocates. Engaging men in prenatal care, infant care, and family planning is linked to higher maternal and newborn health, with downstream outcomes including improved child development and satisfaction with family life (Tokhi et al. 2018). Moreover, men and women alike feel a shared responsibility to prevent pregnancy, and the ideal involvement for many couples includes a common desire for male partner participation (Campbell, Turok, and White 2019; Storck et al. 2022). This egalitarian approach to family planning may be the standard to reach for, but like many ideals, it is something strived for and rarely achieved. On the opposite side, there are men who may see reproduction in more traditional terms, which may also be related to more reductive, gendered, and binary views of reproductive responsibilities.

However, there are a significant number of men who live in between the two extremes, never taking an active role in family planning, but also never intentionally impeding, imposing, or infringing on the rights of their partner. On the one hand, these men are interested in their partners having responsibility and being empowered to make independent choices in the name of women's bodily autonomy. But on the other hand, these men may also want to be engaged and helpful partners themselves. Unfortunately, they often lack knowledge of, resources for, and examples of how to thoughtfully approach or connect these concepts, and thus naturally drift to a sort of neutral, potentially indifferent middle ground, avoiding the perceived conflict between assuming their own individual responsibility and respecting the bodily autonomy of their partner

(Caddy, Temple-Smith, and Coombe 2023; James-Hawkins, Dalessandro, and Sennott 2019). The outcome of this neutrality is a lack of male participation in which the female partner is not only disproportionately burdened with the physical burdens of pregnancy, but often also the financial, emotional, and mental burdens of the fertility work surrounding pregnancy and pregnancy prevention (Kimport 2018).

How do we get men to be more engaged in the arenas of sperm, health, and politics? How do we get them to start being the effective health care advocates we know they can be? At Male Contraceptive Initiative, we believe that introducing multiple forms of contraception will provide men with an equitable way of participating in reproductive processes, expanding their sense of reproductive identity as more comparable to that of their partners and enabling them to play a larger role in reproductive responsibility. We believe this is transformative for family planning and society at large because new contraceptives for men would allow men to make their reproductive identity actionable in new ways.

Men are currently limited to condoms, vasectomy, and withdrawal as their contraceptive methods, all of which serve a distinct purpose and offer a means to engage men as reproductive agents, but this paucity of methods does not offer a long-acting reversible option. Additionally, these options together make up only 25 percent of contraceptive usage globally. It stands to reason that with more options, we may be able to achieve a more equitable share of contraceptive use. Existing and new acceptability research suggests significant demand for a variety of novel male contraceptive methods among men and their partners across geographic contexts (Heinemann et al. 2005; Male Contraceptive Initiative 2023).

Contraceptive options that respondents showed interest in were based on products currently in development for men, which include long-acting reversible contraceptives, daily transdermal gels, daily oral pills, injectables, implants, and oral on-demand contraceptives. These drugs and devices have a wide range of product forms and profiles and include hormonal approaches, small-molecule drugs, and medical devices that are administered in a procedure very similar to a vasectomy. These projects are generally in the early stages when it comes to developing a product, but some leading methods are in human studies today and may very well be the first contraceptives with a chance to take advantage of a significant market. By generating further novel contraceptive options to meet this latent demand, we will bridge a separator between male and female reproductive responsibilities, acting as a major step toward equity and male engagement in reproduction.

Though, what is there to do while these contraceptive methods for men are being developed? The first of these methods would not be on the market for a time measured in years. Subsequent methods that can access remaining sectors of the market and more deeply address unmet male need are even further away, but we do not have to wait to engage men right now. One of the most important steps we can take toward generating male reproductive identities today is to provide men equal access to existing contraceptive methods. Vasectomy, although a permanent method of contraception, is one of the safest and most reliable methods available. But the Affordable Care Act does not require insurance companies to cover it for men. Instead, the legislation only covers contraceptive services for women as preventive care, which furthers the misconception that reproductive health care, and thus reproductive responsibilities, are reserved for those with a uterus. By taking direct action and making vasectomy a covered service in the Affordable Care Act like other female methods of contraception, we open the door to more male patients in doctors' offices and more equity in contraceptive care (Campo-Engelstein 2017). Moreover, we set the precedent that male contraceptive services are valid, which is especially important as more contraceptive options make their way into the pipeline.

We can also do a much better job of teaching men about reproductive health (Bersamin et al. 2017; Karim et al. 2021). To build an effective and well-informed reproductive identity for men, there is a need for increased education and awareness efforts, especially as less-educated and underinformed men participate in partner contraceptive decision-making and exert their influence in other areas related to reproductive health, such as politics (Dehlendorf et al. 2013). As of this writing, over 75 percent of US Congress is made up of men, meaning that legislatively, those that are making the decisions regarding reproductive health are often ill-informed as well as demographically unrepresentative.

Another way we can engage men through new policy is to provide equal family leave and encourage men to take time away from work with family. This not only would have the benefits on men, their partners, and their offspring established at the outset but may also introduce a positive feedback loop wherein the engagement and education of men on the burden of pregnancy and childcare leads to further advocacy and support for positive male engagement in reproductive health. This concept is reflected in a recent study where men's willingness to use novel male contraceptive methods was linked to gender-equitable attitudes (Nguyen and Jacobsohn 2023). Distributing the burden of childcare and childrearing is not a radical or new idea, but it will likely take significant political and social change for such policies to become mainstream (Reeves 2022).

These interventions will do much more than encourage the development of a male reproductive identity. They also stand to enact deep, systemic change in a health care system that has not been designed with male reproductive health in mind. Men see health care providers irregularly and are often lost to follow ups (Bertakis et al. 2000). By ensuring contraceptive coverage for men and, by proxy, annual well health care visits, we can create a system in which men are given a new incentive to see primary care providers early and often, increasing the potential that other health care issues are discovered and addressed. More far-reaching health care implications might be that providers of new male contraceptive services would likely come from a variety of specialties, and the influx of demand could go so far as to induce the formation of a new, patient-centered, gender-independent reproductive health specialty. Regardless of the specific outcome, male engagement in contraception and contraceptive services will offer new opportunities for health care to adapt and change.

Engaging men to increase their sense of reproductive self is a pathway to a healthier, more equitable future, and that engagement will have to take many forms. Moreover, just as a male reproductive identity is constructed from a variety of sources, influences, and lived experiences, factors that shape preferences for health care, including contraception, are diverse. One new contraceptive option will not appeal to all men, nor will a diverse set of approved products meet all their needs. Some men may remain reticent, and others will never use these products. But a reproductive journey often does not end where it starts, and by educating men, facilitating equity, and introducing new contraceptive methods to the market as soon as possible, we lay the groundwork for a world in which men are educated about their own bodies and the bodies of their partners and able to fluently work their way toward building an identity that includes the ability and responsibility associated with creating life.

REFERENCES

Almeling, Rene. 2020. *GUYnecology: The Missing Science of Men's Reproductive Health.* Oakland: University of California Press.

Athan, Aurélie M. 2020. "Reproductive Identity: An Emerging Concept." *American Psychologist* 75 (4): 445–56. https://doi.org/10.1037/amp0000623.

Baroudi, Mazen, Jon Petter Stoor, Hanna Blåhed, Kerstin Edin, and Anna-Karin Hurtig. 2021. "Men and Sexual and Reproductive Healthcare in the Nordic Countries: A Scoping Review." *BMJ Open* 11 (9): e052600. https://doi.org/10.1136/bmjopen-2021-052600.

Bersamin, Melina, Deborah A. Fisher, Arik V. Marcell, and Laura J. Finan. 2017. "Deficits in Young Men's Knowledge about Accessing Sexual and Reproductive Health Services." *Journal of American College Health: J of ACH* 65 (8): 579–84. https://doi.org/10.1080/07448481.2017.1352589.

Bertakis, K. D., R. Azari, L. J. Helms, E. J. Callahan, and J. A. Robbins. 2000. "Gender Differences in the Utilization of Health Care Services." *Journal of Family Practice* 49 (2): 147–52.

Caddy, Cassandra, Meredith Temple-Smith, and Jacqueline Coombe. 2023. "Who Does What? Reproductive Responsibilities between Heterosexual Partners." *Culture, Health & Sexuality* 25 (12): 1640–58. https://doi.org/10.1080/13691058.2023.2173800.

Campbell, Anthony D., David K. Turok, Kari White. 2019. "Fertility Intentions and Perspectives on Contraceptive Involvement Among Low-Income Men Aged 25 to 55." *Perspectives on Sexual and Reproductive Health*, 51 (3): 125–33. https://doi.org/10.1363/psrh.12115.

Campo-Engelstein, Lisa. 2017. "Make Room for Male Methods: Why We Should Expand the ACA Contraceptive Policy to Include Men." *Fertility and Sterility*, April 11, 2017. www.fertstert.org.

Dehlendorf, Christine, Kira Levy, Allison Kelley, Kevin Grumbach, and Jody Steinauer. 2013. "Women's Preferences for Contraceptive Counseling and Decision Making." *Contraception* 88 (2): 250–56. https://doi.org/10.1016/j.contraception.2012.10.012.

El Ansari, Walid, Mohamed Arafa, Haitham Elbardisi, Ahmad Majzoub, Mohammed Mahdi, Ahmed Albakr, Khalid AlRumaihi, and Abdulla Al Ansari. 2023. "Scoping Review of Sexual and Reproductive Healthcare for Men in the MENA (Middle East and North Africa) Region: A Handful of Paradoxes?" *BMC Public Health* 23 (1): 564. https://doi.org/10.1186/s12889-022-14716-2.

Grady, William R., Koray Tanfer, John O. G. Billy, and Jennifer Lincoln-Hanson. 1996. "Men's Perceptions of Their Roles and Responsibilities Regarding Sex, Contraception and Childrearing." *Family Planning Perspectives* 28 (5): 221–26. https://doi.org/10.2307/2135841.

Grandahl, Maria, Maja Bodin, and Jenny Stern. 2019. "In everybody's interest but no one's assigned responsibility: midwives' thoughts and experiences of preventive work for men's sexual and reproductive health and rights within primary care." *BMC Public Health* 19 (1): 1423. https://doi.org/10.1186/s12889-019-7792-z.

Granzow, Kara. 2007. "De-constructing 'Choice': The Social Imperative and Women's Use of the Birth Control Pill." *Culture, Health & Sexuality* 9 (1): 43–54. https://doi.org/10.1080/13691050600963948.

Hardee, Karen, Melanie Croce-Galis, and Jill Gay. 2017. "Are Men Well Served by Family Planning Programs?" *Reproductive Health* 14 (1): 14. https://doi.org/10.1186/s12978-017-0278-5.

Heinemann, Klaas, Farid Saad, Martin Wiesemes, Steven White, and Lothar Heinemann. 2005. "Attitudes Toward Male Fertility Control: Results of a Multinational Survey on Four Continents." *Human Reproduction* 20 (2): 549–56. https://doi.org/10.1093/humrep/deh574.

Hay, Katherine, Lotus McDougal, Valerie Percival, Sarah Henry, Jeni Klugman, Haja Wurie, Joanna Raven et al. 2019. "Disrupting Gender Norms in Health Systems: Making the Case for Change." *The Lancet* 393 (10190): 2535–49. https://doi.org/10.1016/S0140-6736(19)30648-8.

James-Hawkins, Laurie, Cristen Dalessandro, and Christie Sennott. 2019. "Conflicting Contraceptive Norms for Men: Equal Responsibility versus Women's Bodily Autonomy." *Culture, Health & Sexuality* 21 (3): 263–77. https://doi.org/10.1080/13691058.2018.1464209.

Karim, Syed Irfan, Farhana Irfan, Hussain Saad, Mohammed Alqhtani, Abdulmalik Alsharhan, Ahmed Alzhrani, Feras Alhawas, Saud Alatawi, Mohammed Alassiri, and Abdullah M. A. Ahmed. 2021. "Men's Knowledge, Attitude, and Barriers towards Emergency Contraception: A Facility Based Cross-Sectional Study at King Saud University Medical City." *PLOS ONE* 16 (4): e0249292. https://doi.org/10.1371/journal.pone.0249292.

Kimport, Katrina. 2018. "More Than a Physical Burden: Women's Mental and Emotional Work in Preventing Pregnancy." *Journal of Sex Research* 55 (9): 1096–105. https://doi.org/10.1080/00224499.2017.1311834.

Kumar, Naina, and Amit Kant Singh. 2015. "Trends of Male Factor Infertility, an Important Cause of Infertility: A Review of Literature." *Journal of Human Reproductive Sciences* 8 (4): 191–96. https://doi.org/10.4103/0974-1208.170370.

Male Contraceptive Initiative. "MCI's Lemonade Stand: 'Myth Busting: Demonstrating a Robust Global Market for Male Contraceptives.'" YouTube video, 01:25:52, June 29, 2023. https://www.youtube.com/watch?v=8AoBojJcsaQ.

Marsiglio, William. 2003. "Making Males Mindful of Their Sexual and Procreative Identities: Using Self-Narratives in Field Settings." *Perspectives on Sexual and Reproductive Health* 35 (5): 229–33. https://doi.org/10.1363/3522903.

Mohr, Sebastian, and Rene Almeling. 2020. "Men, Masculinities, and Reproduction—Conceptual Reflections and Empirical Explorations." *NORMA* 15 (3–4): 163–71. https://doi.org/10.1080/18902138.2020.1831156.

Nguyen, Brian T., and Tamar L. Jacobsohn. 2023. "Men's Willingness to Use Novel Male Contraception is Linked to Gender-Equitable Attitudes: Results from an Exploratory Online Survey." *Contraception* 123:110001. https://doi.org/10.1016/j.contraception.2023.110001.

Pazol, Karen, Cheryl L. Robbins, Lindsey I. Black, Katherine A. Ahrens, Kimberly Daniels, Anjani Chandra, Anjel Vahratian, and Lorrie E. Gavin. 2017. "Receipt of Selected Preventive Health Services for Women and Men of Reproductive Age—United States, 2011–2013." *MMWR Surveillance Summaries* 66 (20): 1–31. https://doi.org/10.15585/mmwr.ss6620a1.

Redshaw, Maggie, and Jane Henderson. 2013. "Fathers' Engagement in Pregnancy and Childbirth: Evidence from a National Survey." *BMC Pregnancy and Childbirth* 13 (1): 70. https://doi.org/10.1186/1471-2393-13-70.

Reeves, Richard V. 2022. *Of Boys and Men: Why the Modern Male Is Struggling, Why It Matters, and What to Do about It*. Washington, DC: Brookings Institution Press.

Storck, Kathryn E., Lori M. Gawron, Jessica N. Sanders, Nicolle Wiaderny, and David K. Turok. 2022. "'I Just Had to Pay the Money and Be Supportive': A Qualitative Exploration of the Male-Partner Role in Contraceptive Decision-Making in Salt Lake City, Utah Family Planning Clinics." *Contraception* 113:78–83. https://doi.org/10.1016/j.contraception.2022.04.005.

Tokhi, Mariam, Liz Comrie-Thomson, Jessica Davis, Anayda Portela, Matthew Chersich, and Stanley Luchters. 2018. "Involving Men to Improve Maternal and Newborn Health: A Systematic Review of the Effectiveness of Interventions." Edited by Jacobus P. Van Wouwe. *PLOS ONE* 13 (1): e0191620. https://doi.org/10.1371/journal.pone.0191620.

van Wijk, Cecile M. T. Gijsbers, Katja P. van Vliet, and Annemarie M. Kolk. 1996. "Gender Perspectives and Quality of Care: Towards Appropriate and Adequate Health Care for Women." *Social Science & Medicine* 43 (5): 707–20. https://doi.org/10.1016/0277-9536(96)00115-3.

18

Gendered Language, Pregnant Bodies, and Male Contraceptive Development

FABIAN HENNIG

Contraception, by default, is framed as pregnancy prevention. It is a gendered term. The widespread and nonreflective usage of the term illustrates that "female bodies" are seen as reproductive, while "male bodies" are not (Almeling 2020). In the German language, for example, the term contraception can be translated to *Verhütung* which also means "prevention." Tellingly, it is often used synonymously with *Empfängnis*verhütung. *Empfängnis* is a noun derived from the verb *empfangen*, which means "to receive"—something only bodies with uteruses are presumably capable of (Fichtner 1999).[1]

Due to the gendered implications of current terminology, German women's health activists and sexologists have suggested the term *Zeugungs*verhütung (Leiblein 1984; Sigusch 2005). *Zeugung* can be translated as "procreation." In this sense, *Zeugungsverhütung*—"procreation prevention"—makes male involvement in the reproductive process visible, and it hints at the potential for male responsibility for contraception. In this think piece, I adopt the term *Zeugungsverhütung* to deconstruct gendered implications of contraception as well as to question the feminizing notions of contraceptive efficacy.

Coming to Terms with "Male Contraception"

Unlike "male contraception" (or *männliche Kontrazeption*, in German), which is widely used in the medical field, *Zeugungsverhütung*, as such, does not imply maleness or masculinity. The term, in a queer reading, could serve as an alternative to medical terms, which are being increasingly questioned due to their gendered nature. This is best illustrated by the acknowledgment of the US-based Male Contraception Initiative that "our very name . . . is limited and gendered" (MCI 2021). They rightly point out that transgender women and nonbinary persons might produce sperm, and that they need more inclusive contraceptive options.

The need for a gender-sensitive approach to fertility prevention is further highlighted by discussions within profeminist men's groups in Europe, who craft their own contraceptive devices and experiment with their bodies with the intent of suppressing sperm production. This small movement has been growing in both number and geographic range.[2] "Thermic testicular contraception," as some activists label it, operates by heating the testicles (hence "thermic") and can take the form of a jockstrap (Thomas Bouloù 2018a) or a silicone ring (Labrite 2022).[3] Normal sperm production operates at temperatures several degrees below body temperature. The scrotum provides a natural cooling mechanism for the testicles. By lifting the testicles inside the body (the inguinal canal) and heating the glands to body temperature, jockstraps and silicon rings help surpass this cooling mechanism, thus impairing sperm production. Moreover, some men's groups are turning into men's* groups, welcoming queer people and designing androgynous contraceptive fashion. For example, thermic testicular contraception can also be made of a bra and may even be worn for tucking but does not need to resemble sporty men's slips (Thomas Bouloù 2018c: Thomas Bouloù 2018b).[4]

With this in mind, I suggest the use of the term *Zeugungsverhütung* for devices and drugs that can be used by *everybody* who produces sperm, no matter their gender. Although the term itself is derived from the German context, my argument for a conceptual shift in contraceptive development is not limited to one specific country or region, since contraceptive development is a global, human endeavor.

Approaches to Sperm Suppression

There are a multitude of approaches to experimental contraception for sperm producers, some of which have been developed for decades without ever reaching the final regulatory approval for marketing.[5] They include hormonal technologies such as pills, transdermal gels, injections, and implants as well as nonhormonal approaches based on diverse mechanisms, reversible vasectomies, plugs, sperm valves, ultrasound, and directed heat application. For complexity reduction, I focus my research (as well as this essay) on only two approaches, namely hormonal and thermic technologies.

The development of hormonal male contraceptives started in the 1970s, while the first reports on thermic means of male contraception in humans date back to the 1950s (Oudshoorn 2003; Lissner 2006). In a generally underfunded research field, the hormonal approach is clearly hegemonic, as measured by the amount and scale of clinical trials, the number of publications dealing solely with hormonal male contraception, and the universal recognition of "The Male Pill" as a hormonal one akin to those used by pregnancy-capable people. In contrast, thermic contraception is largely neglected: unknown to many and rarely investigated—and, if it is investigated, it's done so only in small trials.

A comparison of these two approaches is interesting, since hormonal and thermic technologies differ in many regards. Hormonal contraception intervenes in the endocrine feedback mechanism. It is perceived as nonnatural and high-tech. Hormones are regulated substances produced by the pharmaceutical industry and, in most cases, prescribed by doctors. Thermic contraception, on the other hand, operates by heating the testicles, is nonhormonal, sometimes perceived as "natural," and is, in most cases, low-tech. If approved, thermic contraceptives might become regulated as some form of medical device. As of yet, they can be bought on the internet or pieced together with everyday material. They are easy to create and, therefore, lend themselves to lay experiments. Some men are creating their own devices and develop them according to their needs.

Interestingly, hormonal and thermic technologies have more in common than initially meets the eye, since both technologies aim (primarily) at the very same process within the body: a suppression of sperm production (spermatogenesis) to very low levels.[6] Hence, both technologies deal with similar challenges regarding fertility assessment.

Pregnancy Rates as the Principal Metric of Contraceptive Efficacy

As we deconstruct naturalized notions of feminine contraceptive responsibility and acknowledge the sperm-producing body as reproductive, we should question how contraceptive efficacy is usually defined and measured as pregnancy prevention. I contend that the measurement and calculation of contraceptive efficacy reveals a disproportionate focus on female bodies in reproductive medicine.

The most common way to assess the efficacy of contraceptive methods is the Pearl Index, a statistical value named by its inventor, Raymond Pearl (Pearl 1933). The Pearl Index is evaluated by counting the number of pregnancies of a given number of subjects within a year. "The numerator in the Index is the number of pregnancies, and the denominator is the cumulative number of months or cycles of exposure from the start of the method until the completion of the study, discontinuation of the method, or pregnancy. The quotient is multiplied by 1,200 if the denominator is reported in months or by 1,300 if the denominator is reported in cycles" (Trussell and Portman 2013). The Pearl Index can therefore also be described as a "pregnancy rate," since it calculates unintended pregnancies in one hundred person-years of intercourse.[7] The index provides a simple number as a seemingly objective benchmark for a straightforward and quick assessment, and it eases the comparison of distinct contraceptives, "female" and "male" methods alike (a vasectomy has a Pearl Index of 0.1, which means that statistically, of 1,000 couples using it as a contraceptive method for one year, one women will get pregnant; intrauterine device, 0.16; pill, 0.1–0.9; condom, 2–12), hence its wide use.[8]

At the same time, and almost unquestioned in this regard, the Pearl Index ties femininity ever more closely to (the measurement of) reproduction. Given that it is the "female" body which gets pregnant, it seems illogical and almost foolish to suggest otherwise. Yet, this is exactly what I am doing in asking these questions: How can we assess (in)fertility in "male" bodies? Is there a way of predicting contraceptive efficacy in sperm producers?

Sperm and Masculinity

Before I deal with these questions, it is worth mentioning that representations of sperm, fertility, and masculinity are closely linked (Martin 1991; Moore 2007; Karioris and Allan 2017). According to the World Health Organization, one of the leading agents in male contraceptive development as well as fertility assessment, a "healthy" or "normal" sperm concentration amounts to approximately sixteen million sperm/ml (WHO 2021). Popular narrations sensationalize such statistics and vividly portray testicles as natural forces of productivity (Moore 2007)—more productive than General Motors even, since they produce millions of sperm in a shorter period of time (Karioris and Allan 2017). Contraceptive researchers sometimes echo such depictions of male overreproductivity by describing the prevention of "the production of billons of sperm" as "a quantitively challenging problem" of male contraceptive research (Bremner and Kretser 1976, 1115; Bai 2011). The notion that it is much more difficult to prevent large amounts of sperm than one egg per month is popular as well as problematic (Campo-Engelstein, Kaufman, and Parker 2019). It puts into question the technological feasibility of male contraception and justifies the gender asymmetry in contraceptives.

This putative difficulty is further enhanced by the popular myth and overestimation that one sperm is enough to induce a pregnancy. A myth that is still often misleadingly taught in children's books characterizes each sperm as a competitive fighter, eager to impregnate (Moore 2007). As will be described here shortly, some contraceptive researchers subscribe to such an understanding of sperm in assuming that contraceptives should aim at suppressing sperm count to zero.

Male bodies, in short, are portrayed as a challenge for contraceptive development, since they produce millions of sperm, each of which is able to impregnate. This portrayal is misleading as well as problematic since it naturalizes the gendered asymmetry in contraceptive technologies. In order to assure procreative prevention, sperm production does not need to be stopped completely, and sperm suppressing contraceptives should not be expected to achieve such a level.

How Low Do We Need to Go?

The question of exactly how low sperm concentration needs to be to constitute an efficacious means of contraception has troubled researchers for decades (Oudshoorn 2003). In the 1980s, given the difficulties of achieving that aim with hormonal agents, researchers debated whether azoospermia (zero sperm) was truly necessary. Some suggested that severe oligospermia (low sperm count) might be sufficient, but how low remained largely unclear. This is because reliable data on the correlation between sperm count and pregnancy rates did not exist at that time.

This changed when the World Health Organization conducted large scale clinical trials on hormonal male contraception in the 1990s (WHO 1990, 1996). Those trials displayed a clear (almost linear) correlation between sperm counts and pregnancy rates: the lower the sperm count, the lower the chances of pregnancy. The study's authors calculated that suppression to ≤3 million of sperm/ml leads to pregnancy rates "comparable" to modern reversible female methods (such as injectables, oral contraception, or medicated intrauterine devices) and is "superior" to condoms. To minimize the chances of unwanted pregnancies, researchers lowered this threshold even further. A "consensus" paper by virtually all international experts in the field established ≤1 million of sperm/ml as a threshold for effective male contraception (Nieschlag 2002, 2007).

While some challenged the consensus (Grimes et al. 2012), most comprehensive clinical studies on hormonal male contraception followed the expert recommendation (Turner et al. 2003; Mommers et al. 2008; Gu et al. 2009; Behre et al. 2016). Yet, the question "How Low Do We Need to Go?" still seems worth discussing (Wang 2022), as indicated by a talk at the *International Consortium Dedicated to Male Contraception* in 2022.

Pregnancy Rate Is Considered the Best Clinical Endpoint in Male Contraceptive Trials

Hypothetically, the acceptance of the ≤1 million sperm/ml as a threshold would allow sperm counts as a measure of contraceptive efficacy. Nevertheless, in the (medical) discourse of male contraceptive development, the pregnant body is the ultimate proof of (male) reproductivity.

Clinical development of hormonal "male contraceptives" usually follows the same steps.[9] First, there are studies on toxicology and dose finding (Phase I), followed by trials on safety (Phase II). Most of these studies assess sperm counts but, ironically, the "contraceptive efficacy" of "male contraceptives" needs to be established with data on pregnant bodies (Phase III at the latest), when scientists count the number of women getting pregnant within a year of exclusive trial contraceptive use (the Pearl Index) (Oudshoorn 2003).[10]

Within this gendered and institutionalized logic, an experimental contraceptive can only be acknowledged as effective if pregnancy data is gathered. Scientists define the pregnancy rate as the "best clinical endpoint" (Grimes et al. 2004) and declare sperm counts mere "surrogate parameters" (Nieschlag 2002). This hierarchy of fertility measures—pregnancy rate as optimal, sperm count as surrogate—is not apparently disputed within the field of contraceptive research. This might be due to the claim that females bear the burden of unintended pregnancy and so should determine what failure is.

I will counter such views by arguing that knowing the Pearl Index does not necessarily lower the risk of unintended pregnancies, especially in methods of sperm suppression. Additionally, I want to show that the fixation on pregnancy rates complicates and decelerates research on such approaches. This is connected to the problem, that, in terms of logic, measuring male fertility by assessing the body of a man's partner seems inverted. As a matter of fact, the Pearl Index measures male (in)fertility only indirectly, with sperm count being a direct measure (Leiblein 1984).[11]

Sperm Counts

Before I dive deeper into the clinical implications of making sperm counts the primary aim of experimental sperm suppression, it should be noted that the question of sperm thresholds exceeds purely scientific discussions. Activist groups have long propagated ≤1 million of sperm/ml for actual use (Kollektiv Thomas Bouloù 2018). This threshold is already the established orientation for the growing number (thousands!) who practice thermic contraception.[12] Given the almost total lack of funding for thermic contraceptive research, as well as its neglect by large parts of the scientific community, so far only small trials have been conducted (Lissner 2006). Based on such scarce research, the Pearl Index cannot be calculated.

Against this backdrop, a recent guideline by American and European andrological associations advised "against heat or other physical agents to decrease sperm output for male contraception" (Wang et al. 2023, 7). While it seems unlikely that such a warning will stop activists and users, who depend on some measure to indicate contraceptive efficacy, the statement indicates growing awareness by the medical community as well as the need for large scale trials to enhance the acceptability among medical experts. While such trials are in the planning phase (the Male Contraceptive Initiative is currently funding trials on the thermic ring Andro-Switch) and pregnancy rates remain out of reach for users of thermic contraception, sperm counts will continue to be of practical merit.[13]

Nonresponse and Inadequacy of Pearl Index

Both hormonal and heat-based technologies of sperm suppression have been facing an unsolved problem: they fail to consistently lower sperm concentration in all individuals. This "nonresponse" phenomenon is discussed by scientists and activists alike, yet it is not understood, and therefore, it is impossible to predict which individual will or will not respond to the intervention (Ilani et al. 2011).

Scientists have tried to minimize the number of nonresponders by combining agents (adding testosterone as well as a progestin), and some users of thermic contraception increase the "dosage" of heat, such as by wearing the underwear longer or by using two kinds of thermic contraceptives. While this indeed diminishes the number of nonresponders, it does not seem to resolve the problem entirely. Some individuals continuously produce more sperm than is deemed efficacious for contraception.

The Pearl Index is a statistical value. It indicates the probability of (not) getting pregnant based on data of a whole study population. The pregnancy rate is inadequate to detect individual cases of nonresponse, and it might create illusions of safety for those individuals. In other words, as a sperm producer, you might know the Pearl Index of the drug you are taking, but you cannot be certain that it works for your body—at least until you perform sperm analysis. Sperm counts are therefore more feasible for assessing "male" fertility. Moreover, and maybe counterintuitively, sperm counts in practical use decrease the female burden of male contraceptive failure better than the Pearl Index. Given the current state of hormonal as well as thermic contraceptive development, any such contraceptive regimen will necessarily be accompanied by repeated assessments of sperm counts.

Complexity Reduction

The analysis of gametes prior to conception should be viewed as a unique possibility to determine the efficacy of contraceptives. Given that this opportunity does not exist in females (eggs are much harder to extract and counting them does not help anyway), the sidelining of sperm counts in male contraceptive development is even more puzzling.

Measuring the fertility of the sperm-producing individual indirectly— that is, by assessing pregnancy rates instead of sperm counts—leads to further problems, making clinical development for male contraception more imprecise, complex, time consuming, and costly. By assessing contraceptive efficacy through the female body instead of the sperm-producing subject, their relationship status becomes an issue. If researchers aim at assessing the efficacy of "male" contraception by evaluating pregnancy rates, they need to include only monogamous couples in clinical trials. Otherwise, they cannot be sure whether a pregnancy is induced by the sperm producer who is included in the trial or by another person. Researchers therefore exclude couples in nonmonogamous partnerships. Nevertheless, they cannot account for female infidelity within such trials.

Conversely, researchers must assume or advise the couple to be sexually active during the trial. If a couple does not have (frequent) intercourse, the efficacy of the experimental contraceptive technology is overestimated. Due to the necessity of accounting for relationship status, infidelity, and sexual activity, assessing "male" fertility by counting pregnancies is therefore more effort and less precise than counting sperm.

Reducing the Sample Sizes and Study Costs

One important obstacle for developing new male contraceptives is the expense of clinical trials. This is especially true for the late stages of clinical trials, which are large in scale and long in duration. Phase IIb and III clinical trials are aimed at calculating the Pearl Index, which is based on the observation of couples having otherwise unprotected intercourse for one year—the so-called "efficacy phase." Sperm producers *and* their partners need to be included, advised, and monitored in such trials, which doubles the study population as compared with trials on sperm producers alone. A large amount of data on females needs to be gathered, their fertility history reconstructed, their pregnancy rates calculated, and their cycles traced, since females with impaired fertility need to be excluded. The "efficacy phase" itself exposes the female study subjects to the risk of unwanted pregnancy or abortion and at the same time adds more complexity to such trials, making them more extensive and costly. The assessment of sperm counts can be achieved with half the study population—sperm producers.

Speeding Up Development

To calculate the Pearl Index, a clinical trial's "efficacy" phase requires one year of waiting for potential pregnancies to occur among participants. Counting sperm, on the other hand, is possible immediately after therapeutic effect of a trial drug and ejaculation. In order to be sure, several sperm counts are needed before and after the medical intervention to determine baseline counts, as well as to assure the consistent suppression of sperm production over a certain period. This period, if sperm counts are to be accepted as the primary outcome for the aim of sperm suppression methods, could be much shorter than one year (one might call them "reproductive months"). Maybe, for the assessment of male fertility, the late and costly stages of clinical contraceptive efficacy trials could be canceled altogether. This would drastically speed up development of new drugs and devices aiming at sperm suppression.

Reproductive Justice and Autonomy for All

The term *Zeugungsverhütung* might appear somewhat awkward and cumbersome, but it can make research easier. It can be used as a conceptual tool for deconstructing feminized notions of contraception and contraceptive efficacy. Furthermore, establishing sperm counts as a contraceptive measure can simplify and accelerate research progress. In accounting for the reproductive capacities of sperm-producing bodies, *Zeugungsverhütung* alters our understanding of masculinity as reproductive and can help men to actively take responsibility for their sexuality, act in their own best interest, and act as caring partners. This, in turn, would lessen the reproductive burden on women, thus enhancing contraceptive justice in cis heterosexual couples (Campo-Engelstein 2012).

Since *Zeugungsverhütung* could be used by everybody who produces sperm (cis men, nonbinary persons, and trans individuals alike), it offers a new option to a queer community, historically underserved by a highly gendered and female-focused contraceptive research paradigm.[14] In clinical practice, this would imply not recruiting self-identified or clinician-identified "men" only but including a wider array of sexes and genders in the design of research of contraceptive clinical and acceptability studies. In that way, *Zeugungsverhütung* would support reproductive autonomy for all.

NOTES

1 The German translation is in line with its original meaning in Latin. "Contraception" is a combination of "contra" (against) and "concipere, conceptus" (to take in and hold, become pregnant, receive). In English "contraception" is used as a general term, including "female" and "male" methods. Nevertheless, its default adjective is "female," as discussed in the introduction to this volume.

2 During the 1980s, a small movement existed in France (and one group in Switzerland). Today, there are more than ten activist groups all over France, and some in other European countries such as Austria, Belgium, and Germany. Historically, thermic contraception was used by individuals in the U.S. as well (Jenks, n.d.; Monkey Man 2007–2008; Hansen Datz, August 07, 2013).

3 Pictures and animations can be found on pages such as GARCON, n.d.

4 Tucking is practiced by trans women, nonbinary people who are assigned male at birth, as well as drag queens. Tucking elevates the testicles into the inguinal canal. In the same manner, "artificial cryptorchidism" (Mieusset and Bujan 1994) is one of the most common ways to practice thermic contraception in cis males. The cis-trans distinction is thus further blurred.

5 The reasons for this are manifold and will not be reconstructed in detail here. They include the reluctance of pharmaceutical industry due to a disbelief that a market for such a product exists, the correlating assumption of male disinterest, hegemonic perceptions of masculinity, the high costs of developing drugs for healthy people, unclear regulations concerning new drugs, the fear of diminishing male sexuality, a more general concern of side effects and a gendered double standard in risk assessment, problems with developing a suitable form of application, the missing of a science of male reproductive health, and the historical lack of research institutions (Oudshoorn 2003; Almeling 2020).

6   Heat also changes other sperm parameters (Mieusset et al., "Hyperthermia and Human Spermatogenesis," 1987). The sperm appear more immobile, their shape is sometimes altered in a dysfunctional way (Mieusset et al., "Effects of Artificial Cryptorchidism on Sperm Morphology," 1987), and their genetic information can be impaired (Ahmad et al. 2012; Abdelhamid et al. 2019; Zhang et al. 2018). All these effects are reversible according to current knowledge. It is much harder to establish how those additional changes effect fertility. Given that counting sperm, therefore, is the easiest way of assessing infertility in sperm producers, and most data on the effect of heat on spermatogenesis focuses on the effect on sperm counts, I focus on this aspect for the remainder of this think piece.
7   Tellingly, those years are oftentimes regarded to as "reproductive years" or "women years."
8   The Pearl Index has several limitations. One of the most striking limitations led to the distinction of theoretical and practical Pearl Indexes, illustrating the difference of efficacy in the laboratory and efficiency in real life conditions. Today, regulatory bodies usually expect researchers to combine the Pearl Index with "life table analysis," which is more accurate (Trussell and Portman 2013). As far as life table analysis is analyzing the reproductive life of "females," my criticism of the gendered logic of efficacy measurement applies here as well.
9   This is similar in the United States, Europe, or China, for example.
10 The development of medical devices (for example for thermic contraception) differs in some ways. It is less strict, shorter, and, for that reason, less costly. But the same gendered logic is applied here as well. In the "efficacy phase" of a study thermic contraception (Phase II b), pregnancy rates would be assessed.
11 This argument is borrowed from Helmut Leiblein (1984). The author does not, however, imply to establish sperm counts of one million/ml as a measure for male contraceptive efficacy. In line with many of the contraceptive researchers of the 1980s, he believed zero sperm to be a necessity. The one-million/ml threshold was established two decades later.
12 The actual number of users can only be estimated. A recent dissertation surveyed almost a thousand individuals who used thermic contraception at least for six months. Certainly, this study did not survey all users of thermic contraception, but it underscores the diffusion of the method (Guidarelli 2023). The contraceptive ring Andro-Switch was sold about twenty thousand times, according to its inventor. While France is the center of thermic contraception, the use is spreading to other parts of Europe.
13 Usually, sperm analysis is performed by a medical specialist. Nevertheless, some users performed sperm analysis with a simple microscope. Since sperm analysis is costly in many countries and most medical specialists are uneducated about thermic contraception, activists build their own laboratories and currently aim for further developing at-home tests to increase the usability of thermic technologies.
14 Since hormone therapies for medical transitioning might interact with or counteract high dosages of hormonal agents used in hormonal contraceptives, queer

sensitivity might imply a shift from hegemonic hormonal methods to nonhormonal methods.

REFERENCES

Abdelhamid, Mohamed H. M., Camille Esquerré-Lamare, Marie Walschaerts, Gulfam Ahmad, Roger Mieusset, Safouane Hamdi, and Louis Bujan. 2019. "Experimental Mild Increase in Testicular Temperature Has Drastic, but Reversible, Effect on Sperm Aneuploidy in Men: A Pilot Study." *Reproductive Biology* 19 (2): 189–94. https://doi.org/10.1016/j.repbio.2019.06.001.

Ahmad, Gulfam, Nathalie Moinard, Camille Esquerré-Lamare, Roger Mieusset, and Louis Bujan. 2012. "Mild Induced Testicular and Epididymal Hyperthermia Alters Sperm Chromatin Integrity in Men." *Fertility and Sterility* 97 (3): 546–53. https://doi.org/10.1016/j.fertnstert.2011.12.025.

Almeling, Rene. 2020. *GUYnecology: The Missing Science of Men's Reproductive Health.* Oakland: University of California Press.

Bai, Nina. 2011. "Beyond Condoms: The Long Quest for a Better Male Contraceptive; For Decades New, Reliable Contraceptives for Men Have Seemed Imminent. Why Isn't There One Available Yet?" *Scientific American*. June 14, 2011. www.scientificamerican.com.

Behre, Hermann M., Michael Zitzmann, Richard A. Anderson, David J. Handelsman, Silvia W. Lestari, Robert I. McLachlan, M. Christina Meriggiola et al. 2016. "Efficacy and Safety of an Injectable Combination Hormonal Contraceptive for Men." *Journal of Clinical Endocrinology and Metabolism* 101 (12): 4,779–88. https://doi.org/10.1210/jc.2016-2141.

Bremner, William J., and David M. de Kretser. 1976. "The Prospects for New, Reversible Male Contraceptives." *New England Journal of Medicine* 295 (20): 1,111–17. https://doi.org/10.1056/nejm197611112952005.

Campo-Engelstein, Lisa. 2012. "Contraceptive Justice: Why We Need a Male Pill." *Virtual Mentor: VM* 14 (2): 146–51. https://doi.org/10.1001/virtualmentor.2012.14.2.msoc1-1202.

Campo-Engelstein, Lisa, Suzanne Kaufman, and Wendy M. Parker. 2019. "Where Is the Pill for the 'Reproductive Man?': A Content Analysis of Contemporary US Newspaper Articles." *Men and Masculinities* 22 (2): 360–79. https://doi.org/10.1177/1097184X17707990.

Fichtner, Jörg. 1999. *Über Männer Und Verhütung: Der Sinn Kontrazeptiver Praxis für Partnerschaft und Geschlechterverhältnis*. Internationale Hochschulschriften 299. Münster: Waxmann.

GARCON. n.d. "La méthode thermique." Accessed November 20, 2023. https://garcon.link.

Grimes, D., M. Gallo, V. Grigorieva, K. Nanda, and K. Schulz. 2004. "Steroid Hormones for Contraception in Men." *Cochrane Database of Systematic Reviews*, no. 3, CD004316. https://doi.org/10.1002/14651858.CD004316.pub2.

Grimes, David A., Laureen M. Lopez, Maria F. Gallo, Vera Halpern, Kavita Nanda, and Kenneth F. Schulz. 2012. "Steroid Hormones for Contraception in Men." *Cochrane Database of Systematic Reviews*, no. 3, CD004316. https://doi.org/10.1002/14651858.CD004316.pub4.

Gu, Yiqun, Xiaowei Liang, Weixiong Wu, Minli Liu, Shuxiu Song, Lifa Cheng, Liwei Bo et al. 2009. "Multicenter Contraceptive Efficacy Trial of Injectable Testosterone Undecanoate in Chinese Men." *Journal of Clinical Endocrinology and Metabolism* 94 (6): 1910–15. https://doi.org/10.1210/jc.2008-1846.

Guidarelli, Manon. 2023. "Enquête transversale sur les dispositifs de contraception par remontée testiculaire: sécurté, acceptablilité, efficacité. TESETIS_2021. Étude sur la contraception testiculaire." Unpublished medical doctoral thesis.

Hansen Datz, Meldody. 2013. "My Boyfriend Boils His Balls for Me: After Birth Control Did Scary Things to My Body, My Boyfriend and I Got Desperate. Why Aren't There More Birth-Control Options for Men?" *The Stranger*, August 7, 2013. www.thestranger.com.

Ilani, Niloufar, Peter Y. Liu, Ronald S. Swerdloff, and Christina Wang. 2011. "Does Ethnicity Matter in Male Hormonal Contraceptive Efficacy?" *Asian Journal of Andrology* 13 (4): 579–84. https://doi.org/10.1038/aja.2010.133.

Jenks, Chris. n.d. "Experimental Method of Male Contraception." Accessed June 12, 2020. www.puzzlepiece.org.

Karioris, Frank G., and Jonathan A. Allan. 2017. "Grow a Pair! Critically Analyzing Masculinity and the Testicles." *Journal of Men's Studies* 25 (3): 1–17. https://doi.org10.1177/1060826516671307.

Kollektiv Thomas Bouloù. 2018. "Hodenempfängnisverhütung." Self-published, Kollektiv Thomas Bouloù.

Labrite, Maxim. 2022. "Andro-Switch Ring." Thorme. Accessed November 20, 2023. https://thoreme.com/en/anneau-andro-switch/.

Leiblein, Helmut. 1984. *Zeugungsverhütung: Praxis Und Kritik*. Frankfurt: Johann Wolfgang Goethe Universität.

Lissner, Elaine. 2006. "Frontiers in Nonhormonal Male Contraception: The Next Step." Male Contraception Information Project, January 16, 2006. www.newmalecontraception.com.

Male Contraceptive Initiative (MCI). 2021. "Contraception Beyond the Gender Binary." *Male Contraceptive Initiative* (blog), October 4, 2021. www.malecontraceptive.org.

Martin, Emily. 1991. "The Egg and the Sperm: How Science Has Constructed a Romance Based on Stereotypical Male-Female Roles." *Signs* 16 (3): 485–501.

Mieusset, Roger, and Louis Bujan. 1994. "The Potential of Mild Testicular Heating as a Safe, Effective and Reversible Contraceptive Method for Men." *International Journal of Andrology* 17 (4): 186–91. https://doi.org/10.1111/j.1365-2605.1994.tb01241.x.

Mieusset, Roger, Louis Bujan, Arlette Mansat, Francese Pontonnier, and Hélène Grandjean. 1987. "Hyperthermia and Human Spermatogenesis: Enhancement of the

Inhibitory Effect Obtained by 'Artificial Cryptorchidism.'" *International Journal of Andrology* 10 (4): 571–80. https://doi.org/10.1111/j.1365-2605.1987.tb00356.x.

Mieusset, Roger, Louis Bujan, Arlette Mansat, Francis Pontonnier, and Hélène Grandjean. 1987. "Effects of Artificial Cryptorchidism on Sperm Morphology." *Fertility and Sterility* 47 (1): 150–55. https://doi.org/10.1016/S0015-0282(16)49951-6.

Mommers, Ellen, Wendy M. Kersemaekers, Jörg Elliesen, Marc Kepers, Dan Apter, Hermann M. Behre, Jennifer Beynon et al. 2008. "Male Hormonal Contraception: A Double-Blind, Placebo-Controlled Study." *Journal of Clinical Endocrinology and Metabolism* 93 (7): 2,572–80. https://doi.org/10.1210/jc.2008-0265.

Monkey Man. 2007–2008. "Male Contraceptive via External Wet Heat: My Venture into the Male Contraceptive." *Burningballs* (blog), July 22, 2007–May 26, 2008. https://burningballs.blogspot.com/.

Moore, Lisa J. 2007. *Sperm Counts: Overcome by Man's Most Precious Fluid*. Intersections. New York: New York University Press.

Nieschlag, Eberhard. 2002. "Sixth Summit Meeting Consensus: Recommendations for Regulatory Approval for Hormonal Male Contraception." *International Journal of Andrology* 25 (6): 375. https://doi.org/10.1046/j.1365-2605.2002.00387.x.

Nieschlag, Eberhard. 2007. "10th Summit Meeting Consensus: Recommendations for Regulatory Approval for Hormonal Male Contraception. October 22–23, 2006." *Contraception* 75 (3): 166–67. https://doi.org/10.1016/j.contraception.2006.12.001.

Oudshoorn, Nelly. 2003. *The Male Pill: A Biography of a Technology in the Making*. Durham, NC: Duke University Press.

Pearl, Raymond. 1933. "Factors in Human Fertility and Their Statistical Evaluation." *Lancet* 222 (5741): 607–11. https://doi.org/10.1016/S0140-6736(01)18648-4.

Sigusch, Volkmar. 2005. "Die "Pille"—Jahrzehnte Danach." In *Sexuelle Welten: Zwischenrufe Eines Sexualforschers*, edited by Volkmar Sigusch, 40–44. Beiträge zur Sexualforschung Bd. 87. Giessen: Psychosozial-Verl.

Thomas Bouloù. 2018a. "Tutoriel remonte-couilles: Modèle jockstrap." YouTube, 00:47:11, November 18, 2018. https://www.youtube.com/watch?v=io9frNy31Ts.

Thomas Bouloù. 2018b. "Tutoriel remonte-couilles: Modèle slip." YouTube, 00:33:58, November 18, 2018. https://www.youtube.com/watch?v=AjZBcK4WzI8.

Thomas Bouloù. 2018c. "Tutoriel remonte-couilles: Modèle soutien-gorge." YouTube, 00:19:14, November 18, 2018. https://www.youtube.com/watch?v=fjrMMv7eoio.

Trussell, James, and David Portman. 2013. "The Creeping Pearl: Why Has the Rate of Contraceptive Failure Increased in Clinical Trials of Combined Hormonal Contraceptive Pills?" *Contraception* 88 (5): 604–10. https://doi.org/10.1016/j.contraception.2013.04.001.

Turner, Leo, Ann J. Conway, Mark Jimenez, Peter Y. Liu, Elise Forbes, Robert I. McLachlan, and David J. Handelsman. 2003. "Contraceptive Efficacy of a Depot Progestin and Androgen Combination in Men." *Journal of Clinical Endocrinology and Metabolism* 88 (10): 4659–67. https://doi.org10.1210/jc.2003-030107.

Wang, Christina. 2022. "Sperm Suppression for Male Contraception—How Low Do We Need to Go?" Talk at Third International Congress on Male Contraception, Paris, May 23, 2022.

Wang, Christina, Maria C. Meriggiola, John K. Amory, Christopher L. R. Barratt, Hermann M. Behre, William J. Bremner, Alberto Ferlin et al. 2023. "Practice and Development of Male Contraception: European Academy of Andrology and American Society of Andrology Guidelines." *Andrology.* https://doi.org/10.1111/andr.13525.

World Health Organization (WHO). 1990. "Contraceptive Efficacy of Testosterone-Induced Azoospermia in Normal Men. World Health Organization Task Force on Methods for the Regulation of Male Fertility." *Lancet* 336 (8721): 955–59.

World Health Organization (WHO). 1996. "Contraceptive Efficacy of Testosterone-Induced Azoospermia and Oligozoospermia in Normal Men." *Fertility and Sterility* 65 (4): 821–29.

World Health Organization (WHO). 2021. *WHO Laboratory Manual for the Examination and Processing of Human Semen, Sixth Edition.* Geneva: World Health Organization.

Zhang, Mei-Hua, Li-Ping Zhai, Zhen-Ya Fang, An-Na Li, Wei Xiao, and Yi Qiu. 2018. "Effect of Scrotal Heating on Sperm Quality, Seminal Biochemical Substances, and Reproductive Hormones in Human Fertile Men." *Journal of Cellular Biochemistry* 119 (12): 10228–38. https://doi.org/10.1002/jcb.27365.19.

19

Shepherding Sperm in Catholic Health Systems

LORI FREEDMAN

> PHYSICIAN: You know, we [used to have] the equipment to spin down the sperm and prepare it and do it. We can't do that here . . . Because it's a Catholic facility, we don't do in vitro fertilization or embryo storage, embryo transfers, artificial insemination—none of that . . . Now, they're getting a little crafty with how they get around it and they go off-campus . . . in fact, the chairman of the entire OB/GYN department of all six [Catholic] hospitals is an infertility specialist, who is starting up an in vitro fertilization clinic off-campus.
> LORI: So, you'll have some place to send your patients.
> PHYSICIAN: Yeah. We had somewhere to send them anyway before—it was just out of the system—but now the system wants the business. (Freedman 2023)

Location matters. When anthropologist Mary Douglas famously explored the social construction of purity, she reminded us that dirt is merely matter out of place (Douglas 2003). In the case of Catholic health care, one type of sin is sperm out of place. Much as dirt can mean healthy soil in one location and filth in another, leaders of Catholic health institutions may view sperm as sin in one location and lucrative biomedicine in another.

The US Conference of Catholic Bishops' policies govern the nation's enormous Catholic health systems (USCCB 2018), which are a source of pride for many within the Church, but their charitable and religious roots have long withered. Gone are the days when nuns served as nurses. And despite their reputation, Catholic health facilities treat low-income patients at a rate less than the average in the United States (Solomon et al. 2020; Lown Institute 2023). Nonetheless, under US law, religious entities can restrict reproductive services based upon a legal fiction that ascribes a conscience to institutions (Wicclair 2011; Sepper 2012; Merner et al. 2023). Importantly, institutional conscience rights supersede those of employees and patients. Catholic hospitals and clinics are often indistinguishable from those of other health systems, except when it comes to reproduction (Kutney-Lee et al. 2014; Wascher et al. 2018).

The bishops' policies and restrictions are spelled out in the Ethical and Religious Directives for Catholic Healthcare Services. Catholic hospitals, by definition, adopt and implement these directives in medical practice, as monitored by hospital clergy and ethics committees. Today, four out of the ten largest US health systems are Catholic, and about one in six patients is treated in a Catholic hospital, whether or not they are aware of the religious restrictions and whether or not they have meaningful alternatives due to geographic or insurance limitations (Solomon et al. 2020; Guiahi, Sheeder, and Teal 2014; Stulberg et al. 2019). Additionally, women of color in many states disproportionately birth in hospitals with religious constraints on care (Shepherd et al. 2018). Such constraints serve to compound the intersecting inequalities and reproductive injustice discussed in Krystale E. Littlejohn's essay in this volume.

Male reproductive autonomy is rarely contested in the United States relative to female reproductive autonomy. But the Catholic Church, through their 654 Catholic hospitals and thousands of outpatient facilities, does place restrictions on male bodies. The church's opposition to abortion may be well known, but the Ethical and Religious Directives also prohibit a variety of other reproductive services, including vasectomy—through a directive forbidding sterilization—and fertility treatments in which sperm are taken from the male body to create embryos.

Given the notorious pronatalism of the church, it can be confusing why the bishops would oppose in vitro fertilization (IVF). However, Catholicism formally endorses only one pathway for sperm: sperm should exit the male body in order to enter the female body during procreative, married intercourse (USCCB 2018; Martucci, Stahl, and Vandendriessche 2022). In this paradigm, sperm travel solely for that procreative purpose, unthwarted by contraception, unwasted by masturbation, and undiverted by vasectomy. Therefore, fertility treatments violate Catholic religious tenets when they require ejaculation outside of heterosexual married intercourse, extracorporeal fertilization (mixing egg and sperm in a petri dish), and the potential destruction of life (disposal of extra embryos).

While the Ethical and Religious Directives offer a clear and centralized source of religious authority, they do not represent the beliefs of religious people. Even among Catholic individuals, nonprocreative sex and infertility interventions are enormously popular. For example, a majority of Catholic Americans approve of gay marriage and consensual adult sex outside of marriage, and only 13 percent feel the use of IVF is morally wrong (Diamant 2013, 2020a, 2020b). Among all religious groups, the awkward realities of getting sperm tested or used in clinical treatments, which often involve men masturbating in a doctor's office, are increasingly normalized and utilized (Schenker 2005; Sallam and Sallam 2016).

The bishops implore the public to return to conservative sexual norms in their advocacy against reproductive and transgender rights (Bharath 2023). Using all tools at their disposal, the Ethical and Religious Directives represent the institutional arm of the US Bishops' campaign to push back on broadly liberalized beliefs about sex and sexuality (Vaggione 2020; Plemons 2018). Still, most data suggest the church is not winning this battle for the hearts and minds (or, at least, behaviors) of Americans.

The US Bishops lean further right than most Catholics, many Catholic health care leaders, and even some Catholic bishops in other countries. As just one example, Belgium's Catholic facilities are known to allow IVF (Martucci, Stahl, and Vandendriessche 2022). Because US Bishops do not, health care administrators and doctors of Catholic hospital systems creatively navigate the rules and guide patients to deposit sperm in facilities that somehow elude Catholic governance while still being affiliated with the system. They ultimately shepherd patients through a process of sperm and egg retrieval in non-Catholic buildings, testing and combining that material in a non-Catholic laboratory, placing it back into a patient's body in a non-Catholic building, and bringing the patient back into the Catholic facility for prenatal and obstetric care once they are pregnant. Similarly, patients of Catholic health systems are often quietly able to get a vasectomy in a non-Catholic outpatient setting if they so desire. The institution remains spiritually pure by prohibiting or displacing the specific components of IVF and contraception that religious leaders do not endorse.

Leveraging both the animal rearing and spiritual connotations of the term *shepherd*, I argue that Catholic health systems deftly shepherd sperm around the doctrinal pitfalls that represent little value to most involved. This strategic shepherding is good both for the bottom line of health systems and for those needing medical assistance to procreate or contracept but who are bound to Catholic health systems for whatever reason.

Catholic health systems are major recipients of public funding (Solomon et al. 2020; Lown Institute 2023), and some even run enormous private equity funds to buffer their systems economically (Cohrs 2021). These financial advantages—and the deft shepherding of sperm and the like—allow these health systems to prosper in the competitive business of medicine. Given the religious mission of the US Bishops, compromising mission for margin seems to lack basic integrity and, theoretically, should induce embarrassment and shame. And perhaps it does. Still, if there is shame from this hypocrisy, it has not kept Catholic health systems from continuing to impose religious barriers to reproductive care for millions of men and women.

Such shepherding is certainly not new. Vasectomy has long been provided to the patients referred from Catholic health facilities to non-Catholic outpatient services with relatively little controversy; abortion as well, but with less of a paper trail (Freedman 2023). Still, as health systems continue to grow in size, bringing more services under their auspices to keep money rolling in and not out, accessing non-Catholic options for various reproductive services is growing increasingly complicated. This is especially true when the insurer also happens to be affiliated with the church.

While IVF (including sperm, egg, and ultimately embryo) is out of place in Catholic institutions, neither Catholic health systems nor their patients want to lose out on IVF's promise of fertility, family creation, and a lucrative business enterprise. In US facilities governed by Catholic doctrine, IVF is a sin. But when a Catholic health system's physicians do the prohibited procedures in a building that is somehow left un-Catholic, it is just good business.

REFERENCES

Bharath, Deepa. 2023. "U.S. Bishops' New Guidelines Aim to Limit Trans Health Care." Associated Press, March 24, 2023. https://apnews.com.

Cohrs, Rachel. 2021. "The Catholic hospital system Ascension is running a Wall Street-style private equity fund." *Statnews*, November 16, 2021. www.statnews.com.

Diamant, Jeff. 2020a. "Half of US Christians Say Casual Sex between consenting Adults Is Sometimes or Always Acceptable." Pew Research Center, August 31, 2020. www.pewresearch.org.

Diamant, Jeff. 2020b. "How Catholics around the World See Same-Sex Marriage, Homosexuality." Pew Research Center, November 2, 2020. www.pewresearch.org.

Diamant, Jeff. 2013. "Abortion Viewed in Moral Terms: Fewer See Stem Cell Research and IVF as Moral Issues." Pew Research Center, August 15, 2013. www.pewresearch.org.

Douglas, Mary. 2003. *Purity and Danger: An Analysis of Concepts of Pollution and Taboo*. New York City: Routledge.

Freedman, Lori. 2023. *Bishops and Bodies: Reproductive Care in American Catholic Hospitals*. New Brunswick, NJ: Rutgers University Press.

Guiahi, Maryam, Jeanelle Sheeder, and Stephanie Teal. 2014. "Are Women Aware of Religious Restrictions on Reproductive Health at Catholic Hospitals? A Survey of Women's Expectations and Preferences for Family Planning Care." *Contraception* 90 (4): 429–34. https://doi.org/10.1016/j.contraception.2014.06.035.

Kutney-Lee, Ann, G. J. Melendez-Torres, Matthew D. McHugh, and Barbra Mann Wall. 2014. "Distinct Enough? A National Examination of Catholic Hospital Affiliation and Patient Perceptions of Care." *Health Care Management Review* 39 (2): 134. https://doi.org/10.1097/hmr.0b013e31828dc491.

Lown Institute. 2023. "Fair Share Spending." Video, 00:59:40, April 11, 2023. https://lownhospitalsindex.org.

Martucci, Jessica, Ronit Y. Stahl, and Joris Vandendriessche. 2022. "One Religion, Two Paths: Making Sense of US and Belgian Catholic Hospitals' Approaches to IVF." *Journal of Religious History* 46 (3): 552–79. https://doi.org/10.1111/1467-9809.12878.

Merner, Bronwen, Casey M. Haining, Lindy Willmott, Julian Savulescu, and Louise A. Keogh. 2023. "Institutional Objection to Abortion: A Mixed-Methods Narrative Review." *Women's Health* 19. https://doi.org/10.1177/17455057231152373.

Plemons, Eric. 2018. "Not Here: Catholic Hospital Systems and the Restriction against Transgender Healthcare." *CrossCurrents* 68 (4): 533–49. https://doi.org/10.1111/cros.12341.

Sallam, H. N., and N. H. Sallam. 2016. "Religious Aspects of Assisted Reproduction." *Facts, Views & Vision in ObGyn* 8 (1): 33.

Schenker, Joseph G. 2005. "Assisted reproduction practice: religious perspectives." *Reproductive Biomedicine Online* 10 (3): 310–19. https://doi.org/10.1016/S1472 -6483(10)61789-0.

Sepper, Elizabeth. 2012. "Taking Conscience Seriously." *Virginia Law Review* 98 (7): 1501.

Shepherd, Kira, Elizabeth Reiner Platt, Katherine M. Franke, and Elizabeth Boylan. 2018. "Bearing Faith: The Limits of Catholic Health Care for Women of Color."

Solomon, Tess, Lois Uttley, Patty HasBrouck, and Yoolim Jung. 2020. "Bigger and Bigger: The Growth of Catholic Health Systems." N.p.: Community Catalyst. www .communitycatalyst.org.

Stulberg, Debra B., Maryam Guiahi, Luciana E. Hebert, and Lori R. Freedman. 2019. "Women's Expectation of Receiving Reproductive Health Care at Catholic and Non-Catholic hospitals." *Perspectives on Sexual and Reproductive Health* 51 (3): 135–42. https://doi.org/10.1363/psrh.12118.

United States Conference of Catholic Bishops (USCCB). 2018. *Ethical and Religious Directives for Catholic Health Care Services*. 6th ed. Washington DC: USCCB.

Vaggione, Juan Marco. 2020. "The Conservative Uses of Law: The Catholic Mobilization against Gender Ideology." *Social Compass* 67 (2): 252–66. https://doi.org/10.1177 /0037768620907561.

Wascher, Jocelyn M., Luciana E. Hebert, Lori R. Freedman, and Debra B. Stulberg. 2018. "Do Women Know Whether Their Hospital Is Catholic? Results from a National Survey." *Contraception* 98 (6): 498–503. https://doi.org/10.1016/j .contraception.2018.05.017.

Wicclair, Mark R. 2011. *Conscientious Objection in Health Care: An Ethical Analysis*. Cambridge: Cambridge University Press.

PART V

Regulating Sperm

20

Examining the Politics, Ethics, and Legality of Anonymity in Gamete Donation

REBECCA W. O'CONNOR

According to the Centers for Disease Control and Prevention, one in eight couples (12 percent of married women) have trouble getting pregnant or sustaining a pregnancy (Lepkowski et al. 2010). Approximately 7.3 million American women ages fifteen to forty-four have received some form of medical care for infertility, a disease recognized by authorities including the World Health Organization and the American Medical Association, which is just one of many potential barriers to family building (Berg 2017). Amid scientific advancement and societal shifts, gamete donation has steadily increased in the last thirty years, with donor conception helping many people become parents.[1]

Leading medical organizations, including the American Society for Reproductive Medicine (ASRM), have long encouraged intended parents to disclose the *use* of donor gametes to their children (Ethics Committee of the ASRM 2018). Less settled in the United States is if, when, and how to disclose the *identity* of an anonymous gamete donor. In the early days of gamete donation, anonymity was paramount, but shifting attitudes and norms are reshaping this thinking and enabling new approaches. For example, as access to direct-to-consumer DNA testing services, such as 23andMe and Ancestry, has become routine, so have headlines about donor-conceived people using them and discovering the identities of their donors and half-siblings. In recent decades, support groups for donors, parents, donor-conceived people, and others have multiplied. Media coverage, podcasts, and advocacy organizations have amplified this community's questions, concerns, and desires. Now, as generations of donor-conceived people are coming of age, some are calling for mandatory disclosure of donors' identities.

Against this backdrop, state and federal policymakers are introducing a raft of policies related to gamete donation and anonymity. These proposals, both legislative and regulatory, call for everything from mandatory disclosure of donors' identities to the establishment of state and national donor registries. Navigating a variety of complex legal, ethical, and practical considerations, lawmakers and professionals are doing their best to support individuals who are building families. To that end, in 2022, ASRM announced the formation of a new, multidisciplinary task force on the Needs and Interests of Donor Conceived People and their families. Announcing this initiative, ASRM president-elect Paula Amato said, "We have entered a new paradigm in the practice of gamete and embryo donation, which must accommodate new realities around disclosure and anonymity" (ASRM 2022a).

An Evolving Regulatory Framework

Regulation of donor eggs, sperm, and embryos is nothing new. The US Food and Drug Administration has enforced donor eligibility standards for years.[2] Yet, a central question still needs to be addressed: should donors in the United States continue to hold a right to anonymity?[3]

Starting in the early 2000s, some European countries and Australia have abolished donor anonymity. Several US states have emulated aspects of this approach in their laws by adopting measures that require state-licensed gamete banks and fertility clinics to maintain and share, under set circumstances, specific, identifying information from donors (e.g., the Uniform Parentage Act[4]).[5] Additionally, several states have laws authorizing adult donor-conceived persons to request the identity of their donors.[6]

In 2022, Colorado became the first state to fully adopt the European model of abolishing donor anonymity.[7] The Donor-Conceived Persons Protection Act takes effect in January 2025 and has garnered considerable attention as the most far-reaching law of its type to date. The introduction of similar proposals in other states signals a potential national trend.[8]

While some caution against a piecemeal, state-by-state regulatory framework for donor conception, this issue is front of mind for many state lawmakers and advocates who are passionate and motivated. It is, therefore, critical that policymakers understand the complex legal, ethical, and practical considerations such proposals raise.

Topics of Debate

Advocates on various sides of this issue seemingly agree that the ability to guarantee lasting donor anonymity has eroded, primarily because anyone sending in a DNA sample to online testing companies is likely to find people they are genetically connected to via gamete donation, including the donor. Considering the erosion of actual anonymity in this realm, lawmakers must balance assertions of a right to know one's genetic origins against the privacy rights of all individuals involved.

At the same time, some ask if portraying this as a clean tension between donor-conceived individuals' "right to know" versus donors' and intended parents' "right to privacy" is an oversimplification. One complication is that a "right to know" may represent a nuanced request seeking several different things, including information about one's medical history, one's identity, a potential relationship with one's donor, and "the full *truth* about the circumstances of one's conception" (Ravitsky 2010, 668).

Moreover, motivations and expectations regarding donor identity disclosure are not universal among donor-conceived persons. In a 2020 survey, 67 percent of respondents said they wanted the donor's identity to be available to them from birth. However, just a third of respondents believed donors should be mandated to remain available for a relationship with donor-conceived children (Burke et al. 2021).

Additionally, the interplay between state policies and existing law warrants examination. Does, for example, a policy eliminating donor anonymity violate the Fourteenth Amendment's equal protection clause? It would do so by establishing for those who are donor-conceived a right to know the identity of their biological parent that a person conceived through sexual intercourse would not have. Another set of open questions concerns how mandatory disclosure requirements would fare under HIPAA scrutiny. The Health Insurance Portability and Accountability Act of 1996 (HIPAA) requires covered entities to ensure safeguards are in place to protect personal health information. How, some ask, can sperm clinics and the like uphold a duty to protect personal health information against a state-mandated disclosure of donor identity and other medical information?

Some question the practical feasibility of compliance and the downstream impacts of these laws. For instance, absent a national donor registry to track such details, will individual states or clinics be expected to fund and operationalize tracking systems to ensure compliance? Would related costs be passed along to patients, creating another barrier to fertility treatments? Will eliminating donor anonymity negatively affect donations and make a gamete supply shortage? Will providers be less inclined to deliver this type of care under the auspices of heightened regulation and scrutiny?[9]

Finally, it is essential to distinguish debates about gamete donor identity and "fertility fraud," such as doctors using their own genetic material to impregnate unwitting patients or gamete donors who failed to disclose hereditary health conditions at the time of donation. While acts of "fertility fraud" are not the focus of this piece, some advocates and policymakers are conflating these issues and proposing legislation aimed at fertility fraud that includes provisions related to donor anonymity.

Inclusion and Intent Matter

To ensure a practical approach to anonymity in gamete donation, we must seek perspectives from a diverse, multidisciplinary set of stakeholders, including donor-conceived persons, medical and mental health experts, parents, and attorneys. Clarity in intent and drafting legislation and regulations is critical. To date, relevant case law is limited. Yet, as states act, they should anticipate jurists' role in interpreting novel laws. Policymakers should narrowly tailor such measures to balance underlying goals and individual rights. Policies on donor disclosure should set clear and explicit standards of responsibility and communication between parties, anticipating individual needs, related costs, and administrative challenges.

NOTES

1 "Donor conception" is having a baby using donated sperm, eggs, or embryos. This can entail of using procedures including in vitro fertilization. A "donor" is an individual who donates sperm, eggs, or embryos. "Recipient parent(s)" may also be referred to as "intended parent(s)."

2   Today, most prospective donors are screened for a genetic predisposition to hereditary conditions such as Tay-Sachs disease and cystic fibrosis. The FDA, CDC, ASRM, and American Association of Tissue Banks have also developed related guidance. The FDA standards require, among other things, human cell, tissue, and cellular-based product establishments to screen and test cell and tissue donors for risk factors for, and clinical evidence of, relevant communicable disease agents or diseases, including HIV and hepatitis.
3   This is the central focus of this paper. Related but separate issues include the parental rights and obligations of a donor about a resulting child and the rights and recourse in instances of fertility fraud or failure to disclose specific genetic conditions at the time of donation.
4   See this model legislation, developed by the Uniform Law Commission, "2017 Parentage Act," last updated December 5, 2024, https://www.uniformlaws.org.
5   See, e.g., RCW Title 26, Ch. 26.26A, section 26.26A.005 et seq.
6   These include California, Connecticut, Rhode Island, and Washington.
7   See CO SB 22–224, signed into law May 31, 2022. The Colorado law's donor disclosure requirement extends to out-of-state egg and sperm banks providing gametes for in-state recipients. The law requires donors to consent to the disclosure of their identity, upon specific conditions, to resulting offspring; sets limits on the number of families a donor can assist (twenty-five); and limits egg donors from undergoing more than six egg donation retrieval procedures.
8   Colorado was one of many states to take on the topic of donor disclosures. In 2011, Washington began requiring clinics to collect donors' medical history and mandated the disclosure of such information to resulting donor-conceived persons. In 2021, a New York state senator proposed legislation requiring in-state reproductive tissue banks to verify the medical history of all donors in the preceding five years. Moreover, state legislative proposals to regulate donor conception appear as both stand-alone measures (e.g., NY S. 7602 [2022]) and, at other times, as part of legislation to address the separate but partly related issue of "fertility fraud" (e.g., MN SB 147 [2023]). For further discussion of this, see Cahn and Suter 2022. Notably, ASRM and other organizations opposed the Colorado legislation for reasons enumerated in correspondence to Colorado governor Jared Polis (see ASRM, 2022b).
9   As noted by Courtney G. Joslin, Katherine L. Kraschel, and Doug NeJaime in their essay in this volume, we have already seen a chilling effect on providers' willingness to offer certain care and procedures in the year since the Supreme Court's decision in *Dobbs v. Jackson Women's Health Organization* (No. 19–1392, 597 U.S. 215 (2022)). This trend, as documented in reports of the ASRM Center for Policy and Leadership (CPL) (see ASRM 2023), has already been seen playing out in the field.

REFERENCES

American Society for Reproductive Medicine (ASRM). 2022a. "ASRM Taskforce on the Needs and Interests of Donor-Conceived People and Their Families." Accessed October 25, 2024. www.asrm.org.

American Society for Reproductive Medicine (ASRM). 2022b. "ASRM to Governor Jared Polis." Accessed October 25, 2024. www.asrm.org.

American Society of Reproductive Medicine (ASRM). 2023. "Changes Ahead: Abortion Policy Proposals Affecting Reproductive Medicine." Accessed October 28, 2024. www.asrm.org.

Berg, Sara. 2017. "AMA Backs Global Health Experts in Calling Infertility a Disease," American Medical Association. Accessed October 25, 2024. www.ama-assn.org.

Burke, Rennie, Yvette Ollada Lavery, Gali Katznelson, Joshua North, and J. Wesley Boyd. 2021. "How Do Individuals Who Were Conceived Through the Use of Donor Technologies Feel About the Nature of Their Conception?" *Harvard Medical Center for Bioethics*. Accessed 28 October 2024, https://bioethics.hms.harvard.edu/journal/donor-technology.

Cahn, Naomi, and Sonia Suter. 2022. "Generations Later, the Rights of Donor-Conceived People Are Becoming Law." *The Hill*, April 23, 2022. https://thehill.com.

Catasalan, Ranilo. "Eligibility Determination for Donors of Human Cells, Tissues, and Cellular and Tissue-Based Products (HCT/Ps)." Virtual Workshop, September 29, 2020. www.fda.gov.

Ethics Committee of the American Society for Reproductive Medicine (ASRM). 2018. "Informing Offspring of Their Conception by Gamete or Embryo Donation: An Ethics Committee Opinion." *Fertility and Sterility* 109 (4): 601–5. https://doi.org/10.1016/j.fertnstert.2018.01.001.

Lepkowski, James M., William D. Mosher, Karen E. Davis, Robert M. Groves, and John Van Hoewyk. 2010. *The 2006-2010 National Survey of Family Growth: Sample Design and Analysis of a Continuous Survey*. Hyattsville, MD: National Center for Health Statistics.

Ravitsky, Vardit. 2010. "'Knowing Where You Come From': The Rights of Donor-Conceived Individuals and the Meaning of Genetic Relatedness." *Minnesota Journal of Law, Science & Technology* 11 (2): 655–84.

Uniform Law Commission. "Parentage Act." Uniform Law Commission. Accessed October 28, 2024. www.uniformlaws.org.

21

Masculinity, Eugenics, and American Family Stories

KAREN WEINGARTEN

We all tell stories about ourselves to understand ourselves, regardless of whether we consciously use the language of narrative. Rita Charon (2001, 1,897) has termed this *narrative competence*, or "the competence that human beings use to absorb, interpret, and respond to stories." This recognition has led her, along with other physicians and medical humanists, to establish the field of narrative medicine as a means to train physicians to integrate patients' stories into the care they receive and the choices that are made when deciding on their treatment. In this essay, I build on the field of narrative medicine to argue that we need to do more to interrogate the enduring stories we tell about male infertility and to question how those stories impact those struggling with infertility and the children born through sperm that is sold. I am particularly interested in how Americans in the twenty-first century have been unable to extricate these stories from the entanglements of masculinity and eugenics and how these entanglements become more apparent when you trace the history of sperm donation (and selling) to the early twentieth century, when it first became a more institutionalized practice.

To state my argument more bluntly, the American cultural, medical, and legal insistence on the availability of anonymous sperm donation can be traced historically to the roots of the fertility industry, which was built on a narrative wedded to a eugenic perspective of preserving American norms of masculinity and family.

Sperm Donation in the 1930s

Little writing about donor insemination, or any insemination for that matter, existed in either medical journals or the popular press until the 1930s when Dr. Frances Seymour, a New York City gynecologist, created a maelstrom when she admitted that she not only regularly used "artificial insemination" in her practice but that several of her patients, including two successful single "business women," had given birth to children with her help. The story was splashed on the cover of several major newspapers, including the May 1, 1934, issue of the *Chicago Daily Tribune* with the sensationalist headline "13 Babies in N.Y. have Test Tube as Father." According to the article, Seymour acknowledged that in the previous two years, thirteen babies in her practice were conceived with the help of insemination. Eleven of those babies, she claimed, were born with the husband's own sperm, and two babies were conceived with anonymous sperm for two "prominent business women" who were single.[1]

Seymour distinguished between the conception of these two types of children, and describes the latter, where an anonymous sperm donor is used, as producing "eugenic babies." In a *Boston Globe* article from April 30, 1934, Seymour explains how she was reluctant to talk publicly about her work in artificial insemination, but when the couple with twins leaked the news, she felt compelled to answer questions about her work to clear up any misconceptions.

The link between eugenics and sperm donation was only strengthened during World War II. As young men were dying and seriously injured on the warfront, Seymour warned British leaders that to counter population decline they should resort to donor insemination to repopulate England and the rest of Europe with the help of "eugenic donors." The magazine *Newsweek* picked up the story in an editorial promoting the idea and quoted Seymour's explanation that artificial insemination "offers the only positive hope of improving racial quality" ("Substitute Fathers" 1943, 87–88). Published in 1943, during the height of World War II, her words seemed to contain no irony, even as millions of people were being killed in concentration camps in the name of eugenics and "improving racial quality."

Test Tube Babies in Midcentury Film

A few years after the war, W. Merle Connell's 1948 exploitation film *Test Tube Babies* was released.[2] It begins with assuring its viewers that the shocking new practice of artificial insemination can produce children "free from all taint of heredity," and that "astounding as it may sound," the resulting child "even resembles the parents." In this film, we are told that only artificial insemination can save the marriage of this beautiful, white, seemingly healthy middle-class couple. (He is a junior architect who "makes more than enough to support a family.") In a sequence filmed on a beach, their healthy and fit white bodies in sleek bathing suits are emphasized: they run with ease, they splash in the waves, they lounge on the sand. Yet because they are not able to conceive, Cathy strays from her husband, spends time with men and women who indulge in drinking and free love, and even allows another man to kiss her in a moment of heated passion (and boredom). Male infertility is a threat to the white American family, the film warns, and only children can save this marriage—and in turn the foundation of white, middle-class America. However, the doctor strongly advises the couple never to tell their children of their conception if they want to be truly cured of the ills of male infertility and preserve the husband's masculinity.[3] His advice would be the norm for all patients who used donor sperm until the early 1990s.[4]

Test Tube Babies foreshadows the feminist critic Sophie Lewis's words when she tells us that "pregnancy has long been substantially technofixed already," especially "when it comes to those whose lives really 'matter'" (2019, 3). George and Cathy's white, middle-class lives matter, and the technologies of artificial insemination (and all reproductive technologies that would follow) were created precisely to help people like them. Across two books, Lewis (2019, 2022) has argued for the abolition of the nuclear family because it upholds patriarchal, racist, and capitalist norms. She also believes it seduces us into believing that genetics matter and are the privileged way to make a family. I mention her work because of its influence in feminist circles but also because she rightly points out that pregnancy has long been technologically mediated and that genetics should not make a family. However, I also want to push against Lewis's insistence that genetics do not matter at all.

Donor Conception in a Contemporary Context

Dani Shapiro's bestselling memoir *Inheritance* traces her discovery of finding out she was donor conceived after doing a consumer DNA test;

it brought mainstream attention to the practices of donor conception in ways that are thoughtful and without being sensationalist. For Shapiro, discovering she was donor conceived answered questions she had about herself and explained her relationship with her parents so that pieces of her life finally fit together. Most practically, when Shapiro begins communicating with her donor, she learns she might have an inherited eye disease, which testing reveals that she does indeed have. She also comes to understand why her entire life she had been told "you don't look Jewish" because of her fair hair and features. It turns out her donor is not Jewish and looks a lot like her. This new knowledge gives her a sense of peace and understanding she never had, and creating a relationship with her donor, Ben, becomes of utmost importance to her.

Still, throughout the memoir, Shapiro reminds readers that her father, the man who raised her and whom she still cherishes after his death, is still her father. "I came from two men" (Shapiro 2019, 248), she tells readers in the closing words of her memoir, and the knowledge of the man who helped her father become *her father* does not erase the bond she had with him. Shapiro offers an example of why nonanonymous sperm donation is so emotionally important for many donor-conceived people. It provides closure, an understanding of herself, and, if anything, deepens her love and respect for her father. Learning she was donor conceived and establishing a relationship with her donor helps her create a narrative about herself that makes sense and feels cohesive—as cohesive as the stories we tell about ourselves can be.

Recent legislation in Colorado will require all sperm and egg banks to keep up-to-date donor records and to ban anonymous sperm and gamete donation starting on January 1, 2025. This push follows similar legislation in Australia and the UK and is in part the result of activism organized by donor-conceived people. There are many active social media groups of donor-conceived people expressing outrage, disappointment, and frustration because knowledge about their genetic ancestry has been denied them.[5] Despite the success in Colorado, it has been difficult to pass similar laws in other states because sperm and egg donation is such a booming business, and there is concern that banning anonymous donations will kill or severely curtail the industry. In recent years, the American Society for Reproductive Medicine

(ASRM) has acknowledged that over-the-counter DNA testing will soon make promises of donor anonymity difficult to keep; still, they have not taken a position on banning anonymous—or what they now call "nonidentified"—donors. (See Rebecca O'Connor's essay in this volume for a discussion of the ASRM's current efforts regarding donor anonymity, and their more recent willingness to reconsider their historical positions [Ethics and Practice Committees 2022].)

A short Viewpoint essay in the *Journal of the American Medical Association* (*JAMA*) published shortly after the Colorado legislation passed reflects on the repercussions of the law, which also mandates that donors update their contact information every three years and forbids fertility clinics from using gametes not originating in Colorado (Cohen, Adashi, and Mohapatra 2022). The three authors of the essay, two law professors and a physician, note that some of these clauses may be challenged in court because they reflect such a departure from mainstream US fertility clinics' practices. They also advise physicians and families caring for donor-conceived children to be prepared to handle the questions and concerns that may arise for donor-conceived children in Colorado once this law is enacted.

While the questions raised by this Viewpoint essay are important, I am more interested in the comments this essay generated in response. There are four published comments, and the first two write against nonanonymous gamete donation. The first comment from a physician argues that there are only downsides to nonanonymous gamete donation because it might mean "some person (a biological child) wants to come into donors' lives" and that the "unintended outcome will be that very few people will be sperm or ova donors" (Hoskinson 2022). The dismissal here of the rights of biological offspring ("some person") is noteworthy, but the commenter's concern that the number of people willing to sell sperm or ova will drop is wrong if US trends follow those in the UK. If anything, the number of people willing to sell their sperm and egg *rose* in the UK after anonymous donor conception was banned (Day 2007). Still, it is a widespread belief and concern, as both commenters against open gamete selling share it, and it is the argument most used against banning anonymous gamete donation.

Despite the American fertility industry's attempts to protect donors' identity and promise lifelong anonymity, over-the-counter DNA tests are only becoming more accessible and popular, making it is questionable whether anonymous gamete donation is even possible. Even if a donor does not take a commercial DNA test, a sibling, child, or other close relative might do so and therefore unintentionally reveal the donor's identity. As the therapist writing the second comment against selling anonymous gametes in *JAMA* notes, "If someone helping to create a human with their DNA is not willing to feel some responsibility to at least have their identity revealed to those humans at a later date, they absolutely should not provide their gametes" (LieberWilkins 2022, 971). She compares the selling of human gametes to the history of domestic adoptions. In the United States, closed domestic adoptions became an anomaly fifty years ago because of the importance of knowing one's medical, genetic, and social histories. While gamete selling is different because there is more intentionality and no accidental pregnancy, the underlying argument is the same: children born under these circumstances must have their needs centered so they can access medical and genetic histories, if they wish (LieberWilkins 2022).

I want to note that just as not all adopted children want to know or make contact with their biological parents, not all children born through gamete donation will want to know their biological origins. However, changes in laws and practices give access to this information for those who want to know. Even if it were a small percentage, which according to surveys done by donor-conceived people it is not,[6] giving people who want to know this access is a human right.

If banning anonymous gamete selling likely will not impact the industry, and if there is growing widespread consensus that knowing about your biological origins is critical to donor-conceived people's mental health (as studies of adopted people show), then why has the US fertility industry been so slow to change its practices? Why have more states not followed Colorado's footsteps? In the United States, fertility clinics are profit-motivated, and any change that might upend their business model or that risks cutting into their profit will be viewed as threatening. And while a decline in the number of gamete donors might impact would-be parents, this possibility does not seem like reason enough to outlaw the practice of anonymous donation. I want to return again to the question of narrative because I think the stories we have told about sperm donations since the early twentieth century underlie American anxieties about nonanonymous gamete donations.

Telling New Stories about Making a Family

As long as we allow for anonymous sperm donation (or sale) and prevent donor-conceived children from accessing records about their donors, heterosexual couples can uphold a narrative about the normativity of their families. This secrecy allows two-parent families to maintain a story that fits into a norm about what a family should be and suspend the knowledge that technology mediated the creation of that family. Because ultimately, as much as assisted reproductive technologies like in vitro fertilization and insemination have become normalized in many cases, there is still inherent shame in admitting when pregnancies need a third party, and especially a sperm donor, to make a family.

While it is increasingly queer couples and single people who are turning to gamete donations, there are other factors that might motivate secrecy, even if it is not in the best interest of the child. While shame may play less of a role in the decision to keep the identity of donors secret in queer or single-parent families because the technological mediation is often (but not always!) more apparent, fear can be a powerful motivator in these cases for many of the reasons outlined in Courtney G. Joslin, Katherine L. Kraschel, and Doug NeJaime's essay in this volume. Ry Russo-Young's 2021 HBO documentary, *Nuclear Family*, about the multiple lawsuits her mothers were involved in to prevent her donor from obtaining visitation rights is a prime example of how fear can motivate secrecy. Russo-Young was conceived in an era when queer women were often banned from using sperm from fertility clinics, and so her mothers knew the identity of their donor—as did Russo-Young. However, when the donor decided he wanted to be more involved in Russo-Young's life than her mothers intended, they fought hard to maintain the illusion that they were always a nuclear, two-parent family—as the title of the documentary implies. While Russo-Young had a good childhood, she mourns the fact that her mothers prevented her from having a relationship with the man who helped conceive her. In the end, because her mothers decided to privilege their nuclear family above all else—because of fear, perhaps because of shame too—Russo-Young feels a sense of loss because she did not have the opportunity to get to know the man involved in her conception, especially since he wanted a relationship with her. The loss she feels because her mothers kept her from knowing her donor is ultimately the story she shares in the ironically titled *Nuclear Family*.

There is a narrative history extending to the early twentieth century that demonstrates how the stories we have told about male infertility and sperm donation have been used to uphold the normative, patriarchal, and eugenic American family. Insisting on the necessity of anonymous sperm donation has consistently been part of this narrative. The secrecy surrounding sperm donations has privileged fertility clinics and physicians most of all; it has created a thriving and growing fertility industry in the United States. However, the needs and desires of donor-conceived children have not mattered much at all in the hundred-plus year history of this industry. There are thousands of people who will never learn much about their genetic makeup or background. Unlike Lewis, I believe genetics and genetic connection can matter. And most importantly, perhaps if we address this matter head on, it can finally help us begin to untangle the eugenic and patriarchal underpinnings of the American nuclear family to show there are many ways to make a family.[7]

NOTES

1 People who sell their sperm and eggs are typically called "donors," even though money is almost always exchanged when anonymity and a gamete bank is involved. I will use the terms *donors* and *sellers* interchangeably throughout this essay and will employ the language of "donation" because it is more familiar to most readers and for the sake of clarity.

2 The film was also released under the names *Blessed Are They*, *Sins of Love*, and *The Pill*.

3 I define "masculinity" in this essay as "the naturalized relation between maleness and power," following Jack Halberstam in *Female Masculinity* (1998, 2). Masculinity and patriarchy are closely related terms, which Halberstam links together as well, because they both intend to reify social power traditionally given to men (often white, but not always) and because they are systems built on inheritance and social privilege. In this essay, I often use the terms *patriarchy* and *masculinity* interchangeably.

4 For more of the history about sperm donation, its regulations, and advice given to patients, see Edward T. Tyler's "Artificial Insemination" (1961) and Diane

Tober's *Romancing the Sperm: Shifting Biopolitics and the Making of Modern Families* (2019). Tober focuses on sperm donation beginning in the 1990s when advice about whether to tell children they were donor conceived began to change, especially as more single and queer women began using donor sperm to conceive children.

5   See, for example, the We Are Donor Conceived website and Facebook group of the same name.

6   According to a 2020 survey by the organization We Are Donor Conceived, 94 percent of donor-conceived people would like access to information about the number of donor siblings they have, 99 percent want access to the medical history of their donor, and 94 percent would like to know the identity of their donor. For the full results, see "2020 We Are Donor Conceived Survey Report," September 17, 2020, www.wearedonorconceived.com.

7   Alyssa M. Newman's essay in this volume also asks why Black men are not donating in larger numbers to sperm banks. Perhaps one answer to this question also lies in understanding how the fertility industry and sperm banks are implicated in the history of eugenics in this country.

REFERENCES

"13 Babies in N.Y. have Test Tube as Father." *Chicago Daily Tribune*, May 1, 1934.

"Baby Production Line." *Daily News*, September 12, 1943.

Charon, Rita. 2001. "Narrative Medicine: A Model for Empathy, Reflection, Profession, and Trust." *JAMA* 286 (15): 1,897–902. https://doi.org/10.1001/jama.286.15.1897.

Cohen, I. Glenn, Eli Y. Adashi, Seema Mohapatra. 2022. "The End of Anonymous Sperm Donation in Colorado." *JAMA* 328 (19): 1,903–4. https://doi.org/10.1001/jama.2022.19471.

Connell, W. Merle, dir. 1948. *Test Tube Babies*. Screen Classic, produced by George Weiss, released April 9, 1948.

Day, Michael. 2007. "Number of Sperm Donors Rises Despite Removal of Anonymity in UK." *BMJ* 334 (7601): 971. https://doi.org/10.1136%2Fbmj.39206.514132.DB.

Ethics and Practice Committees of the American Society for Reproductive Medicine 2022. "Updated Terminology for Gamete and Embryo Donors: Directed (Identified) to Replace 'Known' and Nonidentified to Replace 'Anonymous': A Committee Opinion." *Fertility and Sterility* 181 (1): 75–78. https://doi.org/10.1016/j.fertnstert.2022.02.032.

Halberstam, Jack. 1998. *Female Masculinity*. Durham, NC: Duke University Press.

Hoskinson, Mark. 2022. "'Outing' Sperm Donors?" Comment on "The End of Anonymous Sperm Donation in Colorado: A Step Forward to a New Fertility Future in the US?" by I. Glenn Cohen, Eli Y. Adashi, Seema Mohapatra, *JAMA* 328 (19): 1903–4. October 25, 2022. https://jamanetwork.com.

"Laboratory Twins Born." 1934. *Boston Globe*, April 30, 1934.

Lewis, Sophie. 2019. *Full Surrogacy Now*. New York: Verso.

Lewis, Sophie. 2022. *Abolish the Family*. New York: Verso.

LieberWilkins, Carole. 2022. "When We Know Better We Should Do Better." Comment on "The End of Anonymous Sperm Donation in Colorado: A Step Forward to a New Fertility Future in the US?" by I. Glenn Cohen, Eli Y. Adashi, Seema Mohapatra, *JAMA* 328 (19): 1903–4. https://jamanetwork.com/journals/jama/article-abstract/2797964.

Russo-Young, Ry, dir. 2021. *Nuclear Family*. HBO.

Shapiro, Dani. 2019. *Inheritance: A Memoir of Genealogy, Paternity, and Love*. New York: Knopf.

"Substitute Fathers." 1943. *Newsweek*, September 13, 1943.

Tober, Diane. 2019. *Romancing the Sperm: Shifting Biopolitics and the Making of Modern Families*. New Brunswick, NJ: Rutgers University Press.

Tyler, Edward T. 1961. "Artificial Insemination." In *Sterility: Office Management of the Infertile Couple* , edited by Edward T. Tyler. New York: McGraw-Hill.

22

Technoscientific Reproduction, Queer Sperm, and the Politics of Masculinity

MEREDITH P. FIELD

In *Exposing Men: The Science and Politics of Male Reproduction*, Cynthia Daniels (2006, chap. 6) argues that sperm and masculinity are deeply entwined within "Western" cultural scripts of heteronormative reproduction. Sperm are *the* symbol of Western hegemonic masculinity because they enable the essential masculine trait of virility, which implies the ability to reproduce. In Daniels's words, "The ability to biologically father one's children remains the hallmark of one's manhood" (2006, 161). Sperm are characterized as strong, hardy conquerors of the weak and submissive egg (Daniels 2006; Martin 1991). Accordingly, the Western patriarchal gender binary system constructs a duality that values the "strength" of masculinity over the "weakness" of femininity.

Despite the narrowness of these constructions of strength and weakness, a main social consequence of the association is the derogatory labeling of men who demonstrate qualities the binary system defines as *feminine*, such as vulnerability or dependence, as *effeminate*. As Daniels says, such female traits displayed by a man are culturally understood as "an image of the end of manhood, the antithesis of masculinity" (2006, 158). There is a substantial body of work that explores the cultural association between male homosexuality and the effeminate (Kittiwut 2002; Sánchez and Vilain 2012; Zuger 1984). A complementary body of work elucidates the ties between homosexuality and the use of the term *queer* to describe homosexual males.

In *Queer Theory: An Introduction* (1997), Annamarie Jagose writes that the word *queer* once had two primary uses: as a slang word to describe males engaging in homosexual behavior and as a homophobic insult. Those who were once the target of its derogatory use reclaimed it during the late twentieth century, and its applications have since expanded to describe "a coalition of culturally marginal sexual self-identifications" (1). It is this usage, which alludes to subverting sexual norms, that I apply in combination with the broader use of queer to mean anything outside of "normal" or anything strange.

Biologically speaking, sperm are tiny masses of protein surrounded by seminal fluid packed with potential energy in the form of fructose. The chemical package that makes up semen, and the broader context in which semen occurs in cis male bodies, informs the cultural narrative that roots hegemonic masculinity in virility. That narrative tells us that during ejaculation, pressure builds up in the prostatic urethra before semen is launched out of the penis, in an effort to move the sperm toward the uterus of a fertile female (Levin 2005). Upon release, the virile sperm, characterized as powerful and predictable, drive forward with a single focus of finding a human egg to dominate through fertilization. Once fertilization is achieved, the heroic sperm have completed their mission, and the presumed result is human reproduction.

The masculine institutions of Western science and medicine have gone to great lengths to support men in their pursuit of (sustained) virility throughout their lives—no doubt, in part, due to the connection between socially constructed masculinity and virility. One of the ways in which this occurs is through assisted reproductive technologies (ART), which collect, manipulate, store, and relocate sperm to help them achieve the goal of fertilization—and, ultimately, reproduction. But there's a cold irony to ART. The material practices that assist sperm in the fertilization process, both materially and symbolically, move it toward the "effeminate" that Daniels describes—weak, vulnerable, needy, and dependent. In this essay, I argue that such effeminization of sperm represents a symbolic queering of sperm, because the material changes to it make it inconsistent with symbolizing a masculinity based in virility. I conclude by contemplating what this queering of sperm means for the politics of Western hegemonic masculinity. I begin by describing a personal experience with what I consider to be attempts at queer reproduction, which provides evidence of the material and symbolic effeminization and, ultimately, queering of sperm.

Negotiating FDA Regulations, Clinic Policies, and the Commodification of Sperm

When my same-sex partner and I pursued attempts to impregnate me, we immediately agreed on two key issues about the process: (1) we would allow as little medical intervention as possible and (2) we would use a known sperm donor. We naively believed that both decisions would simplify the logistics of the process and decrease the stress on my body.

We came to an agreement with the donor and planned to visit him for fresh samples each month. But this presented a challenge for us because he lived seven hundred miles away. No problem, we thought, he lives in a city with a big medical university and a reputable sperm bank that we could hire to receive his samples, store them, and ship them to us when we wanted them. But we were wrong.

We soon learned that once sperm enters into the medical system, it becomes a product, subject to Food and Drug Administration (FDA) regulations. More specifically, semen submitted to any "place of business under one management, at one general physical location" becomes a "manufacture[d] . . . human cells, tissues, and cellular and tissue-based product" (HTC/Ps) (US Code of Federal Regulations 2023). My partner and I were told that semen could not be transferred to a private individual unless that individual was under the care of a physician. After a long discussion with the clinic director, it was still unclear whether that rule was a clinic policy or if it was the result of FDA regulation.[1] Furthermore, the originating sperm bank would only ship the sperm to another sperm bank with which it had an existing contract. I called a large regional sperm banking company in our state and asked if they would work with the originating sperm bank. They declined. If the sperm could not be shipped to us, maybe we could get our donor to make a deposit at another sperm bank in the state adjacent to ours when he next visited his parents. That would put the sperm within a three-hour drive from our town. I called the new sperm bank and asked. They agreed.

But our desire to avoid medical intervention presented a new problem. The second sperm bank would not allow the sperm to leave the clinic unless it had been placed in another human body. They would work with us only if I agreed to intrauterine insemination. I declined. This commodification of sperm is just one way that sperm loses its symbolic power. Once it is separated from its cis male body, it is separated from the masculine narrative that it defines. Under the purview of the state and medical institutions, sperm is disempowered and dependent on the policies and procedures that determine its fate.

We were not deterred. We discovered we could get a direct flight to our donor's city and be there in just a few hours. Unfortunately, I contracted COVID on the first trip. I was ill for almost eight weeks, and my menstrual cycle was irregular for the next three months. During those months of waiting, my partner and I agreed that it would be incredibly stressful for us to continue making monthly trips during the academic year (she was in law school, and I am a full-time professor). We could travel to the donor during the summer months, but we needed an alternative plan for getting samples once the fall semester began.

A Personal Observation of Technoscientific Reproduction's Assault on Sperm

My partner identified a commercial service, which promised to help men test their sperm quality, improve their fertility, and preserve their sperm for future use. The company would send a collection kit to our donor. He had three days to use the kit. During that time, he would collect a sperm sample and ship it, overnight, to the company. Once it arrived at the company, they would test it for sperm count, volume, motility, and morphology. Then they would "wash" and freeze it in multiple vials. Our donor received a full report about every sample he deposited, and he sent us screenshots of the reports—complete with easy-to-read charts and graphs. We could request up to three vials to be delivered to a doctor, midwife, or doula of our choice, at least seven days in advance of when we needed it. We, and our donor, signed up for the service and began, unknowingly, to participate in the process of queering sperm.

We learned that, once our donor collected a sperm sample, he added it to a container that held a test yolk buffer to stabilize and preserve the semen until it reached the sperm bank lab the next day (Lange and Bormann 2017). The queering of the sperm had already begun through effeminization; no longer in its cis male body, the weakened sperm had to rely on technoscientific solutions to survive the sperm donation process. Research shows that sperm die at a rate of 5–10 percent per hour outside the human body (Cheng et al. 2022). This rate can be improved with the aid of a special medium. Consequently, once removed from its bodily source of ejaculatory power and safety (consistent temperature, pH, etc. of the human body) when the sample was collected, the sperm needed artificial stabilization to survive until it reached the lab. Once it arrived at the lab, it was tested. Then it was "washed" of seminal fluids, thus robbing it of the energy that typically sustains it during its journey to the egg. It needed an artificial force to sustain it as it was manipulated further. A semen extender was applied before the sperm was frozen, to "stabilize its properties" and extend its life during the preservation process (Bustani and Baiee 2021). Once we requested a vial of the sperm, it was shipped overnight, to our doula, in a cryotank, and we thawed it when we were ready to use it, within seventy-two hours of receiving it. We were told that, by the time it reached us, up to 75 percent of it could be dead, immotile, or morphologically damaged. This process significantly reduced the sperm's value as a symbol of hegemonic masculinity. Rather than representing power and sexuality, the process and associated regulations transformed it into a dependent, fragile commodity, slowly dying in transit.

Even in our attempts to minimize technoscientific intervention in the reproductive process, our donor's sperm had been effectively effeminized through the reduction of its strength, hardiness, and ability to conquer—major characteristics of Western hegemonic masculinity. Our donor's sperm was materially disempowered through the technoscientific reproductive process. Symbolically, his virility, and, by extension, his masculinity were weakened too (Dolan et al. 2017). This material and symbolic weakening of sperm effectively effeminizes and queers it, as it is no longer able to perform its functions associated with the hegemonic masculine and it instead takes on characteristics associated with the devalued feminine.

Queer Sperm and Implications for Masculinity

Combining social scientific approaches to sperm as a symbol of virility with my personal experiences trying to acquire sperm for self-insemination, I argue that technoscientific reproduction, both materially and symbolically, queers sperm through effeminization that results from its processing and handling.

So what does this argument mean for the politics of masculinity? Before I answer that question, I want to position myself as a cis queer woman who does not have, and has never had, the capability to produce sperm. Furthermore, I view my masculinity as a relatively small part of my overall gender identity and presentation. This positionality informs my experience with, and analysis of, the technoscientific treatment of sperm and the meaning I attach to the queering of sperm. In the concluding paragraphs, I will attempt to remain conscious of, and articulate, the ways that I see my positionality affecting my work in this project.

Patriarchy, the social system that upholds the gender binary, sexism, and cis heterosexual norms, is deeply invested in maintaining the current form of hegemonic masculinity, which is tied to virility (Connell 1987; Schilt and Westbrook 2009). Consequently, arguing that sperm is being queered is likely to be met with broad hostility and rejection—especially from those individuals and institutions that are explicitly and implicitly committed to protecting the patriarchy but also from anyone with internalized sexism or homophobia (or both), regardless of their situatedness. My argument that sperm is being queered represents a threat to the patriarchy both because it highlights the modification and displacement of an essential masculine symbol and because it applies a label (queer) that has been, and is, used to other those who reject one or more aspects of the patriarchy.

However, for me, a person who embraces the identity of queerness in relation to my sexuality and who experiences it as both empowering and expansive for my gender identity too, the idea of queering sperm, the very symbol of the current form of hegemonic masculinity, is exciting. I wonder what possibilities it might create for a more socially just and inclusive understanding of gender, sexuality, and reproduction. For example, could the subversive reclaiming of the term *queer* be a model for reclaiming sperm by redefining what it symbolizes? Janelle Lamoreaux's essay in this volume, "Sperm as Sentinel," offers us one starting place for a new symbolic framing of sperm. Could the concept of queer sperm open more space for a multitude of masculinities that continue to be marginalized? And might the queering of sperm help deprivilege heteronormative reproduction?

NOTE

1 The interpretation of FDA regulations can be modified based on federal court rulings. At the time of this writing, ART-related companies are awaiting a decision from the US Court of Appeals for the 9th Circuit regarding business carried out at a stem cell clinic in California. If the lower court's ruling were upheld, it would go against key precedent and it could create more uncertainty about the regulation of HTC/Ps. See Oyster, Weinman, and Laroche 2022.

REFERENCES

Bustani, Ghadeer Sabah, and Falah Hasan Baiee. 2021. "Semen Extenders: An Evaluative Overview of Preservative Mechanisms of Semen and Semen Extenders." *Vet World* 14 (5): 1220–33. https://doi.org/10.14202/vetworld.2021.1220-1233.

Cheng, Qingyuan, Liman Li, Min Jiang, Bo Liu, Yang Xian, Shasha Liu, Xiao Liu, Wenrui Zhao, and Fuping Li. 2022. "Extend the Survival of Human Sperm In Vitro in Non-Freezing Conditions: Damage Mechanisms, Preservation Technologies, and Clinical Applications." *Cells* 11 (18): 2845. https://doi.org/10.3390/cells11182845.

Connell, Raewyn. 1987. *Gender and Power: Society, the Person and Sexual Politics*. Stanford, CA: Stanford Univeristy Press.

Daniels, Cynthia. 2006. *Exposing Men: The Science and Politics of Male Reproduction*. Oxford: Oxford University Press.

Dolan, Alan, Tim Lomas, Tarek Ghobara, and Geraldine Hartshorne. 2017. "'It's Like Taking a Bit of Masculinity Away From You': Towards a Theoretical Understanding of Men's Experiences of Infertility." *Sociology of Health and Illness* 39 (6): 878–92. https://doi.org/10.1111/1467-9566.12548.

Jagose, Annamarie. 1997. *Queer Theory: An Introduction*. New York: New York University Press.

Kittiwut, Jod Taywaditep. 2002. "Marginalization Among the Marginalized." *Journal of Homosexuality* 42 (1): 1–28. https://doi.org/10.1300/J082v42n01_01.

Lange, Allison, and Charles L. Bormann. 2017. "Utilization of a Test Yolk Buffer Solution to Maintain the Integrity of Semen Samples for an Extended Period of Time." Supplement, *Fertility and Sterility* 107 (S3): e27.

Levin, Roy J. 2005. "The Mechanisms of Human Ejaculation—A Critical Analysis." *Sexual and Relationship Therapy* 20 (1): 123–31. https://doi.org/10.1080/14681990500037212.

Mamo, Laura. 2007. *Queering Reproduction: Achieving Pregnancy in the Age of Technoscience*. Durham, NC: Duke University Press.

Martin, Emily. 1991. "The Egg and the Sperm: How Science Has Constructed a Romance Based on Stereotypical Male-Female Roles." *Signs* 16 (3): 485–501.

Oyster, Joshua, Beth P. Weinman, and Austin D. Laroche. 2022. "Ninth Circuit Appeal May Significantly Affect FDA's Authority to Regulate Stem Cell Clinics." *Ropes & Gray*, December 9, 2022. www.ropesgray.com.

Sánchez, Francisco J., and Eric Vilain. 2012. "'Straight-Acting Gays': The Relationship Between Masculine Consciousness, Anti-Effeminacy, and Negative Gay Identity." *Archives of Sexual Behavior* 41:111–19. https://doi.org/10.1007/s10508-012-9912-z.

Schilt, Kristen, and Laurel Westbrook. 2009. "Doing Gender, Doing Heteronormativity: 'Gender Normals,' Transgender People, and the Social Maintenance of Heterosexuality." *Gender and Society* 23 (4): 440–64. https://doi.org/10.1177/0891243209340034.

US Code of Federal Regulations. 2023. "Title 21. Food and Drugs. Ch. 1. Food and Drug Administration. Department of Health and Human Services. Part 1271. Human Cells, Tissues, and Cellular and Tissue-Based Products. 21 CFR 1271.3. How does FDA define important terms in this part?" Washington, DC: GPO. https://www.accessdata.fda.gov/scripts/cdrh/cfdocs/cfcfr/cfrsearch.cfm?fr=1271.3

Zuger, Bernard. 1984. "Early Effeminate Behavior in Boys: Outcome and Significance for Homosexuality." *Journal of Nervous and Mental Disease* 172 (2): 90–97. https://doi.org/10.1097/00005053-198402000-00005.

23

Too Much or Not Enough? Genetic Testing of Sperm Donors

MICHELLE J. BAYEFSKY

Much has changed since the era of medical students dropping off sperm samples for artificial insemination. No longer can sperm be introduced, untested, directly into a patient's body. While initial testing focused on preventing transmission of infectious diseases like HIV and gonorrhea, more recent testing of sperm donors also aims to limit transmission of genetic diseases. The American Society for Reproductive Medicine (ASRM) recommends testing gamete donors for a handful of recessive disorders, such as cystic fibrosis and spinal muscular atrophy (Practice Committee of the ASRM and Practice Committee for the Society for Assisted Reproductive Technology 2021). But in the United States and other places where private egg and sperm banks compete for clientele, donors are asked to undergo increasingly comprehensive genetic testing. These tests include karyotypes, which evaluate chromosomal abnormalities, and expanded carrier testing, which check for an array of recessive conditions (Sims et al. 2010; Payne, Skytte, and Harper 2021).

To some, requiring donors to undergo extensive genetic testing is a step too far (Pennings 2020). If members of the general population do not typically perform this kind of testing, why should sperm donors? To others, donor genetic testing has not gone far enough. Why test for recessive conditions but not dominant ones, which are far more likely to cause disease in offspring? And what about polygenic risk scoring, which rates how likely a person is to develop conditions influenced by multiple genes? As the landscape of genetic testing continues to evolve, so too will the testing of sperm donors. This think piece analyzes the current paradigm for genetic testing of sperm donors and presents a more balanced and deliberate alternative.

Although sperm donors do not make up a large proportion of the US population, the question of how much testing they should undergo touches on issues that are central to the infertility industry and our society at large. When it comes to selecting a sperm donor, recipients may feel more like customers purchasing a product (human genetic material), rather than patients trying to obtain the missing puzzle piece to starting a family. In this setting, the donor-recipient relationship is asymmetric, and sperm donors are often asked to undergo more testing than is required of sperm recipients. Moreover, patients with greater financial resources can purchase sperm from the most reputable and selective sperm banks, exacerbating inequalities in access, which have become increasingly stark in the wake of the COVID-19 pandemic due to a decrease in donor supply (Bowles 2021). As Alyssa M. Newman's essay in this volume emphasizes, there is a particular shortage of Black sperm donors, which adds another challenge for Black women seeking well-vetted Black donors through traditional sperm banks.

Another questionable dynamic relates to the selection of sperm donors themselves. To choose a donor, recipients scroll through dozens of profiles, with the implicit or explicit goal of obtaining the "best" sperm. While on an individual level, it is understandable for a recipient to seek a donor with favorable traits, the sperm industry as a whole has been critiqued for incorporating eugenic thinking by promoting the notion that the "fittest" genetic partners are the most handsome, intelligent, and masculine donors (Daniels and Golden 2004). More advanced genetic testing adds an additional dimension in which some donors can be considered "better" or "worse" than others.

When considering what genetic testing sperm donors should undergo, the broader context of reproductive genetic testing must also be addressed. How much genetic testing should the general public perform, and should we, as a society, make a greater effort to prevent genetic disease in future offspring? While preventing disease and disability may seem like a laudable goal, disability scholars raise important concerns about the impact that genetic selection can have on people living with the conditions that are selected against. For example, Erik Parens and Adrienne Asch (2003) argue that using genetic testing to decrease the rate of disease and disability signals a negative attitude toward those with disabilities and an "intolerance of diversity."

The dilemma of how much genetic testing American sperm donors should undergo is a product of our specific political and economic approach to health care. Market forces prevail because there are no public sperm banks in the United States, only private companies, university-affiliated practices, and a small number of nonprofit banks. Federal regulation of the sperm donation process is relatively minimal, beyond laboratory standards, a medical history, physical exam, and requirements to screen for infectious diseases. Recommendations for preconception genetic testing in the general population come from medical professional societies (Committee on Genetics 2017), rather than a governmental body representing a national health care system, which means those recommendations are optional for physicians.

It is possible to envisage a very different model in which there is a single-payer health care system with a standard approach to genetic testing of future parents, regardless of their mode of conception. While some may decline recommended screening for genetic diseases, it is likely that most people would make use of the "default" level of genetic testing (Dusic et al. 2022), especially if covered by insurance, either before or in the early stages of pregnancy. Public sperm banks would have donors undergo the same level of testing recommended for society more broadly. The goal—rather than ensuring that sperm recipients can access the highest "quality" donors—would be to reduce the risk of transmitting genetic disease to the next generation, for the sake of public health. With this goal in mind, it would be reasonable to require sperm recipients to undergo the same testing as sperm donors (and recommended to the whole population), since testing only one genetic partner would be insufficient to achieve this goal. Alternatively, if the concern was too great that the national health care system was pressuring donors and recipients to undergo genetic testing, testing could be forgone for both parties.

In this kind of system, there would be controversy about which diseases qualify for the list of recommended genetic screening tests and understandable concerns about eugenics. For example, some would support testing for a genetic predisposition toward schizophrenia and others would argue that society should be more accepting of people with mental health disease and not seek to limit the birth of people with schizophrenia. There is good reason to be suspicious of any governmental role in decisions about who should or should not be born. Historically, the eugenic movement, when backed by governments, resulted in forced sterilization and, in Nazi Germany, the outright murder of people who did not fit the government's definition of "genetically good" and "normal." But perhaps there may be a sensitive and inclusive way to decide which conditions merit screening. For example, there could be a public process for deciding which diseases to include, incorporating feedback from communities living with the conditions in question.

Of course, it is difficult to imagine such a model functioning in the United States, at present. The United States does not have a single-payer health care system, and in a highly polarized political climate, it may be politically difficult to reach agreement on which diseases should be included in a standard screening panel. Nonetheless, it is worthwhile to reflect on what a unified approach to genetic testing of sperm donors might look like. That is, an approach with a guiding philosophy that helps to minimize asymmetries and inconsistencies. Other possible guiding principles could focus on maximizing the well-being of future offspring or maintaining genetic diversity within our population. How much genetic testing of sperm donors should be performed would vary by approach. For example, if the primary guiding principle was to maintain genetic diversity, perhaps testing would only be performed for the most severe genetic conditions that cause death in infancy. Without such a guiding philosophy, donors will continue to be tested in an illogical manner: more than the rest of the population, for very rare conditions, and for recessive conditions that only manifest if recipients—who may choose not undergo testing—carry the same mutations.

REFERENCES

Bowles, Nellie. 2021. "The Sperm Kings Have a Problem: Too Much Demand." *New York Times*, January 8, 2023.

Committee on Genetics, American College of Obstetricians and Gynecologists. 2017 "Committee Opinion 691: Carrier Screening for Genetic Conditions." *Obstetrics & Gynecology* 129 (3): e41–55. https://doi.org/10.1097/aog.0000000000001952.

Daniels, Cynthia, Janet Golden. 2004. "Procreative Compounds: Popular Eugenics, Artificial Insemination and the Rise of the American Sperm Banking Industry." *Journal of Social History* 38 (1): 5–27. https://doi.org/10.1353/jsh.2004.0081.

Dusic, E. J., Tesla Theoryn, Catherine Wang, Elizabeth Swisher, Deborah Bowen. 2022. "Barriers, Interventions, and Recommendations: Improving the Genetic Testing Landscape." *Frontiers in Digital Health* 4:961128. https://doi.org/10.3389/fdgth.2022.961128.

Parens, Erik, and Adrienne Asch. 2003. "Disability Rights Critique of Prenatal Genetic Testing: Reflections and Recommendations." *Mental Retardation and Developmental Disabilities Research Reviews* 9 (1): 40–47. https://doi.org/10.1002/mrdd.10056.

Payne, Molly, Anne-Bine Skytte, and Joyce Harper. 2021. "The Use of Expanded Carrier Screening of Gamete Donors." *Human Reproduction* 36 (6): 1702–10. https://doi.org/10.1093/humrep/deab067.

Pennings, Guido. 2020. "Expanded carrier screening should not be mandatory for gamete donors." *Human Reproduction* 35 (6): 1256–61. https://doi.org/10.1093/humrep/deaa088.

Practice Committee of the American Society for Reproductive Medicine and Practice Committee for the Society for Assisted Reproductive Technology. 2021. "Guidance regarding gamete and embryo donation." *Fertility and Sterility* 115 (6): 1395–410. https://doi.org/10.1016/j.fertnstert.2021.01.045.

Sims, Charles, Pamela Callum, Marilyn Ray, Jennifer Iger, and Rena Falk. 2010. "Genetic Testing of Sperm Donors: Survey of Current Practices." *Fertility and Sterility* 94 (1): 126–29. https://doi.org/10.1016/j.fertnstert.2009.01.139.

24

Developing a Reproductive Justice Approach to Regulating Formal and Informal Sperm Donation

NAOMI CAHN AND SONIA M. SUTER

The Supreme Court's opinion in *Dobbs v. Jackson Women's Health Organization* presents fundamental threats to reproductive autonomy in the United States, particularly for communities that already face inequity in accessing health care. In reaffirming *Roe v. Wade*, the Supreme Court's 1992 opinion in *Planned Parenthood of Southeastern Pennsylvania v. Casey* situated the right to abortion within the freedom to make "intimate and personal choices" that are "central to personal dignity and autonomy" (505 U.S. 833, 851). But *Dobbs* was entirely dismissive of this line of reasoning, which has implications for assisted reproductive technology (ART) as a form of procreation. In the wake of *Dobbs*, both states and Congress have considered restrictions of, and protections for, ART. Colorado, for example, enacted groundbreaking legislation that recognizes the rights and interests of donor-conceived people (Protections for Donor Conceived People and Families 2022). Congress has considered legislation that would protect access to fertility treatment (Pecorin 2024). And there has been a great deal of attention to potential laws that might prohibit discarding extra embryos or limit how many can be created in the first place (Tracy 2022), a limitation comparable to abortion bans.

At the same time, there are also fears that reproductive rights advocates will become splintered by class and race, with wealthy white people concerned primarily about ART, while the reproductive justice movement focuses on broader issues of reproductive health and "the ability and rights of women to have or not have children, and to parent their children with dignity" (SisterSong n.d.). Consider, for example, that former vice president Mike Pence, a staunch antiabortion advocate, and his wife used assisted reproductive technology (Owens and González 2022).

Less attention has been given to issues of accessibility and the cost of ART; this too is a reproductive justice issue that shows class and race disparities. In this essay, we focus on sperm donation, which raises issues concerning parentage, access, and reproductive justice. We explore the relationship between formal sperm markets, where fertility clinics or sperm banks process and sell sperm and are loosely regulated by the Food and Drug Administration (FDA), and informal sperm markets, where recipients access sperm in more casual settings. This exploration highlights inequities in access to reproductive care and also shows concerns about regulation in the sphere of ART. While we advocate for additional regulations in the formal market, we are cognizant that certain regulations may push people toward the informal market. As we detail in this essay, the actors and incentives in the formal and informal markets are different, and therefore the appropriate role of the law with respect to each market should reflect those differences.

As a preliminary matter, we note that sperm presents distinct issues for reproductive equity for several reasons. First, collecting sperm is a relatively noninvasive procedure that typically does not require medical intervention. Consequently, sperm donation can more easily evade regulation because it can occur outside of medical clinics. Second, although we recognize that an underground market can exist for eggs, like the "open secret" of organ donation (Goodwin 2006, 11), so far, there are few signs of such a market in eggs, one component of the possibly gendered tone to this think piece. Third, and correspondingly, we recognize that it is not just people who identify as cis men who can donate sperm. This is particularly important, given that the field of masculinity and reproduction has typically focused on "cis- and heteronormativity and the assumed reproductive and sexual normalcy of the heterosexual matrix" (Mohr and Almeling 2020, 168).

The Formal Fertility Market

The formal fertility market consists of all types of legally regulated third-party reproduction, meaning the use of gametes or uteruses from people not intending to parent, as well as any involvement by health care professionals. This is broader than the Centers for Disease Control and Prevention's (CDC's) definition of ART, which includes all techniques involving eggs or embryos and does not include assisted insemination. According to the CDC (2023), 2 percent of babies born each year were conceived via ART, but it is unclear how many more children were born through sperm donation. The consumers of ART include medically infertile couples and socially infertile individuals, that is, those who cannot reproduce without assistance from third parties such as physicians, donors, and or surrogates (Sussman 2019).

The formal market is regulated by both governmental and private actors. The FDA imposes requirements for record keeping and for screening gametes, with a focus on sexually transmitted diseases (Cahn and Suter 2021, 41). Professional organizations issue guidelines, including recommended genetic evaluation of donors, that function as a kind of quasi-regulation (American Society for Reproductive Medicine, 2021).

When it comes to accessing the fertility market, there are disparities across various demographics: those with incomes under $25,000 are half as likely as those with incomes over $100,000 to see "a medical provider because they are unable to become pregnant" (Kelley et al. 2019, 562). For people with disabilities, who face twice the poverty rate of people without disabilities, the cost of infertility treatment can be "out of reach" (Davidson 2021). Black women are almost 40 percent less likely than white women to see a medical provider when they face infertility (Kelley et al. 2019), in part because physicians are less likely to refer them to specialists due to biases, such as "Black women can't be infertile" (McFarling 2020). A minority of states have fertility insurance coverage of IVF (Resolve, n.d.).

Pragmatic Reasons for the Informal Fertility Market

With these barriers to access to fertility care for both physically and socially infertile individuals, many recipients and donors may turn away from formal sperm donation—donation that involves sperm banks or fertility clinics and is regulated by the FDA—to informal do-it-yourself (DIY) sperm donation—donation that might occur, for example, through social media postings or through conversations with a friend. Although the legality of the informal market is unsettled, people are using it for several reasons.

First, it is potentially less expensive to purchase sperm through the informal market; a vial of sperm purchased through sperm banks can easily cost more than $1,000 (Xytex Corporation 2023), while sperm from an acquaintance may well be free. Second, DIY sperm donation expands the types of potential donors, especially those who are underrepresented in sperm banks. Black donors make up less than 2 percent of donors in the largest cryobanks, in part because the screening criteria disproportionately exclude them. As the number of Black women turning to sperm banks increases, there is fierce competition among them for the small supply of sperm from Black donors (Newman, this volume). The number of Hispanic and other nonwhite or non-Asian donors is also strikingly small. In addition, the FDA excludes gay male donors from providing their sperm (Ferguson 2022). Third, recipients who have an interest in developing a relationship with their donor might be drawn to the informal market (Jadva et al. 2018). While there is no formal prohibition on doing so in the formal market, purchasing sperm from an anonymous donor makes it unlikely that there will be a relationship (and intending parent[s] may value the security of legal parentage, with no unwanted donor involvement). Genetic testing might lead the intending parent to the donor, but there is no preexisting agreement or relationship with an anonymous donor, nor any obligation to establish such a relationship.

For any of these reasons, some may choose to find sperm from a good friend, on Craigslist, or even a neighborhood listserv. Consider the Facebook group Sperm Donation USA, a private group with more than twenty-three thousand members. Its public-facing page offers: "If you would like to find a sperm donor without the expensive costs of a sperm bank then join Sperm Donation USA!" (Sperm Donation USA, n.d.). Pollentree.com offers a free-matching service, albeit with a subscription fee (PollenTree, n.d.; Yarrow 2014; Russell 2021).

The informal sperm market may also be desirable to donors. Selling sperm directly gives them control over how many families use their sperm, how many children they help create, and even *which* families obtain their sperm. Donors have expressed the desire to ensure that they donate only to families who will care well for the future children (Sony Podcasts 2022). The DIY market also allows donors to earn more money than they might otherwise with cryobanks functioning as intermediaries; others may wish to avoid screening required by many banks (such as genetic screening) or by the FDA (which screens out gay donors). On the other hand, some donors may be drawn to the informal market for altruistic reasons (Graham, Freeman, and Jadva 2019; Russell 2021), that is, some are willing to truly donate, rather than sell, their sperm (Bowles 2021).

Concerns about Lack of Regulation

At the same time, an unregulated informal market in sperm may also produce harms (Butler 2022). First, the lack of oversight raises problematic health risks. The formal sperm market may not provide full protection against the transmission of genetic disease, but it does protect against sexually transmitted diseases. Some donors will only provide sperm through intercourse (Russell 2021), which creates risks not only of sexually transmitted diseases but also sexual violence. Additionally, there is reason to believe that conception might be less successful in the DIY market, which does not involve sperm analysis to assess donor sperm motility (Russell 2021).

Second, informal markets feed into the illusion that parties are free to structure reproductive arrangements with no state role; in fact, the parties rely on the state not just for legal parentage determinations, but also for health care support. Some state laws may not recognize family formations created through sperm donation outside the medical context, whether sperm is obtained through the formal or informal market. Using known donors and doing so without medical assistance increases the risk that donation does not satisfy laws modeled on prior versions of the Uniform Parentage Act, which prevent donors from having parental rights.

In fact, some courts have ruled that the sperm donor is the legal parent instead of the lesbian partner (Kay 2023; Culhane 2015). That is what happened in early 2023, when an Oklahoma court issued such a ruling despite the fact that the lesbian couple was married *and* that the US Supreme Court has found it unconstitutional to have different rules for married same-sex and heterosexual couples with respect to birth certificates for children conceived through ART (Sosin and Luterman 2023). The birth mother had obtained sperm through the informal donation site Just a Baby (Meyer, Breasette, and Raache 2022). The site "allows you to meet and discuss your needs and wants with potential partners rather than relying on a one-night stand, an anonymous donor or an old friend" (Just a Baby, n.d.). Had the lesbian parents used sperm obtained through the formal market, the donor would have likely been anonymous until the child reached the age of eighteen. The bottom line is that using a known donor can be risky.

Third, the lack of regulation may ignore the interests of donor-conceived people, donors, and recipients, which is a problem in the formal market as well, particularly because economic incentives often shape sperm banks' policies. For example, many donor-conceived people want to be able to learn about the medical history and identity of the donors who led to their conception (Gardner 2022). Many also want to limit the number of times individuals can donate, given that professional guidelines in the United States consider it "acceptable to produce 10,000 offspring per donor" (US Donor Conceived Council 2022), which raises the potential for accidental incest (Cahn 2009). Donors may be receptive to initial outreach by offspring but balk when fifty people reach out to them. Donor sibling groups also may feel challenged and commodified by the numbers of potential members (Hertz 2022; Kramer and Cahn 2013, 191–92), and recipients may want to limit how many "diblings"—half-siblings from the same sperm donor—their children have. Thus, both donors and recipients may be invested in limiting the number of families who use a donor's sperm.

Regulating the Formal and Informal Markets

The law can shape the circumstances in which people obtain gametes and ensure that they maximize their reproductive options. This is especially true for the formal market; the informal market, by design, is harder to regulate directly. In the formal market, the law might step in to insulate against health risks and protect the interests of donor-conceived people. It might influence both markets to promote reproductive justice by creating an environment that enables people to understand the legal and personal implications of how they pursue gamete donations, enabling a wide range of options for pursuing ART and ensuring secure determinations of legal parentage.

With respect to the informal market, we acknowledge the challenges of regulation and emphasize that we do not support banning it outright or criminalizing participation in it. We believe such actions would threaten reproductive justice—and would also be difficult to enforce, although the FDA has attempted to require compliance with its regulations for sperm donation (Abbasi 2013). But we do support regulations intended to address some of the harms of this market and to promote reproductive justice by maximizing the ability of participants to fulfill their parental goals through other means. The informality of the market raises the potential that participants may not realize the underlying risks related to health and legal parentage or the potential lack of enforcement of contracts between the parties.

In this context, the law could address some of those threats by reshaping parentage laws, recognizing and enforcing contracts, and sponsoring public announcements or information to be shared through health care providers and clinics to ensure that participants are aware of the informal market's limitations. We situate these proposals within a reproductive justice framework, which emphasizes attention to how systemic inequality affects reproductive access (Murray 2021, 2053). That framework has "three central tenets: the right to have a child, the right to not have a child, and the right to parent one's children in safe and healthy environments" (Mutcherson 2023). It requires coming to terms with how "existing power structures [can be] used to regulate and surveil" reproduction (quoting Littlejohn, this volume). We recognize that some regulations could be perceived as potentially conflicting with reproductive justice, a point we will address.

Objections to Regulation and Responses

Scholars have raised both pragmatic and jurisprudential concerns about efforts to regulate sperm donation—such as imposing family limits, mandating identity release, or penalizing fertility fraud—particularly in a post-*Dobbs* world. In this section, we describe the objections and provide our responses. We acknowledge that the objections raise significant concerns about regulating the sperm market, both formal and informal. But they also reify the status quo, in which all of these objections are equally salient. Instead, as we discuss below, we believe these objections should guide regulations to ensure reproductive equity for multiple groups, including parents, LGBTQ communities, people of color, and donor-conceived people.

Limiting Supply

A pragmatic concern is that various regulations protecting against donors' misrepresentations about their medical history or mandating identity release could lead to potential shortages of donors. As a starting point, we note that a reproductive justice framework should support policies that do not diminish donor supply generally or with respect to certain groups. But the concerns about regulation limiting supply of donors are complicated. Some regulations, like the FDA's ban on gay men, limit supply and equity by prohibiting the participation of certain groups based on presumptions about their sexual behavior. In contrast, we speculate that family-limit regulations might encourage donors to participate who might otherwise be reluctant to provide sperm if they could not be sure they would not have dozens or hundreds of genetically related offspring. Family limits may be especially important to donors when their identity is accessible to donor-conceived people at the age of majority; the prospect of being contacted by large numbers of genetically related offspring could be daunting.

While some donors may not want to provide sperm—or may charge more—under a mandatory identity-release regime, evidence suggests such regulations may not decrease the supply of donors as some fear. For example, the number of donors increased when anonymity protections were removed in Australia, where payment for sperm is banned (Adams, Ullah, and de Lacey 2016). Moreover, with the ability to identify donors through direct-to-consumer genetic testing, anonymity can no longer be promised. Even so, the ability to be identified does not seem to deter donors (Wodoslawsky et al. 2023).

Reproductive Autonomy

The jurisprudential arguments address reproductive autonomy, the exceptionalization of ART, and genetic essentialism. Regarding reproductive autonomy, donors might want to have the power to decide how many offspring can be produced from their gametes, rather than allowing the sperm banks or the government to do so. Recipient families may also have concerns about regulating sperm donation: they may oppose identity release, may want to ensure an adequate supply of gametes for themselves, may worry that regulation would increase prices and make donor gametes unaffordable, and may fear that regulation in this space is the first step along a slippery slope of limiting their reproductive rights. Because *Dobbs* has significantly limited procreative autonomy, another fear is that regulating gametes will further proscribe reproductive liberty for people who use ART to build families. The critique is that regulating forms of ART that do not involve third parties exceptionalizes these types of ART by singling them out and treating them differently (Cahn and Suter 2021, 83).

The arguments that identity disclosure infringes reproductive autonomy are multilayered (Cahn 2018, 1462). It is worth noting that even in the absence of explicit regulation, the law still defines the area, whether it is "hands off" or "highly regulated" (Cahn and Suter 2021, 85). For example, the lack of regulation to ensure that intended parentage is recognized may limit reproductive autonomy; failure to recognize nontraditional family formation limits the ability of same-sex and nonmarital couples to establish legally recognized and protected families. (Hazeldean 2022). Similarly, family limits for donors offer a measure of protection for reproductive autonomy if the goal is to have children without dozens or hundreds of half-siblings (Mroz 2021). Of course, such regulations might restrict the autonomy of any recipients who might want such an outcome as well as donors who want to provide sperm for an infinite number of children. The presence or absence of such a regulation will affect reproductive autonomy in different ways. Regulation inevitably involves balancing interests.

Indeed, without regulation, the interests of donor-conceived people may not be adequately considered because they are not parties to the negotiations concerning sperm donation. Of course, the goal is for the government to get the balance of all interests right and to "adequately" consider the needs of all who are involved, intended parents, donors, donor-conceived people, and the groups who might otherwise be discriminated against without protections.

Genetics Essentialism

Another concern is that some of the potential regulations of sperm donation, such as eliminating anonymity, may privilege genetic relatedness, with the potential to "undermine the social standing and dignity" of more diverse families, that is, those that do not conform to the married heterosexual family (Cahn and Suter 2021, 83; Joslin 2023).

We concede that limiting the number of children born per donor or mandating identity release does recognize the importance of genes to some people. But recognizing that genes are important to some people is entirely separate from recognizing families legally. When donor-conceived people describe their donors as parents or other children conceived by the same donor as siblings, they are not necessarily referencing them as legal family members. Instead, they are using the very limited language we have to describe these connections.

Moreover, to suggest that wanting to know about one's genetic origins means that donor-conceived people care only about genes and not about the families in which they are raised trivializes and essentializes the reasons for identity disclosure. Donor-conceived people have many reasons for wanting to know their donor's identity (Gardner 2022). This criticism also ignores the fact that genetic traits are quite important in the selection of donors. Recipients often choose donors on the basis of many features with genetic components, such as physical and emotional characteristics, health, and so on. But that does not suggest that only genetic relatedness creates family or familial bonds. Instead, it is the commitment to care for a child and time spent nurturing the child that establishes parent-child relationships. The bottom line is that allowing donor-conceived people to learn the identity of their donor does not itself undermine the importance of families formed without genetic connections. While understanding one's genetic origins is important to many people, it does not mean that it defines their relationships. Nor does it imply that genetic connections are important to everyone. In fact, regulation can help ensure that the law recognizes all forms of family, including those without genetic links.

Exceptionalizing ART

Another jurisprudential concern is that regulating in this area treats ART differently from reproduction in the bedroom, where there are no government-mandated tests of gametes. This differential treatment, however, is consistent with the need to develop rules that address families formed both inside and outside of the traditional heteronormative model. For example, the Uniform Parentage Act has categories for the various types of parents and nonparents involved in reproduction. It explicitly states that a donor is "an individual who provides gametes intended for use in assisted reproduction, whether or not for consideration" and is not a "presumed genetic parent." (Unif. Parentage Act §102 [3][C], 9). Different rules for ART are essential to ensure that nontraditional groups have broader access to family formation by providing a mechanism to establish legal recognition of their relationship.

Of course, ART is not the only place in which there is a need to develop new rules. In the adoption world, for example, states are increasingly likely to enact legislation that allows adoptees access to their original birth certificates (Ross 2021). We might, then, begin to think of the heteronormative model as exceptional, or simply recognize that there are alternative methods for forming recognized parental relationships.

Concern about Majoritarian Values

Finally, a critical concern is that regulation in this sphere might expand to harm marginalized groups. In an era when the LGBTQ+ community is under siege by conservative legislatures (Choi 2023), this is a critical concern. For example, in jurisdictions where the law does not adequately recognize legal parentage for intended parents using ART, increased regulation of sperm donation may open the door to further limits on family creation for less traditional families. This risk is greatest for single or same-sex couples (Choi 2023).

We are very sympathetic to these concerns, particularly in a post-*Dobbs* world. While we recognize that legislators may try to undermine families that are not heterosexual married couples, preventing lack of regulation in the gamete-donation context does not protect against these abuses, as we saw in Oklahoma. Regulation itself is not the threat; it is the nature of the regulation.

Conclusion

We want to close by emphasizing the limits and challenges of what we are suggesting in this essay. In the limited space we have, we cannot fully describe the optimal form of regulation for either the formal or informal markets. We are, as we have already noted, cognizant of the way in which each market may be affected by regulation of the other. For example, requiring fertility banks to set family limits could result in higher prices for sperm. Not only would this impact reproductive justice, it also might push people to the informal market. On the other hand, the threat of losing customers to that market might limit the price impact of such a regulation, thereby reducing the incentives to pursue the informal market. Mandating insurance coverage of medical and social infertility would increase accessibility of the formal market and decrease the need for the informal market, especially if coverage included a broad range of ART, including accessing gametes and even surrogacy. Changing donor qualifications, such as including gay sperm donors, might also expand the pool available in the formal market and could affect cost, while decreasing interest in the informal market.

In addition, we believe the various interests of family members—that is, the parents and donor-conceived people—must be accounted for carefully. Requiring identity release, in accordance with the interests of donor-conceived people, is only possible when the intending parents are secure in their legal rights. Given current legal conditions, that means donor-conceived people should only have the right to learn their donor's identity upon the age of majority, not as a child. That distinction is important from a reproductive justice perspective, because allowing donor-conceived people to learn their donor's identity as an adult does not impact the dynamic of childrearing or interfere with parental decisions about what information to share with a child about their donor and when.

In our current legal landscape, we will continue to see discrepancies as to who has access to ART based on wealth, race, class, gender, sexuality, ability, and location, discrepancies that may inspire and support the free sperm movement (Appleton 2015). *Dobbs* has the potential to exacerbate the situation, and it certainly shows the need for solutions that are rooted in a reproductive justice agenda.

REFERENCES

Abbasi, Amber D. 2013. "The Curious Case of Trent Arsenault: Questioning FDA Regulatory Authority Over Private Sperm Donation." *Annals of Health Law* 22 (1): 1–42. https://dx.doi.org/10.2139/ssrn.2129437.

Adams, Damien, Shahid Ullah, and Sheryl de Lacey. 2016. "Does the Removal of Anonymity Reduce Sperm Donors in Australia?" *Journal of Law and Medicine* 23 (3): 628–36.

American Society for Reproductive Medicine. 2021. "Guidance Regarding Gamete and Embryo Donation." *Fertility and Sterility* 115 (6): 1,395–409. https://doi.org/10.1016/j.fertnstert.2021.01.045.

Appleton, Susan Frelich. 2015. "Between the Binaries: Exploring the Legal Boundaries of Nonanonymous Sperm Donation." *Family Law Quarterly* 49 (1): 93–115. https://www.jstor.org/stable/24577604.

Bowles, Nellie. 2021. "The Sperm Kings Have a Problem: Too Much Demand." *New York Times*, January 8, 2021. www.nytimes.com.

Butler, Gavin. 2022. "Rise of the Sperm Bro: The Touring Men Fathering Children and Undercutting the Fertility Industry." *Vice*, July 29, 2022. www.vice.com.

Cahn, Naomi R. 2009. "Accidental Incest: Drawing the Line—Or the Curtain?—For Reproductive Technology." *Harvard Journal of Law & Gender* 32 (1): 59–108.

Cahn, Naomi. 2018. "The New 'ART' of Family: Connecting Assisted Reproductive Technologies & Identity Rights." *University of Illinois Law Review* 2018 (4): 1,443–71.

Cahn, Naomi, and Sonia M. Suter. 2021. "The Art of Regulating ART." *Chicago-Kent Law Review* 96 (1): 29–86.

Centers for Disease Control and Prevention (CDC). "Commonly Asked Questions." Centers for Disease Control and Prevention. Accessed February 21, 2023. www.cdc.gov.

Choi, Annette. 2023. "Record Number of Anti-LGBTQ Bills Have Been Introduced this Year." *CNN*, April 6, 2023. www.cnn.com.

Culhane, John. 2015. "Sperm Donors Are Winning Visitation Rights." *Slate*, February 20, 2015. https://slate.com.

Davidson, Jordan. 2021. "For Disabled People, the Cost of Infertility Care Is Entirely Out of Reach." *Parents*, May 27, 2021. www.parents.com.

Ferguson, Amber. 2022. "Why Gay Men and Other Groups Are Banned from Donating Sperm." *Washington Post*, October 20, 2022. www.washingtonpost.com.

Gardner, Tiffany D. 2022. "Lack of Complete Medical Information Leaves Donor Conceived People with the Unknown." U.S. Donor Conceived Council, January 27, 2022. www.usdcc.org.

Goodwin, Michele. 2006. *Black Markets: The Supply and Demand of Body Parts*. New York: Cambridge University Press.
Graham, S., T. Freeman, and V. Jadva. 2019. "A Comparison of the Characteristics, Motivations, Preferences and Expectations of Men Donating Sperm Online or Through a Sperm Bank." *Human Reproduction* 34 (11): 2208–18. https://doi.org/10.1093/humrep/dez173.
Hazeldean, Susan. 2022. "Illegitimate Parents." *University of California Davis Law Review* 55: 1583–715.
Hertz, Rosanna. 2022. "Sociological Accounts of Donor Siblings' Experiences: Their Importance for Self-Identity and New Kinship Relations." *International Journal of Environmental Research and Public Health* 19 (5): 1–14. https://doi.org/10.3390/ijerph19042002.
Javda, Vasanti, Tabitha Freeman, Erika Tranfield, and Susan Golombok. 2018. "Why Search for a Sperm Donor Online? The Experiences of Women Searching for and Contacting Sperm Donors on the Internet." *Human Fertility* 21 (2): 112–19. https://doi.org/10.1080/14647273.2017.1315460.
Joslin, Courtney. 2023. "Gamete Regulation and Family Protection in a Post-Dobbs World." *Bill of Health* (blog), May 17, 2023. https://blog.petrieflom.law.harvard.edu.
Just a Baby. n.d. "About." Accessed June 14, 2023. www.justababy.com/about/.
Kay, Kaitor. 2023. "Court Rules in Favor of Sperm Donor in Oklahoma Child Custody Case." *Oklahoma News* 4, February 15, 2023. https://kfor.com.
Kelley, Angela S., Yongmei Qin, Erica E. Marsh, and James M. Dupree. 2019. "Disparities in Accessing Infertility Care in the United States: Results from the National Health and Nutrition Examination Survey, 2013–16." *Fertility and Sterility* 112 (3): 562–68. https://doi.org/10.1016/j.fertnstert.2019.04.044.
Kramer, Wendy, and Naomi Cahn. 2013. *Finding Our Families: A First-of-Its-Kind Book for Donor-Conceived People and Their Families*. New York: Avery.
McFarling, Usha Lee. 2020. "For Black Women, the Isolation of Infertility is Compounded by Barriers to Treatment." *STAT*, October 14, 2020. www.statnews.com.
Meyer, Ali, Austin Breasette, and Hicham Raache. 2022. "Birth Certificate Battle: Sperm Donor Petitions Court for Custody of Baby Boy." *Oklahoma News* 4, June 1, 2022. https://kfor.com.
Mohr, Sebastian, and Rene Almeling. 2020. "Men, Masculinities, and Reproduction—Conceptual Reflections and Empirical Explorations." *Norma: International Journal for Masculinity Studies* 15 (3–4): 163–71. https://doi.org/10.1080/18902138.2020.1831156.
Mroz, Jackqueline. 2021. "The Case of the Serial Sperm Donor." *New York Times*, February 1, 2021. www.nytimes.com.
Murray, Melissa. 2021. "Race-Ing Roe: Reproductive Justice, Racial Justice, and the Battle for Roe v. Wade." *Harvard Law Review* 134 (6): 2025–102.
Mutcherson, Kimberly. 2023. "Dobbs as a Catalyst for Reproductive Justice." *Bill of Health* (blog), May 18, 2023. https://blog.petrieflom.law.harvard.edu.

Owens, Caitlin, and Oriana González. 2022. "Republicans' Thorny Path Ahead on Fertility Policy." *Axios*, November 29, 2022. www.axios.com.
Pecorin, Allison. 2024. "Senate IVF Bill Fails to Advance on Mostly Party Line Vote." *ABCNews*, Sept. 17, 2024. www.abcnews.go.com.
Planned Parenthood of Southeastern Pa. v. Casey, 505 U.S. 833 (1992).
PollenTree. n.d. "Sperm Donors." *PollenTree*. Accessed June 14, 2023. https://pollentree.com.
Protections for Donor Conceived People and Families, SB22–224, 74th Gen. Assembly (2022).
Resolve. n.d. "Insurance Coverage by State." Accessed June 5, 2023. https://resolve.org/.
Ross, Andrea. 2021. "How Can U.S. Adoptees Get Their Birth Certificates?" UC Davis, December 10, 2021. www.ucdavis.edu.
Russell, Tonya. 2021. "The Sperm Donation Is Free, but There's a Catch." *The Atlantic*, May 21, 2021. www.theatlantic.com.
Shepherd, Tory. 2023. "Urgent Calls for Australia-wide Register of Sperm Donations amid Concerns about 'Prolific' Donors." *The Guardian*, February 7, 2023. www.theguardian.com.
SisterSong. n.d. "Reproductive Justice." Accessed October 22, 2024. www.sistersong.net
Sony Podcasts. 2022. "BioHacked: Family Secrets | 11. Underground Markets." YouTube video, 00:37:35, August 1, 2022. https://www.youtube.com/watch?v=oekIKck6UbY.
Sosin, Kate, and Sara Luterman. 2023. "An Oklahoma Judge Just Transferred a Lesbian Mom's Parental Rights to Her Son's Sperm Donor." *The 19th*, February 14, 2023. https://19thnews.org.
Sperm Donation USA. n.d. "Sperm Donation USA." Facebook group. Accessed June 13, 2023. www.facebook.com.
Sussman, Anna Louie. 2019. "The Case for Redefining Infertility." *New Yorker*, June 18, 2019. www.newyorker.com.
Tracy, Abigail. 2022. "'This Is the Whole Point of the Movement': Doctors Fear IVF Will Be the Next Target in GOP's Abortion Crusade." *Vanity Fair*, September 28, 2022. www.vanityfair.com.
US Donor Conceived Council. 2022. "Donor Conception in the United States Compared to Other Countries." April 6, 2022. www.usdcc.org.
Wodoslawsky, Sascha, Joy Fatunbi, Rebecca Mercier, and Andrea Mechanick Braverman. 2023. "Sperm Donor Attitudes and Experiences with Direct-to-Consumer Genetic Testing." *Fertility and Sterility Reports* 4 (1): 36–41. https://doi.org/10.1016/j.xfre.2022.12.004.
Xytex Corporation. 2023. "Pricing: Donor Sperm." Last modified January 3, 2023. www.xytex.com.
Yarrow, Allison. 2014. "How to Get Pregnant with a Racquetball." *New Republic*, December 11, 2014. https://newrepublic.com/.

25

The High Stakes of Gamete Regulation in a Post-*Dobbs* World

COURTNEY G. JOSLIN, KATHERINE L. KRASCHEL, AND DOUGLAS NEJAIME

At its inception, "donor" sperm provision constituted a patriarchal and paternalistic practice. In 1884, Dr. William Pancoast infamously called upon the "best looking member of the class" of medical students to use their sperm to inseminate his female patient without her knowledge or consent. He would go on to collude with his patient's husband, agreeing they would not share the truth of the genetic material used to conceive the child (Almeling 2011, 25). Today, most would look upon this history with shock and dismay, as it is inconsistent with modern conceptions of informed consent, bioethics, reproductive autonomy, and feminism.

In contrast to this patriarchal history, more recent uses of assisted reproductive technologies played an important role in facilitating greater diversity in family forms (Pew Research Center 2010). Families created using procured sperm include single-parent families, same-sex parent families, and families headed by unmarried couples; many of these families include nonbiological parents.[1] The existence of these families challenged traditional, gendered definitions of parenthood (NeJaime 2016), and, in turn, prompted legal reform. For example, some states, though not nearly enough, have laws that protect *all families* formed through assisted reproduction, regardless of the parents' gender or marital status or the existence of a genetic connection between parent and child (NeJaime 2017). Despite these advancements, disparities and inequities remain. Nonbiological parents, especially LGBTQ parents and unmarried parents, continue to struggle for legal recognition of their parent-child relationships (NeJaime 2016).

Moreover, the current legal landscape is marked by increasing attacks on reproductive justice, women's rights, LGBTQ equality, and the progressive developments that assisted reproduction facilitated (Movement Advancement Project 2023). In *Dobbs v. Jackson Women's Health Organization* (2022), the US Supreme Court struck down *Roe v. Wade* (1973), the fifty-year precedent protecting a right to abortion under the due process clause of the Fourteenth Amendment of the US Constitution. In his concurring opinion in *Dobbs,* Justice Clarence Thomas explicitly invited the court to extend its reasoning to overrule other due process precedents, including those protecting rights to use contraception, have nonmarital and same-sex sexual relations, and marry a same-sex partner (*Dobbs v. Jackson Women's Health Organization,* 142 S. Ct. 2228 [2022] [Thomas, J., concurring]).

Assisted reproduction, especially the use of assisted reproduction by unmarried people and LGBTQ people, lies squarely in the crosshairs of contemporary attacks on reproductive justice. Many of the advocates who seek to undermine reproductive choice envision a society in which highly gendered roles of reproduction and parenting are enforced by law. Further, as is the case with abortion, the effects of laws that limit reproductive choice in assisted reproduction stand to disproportionately burden communities of color. Income and race shape access to assisted reproduction (Daar 2017, 80, 82). As Alyssa M. Newman discusses in her essay in this volume, sperm from Black donors may already be difficult to procure. Additional regulation has the potential to increase costs and other hurdles to access.

In light of these developments, policymakers should proceed cautiously, carefully considering whether proposals to regulate assisted reproduction might have the effect (whether intended or unintended) of eroding reproductive autonomy, reiterating essentialist views of biogenetic connection, or undermining the security of diverse family forms. Given these concerns, regulatory proposals should be assessed through an intersectional lens that recognizes the ways inequalities operate in concert to maintain hierarchies and systems of oppression (Center for Reproductive Rights 2020). In this essay, we raise concerns about some of the recent proposals to regulate assisted reproduction and show how a more intersectional reproductive justice approach illuminates the impacts that such proposals would have on marginalized individuals and families.

Recent Regulatory Developments

In the past few years, sensational news stories—some about physicians who adopted practices that were normalized in the earliest days of sperm provision but are now correctly viewed as wrongful—led to calls for regulatory interventions. For example, the 2022 Netflix documentary *Our Father* exposed a fertility doctor, Donald Cline, who used his own sperm to inseminate dozens of patients without their knowledge (Jourdan 2022). Not surprisingly, efforts to respond to these egregious practices with legislative interventions gained traction, as noted by Rebecca O'Connor and Naomi Cahn and Sonia M. Suter in their essays in this volume.

Some of the new and proposed laws aimed at sperm and egg provision impose retroactive penalties—civil, criminal, and/or professional discipline—on parties who engaged in forms of "misconduct" during the fertility treatment process. Today, at least twelve states have some kind of "fertility fraud" law,[2] and other states are considering legislation in this area. Some laws, like Utah's Code Ann. § 76-7-402, narrowly address the blatantly fraudulent behavior of inseminating doctors like Dr. Cline. Some pending bills, though, would go *much further*. For example, a New York bill, N.Y. S80 (2023), would greatly expand the potential liability of fertility care providers, as well as donors. Among other things, if enacted, the bill would authorize the imposition of civil damages for "negligently" providing "misleading" information about the "donor's medical history" (N.Y. S80 § 3 [2023]).

Other states, including California, Colorado, Connecticut, Rhode Island, Utah, and Washington, have laws that seek to regulate the policies and procedures of gamete banks and fertility clinics on the front end, that is, before the fertility care services are provided.[3] The laws in several of these states are based on Article 9 of the Uniform Parentage Act (UPA) of 2017. The UPA (2017) is a uniform state law promulgated by the Uniform Law Commission, a nonpartisan group of state judges, state legislators, law professors, and lawyers that produces model acts on state law topics.

The UPA (2017) is a comprehensive and inclusive statutory scheme aimed primarily at legal recognition of parents in a wide range of families, including those formed through assisted reproduction. As the UPA (2017) regulates the assisted reproduction process, it simultaneously extends clear protections to families formed through assisted reproduction. It recognizes intended parents as legal parents, regardless of marital status, sex, sexual orientation, gender identity, or genetic connection, and it treats a "donor" as a nonparent (Joslin 2018a; Joslin 2018b). As part of this comprehensive, pluralistic parentage framework, the UPA (2017) included a new article—Article 9—that regulates the collection and dissemination of information about gamete providers. Article 9 requires the disclosure of nonidentifying medical information to parents at any point.

In addition, Article 9 addresses release of identifying information about gamete providers. As originally promulgated in 2017, *if* the gamete provider agreed, Article 9 required the disclosure of identifying information upon request of the person conceived with the procured gametes at or after age eighteen. It left every option on the table for gamete providers and intended parents exercising reproductive choices. It allowed parties to decide that they did not want the donor's identity information shared by the gamete bank—a position that some argue is the optimal role for the law (Groll 2021). As originally drafted, Article 9 also enabled banks to procure sperm from a wider range of donors and, in so doing, avoid exacerbating inequitable supply and access issues (Ferguson 2022).

Some states did not take the measured approach in the original version of Article 9. For example, in 2022, Colorado enacted a more proactive regulatory scheme that goes much further than Article 9 (Colo. S.B. 22–224 [2022]). The Colorado law is the first in the United States to *require* all gamete providers to agree that children conceived with their gametes have access to identifying details about the gamete provider when they reach age eighteen.

In response to calls for change by the same groups who advocated for the Colorado law, the Uniform Law Commission created a study committee in 2023 to revisit Article 9. The committee was asked to consider whether the UPA (2017) should be revised to require banks to release identifying information about gamete providers upon request of the person conceived with the procured gametes at or after age eighteen.

In November 2023, the Uniform Law Commission committee voted to revise Article 9 as requested.

Other proposals would go well beyond Colorado's law or the proposed revision to Article 9. Some advocates have called for the enactment of laws requiring the disclosure of identifying information *prior* to the child's eighteenth birthday. The aim is to allow, and indeed facilitate, contact between the child and the gamete provider during their childhood (US Donor Conceived Council 2023). A New York bill would require gamete providers to agree to the release of all their medical records from the last five years (N.Y. S2122 [2023]). This proposal raises significant medical privacy and racial equity concerns (Jiménez 2023; Hug and Wexler 2023).[4] If enacted, this legislation would require all gamete providers to waive their medical privacy protections. This could result, for example, in the disclosure of intimate information that the person would prefer to keep confidential and that is not relevant to the health of any resulting child conceived using the person's gametes, such as a past sexual assault. This is especially troubling in a post-*Dobbs* world in which private information about reproductive health care decisions can lead to civil and criminal penalties. Moreover, this requirement may exacerbate existing equity concerns. For example, since those who are Black, Indigenous, and People of Color (BIPOC) have less access to health care and are less likely to access health care, screening prospective sperm providers by requiring this type of information may disproportionately exclude BIPOC sperm providers.

Implications and Considerations Moving Forward

To be sure, there are practices in the assisted reproduction space—like the behavior of Dr. Cline and other inseminating doctors—that are extremely troubling. Some reforms may be necessary and appropriate. It is important that policymakers considering responses view this set of issues through a reproductive justice lens that centers the experiences of those on the margins of reproduction, family formation, and parental recognition—including LGBTQ people, single women, low-income people, and racial minorities.

For the purposes of this brief essay, we note, but do not fully unpack, the multiple ways in which many of the interventions discussed may reduce access to reproductive health care and worsen racial disparities in access. For example, increasing potential liability for gamete providers—as one of the pending New York bills would do—could reduce (perhaps substantially) the number of people willing to be sperm and egg donors, thereby decreasing supply and increasing cost. At the same time, expanding the potential civil and criminal liability for clinicians, including for unintentional conduct, might reduce the number of physicians willing to provide this care. From this perspective, we see how some of the proposed policies may reduce access, especially for low-income and other marginalized people. This consequence—reduction of access in the face of increased legal liability—is already evident in the abortion context (Chang 2022). For example, it has been reported that, in the face of increasing legal liability, more than half of the ob-gyns in Idaho who specialize in high-risk pregnancies have left the state or will do so by the end of 2023 (Diaz, Kegu, and Novak 2023). As one Idaho doctor who performs abortions put it, her greatest fear is "being tried as a felon simply for saving someone's life" (Kaye and Samaniego 2023). This is not a legal risk that all doctors are willing to take. As more states enact these "fertility fraud" statutes, we may see a similar trend of doctors choosing to leave the practice or limit their fertility care services in the face of increased potential legal liabilities.

We also draw attention to another set of concerns that must be considered—the impact of these interventions on the legal recognition and social standing of families formed through assisted reproduction, especially those created with procured sperm or eggs. As we noted at the outset, robust modern sperm provision in the United States has facilitated a more egalitarian and inclusive understanding of the family. Yet, while there has been progress, many states' laws address and protect only children born to married couples through assisted reproduction (NeJaime 2017, Appendix A; Joslin 2021, Appendix B).

In the many states that still have exclusionary parentage statutes in the context of assisted reproduction, a child's legal relationship with one or both of their intended parents remains vulnerable and may not be legally recognized. The risk that the child's parent is not treated as a *legal* parent, as well as the converse risk that the court *will* recognize the gamete provider as the child's parent, is heightened when there is contact between the child and the gamete provider. This legal risk is heightened if the law seeks to facilitate contact between the donor and the child *during the child's minority*—a proposal that some advocates are pushing (US Donor Conceived Council 2022). This concern is not merely theoretical. A 2023 Oklahoma decision found that the child's known sperm donor was the second parent, and the intended parent, who was the birth parent's spouse, was not (Wilson v. Williams, D-2021-3681 [Okla. 7th Jud. Dist.] Letter Ruling [Feb 13, 2023]).

Emerging proposals also have the potential to undermine the social standing and dignity of families formed through assisted reproduction with donor gametes. By directing attention to biogenetic connection, these laws run the risk of re-privileging the view that "real" parent-child relationships are those that are biologically based (Groll 2021; NeJaime 2017). This view is presented in stark relief in the writings of some proponents who expressly use biogenetic language—for example, referring to gamete providers as "genetic parents" and to children conceived using gametes from the same person as "siblings" (Zang 2021). Some proponents not only elevate biogenetic relationships but also denigrate non-biological ones; they argue that families created with procured gametes are inherently harmful because they separate children from their "true," that is, biological, parents (Breckenridge 2021).

In this way, these arguments may be examples of what the legal scholar Reva Siegel calls "preservation through transformation"—the idea that when justifications for status inequalities become socially untenable, they reemerge in new forms (Siegel 1997). In the past, some sought to justify the legal privileging of married different-sex parents by disparaging other parents as immoral or unfit. Now that there is more social acceptance and legal recognition of LGBTQ and single parents, these newly emergent claims based on the lack of biogenetic family ties offer a basis for denigrating these families, regardless of the worth or capabilities of the people in them (NeJaime 2017). To be sure, perpetuating systems of subordination may not be the intention of proponents who champion identity release. Nonetheless, in this post-*Dobbs* world, laws premised on the importance of donor connection risk reifying essentialist and exclusionary notions of family.

* * *

Of course, the behavior of inseminating doctors like Dr. Cline is deeply troubling. And other objectionable practices deserve our attention. Certainly, there are steps states can and should take to address abuses and to better regulate sperm provision. As states step into this space, however, it is important not to regulate rashly and, in so doing, jeopardize access to reproductive health care, perpetuate inequalities, or undermine existing families and established family law principles.

NOTES

This chapter draws on Professor Joslin's previously published work, Courtney Joslin, 2023, "Gamete Regulation and Family Protection in a Post-*Dobbs* World," *Bill of Health* (blog), May 17, 2023, https://blog.petrieflom.law.harvard.edu.

1. We use "procured" as an umbrella term to describe sperm purchased or donated (informally or commercially through intermediaries or banks) and whether or not the identity of the person providing sperm is known to the intended parents or to be disclosed to the resulting children at a later date.
2. Ark. Code Ann. § 5-13-212; Ark. Code Ann. § 5-37-220; Ark. Code Ann. § 16-118-117; Ariz. Rev. Stat. Ann. § 12–567; Cal. Penal Code § 367g; Cal. Civ. Code § 1708.5.6; Colo. Rev. Stat. Ann. § 18-13-131; Colo. Rev. Stat. Ann. § 13-21-132; Colo. Rev. Stat. Ann. §§ 12-240-121(gg) & 12-255-120(hh); Fla. Stat. Ann. § 784.086; Fla. Stat. Ann. § 456.072; Fla. Stat. Ann. § 459.015(yy); Fla. Stat. Ann. § 458.331; Ind. Code Ann. § 34-24-5-3; Iowa Code Ann. § 714I.3; Ky. Rev. Stat. 311.373; La. Stat. Ann. § 14:101.2; Ohio Rev. Code Ann. § 2907.13; Ohio Rev. Code Ann. § 4731.861; Tex. Penal Code Ann. § 22.011; Utah Code Ann. § 76-7-402.
3. Cal. Health & Safety Code § 1644 et seq.; Colo. Rev. Stat. Ann. § 25-57-101 et seq.; Conn. Gen. Stat. Ann. § 46b-542 et seq.; 15 R.I. Gen. Laws Ann. § 15–8.1–901 et seq.; Utah Code Ann. § 78B-15–708; Wash. Rev. Code Ann. § 26.26A.800 et seq.
4. While health care adjacent, sperm banks are not considered "covered entities" under the Health Insurance Portability and Accountability Act (HIPAA) and, much like many health care apps, pose privacy risks that donors and intended parents may not appreciate or may incorrectly assume are protected under HIPAA. See, e.g., Westman 2022.

REFERENCES

Almeling, Rene. 2011. *Sex Cells: The Medical Market for Eggs and Sperm.* Berkeley: University of California Press.

Breckenridge, Katie. 2021. "Harvard Confirms What We Knew to be True: Commercial Separation of Kids from Their Parents is Harmful." Them Before Us, May 5, 2021. https://thembeforeus.com.

Center for Reproductive Rights. 2020. *Ensuring Equitable Access to Infertility Care in the United States: Guiding Principles for Policies Mandating Insurance Coverage.* N.p.: Center for Reproductive Rights. https://reproductiverights.org.

Chang, Ailsa. 2022. "Bleeding and in Pain, She Couldn't get two Louisiana ERs to Answer: Is it a Miscarriage?" NPR, December 29, 2022. https://www.npr.org.
Daar, Judith. 2017. *The New Eugenics*. New Haven: Yale University Press.
Diaz, Adriana, Jessica Kegu, and Analisa Novak. 2023. "'Hopeless and Frustrated': Idaho's Abortion Ban is Driving OB/GYNs Out of State." *CBS News*, October 31, 2023.
Ferguson, Amber. 2022. "America Has a Black Sperm Donor Shortage: Black Women are Paying the Price." *Washington Post*, October 20, 2022.
Groll, Daniel. 2021. *Conceiving People: Genetic Knowledge and the Ethics of Sperm and Egg Donation*. Oxford: Oxford University Press.
Hug, Aziz Z., and Rebecca Wexler. 2023. "Digital Privacy for Reproductive Choice in the Post-*Roe* Era." *New York University Law Review* 98 (2).
Jiménez, Jesus. 2023. "Mother Who Gave Abortion Pills to Teen Daughter Gets 2 Years in Prison." *New York Times*, September 22, 2023. www.nytimes.com.
Joslin, Courtney. 2018a. "Nurturing Parenthood through the UPA (2017)." *Yale Law Journal* (forum) 589.
Joslin, Courtney. 2018b. "Preface to the UPA (2017)." *Family Law Quarterly* 52 (3): 437.
Joslin, Courtney. 2021. "(Not) Just Surrogacy." *California Law Review* 109: 401.
Jourdan, Lucie, dir. 2022. *Our Father*. Blumhouse Productions. 01:37:00 min. www.netflix.com.
Kaye, Randy, and Stephen Samaniego. "Idaho's Murky Abortion Law Is Driving Doctors Out of the State." *CNN*, May 13, 2023. www.cnn.com.
Movement Advancement Project. 2023. *Under Fire: The War on LGBTQ People in America*. Boulder, CO: Movement Advancement Project. www.mapresearch.org.
NeJaime, Douglas. 2016. "Marriage Equality and the New Parenthood." *Harvard Law Review* 129 (5): 1185.
NeJaime, Douglas. 2017. "The Nature of Parenthood." *Yale Law Journal* 126 (8): 2260.
Pew Research Center. 2010. *Report: The Decline of Marriage and Rise of New Families*. N.p.: Pew Research Center. https://www.pewresearch.org/social-trends/2010/11/18/iv-family/.
Roberts, Dorothy. 1996. "Race and the New Reproduction." *Hastings Law Journal* 47 (4): 935, 941–43.
Siegel, Reva. 1997. "Why Equal Protection No Longer Protects: The Evolving Forms of Status-Enforcing State Action." *Stanford Law Review* 49 (5): 1111.
Uniform Law Commission. "Parentage Act of 2017." Accessed June 3, 2023. www.uniformlaws.org.
Westman, Nicole. "Mental Health Apps Have Terrible Privacy Protections, Report Finds: Prayer Apps Were Also Worse Than Other Categories." *The Verge*, May 2, 2022. www.theverge.com.
Wilson v. Williams, D-2021–3681 (Okla. 7th Jud. Dist.) Letter Ruling (Feb 13, 2023). https://s3.documentcloud.org.
US Donor Conceived Council. 2022. "2022 Advocacy Survey Results." November 16, 2022. www.usdcc.org.

US Donor Conceived Council (@dccouncilusa). 2023. "Last year, we asked our community what their legislative priorities were. . . ." Twitter, February, 3, 2023, 11:32 a.m. https://twitter.com/dccouncilusa/status/1621592533246558215.

Zang, Sarah. 2021. "The Children of Sperm Donors Want to Change the Rules of Conception." *The Atlantic*, October 15, 2021. www.theatlantic.com.

PART VI

Embodying Sperm

26

Why Men Are Missing from Discussions of Infertility and What to Do about It

WILLIAM D. PETOK

Regardless of where one looks, whether to religious texts or to the most recent examples of pop culture, discussions of infertility tend to focus on women and erase men. In the Judeo-Christian Bible, we learn about the struggles of Sarah and Hannah to conceive, but we know little about their male partners thoughts or feelings on the topic (Petok 2015, 260). Contemporary accounts of infertility are similarly missing the male voice. Gordon Ramsey, the celebrity chef, stands out as an exception who has discussed his struggles (WENN 2007). Male factor infertility, sometimes in combination with a female factor, is present in about 50 percent of reported cases. Why then are men so underrepresented in these discussions? How do men feel about a diagnosis of male factor infertility? What can we do to change this lack of attention to male infertility?

Psychological Perspective on Men's Experiences of Infertility

My experience as a psychologist working in the reproductive medicine space since 1985 has provided opportunities to learn how men (with most of my patients being white, cisgender, and/or heterosexual) react to a diagnosis of male factor infertility. They report feeling blindsided in that they knew so little about reproductive health and had no idea they could be responsible for the lack of conception. After all, they got erections and had intercourse that ended in ejaculation. They are embarrassed and guilt ridden that something is wrong with their ability to reproduce. And they often conflate this inability with a sexual problem (Fisher and Hammarberg 2012, 122–27). Somehow, in their minds, the lack of viable sperm or a path to deliver them becomes a manifestation of a sexual failure. By way of contrast, when women experience reproductive difficulty related to eggs, there is no sexual connotation. No arousal or orgasm is required to create a pregnancy for a woman. While aspects of her feminine identity may be challenged because she does not conceive (Petok 2006), there is no conflation with sexual function.

My patients often speak of isolation as well. They are afraid to discuss their infertility with their friends or family members and are therefore alone in their emotional pain. Many of my patients have talked about the isolation as doubly difficult, because after a diagnosis and, in some cases, unsuccessful interventions that involve medication or surgery, the rest of the treatments generally focus on the reproductive systems of their female partners and in the offices of obstetricians or reproductive endocrinologists. Their wives or partners are more conversant in their own reproductive systems, the subsequent interventions take place with their wife's or partner's bodies, and the medical team tends to focus the conversation on the female member of the couple.

An essential element of diagnosis and treatment for male factor infertility is a semen analysis. Men who provide the specimen at a reproductive endocrinology clinic are usually sent to a specimen collection room equipped with appropriate "stimulus materials." Men report that walking into that room, sometimes carrying a specimen cup, feels like they are telling everyone in the clinic about their male incompetence. Because he is less knowledgeable about conception and pregnancy, he does not ask questions and finds the medical team ignoring him, leaving him feeling "less than," or as an accessory rather than a full partner.

To further complicate matters, many men feel an obligation to be strong for their female partners because she is the one enduring invasive procedures. He may be afraid to voice his own negative feelings about the situation because it feels like a weakness that is inconsistent with being strong for her. Sometimes I hear reports that, after the male factor diagnosis is made, and the initial shock of it wears off, a man's partner neglects to ask how he is feeling in the weeks or months that follow. So he struggles alone, feeling that there is no one with whom to share his pain. For these men, the idea of therapy can often be anathema, because it is marked by a cultural "feminization"; in therapy, you talk about being sad, are supposed to weep and feel bad, all in the presence of a stranger. This is not manly! And finally, while there are many books written for women struggling with fertility challenges, there is limited self-help literature available for men, further isolating them (Wischmann and Thorn 2013, 237; Wischmann 2013, 36).

For those heterosexual couples who elect to use a sperm donor to create a family, the isolation, embarrassment, and shame can be even worse. In addition to grief at his genetic line ending with him, men report feeling distressed with the idea that another man will be the source of his partner's impregnation. They describe a sense that another man is "metaphorically having sex" with his female partner to create a child that he will raise as his own. Common questions include: "How can I share this with anyone else?" "Will I be able to bond with this child?" and "What will my child think about me as a man?" (Petok 2014).

How to Create More Support for Male Infertility Patients

From a mental health professional view, the "odd man out" is the male therapist. The Mental Health Professional Group of the American Society for Reproductive Medicine (ASRM) is an organization of over seven hundred licensed professionals who have specialized training working with infertility patients. A 2020 survey of the membership found that almost 95 percent were female. While membership in the organization had almost tripled since the prior survey in 2000, male membership was down 7 percent. If a man with male factor infertility did want to meet with a male therapist, he would have a slim chance of finding one.

There are also gendered discrepancies among medical professionals. Physician membership in ASRM is overwhelmingly composed of those trained as obstetrician-gynecologists, many of whom have done fellowships in reproductive endocrinology. There is an affiliate society within ASRM, the Society for Male Reproduction and Urology, but their membership constitutes less than 2.5 percent of the organization. So while male factor infertility constitutes approximately 50 percent of infertility cases, the number of specialists treating men is far less than half.

On the mental health side, few, if any, graduate programs offer coursework in infertility counseling, much less with a focus on male factor infertility, despite the fact that reproductive challenges impose a huge burden on individuals and couples. So, with limited opportunities to learn about infertility on a graduate level, budding professionals have no exposure to the significant impact that infertility can have on either member of a couple or the couple as a whole.

Are community-based support groups filling in some of these gaps? No. Resolve is a national support organization for infertility patients that began in 1974. Today, their website lists 146 support groups nationwide. There are just three groups exclusively for men and two others are listed as "open to men." Facebook offers two groups for men, one of them run by women. There is a Men's Fertility Forum in the UK. Rhod Gilbert, a British comedian with male factor infertility created HIM Fertility, a support and information organization. And one can find a few religiously based male support groups. But given that male factor accounts for about 50 percent of infertility cases, support for men is extremely limited.

How to Create More Awareness of Male Infertility

In sum, there are many factors that contribute to the lack of public attention to male infertility, including limited reproductive health education for men, a reluctance among men to discuss their infertility (in comparison to their female counterparts), and female-centric reproductive health care. In addition, the first donor insemination was kept secret from the wife and most of the professional world set a standard for secrecy that is counterproductive to creating acceptance and awareness of male factor infertility (Hard 1909). There is a clear need to increase awareness and provide accurate information so that men can make informed decisions about their reproductive health. Following are suggestions based on years of experience working with men dealing with their fertility challenges.

One solution to this lack of public awareness might include encouraging male celebrities to talk about "the need for male reproductive health care." Picture a famous football player standing with his children and partner and saying, "My family is incredibly important to me. If you think a family is in the cards for you, talk to your doctor today about making sure it is." When I was on the board of Path 2 Parenthood, a support and information organization for people trying to build a family, we pitched such an idea to a National Football League team through their player organization. We received no bites! Contrast this with the number of female celebrities who have discussed their infertility and use of donors or gestational carriers.

We also need to do a better job of discussing puberty and reproductive health with adolescents. When girls are removed from the classroom in middle school to talk about menstruation, a similar conversation for boys could take place regarding sperm and preserving sperm health. Sexuality education must become more than "how not to get pregnant or get a disease." However, to accomplish this, attitudes about sexual health education and the regulations that govern it in various states must be brought in line with the idea that reproductive health is important for men as well as women (Petok and Marcell 2022, 14–17).

How to Create More Professional Support for Male Infertility

Increasing the number of male therapists with whom men may feel more comfortable discussing infertility is another challenge. To increase male membership in organizations like ASRM's Mental Health Professional Group, a concerted effort must be made to create professional awareness of the needs of men who will benefit from counseling and support services. To that end, those of us who work on male infertility must make an extra effort to speak at meetings of professional organizations such as the American Psychological Association, particularly to Division 51, the Society for the Psychological Study of Men and Masculinities. Similar professional organizations, such as the National Association of Social Workers, would also be useful forums for further engagement. To that end, Steven Miller, a graduate student at the University of Wisconsin School of Social Work, has initiated a campaign to inform social work students and professionals about infertility and has a podcast, MILES (Men, Infertility, and Life Experiences). Finally, professionals involved with male infertility can volunteer to speak to their training programs and encourage therapists and counselors in training to attend workshops and courses that offer content related to working with this underserved population.

The science of reproduction is clear: babies are born after male *and* female factors combine to produce a child. The impact of infertility is significant globally, with the World Health Organization estimating that 17.5 percent of the adult population will be affected by it (WHO 2023).

While representations of female infertility and its treatment both medically and psychologically are abundant, information, awareness, and resources of the corresponding problem for men is limited. There are multiple determinants of this discrepancy. In order for parity to exist, a significant effort must be made to incorporate the contribution of men and sperm to the discussion of reproductive health. Current avenues to do this exist, but a concerted effort has yet to be made to rectify this inequality.

REFERENCES

Bennett, Jessica. 2015. "A Master's Degree in . . . Masculinity?" *New York Times*, August 8, 2015.

Fisher, Jane R. W., and Karin Hammarberg. 2012. "Psychological and Social Aspects of Infertility in Men: An Overview of the Evidence and Implications for Psychologically Informed Clinical Care and Future Research." *Asian Journal of Andrology* 14 (1): 121–129. https://doi.org/10.1038/aja.2011.72.

Hard, David Addison. 1909. "Artificial Impregnation." *Medical World* 27:163–64.

Petok, William D. 2006. "The Psychology of Gender Specific Infertility Diagnoses." In *Infertility Counseling: A Comprehensive Handbook for Clinicians*, 2nd ed., edited by Sharon N. Covington and Linda Hammer Burns, 37–60. Cambridge: Cambridge University Press.

Petok, William D. 2014. "Sperm Donation: Psychological Aspects." In *Third-Party Reproduction: A Comprehensive Guide*, edited by James M. Goldfarb, 159–68. New York: Springer.

Petok, William D. 2015. "Infertility Counseling (or the Lack Thereof) of the Forgotten Male Partner." *Fertility and Sterility* 104 (2): 260–66. https://doi.org/10.1016/j.fertnstert.2015.04.040.

Petok, William D., and Arik V. Marcell. 2022. "The Acquisition of Sexual and Reproductive Health Knowledge." In *Psychological and Medical Perspectives on Fertility Care and Sexual Health*, edited by Kim Bergman, William D. Petok, 3–20. Amsterdam: Elsevier.

WENN. 2007. "Ramsay's Job Made Him Infertile." Contactmusic.com, September 28, 2007. www.contactmusic.com.

Wischmann, Tewes. 2013. "'Your Count is Zero': Counseling the Infertile Man." *Human Fertility* 16 (1): 35–39. https://doi.org/10.3109/14647273.2013.776179.

Wischmann, Tewes, and Petra Thorn. 2013. "(Male) Infertility: What Does It Mean to Men? New Evidence from Quantitative and Qualitative Studies." *Reproductive Biomedicine Online* 27 (3): 236–43. https://doi.org/10.1016/j.rbmo.2013.06.002.

World Health Organization (WHO). 2023. "1 in 6 People Globally Affected by Infertility: WHO." News Release, April 4, 2023. www.who.int.

27

Sperm Troubles and Infertility Technologies in the Middle East and Arab America

MARCIA C. INHORN

In this chapter, located at the interdisciplinary intersection of medical anthropology, masculinity studies, and Middle East studies, I attempt to answer eight key questions regarding "sperm troubles," which I define here as problems with sperm themselves, leading to medical and social problems for men. These questions are as follows:

(1) Why do sperm troubles cause male infertility?
(2) Why is male infertility so troubling to men?
(3) Why is male infertility so troubling to men in the Middle East?
(4) Why is male infertility even more troubling to Middle Eastern–born men in the United States?
(5) Why is intracytoplasmic sperm injection (ICSI) a hope technology for men with sperm troubles?
(6) What are the troubles caused by ICSI itself?
(7) Why is ICSI still the "only hope" for infertile Middle Eastern Muslim men with sperm troubles?
(8) Why is access to ICSI a troubling reproductive justice issue for infertile men, especially for Middle Eastern–born men living in the United States?

I base my answers to these questions on more than three decades of anthropological research conducted in the Middle East and Arab America. I have interviewed hundreds of infertile Middle Eastern men, including in Egypt (Inhorn 2003), Lebanon (Inhorn 2012), the United Arab Emirates (Inhorn 2015), and Arab America (Inhorn 2018). Most were Muslims (both Sunni and Shia), and they came from a variety of countries of origin (Egypt, Iraq, Lebanon, Palestine, Syria, United Arab Emirates, Yemen). Through in-depth reproductive life histories and ethnographic interviews, I have learned why sperm troubles are so very difficult for men, but especially Middle Eastern Muslim men within their "local moral worlds" (Kleinman 1992).

Why Do Sperm Troubles Cause Male Infertility?

Infertility is generally defined as the inability to conceive after twelve months of regular, unprotected sexual intercourse. This reproductive health problem affects 8–12 percent of all reproductive-age couples worldwide and can involve female infertility, male infertility, or both.

Male infertility involves four major categories of sperm defects, any one of which leads to a diagnosis of male infertility. These include low sperm count (oligozoospermia), poor sperm motility (asthenozoospermia), defects of sperm morphology (teratozoospermia), and total absence of sperm in the ejaculate (azoospermia). Azoospermia may be due to lack of sperm production (nonobstructive azoospermia) or blockages in sperm transport (obstructive azoospermia).

These sperm troubles contribute to *more than half* of all cases of infertility worldwide. Male infertility is, in fact, a very common male reproductive health condition, affecting millions of men around the globe. Yet, it has been called a "neglected" reproductive health problem, one that is overlooked in reproductive health circles and deeply hidden in many societies, including in the West (Inhorn and Patrizio 2015).

Why Is Male Infertility So Troubling to Men?

Studies in the United States have shown male infertility to be among the most stigmatizing of all male health conditions (Barnes 2014; Greil, Slauson-Blevins, and McQuillan 2010). The depth of this stigmatization may be even deeper in non-Western settings; infertility can cast a permanent shadow on a man's community standing. Such stigmatization is clearly related to issues of sexuality. Male infertility is popularly, although usually mistakenly, conflated with impotency (i.e., erectile dysfunction). This "fertility-virility linkage" means that men who are infertile are assumed to be impotent, even though most are not (Lloyd 1996).

Male infertility also prevents millions of men from achieving fatherhood (Inhorn and Patrizio 2015), which, in many societies, is considered a major signifier of adult manhood, and something that many men desire as part of their masculine life trajectories (Hadley 2021). Rates of male childlessness have been shown to be increasing rather dramatically in many countries, including in the West. For example, in the United States, more than half of all men age fifteen to forty-nine have not fathered a biological child, including nearly one-quarter of men in their forties (Martinez, Daniels, and Febo-Vazquez 2018). Yet, among childless American men, more than one-third reported that they would have wanted to have children, but were unable to do so, for either medical or social reasons (Maximova and Quesnel-Vallée 2009).

Why Is Male Infertility So Troubling to Men in the Middle East?

In the Muslim Middle East, male infertility is especially disruptive. On the one hand, fatherhood is a social mandate in this "most married" region of the world, where more than 90 percent of adults will marry at some point in their lifetimes (Rashad, Osman, and Roudi-Fahimi 2005). Middle Eastern societies are also patrilineally organized, with surnames, descent, and inheritance bestowed from fathers to their children. Thus, paternity is critical, given that all children receive their *nasab*, or genealogical origins, from their fathers. Beyond the realm of kinship, Middle Eastern men take great pride and joy in their children (Inhorn 1994, 1996, 2003). It is rare to find a man who does not want to become a father. Thus, when marital infertility problems ensue, men are often shocked and devastated to receive a male infertility diagnosis (Inhorn 2012, 2015, 2018).

Nevertheless, male infertility is prevalent in the Middle East. While male infertility accounts for about 40 percent of all cases of infertility presenting to in vitro fertilization centers in Western countries, in the Middle East, 60–90 percent of all cases involve a diagnosis of male infertility. Moreover, nonobstructive azoospermia is highly prevalent in the Middle East, as are cases of severe oligoasthenozoospermia (i.e., very low sperm count and poor motility) (Inhorn 2012).

Because of advances in the field of genetics, it is now known that a significant percentage of these kinds of severe cases are due to genetic abnormalities. In the Middle East, severe cases of male infertility tend to run in families and are probably related to intergenerational patterns of consanguineous (cousin) marriage, which increase the chances for genetic mutations, including microdeletions of the Y chromosome linked to male infertility (Inhorn et al. 2009).

Because male infertility is often related to genetic sperm defects, the condition is recalcitrant to prevention and is among the most difficult forms of infertility to treat. Male infertility is generally not a condition that can be cured per se. Instead, it represents a chronic reproductive health condition, affecting thousands of Middle Eastern men and millions of other men worldwide.

Why Is Male Infertility Even More Troubling to Middle Eastern–Born Men in the United States?

Millions of Middle Eastern men have been exposed to the toxic legacies of warfare, among them radioactive heavy metals that have been shown to produce negative reproductive health effects. In particular, both the First and Second Gulf Wars in Iraq—Operation Desert Shield and Desert Storm (1990–1991) and Operation Iraqi Freedom (2003–2011), respectively—left a toxic residue of depleted uranium over much of Iraq, due to billions of exploded and unexploded rounds fired by US troops. When depleted uranium explodes, it creates a fine, respirable size radioactive dust that contaminates an impact site and presents a long-term health hazard, given its radioactive decay chain of 4.5 billion years. American and British servicemen exposed to depleted uranium in Iraq have suffered myriad health effects, including male infertility and erectile dysfunction (Doyle, Maconochie, and Ryan 2006). Iraqis exposed to depleted uranium have suffered even more, with growing epidemics of cancer, renal disease, and birth defects (Jones 2014; Surdyk et al. 2021).

These toxic legacies have left their mark on Iraqi refugee men in the United States, many of whom served with the US military in the two wars against Saddam Hussein. Among Iraqi refugee men living in Arab America, their "war stories" include exposure to depleted uranium and other war-related traumas, which they deem responsible for their ongoing male infertility problems. In my own study of Iraqi refugee men living in Detroit, Michigan, Arab America's largest ethnic enclave, one man, Kamal, put it this way: "We heard that there is uranium everywhere . . . I know a lot of men like me. They don't have kids, and they take a long time to get a baby. I know about fifteen to twenty people like that, here in Michigan. Some are friends of mine. We are all refugees" (Inhorn 2018, 46).

Why Is Intracytoplasmic Sperm Injection a Hope Technology for Men with Sperm Troubles?

Now a proud father of an infant son, Kamal was fortunate in that he had been able to solve his male infertility problem through ICSI. A variant of IVF, ICSI (pronounced "ick-see") solves the problem of male infertility in a way that IVF cannot. With standard IVF, spermatozoa are removed from a man's body through masturbation, and oocytes are surgically removed from a woman's ovaries following hormonal stimulation. Once these male and female gametes are retrieved, they are introduced to each other in a petri dish in an IVF laboratory, in the hopes of fertilization.

However, "weak" sperm (i.e., low numbers, poor movement, misshapen) are poor fertilizers. Through "micromanipulation" of otherwise infertile sperm under a high-powered microscope, they can be injected directly into human oocytes, effectively "forcing" fertilization to occur (figure 27.1). As long as one viable spermatozoon can be extracted from an infertile man's body, it can be ICSI-injected into an oocyte, leading to the potential creation of a human embryo. With ICSI, then, otherwise sterile men can father biogenetic offspring. This includes azoospermic men, who produce no sperm in their ejaculate. But through ICSI-related technologies including percutaneous epididymal sperm aspiration, testicular sperm extraction, and testicular biopsy, men who are azoospermic can have their testicles (often painfully) aspirated or biopsied in the search for sperm for the ICSI procedure. In short, ICSI and the sperm extraction techniques it has cocreated can be considered "hope technologies" (Franklin 1997)—namely, assisted reproductive technologies that give infertile men the world over a greater chance of producing a "take-home baby."

Following the introduction of ICSI in Belgium in 1992, ICSI quickly made its way to the Middle East, where it was introduced in an IVF clinic in Cairo in in 1994 (Inhorn 2003). Since then, ICSI has led to a virtual "coming out" of male infertility across the region, as men acknowledge

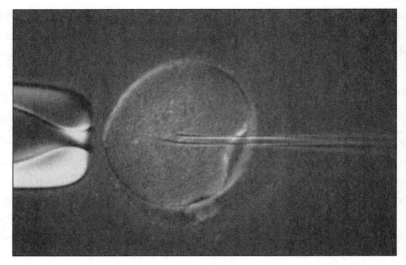

Figure 27.1: Intracytoplasmic sperm injection (ICSI). Courtesy of Spike Walker/Stone/Getty Images (purchased by author for Inhorn 2012).

their infertility and seek the ICSI solution (Inhorn 2012). This masculine hope technology has repaired diminished masculinity in men who were once silently suffering from their infertility. In the Middle East, male infertility is no longer widely perceived as a social problem, but rather as a medical condition that can be treated and overcome.

Furthermore, ICSI is being used in the Middle East and elsewhere as the assisted reproductive technology of choice, effectively replacing its predecessor, IVF. Basically, IVF leaves fertilization up to chance, whereas ICSI does not. Thus, ICSI provides a more guaranteed way of creating "the elusive embryo" (Becker 2000). With ICSI then, human fertilization is increasingly aided and abetted by embryologists working in IVF laboratories around the world. However, some studies from the Middle East suggest that ICSI is being overused for nonmale factor infertility cases and in those cases does not, in fact, improve fertilization or pregnancy rates (Eftekhar et al. 2012).

What Are the Troubles Caused by ICSI Itself?

ICSI may be a breakthrough technology for male infertility, but it is by no means a panacea. For one thing, the precisely timed collection of semen through masturbation can produce deep anxiety and even erectile dysfunction, but it is imperative for most ICSI procedures. In the Muslim world, masturbation itself is generally viewed as *haram*, or religiously forbidden. Thus, masturbation for the purposes of semen collection can be extremely troubling for Muslim men, who often have difficulties producing the required specimen on the day of the procedure (Inhorn 2012, 2015).

In addition, the success of ICSI is quite variable. For azoospermic men who produce no sperm within their testicles, ICSI is not an option; for men with very poor sperm profiles, ICSI may be tried repeatedly, but with no or limited success. When ICSI does succeed, it may be perpetuating genetic defects into future generations, through mutations of the Y chromosome and other inherited disorders (e.g., cystic fibrosis) that may be passed by ICSI to male offspring (Belva et al. 2020). The ethics of passing infertility-related genetic mutations to children—who will then require ICSI in the future to reproduce—has been an increasing cause for concern. In some clinics in the Middle East, preimplantation genetic diagnosis is also being regularly practiced, so that couples affected by severe male factor infertility may be given a choice of culling all of their male embryos to produce female-only offspring (Inhorn 2015).

Why Is ICSI the Only Hope for Infertile Middle Eastern Muslim Men with Sperm Troubles?

Despite these many challenges, ICSI represents the "only hope" for most infertile Middle Eastern men, the vast majority of whom are Muslim. Sperm donation, which has been used in the United States for over a century, is the only other solution for male infertility. But with the exceptions of Shia-dominant Iran and Lebanon, sperm donation is widely prohibited across the Muslim world. Almost all Muslim religious authorities consider sperm donation to be haram, given that it creates genealogical confusion, mistaken paternity, and is also seen as tantamount to *zina*, or equivalent to adultery with a sperm donor. Not surprisingly then, sperm donation, if offered as a solution to male infertility, is almost always refused by Muslim men, who argue that a sperm donor child "won't be my son" (Inhorn 2006, 2012).

Similarly, legal adoption as practiced in the West—where a child takes the adoptive father's (or mother's) surname, can legally inherit from adoptive

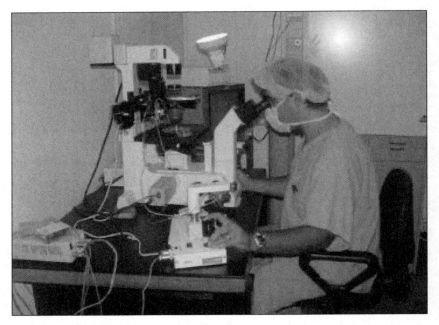

Figure 27.2: ICSI being performed by an embryologist in Beirut, Lebanon. Courtesy of the author.

parents, and is treated as if he or she is a biological child—is also religiously prohibited in most of the Muslim world over concerns about genealogical confusion and the rights of the child to know its biological parents.

In the absence of sperm donation and child adoption then, most infertile Muslim men are left with no other avenues to fatherhood. This makes ICSI the only legitimate solution to male infertility among Muslim men, because it uses their own sperm, no matter how troubled their sperm may be. As one infertile Muslim man in my Lebanese study described his ICSI quest, "I will try again and again and again. I will never lose hope." Or, as another concluded, "I will try until I die" (Inhorn 2012).

Why Is Access to ICSI a Troubling Reproductive Justice Issue for Infertile Men, Especially for Middle Eastern–Born Men Living in the United States?

Not surprisingly then, the emergence of ICSI in the Middle Eastern region in the mid-1990s led to an immediate boom in demand for this technology—a demand that has never waned. IVF clinics today are filled with ICSI-seeking Muslim couples. ICSI is by far the most common assisted reproductive technology now undertaken in the Middle East and in the broader Muslim world, including among diasporic communities in Arab America (Inhorn 2018).

However, ICSI is expensive, usually costing anywhere from $2,000–6,000 per cycle in the Middle East, but $12,000–15,000 per cycle in the United States—the most expensive country in the world, with costs three times the global average. Thus, for many infertile men in the Middle East and Arab America, ICSI is often a last resort, sometimes tried after years of less expensive but failed treatment options (e.g., varicocelectomies to surgically remove varicose veins from the scrotum). For others, ICSI is no option at all because of its exorbitant cost (Inhorn 2012, 2018).

Indeed, lack of ICSI access is a troubling reproductive justice issue, given that reproductive justice entails the right to have children and to parent them safely in healthy environments (Luna 2020). Access to ICSI is the only way for many infertile men to accomplish this goal. But for infertile Muslim men in particular, access to ICSI is also vital for accomplishing this goal in a religiously permitted and morally acceptable manner.

Unfortunately, the achievement of reproductive justice is a fleeting mirage for many Muslim men, as ICSI is well beyond their means. This is especially true for infertile Arab refugee men, many of whom were forced out of their home country by the brutal US-led wars in Iraq, but then found themselves stranded in the United States with its inequitable fee-for-service health care system. This state of "reproductive exile" for many infertile refugees is one for which the United States bears significant moral responsibility, especially given the reproductive damage incited by toxic warfare (Inhorn 2018).

To repay this debt, the US health care system should strive to achieve two significant policy amendments. First, affordable and equitable ICSI access should be guaranteed through an improved Affordable Care Act—one that truly attends to the reproductive health care needs of minority communities, including refugees in this country. Second, the cost of ICSI must be brought down within the private US reproductive health care sector.

Together, reduced ICSI costs and increased ICSI insurance coverage will improve the lives of all infertile men—not only in the United States, but in other nations where lack of ICSI access represents a potent form of reproductive injustice facing men. But among infertile Arab refugee men living in the United States, overcoming this injustice is particularly important. For men like Kamal, fatherhood of an ICSI baby represents a cherished way of rebuilding a meaningful life after so much else has been lost.

Conclusion

This chapter has posed eight key questions about "sperm troubles"— namely, problems with sperm themselves, which lead to medical and social problems for men. These questions are of particular relevance to the Muslim Middle East and Arab America, where male infertility rates are high. As shown through long-term ethnographic research carried out in numerous Middle Eastern countries and in Arab America, ICSI represents a masculine hope technology for infertile men who ardently desire to become fathers using their own sperm. In fact, ICSI represents Muslim men's "only hope," because Islam prohibits both sperm donation and child adoption as solutions for male infertility. Yet, as shown in this chapter, ICSI poses many physical, clinical, and ethical challenges. These include religious concerns over masturbation for semen collection; the variability of ICSI success, especially among azoospermic men who require additional techniques of sperm extraction; and the potential perpetuation of genetic defects among ICSI-conceived male offspring. In addition, the high cost of ICSI is a significant barrier to access, especially among Arab refugee men in the United States who have been made infertile by US-led wars in the region. Indeed, the inability to overcome male infertility because of ICSI's unaffordability represents a potent form of reproductive injustice, thwarting the desire of men to become fathers not only in the Middle East and Arab America but in the world as a whole.

REFERENCES

Barnes, Liberty Walther. 2014. *Conceiving Masculinity: Male Infertility, Medicine, and Identity*. Philadelphia: Temple University Press.

Becker, Gay. 2000. *The Elusive Embryo: How Men and Women Approach New Reproductive Technologies*. Berkeley: University of California Press.

Belva, F., M. Bonduelle, A. Buysse, A. Van den Bogaert, F. Hes, M. Roelants, G. Verheyen, H. Tournaye, and K. Keymolen. 2020. "Chromosomal Abnormalities after ICSI in Relation to Semen Parameters: Results in 1114 Fetuses and 1391 Neonates from a Single Center." *Human Reproduction* 35 (9): 2149–62. https://doi.org/10.1093/humrep/deaa162.

Doyle, Patricia, Noreen Maconochie, and Margaret Ryan. 2006. "Reproductive Health of Gulf War Veterans." *Philosophical Transactions of the Royal Society B* 361 (1,468): 571–84. https://doi.org/10.1098/rstb.2006.1817.

Eftekhar, Maryam, Farnaz Mohammadian, Fariba Yousefnejad, Behnaz Molaei, and Abbas Aflatoonian. 2012. "Comparison of Conventional IVF versus ICSI in Non-male Factor, Normoresponder Patients." *Iranian Journal of Reproductive Medicine* 10 (2): 131–36. doi: 10.18502/ijrm.v19i4.9067.

Franklin, Sarah. 1997. *Embodied Progress: A Cultural Account of Assisted Conception*. London: Routledge.

Greil, Arthur L., Kathleen Slauson-Blevins, and Julia McQuillan. 2010. "The Experience of Infertility: A Review of Recent Literature." *Sociology of Health and Illness* 32 (1): 140–162. https://doi.org/10.1111/j.1467-9566.2009.01213.x.

Hadley, Robin. 2021. *How Is a Man Supposed to be a Man?: Male Childlessness—A Life Course Disrupted*. New York: Berghahn.

Inhorn, Marcia C. 1994. *Quest for Conception: Gender, Infertility, and Egyptian Medical Traditions*. Philadelphia: University of Pennsylvania Press.

Inhorn, Marcia C. 1996. *Infertility and Patriarchy: The Cultural Politics of Gender and Family Life in Egypt*. Philadelphia: University of Pennsylvania Press.

Inhorn, Marcia C. 2003. *Local Babies, Global Science: Gender, Religion, and In Vitro Fertilization in Egypt*. New York: Routledge.

Inhorn, Marcia C. 2006. "'He Won't Be My Son': Middle Eastern Men's Discourses of Adoption and Gamete Donation." *Medical Anthropology Quarterly* 20 (1): 94–120. https://doi.org/10.1525/maq.2006.20.1.94.

Inhorn, Marcia C. 2012. *The New Arab Man: Emergent Masculinities, Technologies, and Islam in the Middle East*. Princeton, NJ: Princeton University Press.

Inhorn, Marcia C. 2015. *Cosmopolitan Conceptions: IVF Sojourns in Global Dubai*. Durham, NC: Duke University Press.

Inhorn, Marcia C. 2018. *America's Arab Refugees: Vulnerability and Health on the Margins*. Stanford, CA: Stanford University Press.

Inhorn, Marcia C., Loulou Kobeissi, Zaher Nassar, Da'ad Lakkis, and Michael Hassan Fakih. 2009. "Consanguinity and Family Clustering of Male Infertility in Lebanon." *Fertility and Sterility* 91 (4): 1,104–9. https://doi.org/10.1016/j.fertnstert.2008.01.008.

Inhorn, Marcia C., and Pasquale Patrizio. 2015. "Infertility Around the Globe: New Thinking on Gender, Reproductive Technologies, and Global Movements in the 21st Century." *Human Reproduction Update* 21 (4): 411–26. https://doi.org/10.1093/humupd/dmv016.

Jones, Toby C. 2014. "Toxic War and the Politics of Uncertainty in Iraq." *International Journal of Middle East Studies* 46 (4): 797–99. https://doi.org/10.1017/S0020743814001123.

Kleinman, Arthur. 1992. "Local Worlds of Suffering: An Interpersonal Focus for Ethnographies of Illness Experience." *Qualitative Health Research* 2 (2): 127–34. https://doi.org/10.1177/104973239200200202.

Lloyd, Mike. 1996. "Condemned to Be Meaningful: Non-response in the Studies of Men and Infertility." *Sociology of Health and Illness* 18 (4): 433–54. https://doi.org/10.1111/1467-9566.ep10939057.

Luna, Zakiya. 2020. *Reproductive Rights as Human Rights: Women of Color and the Fight for Reproductive Justice*. New York: New York University Press.

Martinez, Gladys M., Kimberly Daniels, and Isaedmarie Febo-Vazquez. 2018. "Fertility of Men and Women Aged 15–44 in the United States: National Survey of Family Growth, 2011–2015." *National Health Statistics Reports* 113:1–17. https://dx.doi.org/10.15620/cdc:122080.

Maximova, Katerina, and Amélie Quesnel-Vallée. 2009. "Mental Health Consequences of Unintended Childlessness and Unplanned Births: Gender Differences and Life Course Dynamics." *Social Science and Medicine* 68 (5): 850–57. https://doi.org/10.1016/j.socscimed.2008.11.012.

Rashad, Hoda, Magued Osman, and Farzaneh Roudi-Fahimi. 2005. *Marriage in the Arab World*. Washington, DC: Population Reference Bureau.

Surdyk, Shelby, Moustapha Itani, Mais Al-Lobaidy, Lara A. Kahale, Aida Farha, Omar Dewachi, Elie A. Akl, and Rima R. Habib. 2021. "Weaponised Uranium and Adverse Health Outcomes in Iraq: A Systematic Review." *BMJ Global Health* 6:e004166. http://dx.doi.org/10.1136/bmjgh-2020-004166.

Wischmann, Tewes, and Petra Thorn. 2013. "(Male) Infertility: What Does It Mean to Men? New Evidence from Quantitative and Qualitative Studies." *Reproductive BioMedicine Online* 27 (3): 236–43. https://doi.org/10.1016/j.rbmo.2013.06.002.

28

Sex, Gender, and the Biological and Mental "Load" of Reproduction

JULIE BINDEMAN

Author's Note: For this piece, it was important to me to try to "ungender" pregnancy and parenting where I could. While most academic literature in the past was written within the paradigm of a gender and parenting binary, newer writings are working to adopt a more expansive framework as the concept of a gender continuum has become more accepted. When quoting past articles directly, I will use the language of the article.

Introduction

"It takes two to tango" is an often-used euphemism for heterosexuality, particularly if a pregnancy results from a sexual encounter. While this expression acknowledges that pregnancy does not occur within a vacuum, it is often understood that pregnancy exists as a time and state that is centered primarily in cisgender women and, less often, in pregnant trans men. While it does take two to conceive, once conception occurs, there is an automatic and seemingly unconscious shift in responsibility. This extends to the burden of the mental load, often the unseen time and energy spent preparing and executing the work within a family. Women more often feel this burden, and with pregnancy occurring in a woman's body, the mental load begins at conception. So, though both sperm and egg create a baby-to-be, the mental load begins very lopsided, particularly when the State has eliminated choice around pregnancy.

What Is the "Mental Load" of Reproduction?

A biological act that required coequal participation—fertilization—becomes unequal in the next stage—pregnancy—since females are biologically required to do 100 percent of the work of pregnancy. Not only is there a biological inequality, but even the most egalitarian heterosexual couples, who split chores and do not adhere to the gendered roles of their parents' or grandparents' time, become flummoxed and often default to the gender roles of generations past when it comes to taking care of a baby. Charlotte Faircloth writes about these competing "strata" (or stages) that couples experience, where, on the one hand, relationships are "idealized as equitable and intimate" and, on the other hand, once they begin to parent, the relationships shift to an idealization that centers around "intensive[ness] and gendered [roles]" (Faircloth 2021).

Indeed, inherent to parenting comes work that is often unseen, and in the psychological research literature, this is referred to as "the mental load." Liz Dean, Brendan Churchill, and Leah Ruppanner (2022, 13) encapsulate the mental load as "the combination of the cognitive labor of family life—the thinking, planning, scheduling, and organizing of family members and the emotional labor associated with this work, including the feelings of caring and being responsible for family members but also the emotional impact of this work." Yet, coming up with a uniformly accepted definition of the mental load has proved difficult. Lindsey G. Robertson et al. (2019) identified six aspects of the mental load (they used the term "mental labor"): planning and strategizing; monitoring and anticipating needs; meta parenting; knowing (learning and remembering); managerial thinking (including delegating and instructing); and self-regulation.

Historically, the mental load has been inherently shouldered by women in all aspects: cognitive, emotional, and, of course, physical, and this work is seemingly invisible to men. The mental load is an aspect that is often conferred from the beginning of pregnancy, where the idea that is conditioned and reinforced is that the act of gestation is solely the responsibility of the person who is pregnant. Certainly, this assigning of the mental load is true in its most biological sense and is often true in a social sense as well. It is the pregnant person who experiences physical changes in their body and who is encouraged to take daily prenatal vitamins, as well as attend doctor appointments, among various other tasks. All of these can lead to additional burdens, such as time off from work and the expense of doctor's appointments; time off from work for bedrest, should complications arise; and, if they have older children, additional childcare expenses as children are not welcome at many physician offices. Often, women know about these exigent factors that come with pregnancy, which might make them consider or reconsider if they really want to be pregnant.

Making Pregnancy Decisions

When people are unsure about continuing a pregnancy, there may be a conversation within the couple (for those who are partnered) about how to proceed. From my experience counseling those in this situation, they might face a range of questions: Who's choice is it, actually? Does the person who provided sperm have any say? Or should the choice solely be that of the person who is pregnant? Can it truly be a mutual decision?

There is scant research on men and their emotional experiences of unintended pregnancies. By definition, the intention (or lack thereof) of a pregnancy is in the eye of the beholder, as partners might not be aligned. According to a review by Beáta Nagy and Adrien Rigó (2021), men under twenty-five years old and those not living with their partner at the time of pregnancy are more likely to label a pregnancy as "unintended." Other factors also contributed to this labeling, such as financial security, whether their education was still in progress, and the relationship's stability. Interestingly, this review found that, in about a third of the cases, women followed their partners' labeling of pregnancies as unintended.

The stigma that surrounds abortion as a decision (within the three domains of perceived stigma, enacted stigma, and internalized stigma) tends to be based on (at best) "disrespect" and, at worst, misogyny, as Rachel L. Dyer, Olivia R. Checkalski, and Sarah J. Gervais (2023) explicate. Regardless of who makes the choice or what choice is made, or even if the choice is agreed upon, there is a gendered inequality in how each partner is perceived within society, which can be crisscrossed with socioeconomic and racial inequalities. For example, a woman choosing abortion may be viewed as a "slut," or some other shaming type of language, and that same language might also be applied if she continues the pregnancy, as it offers visible proof of sexual activity. However, her male partner has no pregnancy identifier and might even be celebrated as a "stud" for his "strong swimmers," given the positive language often used to describe a male's role in conception.

It does not matter how the decision to end a pregnancy is made: societally and legally, the male's options remain significantly more flexible than the female's options. Because of how society sets up the demand and responsibility on women around pregnancy, there are few, if any, consequences set up and enforced that impact men in this decision. Men can leave and not participate in the emotional, financial, or hands-on bearing or rearing of a child. Few states have mandatory paternity testing with the follow-through of child support (which tends to begin at birth). Even if states have this protection, the enforcement often lacks actual teeth for this to be effective or, in many cases, real. However, as in Lynne Haney's essay in this volume, this supposition and stereotype is not necessarily true, particularly for fathers who have been incarcerated and have had to be entangled with two systems: the penal system and the child support system. This all being said, giving men too much say can also be seen as fraught, as noted in Jennifer A. Reich's essay in this volume.

The Bodily and Psychological Load of Pregnancy, Birth, and Breastfeeding

If people do continue with a pregnancy, the bodily and psychological division of labor continues to be disproportional for the person giving birth. Pregnancy and childbirth are inherently risky, and the magnitude of risk differs based on race and socioeconomic status (Njoku et al. 2023). Paula Braveman (2023) outlines specific systemic factors that contribute to increased mortality and morbidity for Black, Latine, and Indigenous Americans (Braveman 2023). There are strong and repeated correlations between a lack of college education, teen pregnancies, and being a single parent as well as other social determinants including low income, which factors into situations such as food or housing insecurity, poor nutrition, and chronic stress (Braveman 2023; Njoku et al. 2023). Regardless of the different risk profiles, women and pregnant people subject themselves to potential risk in the act of giving birth with each pregnancy they undertake.

After birth, a female's biological load does not end. While, in theory, lactation could potentially be induced in males (given that they have mammary glands), it is an exceedingly rare occurrence and is now usually discussed with reference to trans women (García-Acosta et al. 2019). Often, breastfeeding is seen as an easy decision for both members of a heterosexual couple, given the appearance of its economic and often-touted health benefits. However, an in-depth article looking at the supposed benefits of breastfeeding showed something surprising: the association between breastfeeding and positive health outcomes in children is weak rather than causal (Colen and Ramsey 2014). Additionally, the costs of breastfeeding are often invisible (such as the time it takes a person to nurse), seen as a single-time investment (for example, breast pumps and parts), or perceived as easy (whereas there can be a steep learning curve for both parent and child) (Mahoney, Taylor, and Forman 2023).

For the person who just gave birth, breastfeeding might feel like a sustained emotional tie with the baby that is unique to this particular dyad (Tucker and O'Malley 2022). There are public campaigns that enforce this idea and have emphasized the importance of breastfeeding, perhaps a little too well (Barnhill and Morain 2015). Human breastmilk has the ability to be pumped, therefore giving nonbirthing parents such as fathers an opportunity to bottle feed the baby without couples needing to choose formula if they are hoping to breastfeed (Felice et al. 2017). Potentially, for cisgender heterosexual couples, bottle feeding can free up a mother as well as enable her partner to share in the intimate attachment experience of feeding (Dagla et al. 2023).

Conclusion

In addition to the biological requirements of pregnancy, birth, and beyond, the mental load becomes another burden for many cis women. Over time, it is possible for this load to be shared in more gender-egalitarian ways, even in the face of significant societal pressures and systems. For example, *Fair Play* is a program, book, and documentary by Eve Rodsky (2019) that guides how families might shift the load to make it more equitable within a family system. One suggestion she makes is to write down every single task that each person does on cards, and then together, they can be divided (based on choice and preference) equitably.

Even as women and other pregnant people carry most of the biological and often mental loads of pregnancy and childrearing, the question of "who decides" (lawmakers, individuals, couples) can linger. In most state legislatures across the nation, men still constitute the majority. This is exactly the part of the population least bodily impacted by pregnancy, birth, and childrearing, yet they are responsible for introducing and passing laws that disproportionately affect women. And at the moment, state after state is rolling back abortion laws and creating new incentives to curb abortion. While it takes two actually to conceive a child, women bear the bodily and psychological load even as they are being shut out of legal decision-making about reproduction.

REFERENCES

Barnhill, Anne, and Stephanie R. Morain. 2015. "Latch On or Back Off? Public Health, Choice, and the Ethics of Breast-Feeding Promotion Campaigns." *International Journal of Feminist Approaches to Bioethics* 8 (2):139–71. https://doi.org/10.3138/ijfab.8.2.139.

Bos, Henny M. W., Lisette Kuyper, and Nanett K. Gartrell. 2018. "A Population-Based Comparison of Female and Male Same-Sex Parent and Different-Sex Parent Households." *Family Process* 57 (1):148–64. https://doi.org/10.1111/famp.12278.

Braveman, Paula. 2023. "Preventing Maternal Mortality." *Medical Care* 61 (5): 255–57.

Colen, Cynthia G., and David M. Ramey. 2014. "Is Breast Truly Best? Estimating the Effects of Breastfeeding on Long-Term Child Health and Wellbeing in the United States Using Sibling Comparisons." *Social Science & Medicine* 109:55–65. https://doi.org/10.1016/j.socscimed.2014.01.027.

Dagla, Calliope, Evangelia Antoniou, Antigoni Sarantaki, Maria Iliadou, Irina Mrvoljak-Theodoropoulou, Ewa Andersson, and Maria Dagla. 2023. "The Effect of Antenatal Education on Expectant Fathers' Attitudes Toward Breastfeeding and Attachment to the Fetus." *Nursing Reports* 13 (1): 243–54. https://doi.org/10.3390/nursrep13010023.

Dean, Liz, Brendan Churchill, and Leah Ruppanner. 2022. "The Mental Load: Building a Deeper Theoretical Understanding of How Cognitive and Emotional Labor Overload Women and Mothers." *Community, Work & Family* 25 (1): 13–29. https://doi.org/10.1080/13668803.2021.2002813.

Dyer, Rachel L., Olivia R. Checkalski, and Sarah J. Gervais. 2023. "Abortion Decisions as Humanizing Acts: The Application of Ambivalent Sexism and Objectification to Women-Centered Anti-Abortion Rhetoric." *Psychology of Women Quarterly* 47 (4): 528–46. https://doi.org/10.1177/03616843231173673.

Faircloth, Charlotte. 2021. "When Equal Partners Become Unequal Parents: Couple Relationships and Intensive Parenting Culture." *Families, Relationships and Societies* 10 (2): 231–48. https://doi.org/10.1332/204674319X15761552010506.

Felice, Julia P., Sheela R. Geraghty, Caroline W. Quaglieri, Rei Yamada, Adriana J. Wong, and Kathleen M. Rasmussen. 2017. "'Breastfeeding' but Not at the Breast: Mothers' Descriptions of Providing Pumped Human Milk to Their Infants via Other Containers and Caregivers." *Maternal and Child Nutrition* 13:e12425. https://doi.org/10.1111/mcn.12425.

García-Acosta, Jesús Manuel, Rosa María San Juan-Valdivia, Alfredo David Fernández-Martínez, Nieves Doria Lorenzo-Rocha, and Maria Elisa Castro-Peraza. 2019. "Trans Pregnancy and Lactation: A Literature Review from a Nursing Perspective." *International Journal of Environmental Research and Public Health* 17 (1): 44. https://doi.org/10.3390/ijerph17010044.

Mahoney, Sarah E., Sarah N. Taylor, and Howard P. Forman. 2023. "No Such Thing as a Free Lunch: The Direct Marginal Costs of Breastfeeding." *Journal of Perinatology* 43:678–82. https://doi.org/10.1038/s41372-023-01646-z.

Nagy, Beáta, and Adrien Rigó. 2021. "The Psychosocial Aspects of Induced Abortion: Men in the Focus." *Men and Masculinities* 24 (4): 671–89. https://doi.org/10.1177/1097184X19856399.

Njoku, Anuli, Marian Evans, Lillian Nimo-Sefah, and Jonell Bailey. 2023. "Listen to the Whispers before They Become Screams: Addressing Black Maternal Morbidity and Mortality in the United States." *Healthcare* 11 (3): 438. https://doi.org/10.3390/healthcare11030438.

Robertson, Lindsey G., Tamara L. Anderson, M. Elizabeth Lewis Hall, and Christina Lee Kim. 2019. "Mothers and Mental Labor: A Phenomenological Focus Group Study of Family-Related Thinking Work." *Psychology of Women Quarterly* 43 (2):184–200. https://doi.org/10.1177/0361684319825581.

Rodsky, Eve. 2019. *Fair Play: A Game-Changing Solution for When You Have too Much to do (and More Life to Live)*. New York: Putnam.

Tucker, Zachary, and Chasity O'Malley. 2022. "Mental Health Benefits of Breastfeeding: A Literature Review." *Cureus* 14 (9): e29199. https://doi.org/10.7759%2Fcureus.29199.

29

Direct-to-Consumer Digital Health, Hybrid Masculinities, and the "Straighting" of Sexual Intimacy

BEN CURRAN WILLS

In mid-2018, images of pokey, prickly, and decidedly phallic cactuses were plastered across New York's subway stations by a new startup called Hims in a highly visible ad campaign for erectile dysfunction (ED) treatment (Mascarenhas 2021). With clever marketing backed by venture capital, Hims has sold generic Viagra (sildenafil) and similar drugs to likely millions of men across the United States, achieving a multi-billion-dollar valuation (Brown and De Vynck 2020). Ro, another major player in this space, has had similar success with viral advertisements and high-visibility sponsorship of organizations like Major League Baseball.

Although these companies represent a slice of the US health care industry, they have had an outsize impact on consumers, especially the digital-native Millennials they primarily target (De Vynck and Huet 2018). Hims spends roughly *half* of its gross revenue on marketing (Ro is likely similar; most companies spend in the single digits). It is no surprise, then, that 40 percent of respondents in a pilot survey had heard of one or both (Wills 2023). Analyzing the marketing of Hims, Ro, and other direct-to-consumer digital health companies that focus on men's sexual health, then, is critical for understanding the present and future of masculinities, men's sexual health care, and their intersections. These companies exploit classic anxieties around masculinity and sex, repackaging them in pastel hues to market pharmaceutical and over-the-counter treatments for ED and premature ejaculation to young men. When marketing frames on-demand, hyperfirm erections and infinite ejaculatory latency not as normal differences, but "options" that men choose, the possibilities for subversive masculinities and diverse sexual intimacies are constricted.

What are these companies exactly? Hims and Ro are two of the largest direct-to-consumer digital health companies and exemplars of a new health care business model. Such companies sit at the intersection of three lines of business: telehealth, mail-order pharmacies, and direct-to-consumer lifestyle and wellness goods. First, company-employed or -contracted telehealth physicians evaluate potential patients for a limited range of minor conditions promoted by the companies; typically, this involves reviewing electronic forms and asynchronously messaging with the patient. Upon diagnosis and purchase, companies then mail consumer-patients their prescriptions, which are often bundled with over-the-counter treatments—direct-to-consumer digital health companies are not only medical providers, but subscription-based consumer goods businesses as well. Like many of the other direct-to-consumer startups familiar to anyone who has scrolled on Instagram in the last decade (for example, Allbirds, Birch Box, Glossier, Hello Fresh, Smile Direct Club, and Warby Parker), direct-to-consumer digital health companies spend heavily on marketing to gain new customers and recoup their costs by establishing long-term relationships with customers (Schlesinger, Higgins, and Roseman 2020).

Though there are many direct-to-consumer digital health brands and foci, cis men's health and wellness has been a core focus since the industry began.[1] Indeed, the category took off when Viagra went off-patent in 2017 (Barnett 2021). Generic ED medication is a major sales driver in this segment (Mascarenhas 2021), alongside treatment for premature ejaculation with lidocaine wipes and antianxiety drugs like escitalopram (generic Lexapro).

Over the past five years, I have immersed myself in industry news coverage, listened to interviews with direct-to-consumer digital health executives, and built a collection of photos of advertisements. These materials, along with visual content analysis of a subset of social media advertisements from Hims and Ro (Wills and Gottlieb 2025), suggest that these companies aim to expand the target audience for treatment of erectile dysfunction and premature ejaculation. Twenty-five years ago, the archetypal Viagra patient was a white, cisgender, heterosexual, middle-aged-to-older man. Direct-to-consumer men's digital health advertising campaigns, however, target men as young as their twenties.

To understand why advertising to younger men about erectile dysfunction and premature ejaculation may be problematic, it is important to understand what they "are." What sounds self-explanatory are in fact intricate histories. As they are known today, erectile dysfunction and premature ejaculation are relatively recent, social-medico-pharmaceutical creations. In the early 1900s in the United States, erectile dysfunction was understood to be a problem in young men but expected for older men (Fishman 2010). Later in the twentieth century, erectile dysfunction was conceptualized as a barrier to a new idea of "successful aging." Encouraged by a colleague's demonstration proving the effectiveness of physiological (instead of psychiatric) treatments, in the 1980s urologists claimed erectile difficulties as within their treatment domain. By the mid-1990s, the term "erectile dysfunction" was established (Mamo and Fishman 2001). Premature ejaculation, on the other hand, has long been understood as problematic. Recently, it has been the subject of increased medical attention, elevated by quantifiable diagnostic criteria and routinely treated by off-label antianxiety drugs as a first line of treatment (Grunt-Mejer 2022b).

In their current guise, erectile dysfunction and premature ejaculation share three common threads. First, they are now understood to be pathological at any age. Second, they have been pharmaceuticalized—that is, constructed as diseases for which medication (and not talk therapy or surgery, for example) is understood to be the most logical treatment.[2] And third, they have been tightly attached to particular visions of masculinity.

The success of sexual dysfunction treatments has in large part been due to pharmaceutical companies' early successes in marketing sexual health conditions and motivating treatment-seeking by appealing to masculine anxieties (Mamo and Fishman 2001). Featuring politically and athletically dominant celebrity spokesmen, as well as graying men and their wives cavorting on beaches, advertisements from the early- and mid-2000s linked masculine power and intimate partnership with penile turgidity (Loe 2004; Lexchin 2006). Initial marketing focused on expanding "awareness" of erectile dysfunction but progressively widened to target younger men, emphasizing erectile "quality" and "difficulties" over "dysfunction." This further expanded the population of medicalized penises, or those deemed appropriate for medical intervention (Lexchin 2006).

Today's direct-to-consumer digital health advertising for erectile dysfunction and premature ejaculation extends these links in a social milieu that has at least superficially evolved since the turn of the millennium. The audience for yesteryear's ads held different ideals of masculinity than the HENRY ("high earner, not rich yet") men who are the targets of current advertising campaigns (Daly 2019). For the latter group, contemporary embodiments of masculinity are more complex and subtle. In this regime of "hybrid masculinities" (Bridges and Pascoe 2014), where men strategically adopt aesthetic or other characteristics of subordinated masculinities while maintaining rhetorical distance, expressions of (particularly white) masculinity present in self-aware, symbolically distant relation to more obvious, stereotypical masculine aesthetics that pervade the first generation of ED ads.

In their ads, direct-to-consumer men's digital health companies recruit hybrid masculine aesthetics while hammering on durable masculine insecurities around sexual performance. Models appear young, of various ethnicities, handsome but not intimidatingly so, and dressed in outfits seemingly picked from the digital racks of Everlane, another millennial-targeting direct-to-consumer company. One social media ad shows a cisgender, heterosexual-seeming couple in their twenties excitedly pointing toward text reading "Last up to 5x longer" (Hims & Hers Health, Inc. 2023). Another shows a man and woman happily embracing; the woman holds a tin of Hims' "Hard Mints" chewable tablets and superimposed text reads, "GET HARDER, GO LONGER / Light her fire" (Hims & Hers Health, Inc. 2024a). A third is "for your wild side . . . and hers," enabling men to "have better sex whenever you want" and "go hard. Go long. Go chewable" (Hims & Hers Health, Inc. 2024b). By tying partnered happiness to phallic potency and mastery of ejaculation, these ads exploit and reinforce age-old masculine insecurities regarding sexual performance (see also Almeling 2020).

As these examples show, not only do direct-to-consumer men's digital health advertisements expand the age range of men targeted by sexual health marketing, but they also reestablish which bodily variations merit treatment. Erectile dysfunction marketing of the past shifted from dysfunction to quality and difficulties. Current direct-to-consumer men's digital health advertisements continue this trend, reframing the purpose of medicine from *treatment* to *enhancement* (cf. Marshall 2006). Rather than use the medical languages of physical issues ("Do you have problems with erections?") or even diagnostic categories ("Do you have ED?"), which imply a goal of restoring normal function, such advertisements offer the potential to improve—that is, enhance—performance ("last long*er*"), regardless of the starting point. By recruiting tropes of comparative, performance-based masculinity, they shift the goalposts, normalizing "better and better" over "well and good."

Targeting twenty-somethings' insecurities in erectile dysfunction and premature ejaculation advertising reinforces performance insecurity as a normative part of male, masculine experience (though if you have generalized or performance anxiety, Hims sells antianxiety medication, off-label antidepressants, and beta-blockers, too). Moreover, for an even younger generation of men, it reinforces the sexual encounter as a site of self-consciousness and performance evaluation. This can lead to sexual experiences that, ironically, are less intimate and fulfilling for all involved (Mamo and Fishman 2001).

That improved "access" to erectile-dysfunction- and premature-ejaculation-affecting substances is not as felicitous as it might at first sound is brought into further relief when the kinds of sex they imply is contrasted with queer sexual practices. With an appreciation of myriad sizes, abilities, embodiments, and desires, queer sex can be a liberatory, expansive contradiction to the phallocentric, penetration-focused, well-worn script of normative heterosex (cf. Potts 2000). Penetration may occur (by any number of things, bodily or otherwise), or not; orgasm may occur, or not; erections and ejaculations may feature prominently, or not at all. Queer sex is certainly not without its own scripts (and occurs detached from neither cis-heteronormative sexual scripts nor normative masculinities) but starting from a blanker page affords a greater variety of emotions, intimacies, and bodily (mal)functions.

Queer in this sense is used expansively, in terms of deviance from cultural expectations of whom to love, how to be intimate, how to present and identify—in short, how to be. From this lens, cisgender, heterosexual couples can and do engage in behavior that one can perceive queerly (the politics of identifying as queer being another matter entirely). Studies looking at the impact of ED drugs on their original market—older couples—are helpful in this regard. Some female partners found they had mixed feelings when Viagra popped up in their bedrooms. While appreciated by those who enjoyed the revival of penetrative sex with their partners, for others, the introduction of Viagra recentered masculine performance and physicality in sex at the cost of the affectionate dimensions of sexual intimacy that had bloomed in the absence of omnipresent erections (Loe 2004; Grunt-Mejer 2022a). Similarly, and contrary to cisgender, heterosexual norms, some older cishet men appreciate being relieved of the duties of penetrative heterosex and enjoy the opportunities for intimacy that emerged in the absence of this expectation (Towler et al. 2022).

Considering cisgender heterosexual intimacy through a queer lens and alongside the experience of older adults suggests that lasting "5x longer" is not necessarily the marriage-saving panacea that Hims and Ro make it out to be. Instead, it is likely to accentuate stresses of intimate partnerships. It would seem, then, that despite approachable, relatable ads and rhetorics of "democratizing access," Hims and Ro exploit and reinscribe age-old anxieties through the aesthetics of hybrid masculinities. The recent expansion of direct-to-consumer men's sexual digital health ultimately "straights," not queers, normative male self-understanding and sexual imaginaries, to the detriment of cis men and their intimate partners.

NOTES

1 These companies also treat women, e.g. through "sister" brand Hers. At no point, however, do they earnestly engage with non-cis people. There are direct-to-consumer digital health companies like Folx Health and Plume that specifically focus on trans+ people and gender-affirming care.

Also important to consider, but outside of the scope of this essay, are the differences between direct-to-consumer digital health brands marketed toward men and women. While erections, ejaculation, and balding are the primary focuses of male-focused brands, women's brands emphasize anxiety and depression. Mental health treatment may be a tougher sell for men, but they are not as far apart as one might think—for a yet-unclear amount of time, Hers was a sales channel for Addyi (flibanserin), a failed antidepressant that was rebranded and approved by the Food and Drug Administration for "female hypoactive sexual desire disorder" despite sustained skepticism of the condition, flibanserin's efficacy, and the drug's safety, given the side effects of extreme drowsiness when paired with alcohol. There is much to say (and much has been said) about the differences between erectile dysfunction treatment, which provides physiological effect but presumes desire, and female-targeted equivalents, which generally focus on a lack of desire.

2 Indeed, the effectiveness of sildenafil and other PDE5 inhibitors is itself an element of the diagnostic process, and failure of these drugs is indication of further pathology (Hackett et al. 2018). This, however, can mask the many causes of erectile dysfunction. Thank you to Brian T. Nguyen for this point.

REFERENCES

Almeling, Rene. 2020. *GUYnecology: The Missing Science of Men's Reproductive Health*. Oakland: University of California Press.

Barnett, Kendra. 2021. "Hims, Nurx and Ro's New Prescription for Pharma Sales and Marketing." *The Drum*, April 6, 2021. www.thedrum.com.

Bridges, Tristan, and C. J. Pascoe. 2014. "Hybrid Masculinities: New Directions in the Sociology of Men and Masculinities." *Sociology Compass* 8 (3): 246–58. https://doi.org/10.1111/soc4.12134.

Brown, Kristen, and Gerrit De Vynck. 2020. "Hims Built a $1.6 Billion Online Empire by Pushing Prescriptions." *Bloomberg*, October 30, 2020. www.bloomberg.com.

Daly, Dominique. 2019. "Hack HENRY: Maximise Millennial Marketing with Demographic Segmentation." *Hurree* (blog), October 14, 2019. https://blog.hurree.co.

De Vynck, Gerrit, and Ellen Huet. 2018. "This Startup Is Selling Generic Viagra and Rogaine to the Instagram Crowd." *BNN Bloomberg*, July 18, 2018, sec. Company News. www.bnnbloomberg.ca.

Fishman, Jennifer R. 2010. "The Making of Viagra: The Biomedicalization of Sexual Dysfunction." In *Biomedicalization: Technoscience, Health, and Illness in the U.S.*, edited by Adele E. Clarke, Laura Mamo, Jennifer Ruth Fosket, Jennifer R. Fishman, and Janet K. Shim, 289–306. Durham, NC: Duke University Press. https://doi.org/10.1215/9780822391258-011.

Grunt-Mejer, Katarzyna. 2022a. "'Disordering' Sex Through Medicine." In *The Routledge Handbook of Philosophy of Sex and Sexuality*, edited by Brian D. Earp, Clare Chambers, and Lori Watson, 375–92. New York: Routledge. https://doi.org/10.4324/9781003286523-32.

Grunt-Mejer, Katarzyna. 2022b. "The History of the Medicalisation of Rapid Ejaculation—A Reflection of the Rising Importance of Female Pleasure in a Phallocentric World." *Psychology & Sexuality* 13 (3): 565–82. https://doi.org/10.1080/19419899.2021.1888312.

Hackett, Geoff, Mike Kirby, Kevan Wylie, Adrian Heald, Nick Ossei-Gerning, David Edwards, and Asif Muneer. 2018. "British Society for Sexual Medicine Guidelines on the Management of Erectile Dysfunction in Men—2017." *Journal of Sexual Medicine* 15 (4): 430–57. https://doi.org/10.1016/j.jsxm.2018.01.023.

Hims & Hers Health, Inc. 2023. "Last up to 5x longer." Digital advertisement shown on Meta social media platforms. Meta Ad Library, 1374250639872193. https://www.facebook.com/ads/library/?id=1374250639872193.

Hims & Hers Health, Inc. 2024a. "Light her fire." Digital advertisement shown on Meta social media platforms. Meta Ad Library, 1509195973110583. https://www.facebook.com/ads/library/?id=1509195973110583.

Hims & Hers Health, Inc. 2024b. "Go hard. Go long. Go chewable." Digital advertisement shown on Meta social media platforms. Meta Ad Library, 1526382391480729. https://www.facebook.com/ads/library/?id=1526382391480729.

Lexchin, Joel. 2006. "Bigger and Better: How Pfizer Redefined Erectile Dysfunction." *PLOS Medicine* 3 (4): e132. https://doi.org/10.1371/journal.pmed.0030132.

Loe, Meika. 2004. "Sex and the Senior Woman: Pleasure and Danger in the Viagra Era." *Sexualities* 7 (3): 303–26. https://doi.org/10.1177/1363460704044803.

Mascarenhas, Natasha. 2021. "Employees Detail Rising Tensions at Ro as Healthcare Unicorn Struggles to Grow beyond First Win." *TechCrunch*, October 27, 2021. https://social.techcrunch.com/2021/10/27/ro/.

Mamo, Laura, and Jennifer R. Fishman. 2001. "Potency in All the Right Places: Viagra as a Technology of the Gendered Body." *Body & Society* 7 (4): 13–35. https://doi.org/10.1177/1357034X01007004002.

Marshall, Barbara L. 2006. "The New Virility: Viagra, Male Aging and Sexual Function." *Sexualities* 9 (3): 345–62. https://doi.org/10.1177/1363460706065057.

Potts, Annie. 2000. "'The Essence of the Hard On': Hegemonic Masculinity and the Cultural Construction of 'Erectile Dysfunction.'" *Men and Masculinities* 3 (1): 85–103. https://doi.org/10.1177/1097184X00003001004.

Schlesinger, Leonard A., Matt Higgins, and Shaye Roseman. 2020. "Reinventing the Direct-to-Consumer Business Model." *Harvard Business Review*, March 31, 2020. https://hbr.org.

Towler, Lauren B., Cynthia A. Graham, Felicity L. Bishop, and Sharron Hinchliff. 2022. "Sex and Relationships in Later Life: Older Adults' Experiences and Perceptions of Sexual Changes." *Journal of Sex Research* 60 (9): 1,318–31. https://doi.org/10.1080/00224499.2022.2093322.

Wills, Ben Curran. 2023. "Paging Dr. Bezos: Health Equity and the Rise of Direct-to-Consumer Digital Health." MS thesis, Georgia Institute of Technology, 2023.

Wills, Ben Curran, and Jeremy Gottlieb. 2025. "After Viagra®: Multivalent Medicalization, Hybrid Masculinities, and Direct-to-Consumer Digital Health." Under Review at *NORMA* International Journal for Masculinities 1–21. https://doi.org/10.1080/18902138.2025.2451509.

30

Speculating about Sperm for Trans Reproductive Futures

CARLO SARIEGO

Sperm is stuck. In the historical context, it is stuck in histories of violent paternal lineages that have established and maintained power in many national contexts, and it has been an important adhesive between colonial and imperial conquest (Preciado 2015; Yuval-Davis 1997). Culturally, sperm is stuck under the heavy weight of masculinity, virility, and fatherhood. In reproductive health and science, sperm is stuck on one side of a biological binary. What all these contexts have in common is that sperm is stuck in the association of male, men, and fathers and in a reproductive hierarchy that centers whiteness (Valdez and Deomampo 2019).

To unstick sperm, this essay makes two arguments: (1) sperm is conceptually trapped by notions of sex, masculinity, and fatherhood (at the exclusion of fathers who do not produce sperm and mothers who do), and (2) using the tool of reproductive speculation, transgender women have unstuck sperm and reappropriated it as a metonym for reproductive intimacy and a tool for seeing the future. By taking sperm outside of its normal context and centering trans and queer reproductive desires, this essay shows how sperm's association with fatherhood and its gendering as male traps its utility in reproductive justice and possibility. By troubling knowledge about sperm and its potentialities I argue that speculation is the best tool for addressing reproductive stickiness, and reproductive desire should be prioritized as much as reproductive need. This essay concludes, following the work of transgender women, that all reproduction is a speculative miracle.

What Is Sperm?

Centering a reproductive material like sperm in questions of transgender inclusion in reproductive studies troubles the idea that such inclusion could be resolved through a change in language alone. Scholars of transgender health care have called for research that is more inclusive of transgender people, specifically in reproductive health (Pfeffer et al. 2023). Researchers have heeded this call by utilizing gender-neutral language in discussions of reproduction (Rowlands and Amy 2018).

While necessary for the advancement of trans health and thriving, changing terminology does little to address the ways in which a reproductive material like sperm circulates in cultural and scientific realms of strict sexual divisions that do not reflect the reproductive miracles transgender people's bodies can perform. Within these strict divisions, sperm is something male-sexed bodies produce, and eggs are something female-sexed bodies produce, an example of "cis-normativity" (Aultman 2014). Scholars and doctors alike have pivoted to phrases such as "pregnant person" in lieu of "pregnant woman" to indicate the variety of people with various gender identities engaged in the activity of pregnancy, but reproduction remains bifurcated by the categories of male and female, sperm and eggs.

Sperm, as a substance, is difficult to think about outside of its context in reproduction. Stripping away any sexed or reproductive context, it would be hard to describe what sperm is. In reproductive health and science, it is a substance ultimately defined by its reproductive role, and sperm never takes on cross-sex associations (like female sperm) or cross-gender ones (like girl sperm). Inclusive language alone does not directly address the failure of strict divisions between reproductive materials to describe the reproductive needs for trans family making. Transgender people—and their reproductive lives—are more than just a problem of adjusting for inclusive language, and sperm's cultural stickiness exemplifies this. If sperm is fundamentally tied to reproductive sexual difference, then an adjustment in language will hardly begin to untie it.

Sperm Is Sticky

Sperm is sticky. Not just as a substance. As Sara Ahmed describes it in her book, *The Cultural Politics of Emotion*, certain objects become "stuck" with histories of association that are "reopened in each encounter" (Ahmed 2014). Sperm is one such object, stuck in this history of its association with sexed bodies. Understood through the history of reproductive science and shaped by the affective economy of sex and gender, sperm is an example in which sex and reproduction are stuck to gender and reproductive normalcy (Almeling 2020; Halberstam 2016).

In the world of sperm, particular kinds of associations "stick" as it circulates through reproductive medicine, sex, and popular culture. These circulations produce a connection between people who encounter sperm, such as physicians and intended parents. But these circulations are not neutral. They are governed by a history of reproductive normativity (culturally accepted forms of reproduction such as the nuclear family, legal marriage, and heterosexuality) maintained by the social and political order under which sperm is understood (Hong 2015). As such, sperm remains stuck in its association with men, with male bodies, and with a white, cisgender framework of reproduction. To unstick sperm, we must recognize the malleability of sexed bodies and their reproductive roles. This recognition can help us begin to reimagine what reproduction can look like without all the sticky substances keeping it in place.

Unsticking Sperm

One of the ways to begin unsticking sperm is to examine the exclusion of transgender women from any reproductive contributions to childbearing outside of their potential abilities to produce sperm. For example, the recent outrage over a transgender mother's breast pump demonstrates how the substances produced by the reproductive bodies of transgender people are always understood through inflexible sex categories and their corresponding gender and familial roles.

On June 29th, 2023, ITV news released a segment about the impact of soaring water bills on everyday families in Thames, England. The clip features a mother describing the toll the increase in price would have on her chores and the functioning of her family. Mika Minio-Paulello told the *News at Ten* program that the soaring water bills would be "tough if you're a mum." Within hours of being posted, the clip had gone viral, rapidly circulating on Twitter in an explosion of outrage, not over the rising costs of water and increasing financial pressure on mothers but because Mika Minio-Paulello had been identified as a transgender woman (Hill 2023).

Those who were outraged at the clip were particularly upset that Minio-Paulello had described herself as a "mother," an identity they argue is impossible for a transgender woman to claim. Further, a breast pump was visible in one of the video clips, which Minio-Paulello addressed by affirming that she had been able to feed her child by breastfeeding, something that is possible for transgender women (Hill 2023). This further fueled the harassment and online vitriol of transphobic commentators who were particularly disgusted by the possibility of a transgender woman breastfeeding. Comments flooded the *Daily Mail* coverage, calling Minio-Paulello a pervert and accusing her of child abuse by equating her desire for producing milk to a perversion of her relationship to her "male body."

Sperm v. Milk

Transgender women can safely breastfeed babies by lactating from their own breasts. This has been true for decades, and has been reaffirmed by the Centers for Disease Control and Prevention in response to the outrage precipitated by Minio-Paulello's interview (Rogers 2023). The public reception of Minio-Paulello's motherhood demonstrates an important contradiction: on the one hand, those who deny transgender women can be mothers insist that any production of milk is not a function of feeding a baby, but a perversion (Hill 2023), and that the act must be sexual in nature. The denial that transgender women can be mothers is often predicated on the idea that a biological function (via things such as lactation) is impossible. On the other hand, the same critics deny that transgender women can be mothers because of their biological contribution, often attributed to their ability to produce sperm, something that would only allow them to be fathers. Mothers make milk, fathers make sperm. When transgender women make milk to feed their babies, the transphobic argument goes that they are either producing a sexual fluid or they are in denial of their true biological role in parenting: sperm producers, fathers.

Sperm sticks not only to sex and gender, but to parental roles as well. Thus, to begin to unstick sperm, I argue that we can learn about sperm by examining how it is understood outside of reproductive normalcy: in queer reproductive contexts. Sperm is trapped. It is defined as either (1) disembodied biological contribution or (2) an indication of fatherhood. We must liberate sperm beyond its role as a biological contribution to reproduction, and learning more about the reproductive lives of queer and trans people can help us do so.

Reproduction, Queer Theory, and Transgender Studies

Some strands of queer theory have positioned reproduction as antiqueer, rendering sperm solely into the sexual realm. For example, Lee Edelman's (2004) landmark essay describes reproductive desire as antithetical to queerness, and Jack Halberstam (2005) has argued that queer time and space are different because they operate outside the organizing structure of heterosexual reproduction. However, in contrast to queer theory, reproduction is an important object for transgender studies due to the shared project of reproductive and transgender rights, as well as the expansion of reproductive techno-possibilities. Transgender women writing fiction and poetry have rearranged sperm's significance, figuring sperm as a substance of reproductive intimacy and an object of future possibility.

In Torrey Peters's *Detransition, Baby* (2021), sperm transverse sexual, gendered, and reproductive categories. Sperm for the transgender women in the novel acts as a metonym for sexual and reproductive intimacy. The main character, a transgender woman named Reese, dreams of pregnancy and motherhood. To gain proximity to cis women's fertility, she utilizes unprotected sex with an HIV positive partner (whose viral load has been reduced to undetectable levels): "Only now, with his HIV, had she found an analogue to a cis woman's life changer . . . He liked to play close to the edge too, pushing to knock her up, to impregnate her with a viral seed. Make her the mommy, her body host to new life, part of her but not, just as mothers eternal" (Peters 2021, 8). The chance that she could contract HIV, however slim, simulates the fear of an unintended pregnancy. Sperm, in this context, functions as a vessel for reproductive risk and vulnerability that transverses cis and trans women's experiences.

Further, sperm transcends its association with fatherhood in Peters's book. As Reese desperately desires being a mother, her ex-lover Ames (a transgender woman who detransitioned) accidentally impregnates his boss under the false assumption that he would be sterile after years of using hormone replacement therapy as a transgender woman. Ames began his transition by rejecting the "enormous weight of fatherhood" (Peters 2021), and it is only when he is accidentally implicated in a pregnancy by getting someone else pregnant that he begins to see his role as more than the individual who provided sperm and therefore the "father."

For trans women, reproduction is also hindered by the hyperviolence that comes with being trans in a world that is not only transphobic but also misogynistic. Violence against transgender women forecloses their abilities to secure their reproductive desires, making it an issue of reproductive justice. In the context of such vulnerability and precarity, reproductive possibility and potential for trans women of color is often only accessible when taken into their own hands. In micha cárdenas's article and artwork *Pregnancy Poems*, she describes her experience going off hormone therapy to produce sperm and documents her journey to motherhood using various DIY tools, such as a children's microscope to monitor her growing sperm count. Accounts of transgender reproduction, she argues, have largely focused on transgender men at the exclusion of transgender women's experiences, particularly the generation of sperm. "I have to take my vitamins everyday, all to make a baby. I'm a trans woman and I'm pregnant," she writes (cárdenas 2016).

Transgender women, when seeking gender-affirming care, are often misinformed about their reproductive possibilities due to the misattribution of sperm to fatherhood and masculinity (Fiorilli 2019). cárdenas describes how her doctors told her she would be sterile after going on hormone replacement therapy: "They told me I would be sterile, the doctors and brochures . . . but they don't know, and they lied to me, and other trans women have done it" (cárdenas 2016, 52). The association between sperm and masculinity and virility runs the risk of rendering reproductive desires as invalidating of transgender identity, an effort to divorce the body and the mind, something Julian Gill-Peterson (2014, 203) describes as a result of the "restriction of transgender agency to psychic identity" which "renders the matter of the trans body inaccessible, and ultimately separate from the subjectivity that is meant to be its anchor."

Thus, sperm appears in such trans contexts as more than just a biological substance that indicates genetic parentage and operates within and against its social designation as male and father-bound. Sperm can instead be used to pursue a theory of reproduction that seeks to transcend beyond a biological or symbolic role and into the realm of desires. I am writing now about the realm of transgender theory but, ultimately, I believe this point is applicable to all reproductive desires.

Absent Sperm

Finally, trans women have utilized sperm to highlight the racialized order of cisgender reproduction. In this case, it is the absence of sperm that troubles its centrality in reproduction. The artist Vaginal Creme Davis has provided a rich text exploring trans reproduction in the speculative realm through her performance art. In 1986 she starred in her short film, *That Fertile Feeling*, a video which follows Davis and friend Fertile La Toya Jackson through their reproductive exploits. After Fertile's water breaks while the pair are watching television, Fertile is rushed to the hospital where she is turned away because she does not have state health insurance. Eventually, back at her apartment, Fertile's boyfriend (who happens to always be naked) and Davis act as midwives as Fertile gives birth to eleven babies. Post delivery, Fertile hops on a skateboard and rides away down a Los Angeles street. Davis calls after her, "Fertile! You're so fertile! You're the first woman in the world to give birth to eleven-tuplets!"

Fertile's pregnancy and delivery is an example of a speculative reproductive miracle: "both in the quantity" of babies and how Davis and Fertile come to womanhood via hyperfertility (Dunham 2015). As Dunham puts it, the fact that "they have bodies that may not be able to give birth" but are, in the same moment, rendered hyperfertile (as women of color) makes the way for their performance to articulate the "cultural fixation on pregnancy as the marker of womanhood." Their contribution to reproduction eclipses sperm, focusing instead on the hyperfertility of Black women in American culture, highlighting how the organization of reproductive materials is always already punctuated by racial hierarchies.

As discussed in the vignette above, transgender women are expected to adhere to the most conservative expectations we have of mothers. Any step outside of the norm is considered a means for criticism and accusations of perversion. For straight, cisgender people, sexuality and reproduction are considered inextricably linked and understood as part of the natural order. For those seeking to parent outside of heteronormative contexts, any relationship to reproduction that might include sexuality produces a vulnerability. However, this vulnerability includes the opportunity and necessity to unstick the stickiest substance by utilizing it to approximate cis intimacy (as in Peters 2021), to create a trans future (as in cárdenas 2016), or to exaggerate a racialized absence (as in Davis 1986).

All Reproduction Is Speculative Miracle

Trans women may be particularly positioned to think critically about sperm, but I follow Merve Emre (2018) in arguing for an insistence that all reproduction is assisted by our belief in cultural scripts. It is not just trans people who are crafting their reproductive realities. Even reproduction that appears "natural" (such as cis, heterosexual reproduction) only operates through the assumed naturalness of heterosexuality. The same logic can be extended to sperm: sperm is as much a metonym for sexual and reproductive intimacy in straight and cis contexts as it is in queer and trans ones. Emma Heaney (2021) writes, on her own complicated quest to get pregnant, "The cervix is not the threshold to a holy vessel. . . . Structures are ever-evolving biological entities, who sometimes function as you wish them to, and sometimes do not." Heaney emphasizes how, regardless of how you might choose to get pregnant, our flesh is not foolproof. Not every attempt at pregnancy will succeed. The cervix is a structure that changes with each turnover of our genetic material and is as responsive and flexible as the rest of us. Cis, straight, queer, and trans reproduction share the same raw materials and the same unreliability.

Much of the writing on reproductive technology and its feminist futurity excludes the phenomenon of sperm, a substance often rendered freely available. However, following Heaney, sperm is not a pathway to a particular parental role or outcome. Sometimes sperm functions to create the material ends we desire, sometimes it does not, and these successes and failures are not necessarily consistent across cis or trans reproductive contexts. As Kalindi Vora (2014) has argued, questions about reproduction include questions about what we recognize as human and, as such, who is designated as worthy of creating life. Sperm has held the potential for life in its definition for many years, it is often seen as liquid containing tiny specs of the start of the reproductive process. But such potential has not been evenly distributed. Expanding "men's reproductive health" to include trans women does not come close to unpacking the ways in which sperm circulates in the economy of baby making outside of the narrow heteronormative context.

Ultimately, I would like to emphasize that sperm is a tool for anyone seeking to create a baby. This may appear obvious, but I intend this assertion to be taken seriously as a way of reorganizing the way sperm is understood in reproductive processes in order to imagine new reproductive futures. So, how do we write a future for sperm? Following in the tradition of transgender women, we need to speculate. Speculative thinking empowers sperm to move beyond just material and into the realm of the desires we might have for family making, our communities, and our futures together.

If those of us seeking to improve reproduction through reproductive health and justice can move to the realm of desire and away from the strict realm of the material, we may be able to address some of what seem to be addressable "nuances," "complications," and "differences" in how to think about sperm that crop up throughout this volume. This is not a wholesale denial of the utility and interconnection between desire and materiality; I will not turn against the flesh or, in this context, the sticky wetness that unites our thinking. However, I aim to push the limits of what the material provides for us when it is read through that which is already presumed. By using speculation and desire-based thinking, we might see sperm change shape before our very eyes.

So, imagine this. You enter the clinic, hand in hand with your partner. Perhaps this clinic is on earth, perhaps it is elsewhere. I don't know what the future holds. You are a person, and you want a family. Pushing through the doors (if we even have doors still), you enter a waiting room and approach the front desk. "I'm here to discuss my desires for family," you tell the individual who works at the front desk. "We are looking forward to helping you," they responded, "please take a seat, and we will be right with you." The television in the corner is playing a recording of a Talking Heads video—"retro," you think to yourself. You relax into your seat (which is comfortable, we have finally figured out how to make seats comfortable). A young woman steps through another set of doors and calls your name. "Follow me, please," she says. Her face is bright and welcoming, she walks you to a room and you step inside, where you are greeted by a team of community members with various specialties seated at a round table, welcoming you. Each person takes turns introducing themselves. No need to go into exhaustive detail but, at least initially, you are greeted by a mental health professional, an endocrinologist, a fertility specialist, a gender theory graduate student, a local daycare provider, a teacher, a nutritionist, an artist, your lovers, and your friends. You sit at the table, and the artist takes your hand. "Tell me," the artist says. "Tell me what you want." Your body has the ability to make sperm, your partner's doesn't—that doesn't matter here. You close your eyes, take a deep breath, and begin to describe your dreams . . .

REFERENCES
Ahmed, Sara. 2014. *Cultural Politics of Emotion*. Edinburgh: Edinburgh University Press.
Almeling, Rene. 2020. *GUYnecology: The Missing Science of Men's Reproductive Health*. Oakland: University of California Press.
Aultman, B. 2014. "Cisgender." *TSQ: Transgender Studies Quarterly* 1 (1–2): 61–62. https://doi.org/10.1215/23289252-2399614.
cárdenas, micha. 2016. "Pregnancy: Reproductive Futures in Trans of Color Feminism." *TSQ: Transgender Studies Quarterly* 3 (1–2): 48–57. https://doi.org/10.1215/23289252-3334187.
Dowland, Douglas. 2021. "Barebacking's Late Style." *GLQ: A Journal of Lesbian and Gay Studies* 27 (1): 152–54. https://doi.org/10.1215/10642684-8776946.
Dunham, Cyrus Grace. 2015. "The Terrorist Drag of Vaginal Davis." *The New Yorker*, December 12, 2015. https://www.newyorker.com/culture/culture-desk/terrorist-drag-vaginal-davis.
Edelman, Lee. 2004. *No Future: Queer Theory and the Death Drive*. Durham, NC: Duke University Press.
Emre, Merve. 2018. "All Reproduction Is Assisted." *Boston Review*, August 10, 2018. http://bostonreview.net.
Fiorilli, Olivia. 2019. "Reproductive Injustice and the Politics of Trans Future in France." *TSQ: Transgender Studies Quarterly* 6 (4): 579–92. https://doi.org/10.1215/23289252-7771737.

Gill-Peterson, Julian. 2014. "The Technical Capacities of the Body: Assembling Race, Technology, and Transgender." *TSQ: Transgender Studies Quarterly* 1 (3): 402–18. https://doi.org/10.1215/23289252-2685660.

Halberstam, Jack. 2005. *In a Queer Time and Place: Transgender Bodies, Subcultural Lives*. New York: New York University Press.

Halberstam, Jack. 2016. "Trans*—Gender Transitivity and New Configurations of Body, History, Memory and Kinship." *Parallax* 22 (3): 366–75. https://doi.org/10.1080/13534645.2016.1201925.

Heaney, Emma. 2021. "Is a Cervix Cis?: My Year in the Stirrups." *Aster(ix) Journal*, February 18, 2021. http://asterixjournal.com.

Hill, Milli. 2023. "Can a Person Born a Male Really Breastfeed a Baby? The Answer Will Shock You." *Daily Mail*, July 7, 2023. www.dailymail.co.uk.

Hong, Grace Kyungwon. 2015. *Death beyond Disavowal: The Impossible Politics of Difference*. Difference Incorporated. Minneapolis: University of Minnesota Press.

Nixon, Laura. 2013. "The Right to (Trans) Parent: A Reproductive Justice Approach to Reproductive Rights, Fertility, and Family-Building Issues Facing Transgender People." *William & Mary Journal of Race, Gender, and Social Justice* 20:73–103.

Peters, Torrey. 2021. *Detransition, Baby*. New York: One World.

Pfeffer, Carla A., Sally Hines, Ruth Pearce, Damien W. Riggs, Elisabetta Ruspini, and Francis Ray White. 2023. "Medical Uncertainty and Reproduction of the 'Normal': Decision-Making around Testosterone Therapy in Transgender Pregnancy." *SSM—Qualitative Research in Health* 4:100297. https://doi.org/10.1016/j.ssmqr.2023.100297.

Preciado, Paul B. 2015. "Restif de la Bretonne's State Brothel: Sperm, Sovereignty, and Debt in the Eighteenth-Century Utopian Construction of Europe." *South as a State of Mind*. www.documenta14.de.

Rogers, Zachary. 2023. "CDC Says Trans People Can 'Chestfeed' Babies in published Guidance, Critics Warn of Health Risks." *ABC7*, July 6, 2023. https://katv.com.

Rowlands, Sam, and Jean-Jacques Amy. 2018. "Preserving the Reproductive Potential of Transgender and Intersex People." *European Journal of Contraception & Reproductive Health Care* 23 (1): 58–63. https://doi.org/10.1080/13625187.2017.1422240.

Valdez, Natali, and Daisy Deomampo. 2019. "Centering Race and Racism in Reproduction." *Medical Anthropology* 38 (7): 551–59. https://doi.org/10.1080/01459740.2019.1643855.

Varghese, Ricky, and Tim Dean, eds. 2019. *Raw: PrEP, Pedagogy, and the Politics of Barebacking. The Exquisite Corpse*. Regina, Canada: University of Regina Press.

Vora, Kalindi. 2014. "Experimental Sociality and Gestational Surrogacy in the Indian ART Clinic." *Ethnos* 79 (1): 63–83. https://doi.org/10.1080/00141844.2013.770744.

ACKNOWLEDGMENTS

The editors thank Ilene Kalish and the whole team at NYU Press for the extraordinarily smooth process from idea to publication, and we are grateful to series editor Jennifer Reich for her early enthusiasm and ongoing support of this book. We also thank Victoria Baker for doing an excellent job constructing the index.

Rene Almeling expresses gratitude to Yale University for funding to support the conference during which this volume was developed. She is grateful to graduate student Carlo Sariego and staff members Lauren Gonzalez and Barbara Ruth for their assistance with the conference, and she offers special thanks to graduate student Zahra Abba Omar for her efforts at all stages of this project, from the initial conference planning to assisting with the logistics of assembling the edited volume.

Lisa Campo-Engelstein thanks her parents for their unwavering support and for raising her a feminist.

Brian T. Nguyen would like to thank all the women whose experience and endurance of gender-based disparities inspired him to dedicate his career to addressing gender inequity and protecting reproductive rights. He is grateful to his mother Hang Nguyen, who has made everything possible; his wife, Amy Li, whose combination of love and leadership has offered a safe and supportive space to be vulnerable and grow as a husband, father, and scholar; and his sister, Julie Nguyen, who has pushed boundaries and redefined priorities personally and professionally in ways that will empower his daughter, Charlotte Nguyen, to do the same. The future is bright because of women.

ABOUT THE EDITORS

RENE ALMELING is Professor of Sociology at Yale University. Her primary research and teaching interests are in gender, medicine, and reproduction. Using a range of qualitative, historical, and quantitative methods, she examines questions about how biological bodies and cultural norms interact to influence scientific knowledge, medical markets, and individual experiences. She is the author of two award-winning books: *Sex Cells*, which offers an inside look at the American market for egg and sperm donors, and *GUYnecology*, which examines the causes and consequences of inattention to male reproductive health. She has conducted two original surveys, the first on Americans' attitudes toward genetic risk (with political scientist Shana Kushner Gadarian), and the second on women's bodily experiences of in vitro fertilization. Professor Almeling's research has been funded by the National Science Foundation, the Robert Wood Johnson Foundation, and the Center for Advanced Study in Behavioral Sciences at Stanford University. At Yale, she holds courtesy appointments in American Studies; Women's, Gender, and Sexuality Studies; the Institution for Social and Policy Research; the School of Public Health; and the School of Medicine.

LISA CAMPO-ENGELSTEIN is Director and Chair of Bioethics and Health Humanities and the Harris L. Kempner Chair in the Humanities in Medicine Professor at the University of Texas Medical Branch. She is an Elected Board Member for the International Network on Feminist Approaches to Bioethics and the America Society for Bioethics and Humanities Board. She also serves on the Advisory Board for the Male Contraceptive Initiative and Alliance for Fertility Preservation. She specializes in reproductive ethics, especially fertility preservation and male contraception, and feminist and queer bioethics. She is the coeditor of two books on reproductive ethics and has been published in leading journals in medicine, science, bioethics, feminist theory, and queer health. Dr. Campo-Engelstein has been interviewed by premier national and international news organizations including National Public

Radio, the *New Yorker*, the Canadian Broadcasting Corporation (CBC), and the British Broadcasting Corporation (BBC). The BBC recognized her research as engendering a better future for women, naming her as one of the "inspiring and influential" women on their 100 Women 2019 list.

BRIAN T. NGUYEN, MD, MSc, is Associate Professor of Obstetrics & Gynecology at the Keck School of Medicine of the University of Southern California. As Program Director for the Fellowship in Complex Family Planning, he trains obstetrician-gynecologists to become specialists in abortion and contraception within the framework of reproductive justice. His EMERGE (Expanding Male Engagement in Reproductive and Gender Equity) Lab recognizes the disproportionate burden of pregnancy planning and prevention that is often shouldered by cisgender heterosexual women and reimagines a more progressive role for cisgender, heterosexual men in conventional women's sexual and reproductive health—including involving men in prenatal care, helping men prevent pregnancy, screening for postpartum paternal depression, defining paternity, counseling on advanced paternal age, and providing male partner treatment for STIs. He has published on topics including men's access to emergency contraception, the underutilization of vasectomy, and cis men's experience of abortion. Dr. Nguyen is currently focused on developing new male contraceptives and is a subinvestigator for an international multicenter clinical trial of a topical hormonal male contraceptive gel funded by the National Institutes of Child Health and Human Development. He additionally conducts research on men's willingness to use male contraceptives as a consultant to the World Health Organization.

ABOUT THE CONTRIBUTORS

MICHELLE J. BAYEFSKY, MD, is a fellow in Reproductive Endocrinology and Infertility at RMA of New York and Mount Sinai School of Medicine. She completed her residency training in Obstetrics & Gynecology at NYU Langone Health. She graduated cum laude from Harvard Medical School and summa cum laude from Yale College. Previously, she was a fellow in the Department of Bioethics at the National Institutes of Health. She is a member of the American Society for Reproductive Medicine Ethics Committee. Her research has focused on ethical issues in reproductive health, with a particular emphasis on the intersection of genetics and reproductive medicine. Her work has been published in a variety of academic journals including the *Journal of the American Medical Association, Obstetrics and Gynecology,* the *American Journal of Bioethics,* and the *Journal of Law, Medicine and Ethics.* She is coauthor of the book *Regulating Preimplantation Genetic Diagnosis in the United States: The Limits of Unlimited Selection (Palgrave Pivot, 2015).*

ANDRÉA BECKER, PhD, is Assistant Professor of Sociology at Hunter College, City University of New York. As a medical sociologist with expertise in gender and feminist science and technology studies, Becker's work critically examines every aspect of human reproduction—from sexuality and contraception to birth, abortion, and sterilization. Becker received their PhD from the CUNY Graduate Center in 2022 and was a postdoctoral research fellow at UC San Francisco in the ANSIRH (Advancing New Standards in Reproductive Health) research program. Becker's research has been published in a range of academic journals, including *Social Science and Medicine, Contraception,* and *Gender & Society.* Her forthcoming book, *Get It Out: On the Politics of Hysterectomy,* examines what it means to choose hysterectomy in a culture that devalues the uterus and the people who have them. In addition to academic work, Becker engages in public sociology and has written for the *New York Times, Slate, The Nation,* and other publications.

DAVID L. BELL, MD, MPH, is Professor of Pediatrics and Population and Family Health at Columbia University Irving Medical Center. As an adolescent medicine physician, Dr. Bell has been Medical Director of the Young Men's Clinic at New York Presbyterian Hospital since 1999. This clinic focuses on primary care for adolescent and young adult males, emphasizing high-quality, respectful services, including sexual and reproductive health care. Dr. Bell is a past president of the Society for Adolescent Health and Medicine and cofounder and Board Chair of the Partnership for Male Youth. He has consulted for the United States Agency for International Development (USAID) and has served on expert working groups for the US Department of Health and Human Services' Title X National Clinical Guidelines. His achievements have earned him numerous honors, including the Lawrence S. Neinstein Award in Young Adult Health, inclusion in MSNBC's The Grio's 100 history makers, the 2012 Physician of the Year Award from NewYork-Presbyterian Hospital, and consistent recognition as a regional and New York metro area Castle Connolly Top Doctor since 2014.

JULIE BINDEMAN graduated from George Washington University and is the co-owner of Integrative Therapy of Greater Washington in Rockville, Maryland. Her specialty is in the field of reproductive psychology, where she actively writes, lectures, and presents. She is an approved consultant in Eye Movement Desensitization and Reprocessing through EMDRIA. She has served on several committees within the Mental Health Professional Group of the American Society for Reproductive Medicine and was elected in 2021 to its Executive Committee. She served as a former Board Member of the Maryland Psychological Association for over ten years. Dr. Bindeman is a member of multiple organizations focused on Maternal and Reproductive Mental Health and was appointed by the Governor of Maryland to serve on its Maternal Mental Health Task Force. She was recently awarded the Karl Heiser Award for her legislative efforts on behalf of psychology. Dr. Bindeman has published several chapters and articles about reproductive psychology and is the editor of a forthcoming book about abortion.

MARION BOULICAULT is a feminist philosopher of science and technology. She is Assistant Professor at the University of Edinburgh and serves as Director of Interdisciplinary Research at the Harvard Gender-Sci Lab. Prior to Edinburgh, she was Distinguished Postdoctoral Scholar in Ethics & Technology at the MIT College of Computing and a Junior Research Fellow at Trinity Hall College, University of Cambridge. In her research, she develops and employs feminist tools to analyze the normative dimensions of scientific measurement and data collection practices. Her dissertation research (completed in 2021 at MIT) examined how widely used fertility measurement technologies—such as ovarian reserve testing and semen analysis—reflect and enact social norms and ideologies. Her work has appeared in academic journals including *Human Fertility*, *Social Studies of Science*, and the *American Journal of Bioethics*, as well as popular media venues such as *Slate* and the *Guardian*.

TRISTAN BRIDGES is Associate Professor of Sociology at the University of California, Santa Barbara. He currently serves as coeditor of the interdisciplinary journal *Men and Masculinities*, coedited the interdisciplinary anthology *Exploring Masculinities: Identity, Inequality, Continuity, and Change*, and coauthored *A Kaleidoscope of Identities: Reflexivity, Routine, and the Fluidity of Sex, Gender, and Sexuality*. His research focuses on contemporary transformations in masculinities, men's identities, relationships, and gender and sexual politics. He has studied communities of male bodybuilders, fathers' rights activists, feminist men, American couples with "man caves" in their homes, the relationship between masculinity and mass shootings in the United States, gendered disparities in search patterns on Google, and gendered demographic shifts in sexual identities in the United States. His work has appeared in *Gender & Society*, *Signs*, *Sociology Compass*, *Body & Society*, *Contexts*, *Frontiers in Psychology*, *Sociological Perspectives*, the *Lancet Regional Health—Americas*, and more.

NAOMI CAHN is Justice Anthony M. Kennedy Distinguished Professor of Law and Codirector of the Family Law Center at the University of Virginia School of Law. She has written numerous books, articles, and book chapters about assisted reproductive technology, including *Test Tube Families: Why the Fertility Markets Need Legal Regulation* and a chapter in the edited collection *Donor-Linked Families* as well as several articles with Professor Sonia Suter. With June Carbone and Nancy Levit, she is coauthor of *Fair Shake: The Fate of Women in a Winner-Take-All World*, and with Bridget Crawford and Emily Gold Waldman, *Hot Flash: How the Law Ignores Menopause and What We Can Do About It*.

CHRISTOPHER DE JONGE, PhD, HCLD, is Former Director of the Andrology Program at the University of Minnesota Medical Center and past Adjunct Professor in the Department of Urology at the University of Minnesota. He is a board-certified high-complexity clinical laboratory director and the first individual to be certified as an Embryologist by the American College of Embryology. In 1989, Christopher received his doctorate in Physiology and the Graduate College Award from Rush University in Chicago. In 1995, he received the American Society of Andrology Young Andrologist award in recognition of his significant contributions to the field of andrology. He was coinvestigator and author of a research publication cited by *TIME* magazine as a 2010 Top Ten Medical Breakthrough. He has twice served on the Editorial Committee for the WHO Laboratory Manual for the Examination of Human Semen and Sperm–Cervical Mucus Interaction. He is a member of the WHO Guideline Development Group for the *WHO Guidelines on Fertility Care, Infertility and Subfertility*. He is a member of the Practice Guidelines Committee—Male Infertility Panel—American Urological Association. Along with Christopher L. R. Barratt, he is a founder of the global Male Reproductive Health Initiative (MRHI).

MEREDITH P. FIELD, PhD, MSEd, is a medical sociologist who has served as Assistant Professor of Sociology at Alfred University since completing an Ohio Policy Evaluation Network Postdoctoral Research Fellowship in the Department of Sociology at University of Cincinnati in 2020. She completed her dual title PhD in Rural Sociology and Women's and Gender Studies at the Pennsylvania State University. She holds a Graduate Certificate in International Education from the School for International Training Graduate Institute, and both a MSEd and a BA in Environmental Studies from Bucknell University. Dr. Field's research focuses on health care access and equity issues, especially the ways that policy affects access to reproductive health care. Her past research projects explored access to maternal health care in rural areas of Pennsylvania and how policy changes shaped access to abortion care in Ohio and Kentucky. She has published in medical journals such as *Obstetrics & Gynecology*, *Health Education Online*, and the *Lancet Regional Health—Americas*.

LORI FREEDMAN is Professor of Obstetrics, Gynecology & Reproductive Sciences and a sociologist and bioethicist at the University of California, San Francisco, who investigates the ways in which reproductive health care is shaped by our social and medical structures. Author of *Willing and Unable: Doctors Constraints in Abortion Care* and *Bishops and Bodies: Reproductive Care in American Catholic Hospitals*, she researches and writes about the intersection of religion and health care, especially in the case of Catholic hospitals, with an interest in how conscientious objection in medical practice operates at the institutional level. Through qualitative interviews with Catholic hospital physicians and patients, as well as national surveys of American women, her research lends insight into how institutional policies for reproductive care can be hidden from view, malleable, and obstructive to patient autonomy and well-being. Freedman conducts her research with Advancing New Standards in Reproductive Health (ANSIRH), a program of the Bixby Center for Global Reproductive Health at UCSF. In addition to being a Greenwall Faculty Scholar alumna, she was also designated an Emerging Leader in Health and Medicine at the National Academy of Medicine.

JEREMY A. GOTTLIEB is an MD-PhD student in Medical Anthropology at University of California, San Francisco, and University of California, Berkeley. They are interested in gender diverse health care and have conducted and published previous ethnographic research in pediatric Trans health care, including contributing the chapter "Trans in Practice, Transition in Sequence: Providing Medical Assistance for Gender Transitions in Trans and Gender Non-Conforming Youth" in *Trans Health*, edited by Max Nicolai Appenroth and María do Mar Castro Varela. In addition to further work on Trans health care, they are pursuing projects on digital standardized patient technologies and deep brain stimulation as a treatment for psychiatric illnesses.

LYNNE HANEY is Professor of Sociology at New York University, where she also directs the Law and Society Undergraduate Program and the Prison Education Program Research Lab. She has published several award-winning books and articles in gender studies, punishment, and law. Her most recent book, *Prisons of Debt: The Afterlives of Incarcerated Fathers*, examines the criminalization of child support in the contemporary United States and its effects on men's lives as parents.

FABIAN HENNIG is a gender studies scholar based in Germany who studied in Göttingen (BA), Berlin (MA), and Basel, Switzerland, and is currently working as a teaching assistant at the Gender & Diversity Working Group at Kiel University. Hennig is a PhD student in Sociology in Frankfurt, a member of the DFG-Research Training Group "Life Sciences – Life Writing" at the medical center at the University of Mainz and former recipient of the German Research Foundation (DFG) scholarship. Additionally, Hennig is the Postdoctoral Fellow Junior Scholar Awardee of the 2022 Reproductive Ethics Conference in Galveston. Hennig examines the history (since the twentieth century) and present situation of contraceptive development with a focus on hormonal and thermal research approaches. This study draws on a diverse set of materials, such as clinical studies, expert interviews, manifestos, publications of the women's health movement and men's groups, autobiographies, and online blogs. Hennig's PhD project is situated at the intersection of gender studies, science and technology studies, history of medicine, and sociology of knowledge. Objectives include a critical reflection on masculinity, further development of medical ethics in contraceptive studies, conceptual impulses for research development, and an enhancement of reproductive justice. Hennig speaks at academic conferences and is always happy to share thoughts with a broader public, medical students, and sexual education experts.

STANTON HONIG, MD, is Professor of Urology; Director of Men's Health in Urology; Chair of the Reproductive & Sexual Health Committee in Urology; and Chief of Sexual Medicine and Reproductive Health at Yale University. He is a nationally and internationally recognized expert on sperm-related fertility and sexual medicine and surgery. He is the past president of the Society for the Study of Male Reproduction, a sub society of the American Urological Society. He was formerly President of the Society for Male Reproduction/Urology, a subsociety of the American Society of Reproductive Medicine. He is currently on the American Urology Association's Vasectomy Guidelines Committee. As Chairman of the Reproductive and Sexual Medicine Council of the Urology Care Foundation, he was able to simplify information given directly to patients about conditions that are treatable and reversible in male infertility.

MARCIA C. INHORN, PhD, MPH, is William K. Lanman Jr. Professor of Anthropology and International Affairs in the Department of Anthropology and the Whitney and Betty MacMillan Center for International and Area Studies at Yale University, where she has served as Chair of the Council on Middle East Studies. A medical anthropologist specializing in gender, technology, and reproductive health issues, Inhorn has conducted research on the social impact of infertility and assisted reproductive technologies in the Middle East (Egypt, Lebanon, the United Arab Emirates) and Arab America over the past forty years. She is the author of six award-winning books on the subject, including *The New Arab Man: Emergent Masculinities, Technologies, and Islam in the Middle East*. Her latest book, *Motherhood on Ice: The Mating Gap and Why Women Freeze Their Eggs*, is based on a US National Science Foundation study of 150 American women who froze their eggs. She is also the (co)editor of fourteen books, including *The New Reproductive Order: Technology, Fertility, and Social Change around the Globe*.

COURTNEY G. JOSLIN is Martin Luther King Jr. Professor of Law at UC Davis School of Law, where she teaches in the areas of constitutional law, family law, and antidiscrimination law. Joslin is a leading expert and scholar in the areas of family and relationship recognition, with a particular focus on same-sex and unmarried couples. She is a two-time recipient of the Dukeminier Award for her articles "Protecting Children(?): Marriage, Gender, and Assisted Reproductive Technology," in the *Southern California Law Review*, and "Discrimination In and Out of Marriage," in the *Boston University Law Review*. She is a coauthor (with William N. Eskridge Jr. and Nan D. Hunter) of the textbook *Sexuality, Gender, and the Law* and a coauthor (with D. Kelly Weisberg) of the eighth edition of the *Modern Family Law* textbook. Professor Joslin served as the Reporter for the Uniform Parentage Act of 2017, and she is an elected member of the American Law Institute.

KATHERINE L. KRASCHEL is Assistant Professor of Law and Health Sciences at Northeastern University School of Law and Bouvé College of Health Sciences at Northeastern University. She also holds a faculty appointment in the Department of Obstetrics, Gynecology and Reproductive Sciences at Yale School of Medicine. She was the founding codirector of the Reproductive Rights and Justice Project Clinic at Yale Law School. Kraschel's scholarship focuses on the intersection of reproduction, gender, bioethics, and health policy with a particular concentration on reproductive technologies. Her work has appeared in prominent journals including the *Journal of the American Medical Association*, the *Harvard Journal of Law and Gender*, the *American Journal of Obstetrics and Gynecology*, and the *Journal of Law, Medicine and Ethics*. She is a coeditor (with Glenn Cohen, Abbe Gluck, and Carmel Shachar) of *COVID-19 and the Law: Disruption, Impact, and Legacy*. In 2016, the National LGBT Bar Association named Kraschel one of the Best LGBT Lawyers Under 40, and in 2018, she was named one of the top 40 Lawyers under 40 by the American Bar Association.

JANELLE LAMOREAUX is Associate Professor of Anthropology at the University of Arizona with affiliations in East Asian Studies and Social, Cultural & Critical Theory. Her book, *Infertile Environments*, is an interdisciplinary account of how epigenetic toxicologists in China study male infertility at a moment of rising concern about men's reproductive health. She is currently researching environmental aspects of reproductive decision-making and directing the Collaborative Anthropology of Reproduction and the Environment Lab. Her work has appeared in *Science, Technology & Human Values*, *Medical Anthropology Quarterly*, *Environmental Humanities*, and *Cultural Anthropology* and has been supported by the National Science Foundation, the Social Science Research Council, and the Wenner Gren Foundation.

ANNE LE GOFF is an Associate Professor of Science and Technology Studies and Bioethics at the SupBiotech Institute in Paris. Her research and teaching interests are primarily in biotechnologies, reproduction, and nature. She uses philosophical and qualitative methods to explore how conceptual, ontological, and moral transformations both prompt and are prompted by contemporary biotechnologies and biological knowledge. She focuses in particular on reproduction and stem cell research and conducted ethnographic work in these areas during her postdoctoral fellowships at the University of California, Los Angeles. She is the author of the French book *L'animal humain*, which offers a new philosophical understanding of human beings as animals, and she has written numerous articles in English and French.

KRYSTALE E. LITTLEJOHN is Associate Professor of Sociology at the University of Oregon and author of *Just Get on the Pill: The Uneven Burden of Reproductive Politics*. She earned her PhD from Stanford University in 2013 and her BA from Occidental College in 2007. Her work examines race, gender, and reproduction, particularly at the nexus between embodiment and biomedical technologies. Her research has been published in *Demography*, *Gender & Society* and *Journal of Health and Social Behavior*, among other outlets. She has received funding from the American Association of University Women (AAUW), the National Institutes of Health, the Society of Family Planning Research Fund, and the American Sociological Association Minority Fellowship program. In her most recent book, *Fighting Mad: Resisting the End of Roe*, she and coeditor Rickie Solinger bring together changemakers from across the United States to examine how people on the ground fought to protect abortion access in the wake of the Supreme Court's decision to overturn *Roe v. Wade*.

ARIK V. MARCELL is Professor at the Johns Hopkins School of Medicine and the Bloomberg School of Public Health. He is a pediatrician and adolescent medicine specialist and Director of Adolescent Services and the Title X program at the Johns Hopkins Harriet Lane Clinic; Title X is a federal program designed to increase family planning services for underserved individuals. Dr. Marcell's research is focused on improving adolescent sexual and reproductive health and access to care, especially for young males by incorporating patient and provider and interdisciplinary approaches. His current projects funded by the National Institutes of Health include examining the efficacy of a mobile health app to promote sexual and reproductive health care for male adolescent patients and texting fathers-to-be to increase infant engagement. Additionally, he has funded projects by the Agency for Healthcare Research and Quality and the Maternal and Child Health Bureau to examine adolescents' well-visit attendance trajectories over time by sex. He directs Y2CONNECT.org, a comprehensive youth resource guide for Baltimore that has also been used by other school jurisdictions. He also led the first men's health updates to the nation's Title X Clinical Guidelines. He has received numerous teaching awards for his Masculinity, Sexual Behavior and Health course at the Bloomberg School of Public Health.

DOUGLAS NEJAIME is Anne Urowsky Professor of Law at Yale Law School, where he teaches in the areas of family law, legal ethics, law and sexuality, and constitutional law. He holds a secondary appointment at the Yale Child Study Center. He is the author of several articles on the legal recognition of parent-child relationships, including "How Parenthood Functions," *Columbia Law Review* (with Courtney Joslin); "The Constitution of Parenthood," *Stanford Law Review*; "The Nature of Parenthood," *Yale Law Journal*; and "Marriage Equality and the New Parenthood," *Harvard Law Review*. NeJaime led the effort to pass comprehensive parentage reform in Connecticut, serving as the principal drafter of the Connecticut Parentage Act, Public Act 21–15, which took effect in 2022.

ALYSSA M. NEWMAN is a Senior Research Scholar at the Kennedy Institute of Ethics and Assistant Professor in the Department of Sociology at Georgetown University. Previously, she was a Hecht-Levi Postdoctoral Fellow at the Johns Hopkins Berman Institute of Bioethics and the Hixon-Riggs Early Career Fellow in Science and Technology Studies at Harvey Mudd College. Her research currently focuses on race and assisted reproductive technologies, as well as on institutional solutions to racial health disparities. She has also published extensively on multiraciality, exploring the topic through a variety of research projects relating to collective identity formation, biology and genetics, the intersection of mixedness and masculinity, immigration, and family relationships and reproduction. Her work can be found in journals such as *Bioethics*, *New England Journal of Medicine*, *Sociology of Race and Ethnicity*, and *Medical Anthropology*. Dr. Newman received her PhD in Sociology with a doctoral emphasis in Black Studies from the University of California, Santa Barbara.

LOGAN NICKELS is Chief Research Officer at Male Contraceptive Initiative (MCI), a leading nonprofit providing funding and advocacy support for the development of new methods of contraception for those that produce sperm. Originally from Oklahoma, and with his PhD from the University of Oklahoma, he has been with MCI since 2017 when he was hired as the organization's first full-time employee. Today, he is responsible for a research portfolio of over $14 million in scientific funding that includes grants and philanthropic investments toward research and development of novel male contraceptive drugs and devices. His portfolio includes partnerships with academic and startup institutions, market research, social science, and robust support for young investigators. Logan is also Chief Scientific Officer at Contraceptive Accelerator Network, a mission-driven subsidiary of MCI aiming to directly develop novel contraceptive methods. He has published in academic journals on topics such as contraceptive development, contraceptive market sizes, and the ethics of risk in contraception. In his free time, Logan enjoys cooking and making music, but he can generally be found surrounded by his family.

REBECCA (BECCA) W. O'CONNOR brings to her role as Director of the American Society for Reproductive Medicine's (ASRM) Center for Policy and Leadership extensive experience within the nonprofit and government sectors and at law firms in Boston, Philadelphia, and Washington, DC. Becca served nearly a decade in Massachusetts state government as counsel to the Senate Committee on Ways and Means and legislative liaison for the Massachusetts Office of Victim Assistance. Additionally, Becca was a lead policy officer in organizations including ASRM; The Rape, Abuse & Incest National Network (RAINN); the Parkinson's Action Network; the District of Columbia Coalition Against Domestic Violence; and the American Association for Justice. Becca received her BA in Sociology and Anthropology from Randolph-Macon

Woman's College and her JD from Vermont Law School, which awarded her its inaugural Social Justice Scholar Award in 2016. She is a member of the Massachusetts and DC bars and resides in Maryland with her husband and their IVF-conceived twin daughters.

WILLIAM D. PETOK is a practicing clinical psychologist and a Clinical Associate Professor of Obstetrics and Gynecology at Thomas Jefferson University. He earned his doctorate at the University of Maryland, College Park, in 1978. He is a past Chair of the Mental Health Professional Group of the American Society for Reproductive Medicine and served on the Executive Council of the Society for Assisted Reproductive Technology from 2009–22. He regularly speaks on the psychosocial component of assisted reproductive technologies and sexuality. His publications include book chapters on infertility counseling and sexuality and gender-based differences as well as journal articles on male factor infertility, the interrelationship of religion and sexuality, and the treatment of sexual dysfunctions. He a regular reviewer for *Fertility and Sterility* and other reproductive health journals. He is also coediter of the book *Psychological and Medical Perspectives on Fertility Care and Sexual Health*.

CARLO SARIEGO is a dual-degree PhD candidate at Yale University in the Women's, Gender, and Sexuality Studies and Sociology departments. Their work examines the cultural, social, and historical processes through which bodies, nations, and their borders take shape in the United States. Their dissertation work brings together the topics of assisted reproductive technologies, genetics, family, gender-affirming care, and queer and transgender theory to examine state reproductive power and control. Sariego received their master's degree from the Reproductive Sociology Research Group (ReproSoc) with distinction at the University of Cambridge in 2019. They are currently a Health Policy Research Scholar with the Robert Wood Johnson Foundation, a graduate fellow of the Yale Ethnography Hub, and organizer for the Women's, Gender, and Sexuality Studies Colloquium and Graduate Policy Fellows Program at Yale. Their work has been published in *Signs, Social Science and Medicine*, and *Population Studies*.

STEF M. SHUSTER is Associate Professor in Lyman Briggs College and Department of Sociology at Michigan State University. Their current research in gender, medicine, and feminist science and technology studies considers how evidence is constructed, mobilized, and weaponized, which is the subject of their book, *Trans Medicine: The Emergence and Practice of Treating Gender*. In *Trans Medicine*, shuster traces the development of this medical field from the 1950s to modern medicine to show how providers create and use scientific and medical evidence to quell uncertainty, "treat" a gender identity, and uphold their authority. Their next book project is supported by a National Science Foundation CAREER grant and will examine the social and reproductive control of trans people over the twentieth century and into contemporary times. shuster currently serves on the editorial boards for *Social Science & Medicine* and *Social Currents* and is a deputy editor for *Gender & Society*.

SONIA M. SUTER is Kahan Family Research Professor of Law, Henry St. George Tucker III Dean's Research Professor of Law, and Founding Director of the Health Law Initiative at The George Washington University School Law School. A former genetic counselor who earned PhD candidacy in human genetics, she writes about issues at the intersection of law, medicine, and bioethics. She has published widely in law reviews as well as peer-reviewed interdisciplinary and science journals, and she has coauthored several articles with Professor Naomi Cahn. In addition, she is coauthor of two leading interdisciplinary textbooks: *Reproductive Technologies and the Law* and *Genetics: Ethics, Law and Policy*.

KAREN WEINGARTEN is Professor of English at Queens College, City University of New York. She published *Pregnancy Test* in March 2023, which tells the history of the pregnancy test and how it changed what it means to be pregnant. Her first book, *Abortion in the American Imagination: Before Life and Choice, 1880–1940*, presented a genealogy of abortion rhetoric in American literature, film, and popular culture. In early 2023, she coedited a forum for *Feminist Studies* reflecting on fifty years since *Roe v. Wade*, and in 2025 she will publish a collection entitled *Abortion Stories*.

BEN CURRAN WILLS, MS, is a PhD student in Sociology and Science Studies at University of California, San Diego. He works on the health equity implications of telehealth, AI, and other emerging technologies and business models in health care, incorporating perspectives from medical sociology, science and technology studies, bioethics, studies of gender and femininities and masculinities, and public health. Before coming to UCSD, Wills worked in the school of public health at Georgia State University; worked at the Hastings Center, a bioethics think tank; and was a Maguire Fellow at the University of Melbourne. He holds an MS in History and Sociology of Technology and Science from Georgia Tech and a BA in Cognitive Science from Vassar College.

INDEX

NOTE: As indicated at the end of the Introduction, we recognize that gendered language (e.g. male, female, men, women, cis, trans, etc.) remains unsettled and is used in different ways by different contributors to this volume. To direct readers to related topics, we have made extensive use of *See also* references in this index. Page numbers in *italics* indicate an illustration.

abbreviations, list of, xi

ableism, as system of oppression, 62

abortion: Catholic health systems prohibiting, 191, 193; elimination of choice and exacerbation of female burdens of pregnancy, 162, 273, 278; EMERGE Framework and male partner involvement in, 26; emotions of men when a pregnancy they coconceived is terminated, 29; as federally protected right, ended by *Dobbs* decision, 9–10, 244; loss of practitioners in wake of *Dobbs*, 203n9, 248; misogyny and domination as motivating antiabortion sentiment, 64; right to, as reproductive justice issue of access and not only choice, 127; right to, but no guarantee of access to, 9–10; state bans on, 10, 22, 278. *See also* abortion decisions; *Dobbs v. Jackson Women's Health Organization* (2022)

abortion decisions: belief that men can walk away from, 117, 276; *Casey* decision reestablishing women's right to decide, 30, 228; gendered inequality in social perception of, 274–275; legal strategies used by men to block women's (and minors') right to, 30, 64; male partner's lack of empathy in recognizing decisions should be female partner's, 26; male partner's vocal support for, importance of, 26; state elimination of choice as exacerbating women's burden in pregnancy, 162, 273, 278; stigma of, 26, 275

—DENIAL OF ACCESS TO: life outcomes of women who obtained abortion fared better than those denied access, 30–31; physical violence risk from man involved, 30–31

accidents, cisgender men's higher mortality rates, 54–55

adolescence: concrete thinking and risk behaviors of, 141; smaller peer networks for males, 40, 41; and spermarche, lack of data about, 141. *See also* masculinity beliefs, traditional—adolescents and

adolescent male sexual and reproductive health: age of first sex experience, 38, 141; condoms used incorrectly, 37; contraceptive options, counseling about, 143; egalitarian attitudes toward shared responsibility for contraception, 41; emergency contraception (female), counseling males about, 143; genital exams and, 39; high rates of STIs, 37, 38; involvement in contraception improves female SRH, 41, 142; and sperm health, patient counseling and testing for, 142; unintended pregnancy and, 37, 38, 41, 141; for young people with intellectual and physical disabilities, 39–40. *See also* sex education

—BARRIERS IN ACCESS TO CARE: affordable services, lack of knowledge of, 39; clinic visits, time spent talking about sex, 43; clinician characteristics preferred by, 39, 46; clinician training needed, 43–44, 47; clinicians, female discomfort with male SRH visits, 43–44; clinicians, lack of, 42, 43–44; lack of knowledge about SRH, 38–39; may not perceive the need to talk to a doctor, 39; mothers expressing discomfort talking with their sons about, prefer male role models or clinicians, 40; nonclinical, professional staff (e.g. school nurses), training for, 40–41, 45; parents and peers, training for, 40–41; primary care provider guidelines for preventive care, and failure to provide, 36–37, 42–43; smaller social networks of males, 40

adolescent male sexual and reproductive health (cont.)
—SOCIOECOLOGICAL FRAMEWORK FOR: overview as multilevel intervention, 37–38, 38, 46–47; cultural context, 41–42; inclusiveness of, 47; need for, 36–37; personal context, 38–40; Project Hombre study (Brazil), and unlearning traditional masculinity beliefs, 45–46; social context, 40–41; structural context: health care, 42–44; structural context: sex education, 44–45
adolescent services: establishment of, 42; girls as focus of cultural attention, 140–141
adoption of children: as haram (prohibited) for Middle Eastern infertile men, 267–268, 270; open adoption, and access to medical and genetic history, 210, 238; as queer family practice, 126–127, 128
advertising and marketing: of HPV vaccine, 32, 33. See also direct-to-consumer digital health companies—marketing of erectile dysfunction (ED) and premature ejaculation treatments
Affordable Care Act (ACA): ICSI (intracytoplasmic sperm injection), proposal to add coverage of, 269–270; male contraception (including vasectomy) excluded from, 27, 33, 44, 159, 169; no-cost contraception mandated for insurance plans, 159
Aftershock (documentary), 31–32
age of father, as paternal effect, 1, 7, 25, 87
Ahmed, Sara, The Cultural Politics of Emotion, 289–290
alcohol intake, cisgender men and, 54
Almeling, Rene, GUYnecology: The Missing Science of Men's Reproductive Health, 7, 98, 158, 174
AMA. See American Medical Association
Amato, Paula, 200
American Academy of Pediatrics, 42
American Association of Tissue Banks, 203n2
American College of Obstetricians & Gynecologists (ACOG), 42, 159
American Family Care (urgent care franchise), Man Up Checkup campaign, 54, 55–56
American Medical Association (AMA): adolescent services, 42; infertility classified as disease, 73, 199
American Psychological Association, Society for the Psychological Study of Men and Masculinities, 259

American Society for Reproductive Medicine (ASRM): overview, 73; clinical guidelines for genetic testing of gamete donors, 223, 230; clinical guidelines on male infertility, 86–89; direct-to-consumer DNA testing making donor anonymity difficult to guarantee, 208–209; inadequate number of male infertility specialists, 73–74; loss of practitioners in wake of Dobbs, 203n9; Mental Health Professional Group, lack of male membership in, 257, 259; Needs and Interests of Donor Conceived People (task force), 200; opposed to abolishing donor anonymity, 203n8; use of donor gametes, disclosure of, 199
American Urological Association (AUA), 74; clinical guidelines on male infertility, 86–89
Ancestry. See direct-to-consumer DNA testing
andrologists (male reproductive health specialists): advising against use of thermic testicular contraception, 181–182; insufficient number to treat male infertility, 75; number of fellowship training programs for, 75; as specialists in acute conditions, 22
Andrology (journal), 97
animals (nonhuman), endocrine-disrupting chemicals as health threat, 94
Arab America, male infertility in: overview, 261–262, 270; high rates among refugees due to depleted uranium exposures in US-led Iraq wars, 264–265, 269; ICSI as "only hope" for, 267–270. See also ICSI (intracytoplasmic sperm injection); Middle Eastern Muslim men, and male factor infertility
ART. See assisted reproductive technologies
artificial cryptorchidism. See thermic testicular contraception (artificial cryptorchidism)
Asch, Adrienne, 224
ASRM. See American Society for Reproductive Medicine
assisted reproductive technologies (ART): class and racial disparities in access, 108, 224, 230, 239–240, 244, 247–248; defined by all types of third-party reproduction, 229–230; embryos, 228, 229–230; failed cycles, and evaluation of male, 86–87; and genetic implications for sperm counts, 94; intrauterine insemination (IUI), 85, 218; lack of male infertility evaluation prior to procedures, 72–73, 74; number of births per year, 230; preparation and handling of sperm/semen, 218–219; profits of, and neglect of diagnosis

and treatment of male factor infertility, 85; as queering sperm, 215–221; state insurance coverage mandates as privileging, 85; surrogacy, 229, 230, 239; testicular sperm extraction, 147, 265; under legal attack, 228, 244–245. *See also* family, diversity of forms facilitated by assisted reproduction; ICSI (intracytoplasmic sperm injection); IVF (in vitro fertilization); IVG (in vitro gametogenesis); sperm banks (sperm donation); sperm donation (DIY/informal market)
— IN THE WAKE OF *Dobbs*: bodily autonomy significantly limited, 228; class and racial disparities in access, 228, 244, 247–248; cost of, 229, 248; federal proposal to protect, 228; legal parentage in diverse family forms, at risk, 238–239, 243–245, 248–249; medical privacy violations that could invite civil and criminal penalties, 247; as reproductive justice issue, 228–229, 244–245, 247–249; state proposals to restrict, 228, 244

AUA. *See* American Urological Association

Australia: declines in sperm counts, 90; donor anonymity abolished, 200, 208, 235

Austria, groups experimenting with thermic testicular contraception, 184n2

autoimmune disease medications, 89

basic resources: the politics of decisions determining access to, 2; racism and poverty precluding access to, 8, 9

behaviors of parents: maternal, as focus of attention in research on epigenetic transformations, 105. *See also* maternal effects on reproductive outcomes
— PATERNAL: lack of programs to aid change in, 25; lifestyle changes by infertility patients, 87–88. *See also* paternal effects on reproductive outcomes

Belgium: Catholic health facilities allow IVF, 192; groups experimenting with thermic testicular contraception, 184n2; ICSI and, 265

biological fables: of active sperm and passive egg, 96, 157, 215, 216; as cultural narrative, 157; of human reproduction as (cis) women's responsibility alone, 157–158, 159, 162–163; male contraceptive methods as too difficult to develop, 177–178; one sperm is enough to induce a pregnancy, 178; public health consequences of, 157

biomedical research: and the biological fable of reproductivity as (cis) women's responsibility alone, 158; cultural beliefs about gender as shaping, 7; establishment of rules requiring inclusion of females, 6–7; "ethos of translation" in seeking research funding, 148; the "inclusion and difference paradigm" (Epstein) and, 6–7, 84

Black men: forced vasectomies of, 161–162; as percentage of US population, 107; as sperm donors in the informal fertility market, 109, 231; traumatized by partner loss to maternal mortality, 31–32. *See also* sperm banks (sperm donation)—Black donor shortage

Black women: bias of physicians ("Black women can't be infertile"), 230; as disproportionately less likely to seek reproductive care, 230; homicide rate during pregnancy significantly higher for, 31; hyperfertility trope imposed on, 230, 294; maternal mortality rates significantly higher for, 31–32, 276; as turning to the informal fertility market, 109, 231. *See also* reproductive justice; sperm banks (sperm donation)— Black donor shortage

blood pressure increases, male-infertility associated, 93

bodily autonomy: eugenics movement seeking to limit, 135, 161–162; and unending legislative attacks on trans and nonbinary people, 2
— OF PREGNANCY-CAPABLE PEOPLE: overview as sacrosanct, 10–11; *Casey* as reaffirming, 30, 228; *Dobbs* as significantly limiting, 228, 236; homicide as leading cause of pregnancy-associated death, 31; men's legal strategies to block abortion choice, 30, 64; men's reproductive justice may not limit, 10–11, 27, 29, 30–31, 34, 64–67; reproductive justice and, 10–11, 61, 127; as under attack, 2, 10–11, 228, 236, 244; (white) male policymakers unable to grasp full extent of burdens of pregnancy making decisions to limit, 22, 169, 278

body fat, associated with male infertility, 93

body mass index, as factor in global decline of sperm counts, 93–94

Borrero, Sonya, 38–39

BPA (bisphenol A) exposure, 149

brain tumors, associated with male infertility, 88

Braveman, Paula, 276

Brazil, Project Hombre study, 45–46

breastfeeding: economic and health benefits, weak association of, 277; induction of lactation in males, 277; public health campaigns supporting, 277; pumping milk, and bottlefeeding by both partners, 277; socioeconomic burdens of, 277; trans women and, 277, 290–291
Brockovich, Erin, 94–95
burdens of reproductivity as gendered inequality: contraception, 25, 33, 167–168; of IVF, 72, 73, 256; of male contraception failures, 180, 181, 183; preventive SRH, 32, 33. *See also* pregnancy and related reproductive burdens

Canada, declines in sperm counts, 90
cancer: adolescent males and, 40; associated with male infertility, 87; cisgender youth with, and fertility preservation, 122, 126, 128–129, 129n4; HPV (human papillomavirus) as cause of cervical cancer, 24, 32; HPV as cause of penile, anal, and oropharyngeal cancers, 24, 32; testicular, associated with male infertility, 73, 76, 85, 87, 93, 95; treatments for, and recommendations to avoid pregnancy for 12 months following, 88; treatments for, and sperm banking to protect future fertility, 89; treatments for, informing patients of effects on sperm production, 88
cárdenas, micha, *Pregnancy Poems*, 293, 295
cardiovascular disease: associated with male infertility, 73, 76; cisgender men's higher rates of, 54
Casey. *See Planned Parenthood of Southeastern Pennsylvania v. Casey*
Cassino, Dan, 55
Catholic health systems: abortion, prohibited in, 191, 193; Catholic individuals, disagreements with US Bishops, 192; and federal law allowing religious entities to restrict reproductive services, 190–191; IVF (in vitro fertilization), prohibited but shepherded through, 191–194; policies and restrictions (Ethical and Religious Directives for Catholic Healthcare Services, US Conference of Catholic Bishops), 190–191, 192, 193; public funding and private equity funds, 193; size of network in the US health care sector, 191; vasectomy, prohibited in, 191, 192–193; women of color disproportionately birthing in, 191
CDC. *See* Centers for Disease Control and Prevention

celebrities, bringing public awareness to male factor infertility, 255, 258–259
Census, US, 74, 107
Centers for Disease Control and Prevention (CDC): ART defined by, 229–230; *Assisted Reproductive Technology Fertility Clinic and National Summary Report*, 72; HPV as nearly ubiquitous, 32; IVF Success Estimator, 72; meeting on male infertility (2010), 85; men's health incorporated under women's reproductive care umbrella, 78–79, 85; *Providing Quality Family Planning Services*, 42–43; suicide rates, 121; support for male infertility research needed from, 85, 86; transgender women safely breastfeeding babies, reaffirmed by, 291
Cermele, Jill, 57
cervical cancer screening, 24
Charon, Rita, 205
Checkalski, Olivia R., 275
Chicane people: forced vasectomies of, 161–162. *See also* ethnicity, and inequalities; Latine people; people of color
child support system: drivers' license revocation and passport suspension for debt in, 117; general lack of male accountability, 276; mandatory wage garnishment for child support, 117; paternity establishment, 117; "public assistance payback," 117; state requirements for paternity testing, 276
—THE AFTERLIFE OF INCARCERATED FATHERS: amounts of debt owed, 114, 117; conflation of parenthood with cycles of punishment and debt, 117; courts and judges, 116, 118, 119; debt is owed to state as "public assistance payback," 114, 117; fathers disappearing into hiding, 119; fear and reproduction entangled in, 118–119; interest on child support debt accrues while incarcerated, 114; intersecting disadvantages of fathers in, 115, 116, 117, 118; James's story, 113–115, 116, 117; number of fathers involved, 116; parenthood as denied to, 118; paternity as compelled and mandated, 117; paternity as monetarized and financialized, 117–118; positionality and methodology of the researcher, 115–116, 119; surveillance and control by the state, 117–119
child welfare system: abrogation of parental rights as reproductive justice issue, 10; removal of children for maternal refusal

of medical care, as threat, 33; removal of children for receiving gender-affirming care, as reproductive justice issue, 66
childbirth: EMERGE Framework and paternal involvement in, 26. *See also* childcare; maternal mortality in pregnancy and childbirth; pregnancy
childcare: benefits of paternal engagement with, 167; denial of paternity leave and female partners assuming responsibilities, 26; of older children during pregnancy, 274–275. *See also* breastfeeding; pregnancy and related reproductive burdens
childlessness due to male infertility: as increasing globally, 263; and social position of men in non-Western countries, 263
children: cisgender youth with cancer, fertility preservation by, 122, 126, 128–129, 129n4; food insecurity of, 8; incarceration of caregivers and separation from, 66. *See also* childcare; trans and gender diverse youth
Children of Men, 90
children's health: benefits of paternal engagement on, 31, 46, 167; breastfeeding and weak association with, 277; effect of paternal age and health on, 1, 7
China: clinical trials of male contraceptives, steps of, 179–180, 185n9, 185n10; fertility insurance, 105; male infertility research, 104, 105; sperm banking, 105
chlamydia, 23–24, 32. *See also* STIs (sexually transmitted infections)
cholesterol problems, male-infertility associated, 93
Churchill, Brendan, 274
cis-normativity: defined, 289; sperm donation and, 229. *See also* heteronormativity
cisgender men: persistent bias against, in reproductive sciences, 136; as term, 12, 166
class: and sperm donor access, disparities in, 224, 230, 239–240, 247–248; as structuring logic of reproductive injustice, 63; as system of oppression, 62; trans people's fertility preservation access as heavily influenced by, 127–128, 135–138; vasectomy access and, 159–160, 161; and vasectomy, forced, 161–162. *See also* poverty; stratified reproduction
—LOW-INCOME PEOPLE: Catholic health facilities serving at rate less than average, 190; and male factor infertility, human right to treatment for, 65

climate change: compared to global decline in sperm counts, 90, 104; environmental activism and, 103. *See also* environmental damage
Cline, Donald, 245, 247, 250
clinical recommendations and guidelines: for adolescent male preventive SRH care, 36–37, 42–43; genetic testing of gamete donors (ASRM), 223, 230; male infertility (AUA and ASRM), 86–89; for postpartum tubal ligation, 159; preconception genetic testing in general population, 225; *Providing Quality Family Planning Services* (CDC), 42–43; trans people's fertility preservation (WPATH and US Endocrine Society), 122, 124, 126–127, 129n2, 129n4, 134, 135
clinical trials, establishment of rules requiring inclusion of females, 6–7
Coleman, Eli, 126, 129n4
Colen, Shellee, 63
colonization, as factor reinforcing traditional masculinity beliefs, 41
conception: the biological fable of active sperm and passive egg, 96, 157, 215, 216; as coequal act, 273, 278; counseling for, as rarely provided in primary care, 22, 43; the egg as agent via chemoattractants, 157
condoms: Affordable Care Act mandating insurance coverage of, 159; contraceptive efficacy of (Pearl Index number), 177; historical commitment of men to using, 25; the human right to use, 65; as incorrectly used by adolescent males, 37; as underused by men in new sexual relationships, 23; and vasectomies, as only male contraceptive methods on market, 25, 168
Congress. *See* federal laws
Connell, W. Merle, *Test Tube Babies* (exploitation film), 206–207, 212n2
contraception: adolescent male attitudes of shared responsibility for, 41; adolescent male involvement in, as improving female SRH, 41, 142; adolescent males and lack of knowledge of, 38–39; as almost exclusively a female burden, 25, 33, 167–168; counseling for men, as rarely provided, 22; EMERGE Framework and male involvement in, 25; emergency (female), male purchases of, 143; as gendered term, 174, 184n1; law and policies defining as female burden, 33, 158–159; men's human right to knowledge and methods of, 65–66; policy of covering costs incurred by men, proposal for, 33;

contraception (*cont.*)
post-*Dobbs* attack on right to, 244; side effects in women, 33, 158; state laws and policies limiting, 10; traditional masculinity beliefs defining as female burden, 41; *Zeugungsverhütung* ("procreation prevention") and male involvement in, 183–184. *See also* contraceptive efficacy, pregnancy rates as principal metric of; male contraception; sterilization; stratified reproduction
—FEMALE METHODS: efficacy of (Pearl Index number), 177; hormonal (the pill), 158, 160, 177; IUDs (intrauterine devices), 160–161, 177; statistics on usage, 158
contraceptive efficacy, pregnancy rates as principal metric of: overview, 176–177; life table analysis, 185n8. *See also* male contraceptive efficacy
—THE PEARL INDEX: overview, 177; of female methods, 177; interpreting as "pregnancy rate," 177, 185n7, 185n8; male contraceptive methods required to use, limitations of and reasons to use sperm counts, 179–180, 181–184
COVID-19 pandemic: cisgender masculinity contributing to spread of, 55; cisgender men's health risk-taking behaviors and mortality rates from, 55; as crisis, 91; men with significant caregiving responsibilities taking risks seriously, 55; sperm donor shortage due to, 107, 108, 224
Craigslist, 231
Crenshaw, Kimberlé, 127
cryobanks. *See* sperm banks (sperm donation)
cryopreservation. *See* sperm banking for preservation of fertility (cryopreservation); transgender people's fertility preservation
cultural beliefs: as barrier for access to male factor infertility care, 75. *See also* biological fables; masculinity beliefs, traditional; sex and gender, traditional categories of
cystic fibrosis, 203n2, 223

Daniels, Cynthia, *Exposing Men*, 95, 215, 216
Davis, Vaginal Creme, *That Fertile Feeling* (video), 294–295
de Nie, Iris, 124
Dean, Liz, 274
Deonandan, Raywat, 98
Department of Health and Human Services, Office of Men's Health, proposed, 78–79

Detransition, Baby (Peters), 292–293, 295
diabetes: associated with male infertility, 85, 87; cisgender men's higher rates of, 54
diet: cisgender men and health risk-taking behavior, 54; as factor in global decline of sperm counts, 93–94; food insecurity, 9; nutritional deficits in, and maternal mortality and morbidity risks, 276; nutritional supplements, informing male infertility patients of limited utility of, 87–88
digital health. *See* direct-to-consumer digital health companies
DiMaggio, Anthony, 64
direct-to-consumer digital health companies: as new health care business model, 281; as subscription-based consumer goods business, 281; telehealth physicians, 281; for trans+ people and gender-affirming care, 285n1; women's "sister" brands focusing on "female hypoactive sexual desire order," 285–286n1
—MARKETING OF ERECTILE DYSFUNCTION (ED) AND PREMATURE EJACULATION TREATMENTS: overview, 280; budget for, 280, 281; as building on pharmaceutical companies' marketing of sexual health conditions, 282–283; expansion of target audience to younger men as goal of, 281, 283–284; as exploiting anxieties around masculinity and sex, 280, 283–285; HENRY ("high earner, not rich yet") men as current targets, 283; "hybrid masculinities" as current aesthetic in, 283, 285; Millennials as target audience for, 280, 283; queer sex as lens of understanding the "straighting" heteronormativity reinforced by, 284–285; as reframing the purpose of medicine from treatment to enhancement, 284; as reinforcing performance insecurity as normative to masculine experience, 284; as social-medico-pharmaceutical creations, 282
—PHARMACEUTICAL SALES: Addyi (flibanserin), 285–286n1; bundled with over-the-counter treatments, 281; generic ED medication, 280, 281, 286n2; off-label antianxiety drugs (e.g. escitalopram), 281, 282; performance anxiety drugs, 284
direct-to-consumer DNA testing, sperm donor anonymity no longer guaranteed due to, 199, 201, 208–209, 210

direct-to-consumer "home sperm tests," 84–85, 185n13
disabilities: ableism as system of oppression, 62; adolescent males with mental or physical, SRH educational interventions with, 39–40; blame of mother for infants born with, 33; eugenics and genetic testing for ART procedures, 224, 225–226; eugenics movement seeking to limit reproductive autonomy of people with, 135; paternal age and risk of birth defects, 87; paternal toxic exposures and risk of birth defects, 150; poverty as disproportionately experienced by people with, 230
DNA of sperm: epigenetic transformations that do not affect, 104; recurrent pregnancy losses or failed IVF cycles and testing of, 86–87. *See also* paternal effects on reproductive outcomes
DNA testing (direct-to-consumer), sperm donor anonymity no longer guaranteed due to, 199, 201, 208–209, 210
Dobbs v. Jackson Women's Health Organization (2022): overview as striking down *Roe v. Wade* (federally protected right to abortion), 9–10, 244; additional due process precedents placed under threat in, 244; based on subjective interpretations of Constitution vs. women's lived experiences, 22; bodily autonomy as significantly limited by, 236; forced vasectomy as rhetorical tactic in wake of, 161–162; Fourteenth Amendment due process precedent dismissed in, 244; increasing legal strategies of men to prevent legal abortion, 30, 64; the LGBTQ+ community as under siege in wake of, 238–239, 244, 249; loss of practitioners for high-risk pregnancies in wake of, 203n9, 248; state bans and restrictions in wake of, 10, 22; and subpar care for women experiencing pregnancy loss, 162; vasectomy rate increasing in wake of, 162. *See also* assisted reproductive technologies (ART)—in the wake of *Dobbs*
donor, definitions of, 202n1, 212n1, 243n1
donor-conceived people: accidental incest as risk for, 233; activism producing regulations, 208; age of majority as identity disclosure date, 239; ASRM task force (Needs and Interests of Donor Conceived People), 200; calls for mandatory disclosure of donors' identities, 199; desire to know biological origins, 210, 213n6; "dibling" groups (half siblings from the same donor), 233; family/kinship language used to refer to donors and other children by same donor, 237, 249; and family limits (number of donations), 233, 235, 236; family of origin, importance of, 237–238; importance of knowing identity, 207–208, 210, 211–212, 213n6, 233, 237; interests may be ignored in both formal and informal sperm donation, 233, 236–237, 239; mental health improvement with knowing origins, 210; social media support groups for, 208, 213n5. *See also* sperm banks (sperm donation); sperm donation (DIY/informal market)
donor conception: definition of terms, 202n1; recommendations to disclose use of to children, 199; support groups for community members, 199
donor insemination: as haram for Middle Eastern Muslim men, 267, 270; perceived or believed to be a form of adultery, 257, 267; secrecy of, as longstanding dysfunction, 207, 258
Douglas, Mary, 190
drag queens, 184n4
Dyer, Rachel L., 275

eating disorders, 140, 141
Edelman, Lee, 292
education about reproductive health. *See* medical schools and residencies; public awareness and education; public health campaigns; sex education
educational attainment: as barrier for access to male factor infertility care, 75; maternal mortality and morbidity correlated to lack of, 276
egg banking, IVF cycles for purpose of, 73
egg donation: overview, 229–230; no apparent informal market in, 229; regulations on, new and proposed, 203n7, 208, 209, 245, 248. *See also* sperm banks (sperm donation)
eggs: agency of, via chemokinesis, 157; biological fable of active sperm and passive egg, 96, 157, 215, 216
Eisenberg, Michael, 103
EMERGE (Expanding Male Engagement in Reproductive and Gender Equity) Framework: overview as based on women's SRH care, 23, 24; issues to cover, 23–27; no diversion of resources from female SRH for, 27; rights of women must remain prioritized, 27; website, 24
emergency contraception (female), males buying for partners, 143

employment: discrimination against trans people, 127; mandatory wage garnishment for child support payments, 117; untenable position of multiply disadvantaged formerly incarcerated fathers with child support debt, 118; women's burden of time off during pregnancy, 274–275

Emre, Merve, 295

endocrine-disrupting chemicals, 94–95, 97, 149

Endocrine Society, US, 122; recommendations for trans people's fertility preservation (with WPATH), 122, 124, 126–127, 129n2, 129n4, 134, 135

environmental damage: activism for the environment, 66, 103, 105; climate change as warning signal, 104; declining sperm counts as warning signal, 104

environmental exposures: as crisis in global decline of sperm counts, 94–95, 104–105; depleted uranium (toxic warfare), 264–265, 269; endocrine-disrupting chemicals, 94–95, 97, 149; genotoxic threats of synthetic chemicals, 105; informing infertility patient of risks, 87; paternal effects on reproductive outcomes and, 7; postgenomic perspective as influential on human health, 103; "shrinking penis" research and reporting, 105. See also epigenetic transformations within sperm due to environmental toxicants

environmental justice, as reproductive justice issue, 66

Epidemiology (journal), 97

epigenetic transformations within sperm due to environmental toxicants: definition of, 104; ICSI (intracytoplasmic sperm injection) and, 150; IVG research and mechanism of, 149–150; law and policy changes in response to studies of, 105, 151; maternal prenatal behavior as focus of attention on, 105; as possible even when sperm counts are normal and male fertility intact, 104, 150; sperm as biological sentinel and, 105–106; sperm banking (cryopreservation) as precaution, 105; transmissible across generations, 104, 105–106, 150. See also environmental exposures; paternal effects on reproductive outcomes

epigenome and epigenetic marks of primordial germ cells, 149–150

Epstein, Steven, 6–7, 84

erectile dysfunction (ED): caused by need for masturbation for ICSI procedures, 267; conflated with male infertility, 262; depleted uranium exposure causing, 264; older couples' mixed feelings about Viagra, 285; pharmaceutical companies' marketing of, by appealing to masculine anxieties and widening the population of medicalized penises, 282–283. See also direct-to-consumer digital health companies—marketing of erectile dysfunction (ED) and premature ejaculation treatments

ethnicity, and inequalities: adolescent males and high rates of STIs, 37, 38; adolescent males and high rates of unintended pregnancies, 37, 38; age of first sex experience, 38; sperm bank donor exclusions, 231, 247. See also Black men; Black women; Indigenous people; Latine people; people of color

eugenics: coercive sterilization and imprisonment to control reproductive capacity of marginalized groups, 135, 161–162; donor insemination and IVF origins in, 205, 206–207, 211, 212, 213n7; and genetic testing of sperm donors, 224, 225–226; in Nazi Germany, 206, 225–226

Europe: clinical trials of male contraceptives, steps of, 179–180, 185n9, 185n10; countries abolishing donor anonymity, 200, 208, 209; declines in sperm counts, 90; groups experimenting with thermic testicular contraception, 175, 184n2, 185n12

European Society of Human Reproduction and Embryology, 77

Facebook: online sperm donation groups (DIY/informal), 231; support groups for donor-conceived people, 213n5; support groups for male factor infertility, 258

Fair Play (Rodsky) (program, book, documentary), 277–278

Faircloth, Charlotte, 274

family: chosen family as longstanding queer and trans community practice, 126–127, 128; *Fair Play* program for equitable division of labor within, 277–278; trans youth and rejection from their family of origin, 126. See also childcare; pregnancy and related reproductive burdens—mental load

family, diversity of forms facilitated by assisted reproduction: overview, 243–244, 248; genetic essentialism as denigrating, 244, 249; known sperm donor given legal parentage rights, 232–233, 249; known sperm donor wants contact, 211–212; legal protection by Uniform

INDEX | 325

Parentage Act, 246; and reemergence of status inequalities, 249; threats to legal parentage in, 238–239, 243–245, 248–249. *See also* lesbian couples; LGBTQ+ parent families; single-parent families; unmarried couples
family planning clinics: clinical guidelines for (federal), 42–43; expansion of male services in, and increase of demand for, 39; vasectomy rarely offered by, 159
fathers, benefits of involvement of: in childbirth, 26; in childcare, 167; children's health, 31, 46, 167; decrease in infant mortality rates, 31; in pregnancy, 31, 46, 167
fathers/fatherhood. *See* child support system—the afterlife of incarcerated fathers; EMERGE (Expanding Male Engagement in Reproductive and Gender Equity) Framework; incarceration—of fathers; male reproductive identity; parenting
Fausto-Sterling, Anne, 3
FDA. *See* Food and Drug Administration (FDA)
federal agencies. *See* Centers for Disease Control and Prevention (CDC); Department of Health and Human Services; Food and Drug Administration (FDA); National Institutes of Health (NIH)
federal laws: child support, 117; HIPAA, 201–202, 250n4; Men's Health Awareness and Improvement Act (proposed), 79; *Planned Parenthood of Southeastern Pennsylvania v. Casey*, 30, 228; protection of ART, proposed, 228; religious entities may restrict reproductive services based on legal fiction of institutional conscience, 190–191. *See also* Affordable Care Act (ACA); *Dobbs v. Jackson Women's Health Organization* (2022); law and policy; *Roe v. Wade*
fertility fraud. *See* sperm banks (sperm donation)—fertility fraud
fertility insurance, 105
fertility preservation. *See* sperm banking for preservation of fertility (cryopreservation); transgender people's fertility preservation
Folx Health (direct-to-consumer digital health company), 285–286n1. *See also* direct-to-consumer digital health companies
Food and Drug Administration (FDA): emergency contraception sold over the counter, 143; flibanserin pharmaceutical approved for "female hypoactive sexual desire disorder,"

285–286n1; gamete donor testing for infectious diseases, 203n2, 223, 225, 230, 232; HPV vaccine, 24; regulation of sperm/semen once it enters a place of business, 217, 221n1
food insecurity, racism and poverty as structural causes of, 8, 9
Fourteenth Amendment: additional due process precedents under attack, 244; due process precedent dismissed for abortion, 244; sperm donor anonymity and equal protection clause, 201
France, groups experimenting with thermic testicular contraception, 184n2, 185n12
fraud. *See* sperm banks (sperm donation)—fertility fraud
Frickel, Scott, 105

gamete banks. *See* egg donation; sperm banks (sperm donation)
gender, dualistic/binary view of: and metaphor of masculine sperm and feminine egg, 96, 157, 215; rejection of, as methodology, 5–6; and the state, feminist scholarship on, 115–116; US health care system organized around belief in, 6. *See also* gender equity; gendered reproductive knowledge (female bodies as reproductive, male bodies as nonreproductive); gendered social inequalities; masculinity beliefs, traditional; sex and gender, traditional categories of; trans reproduction
gender-affirming care: family and medical team support and improved mental health parameters, 121; health insurance and, 125–126, 136; laws banning, 66, 121, 136; male contraceptive hormonal methods interacting with, and suggestion to use nonhormonal methods, 185–186n14; medical system roadblocks to treatment, and fear of expressing a desire to preserve fertility, 125; mid-twentieth century hierarchy of patients "worthy" of receiving care, 134–135; mid-twentieth century requirement of sterilization for those seeking, 135; misinformation about sterility after estrogen treatment, 293; recommendations for providers of, to assess need for fertility preservation, 122, 124, 126–127, 129n2, 129n4, 134, 135; as reproductive justice issue, 66; state law and policy restrictions on, 10, 66; suicide rate of trans youth decreased by, 121. *See also* trans and transgender people

gender-egalitarian heterosexual couples: as ideal, 167; reversion to unequal gender roles in pregnancy and childcare, 168, 274

gender-equitable behavior, men's views on, and interest in male contraception, 25, 160, 167, 170

gender equity, expansion of SRH to men and male bodies as necessary to, 23, 27

gendered reproductive knowledge (female bodies as reproductive, male bodies as nonreproductive): overview, 7; as barrier to male reproductive identity, 166–167; as barrier to scientific understanding of sperm count trends, 98–99; as biological fable, 158–159; and "contraception" as gendered term, 174, 184, 184n1; lack of a medical specialty in men's reproduction and, 158; as naturalizing the gendered asymmetry in contraceptive technologies, 178; as persistent bias in reproductive sciences, 136; and research on men's contraceptive options as sparse, 158

gendered social inequalities: and the political entanglement of SRH, 21–22; in social perception of abortion decision, 274–275. See also biological fables; burdens of reproductivity as gendered inequality; gendered reproductive knowledge (female bodies as reproductive, male bodies as nonreproductive); reproductive justice; stratified reproduction

genetic abnormalities: associated with male infertility, 85, 87; as cause of severe cases of male infertility, 263–264; ICSI (intracytoplasmic sperm injection) may be perpetuating into future generations, 267, 270; as prevalent among Middle Eastern Muslim men with severe male infertility, 263–264; thermic testicular contraception and effects on sperm, 185n6. See also epigenetic transformations within sperm due to environmental toxicants

genetic essentialism, and sperm donor identity disclosure, 237–238, 244, 249

genetic testing for male factor infertility, 25, 86–87

genetic testing of donors. See sperm banks (sperm donation)—genetic testing of donors

Germany: groups experimenting with thermic testicular contraception, 184n2. See also Zeugungsverhütung ("procreation prevention")

Gervais, Sarah J., 275

Gilbert, Rhod, 258

Gill-Peterson, Jules, 293–294

global sperm counts. See sperm counts in global decline

global warming. See climate change

gonorrhea, 23–24, 32, 223. See also STIs (sexually transmitted infections)

Gulf Wars (First and Second) in Iraq, depleted uranium exposures, 264–265, 269

gun violence, as reproductive justice issue, 66

GUYnecology: The Missing Science of Men's Reproductive Health (Rene Almeling), 7, 98, 158, 174

haemocytometry, 97

Halberstam, Jack, 212n3, 292

Handmaid's Tale, The, 90

Hay, Colin, 91–92

health, sperm, and politics: overview of nexus of, 1–3

health care, reluctance of men to obtain: delays due to fear and embarrassment, 84–85; and infertility investigations beginning with women's health care, 72; pattern of visits as declining in adolescence, 44, 84; traditional masculinity beliefs and, 39, 41, 46, 54. See also public health campaigns—"healthy masculinity strategies"

health care system (US): focus on maternal, infant, and child health, 42; male SRH care overlooked in, 42; as organized to place all reproductive responsibility on pregnant-capable people, 159, 166–167; as still largely organized around belief in two separate sexes, 6

health insurance: discrimination against trans people, 127; for gender-affirming health care, 125–126, 136; male factor infertility not covered by, 73, 85; paternal genetic testing not covered, 25; for sperm donation, 230, 239; for trans fertility preservation, 125–126, 136–137, 138; tubal ligation covered while vasectomy is excluded, 27; vasectomy not covered by, 27, 33, 159

Heaney, Emma, 295

heart disease. See cardiovascular disease

hepatitis, gamete donors tested for, 203n2

heteronormativity: as cultural script entwining sperm and masculinity, 215; donor insemination origins as patriarchal and paternalistic, 205, 206–207, 211, 212, 212n3, 213n7, 243, 245; patriarchy as social system upholding, 212n3, 220; performative, queer sex as lens of understanding its reinforcement by direct-to-consumer men's digital health companies, 284–285; queering of sperm and depriveleging of, 220–221; and reemergence of status inequalities, 249; sperm as stuck in reproductive normativity of patriarchal white supremacy, 288, 289–290; of sperm banks, and challenge of non-cisgender sperm-producing people as donors, 229. *See also* masculinity beliefs, traditional

Hims (direct-to-consumer digital health company), 280–281, 283, 284, 285, 285–286n1. *See also* direct-to-consumer digital health companies

HIPAA (medical privacy law), 201–202, 250n4

Hispanic sperm donors, 231. *See also* Latine people

HIV infection: adolescent male rates of infection, 38; gamete donors tested for, 203n2, 223. *See also* STIs (sexually transmitted infections)

Hollis, Rolanda, 161

homelessness: number of people in the US, 8; trans women of color and, 136; trans youth and, 126. *See also* housing insecurity

homicide of pregnant and postpartum women: as leading cause of pregnancy-associated death in the US, 31; women of color and significantly higher risk of, 31. *See also* violence

homophobia. *See* LGBTQ+ people—discrimination against (homophobia)

housing insecurity: discrimination against trans people, 127; maternal mortality and morbidity risk and, 276; racism and poverty as structural causes of, 8, 9. *See also* homelessness

HPV (human papillomavirus) vaccine: advertising and marketing of, 32, 33; approved for girls and women initially, 32; approved for men and male partners (in two phases), 24, 32–33; campaigns emphasizing self-protection from disease vs. protection of female partner, 24–25, 32–33; low uptake by young men and male partners, 24, 32–33; and prevention of cervical cancer, 24, 32; and prevention of penile, anal, and oropharyngeal cancers, 24, 32. *See also* STIs (sexually transmitted infections)

Human Reproduction (journal), 94

Hussein, Saddam, 264

hypogonadotropic hypogonadism, and evaluation of infertility patient, 88

hysterectomy as sterilization: forced, 135, 161, 162; reclaimed as desired procedure, 162; vasectomy as cheaper, safer, and more effective than, 158. *See also* tubal ligation; vasectomy

ICSI (intracytoplasmic sperm injection): access barrier as reproductive justice issue, 269–270; cost of, as barrier to access, 269; cost reduction in the US, recommendation for, 269–270; and epigenetic transformations within sperm due to environmental toxicants, 150; the ethics of passing infertility-related genetic mutations and choice to cull all male embryos, 267; as "hope technology," 265, 266, 270; insurance coverage, recommendation to provide, 269–270; masturbation to obtain specimen, as haram in the Muslim world, 267, 270; may be perpetuating genetic defects into future generations, 267, 270; as "only hope" for most infertile Middle Eastern men, 267–270; and openness about male infertility across the Middle East, 265–266; origins in Belgium, 265; overuse for nonmale factor infertility, 266; process of, 150, 265, 266, 268; pronunciation of, 265; as variant of IVF, 265, 266

—SPERM EXTRACTION METHODS: azoospermic men will require, 265, 267, 270; percutaneous epididymal sperm aspiration, 265; testicular biopsy, 265; testicular sperm extraction, 147, 265

in vitro fertilization. *See* IVF (in vitro fertilization)

in vitro gametogenesis. *See* IVG (in vitro gametogenesis)

incarceration: difficulty of finding employment with criminal record, 118; early releases during COVID-19 pandemic, 114; effects on health and family life, as reproductive justice issue, 10, 66, 115; by eugenics movement of marginalized groups to control reproduction, 135; forced vasectomies of men, 161–162; number of people confined in the US, 116; trans women of color and, 136

—OF FATHERS: and conflation of parenthood with cycles of punishment and debt, 117; emotional pain and loss of, 113–114, 118; James's story, 113–115, 116, 117; number of fathers with minor children confined, 116; parenthood as denied by, 118; race and class inequalities and, 115, 116, 117, 118; "responsible fatherhood" programming in reentry services, 118. *See also* child support system—the afterlife of incarcerated fathers

Indigenous people: forced vasectomies of, 161–162; and risk of maternal mortality and morbidity, 276; sperm bank practices disproportionately excluding, 247. *See also* ethnicity, and inequalities; people of color
individual responsibility, making health a matter of: overview, 2, 9; blame and stigma of those who cannot achieve health, 9; as ignoring the historical, structural, and cultural processes involved, 9, 45–46; individualism as US cultural belief and weakness of the social safety net, 9; surveillance and punishment of the marginalized and, 9; of trans people's reproductive autonomy, 135
infant mortality, paternal involvement with pregnancy lowers rates of, 31
infertility: classified as disease by AMA and WHO, 73, 199; definition of, 71, 262; IVF Success Estimator, 72; medically infertile, 230; number of people seeking treatment, as rising, 72; rates of, 71–72, 199, 259, 262; socially infertile, 230; state laws mandating insurance coverage for, 73, 85. *See also* infertility investigation process; male factor infertility
—FEMALE FACTOR: support groups for, 85, 258; women's response to diagnosis of, 256
infertility investigation process: clinical guidelines for (AUA and ASRM), 86–89; couples who have previously undergone medically assisted procedures, 72–73; lack of male evaluations prior to beginning, 72–73, 74; obstetrician-gynecologist or reproductive gynecologist as starting point, 72; referral to reproductive endocrinologist, 72. *See also* assisted reproductive technologies (ART); male factor infertility; sperm/semen testing
International Conference on Population and Development (1994), 142
International Consortium Dedicated to Male Contraception (2022), 179
International Planned Parenthood Federation, 43
International Symposium on Spermatology, 98
intersectionality: analysis of health policies and practices, 162; defined as multiple systems of oppression reinforcing and constituting each other, 62; of formerly incarcerated fathers with child support debt, 115, 116, 117, 118; and the politics of decisions determining who has access to the basic needs of life, 2; of racism and poverty, 8–9; trans reproductive care as inherently intersectional, 127–128. *See also* gendered social inequalities; poverty; racialized inequalities; reproductive justice
intracytoplasmic sperm injection. *See* ICSI (intracytoplasmic sperm injection)
Iran, 267
Iraq: First and Second Gulf Wars in, depleted uranium exposures, 264–265, 269; refugee men living in Detroit, MI, 264–265
IVF (in vitro fertilization): annual number of cycles in the US, 73; Catholic health systems prohibiting by policy but facilitating for patients, 191–194; Catholic people approving, 192; compared to ICSI, 265, 266; IVF Success Estimator (CDC), 72; male factor infertility as diagnosis, number of cycles per year, 73; and male factor infertility, women bearing burden of treatment, 72, 73, 256; process of, 265; as research tool, 150; state laws restricting, 10; state Medicaid programs covering, for trans reproductive care, 137, 138. *See also* assisted reproductive technologies (ART); ICSI (intracytoplasmic sperm injection)
IVF Success Estimator, 72
IVG (in vitro gametogenesis): overview of production of sperm using stem cells, overview, 145–146; bioethics and, 147–148; process of, 146–147; as research tool for understanding spermatogenesis and infertility, 148–151; for use as assisted reproductive technology producing genetically related gametes, 145, 147–148

Jackson, Fertile La Toyah, 294
Jacobson, Jenna, 58
Jagose, Annamarie, *Queer Theory: An Introduction*, 215–216
Jaleel, Marya, 98
Journal of the American Medical Association (JAMA), 209, 210
Just a Baby, 232–233

Keck, Frédérick, 96, 104
kidney disease medications, 89
Kolata, Gina, 97

Lakoff, Andrew, 96, 104
Latine people: the carceral system and separation of caregivers from children, 66; forced vasectomies of, 161–162; and risk of maternal

mortality and morbidity, 276; as sperm donors, 231. See also ethnicity, and inequalities; people of color
law and policy: contraception defined as female burden, 33, 158–159; costs of contraception incurred by men, coverage of (proposed), 33; epigenetic changes to sperm and responses in, 105, 151; exclusion of men's contraception from Affordable Care Act mandates, 33, 44; male infertility research and policies to support findings, 98; preventive SRH defined as female burden, 32; (white) male policymakers unable to grasp full extent of burdens of pregnancy making decisions on, 22, 169, 278. See also child support system; federal laws; incarceration; state law and policy
Lebanon, 267
Leiblein, Helmut, 185n11
Lerchl, Alexander, 98
lesbian couples: as formerly blocked from using sperm banks, 211; IVG process for children related to both parents, 147; known sperm donor given legal parentage rights, 232–233, 249; known sperm donor wants contact, 211–212; legal parentage as greater risk post-*Dobbs*, 238–239, 243–244, 248–249; and movement to tell children they are donor-conceived, 212–213n4; personal narrative of donor conception, 217–221; sperm bank/formal market anonymous donor, 233; Uniform Parentage Act protecting family formations of, 246. See also family, diversity of forms facilitated by assisted reproduction; LGBTQ+ parent families; LGBTQ+ people
Levine, Hagai, 90, 92–93, 95, 98
Lewis, Sophie, 207, 212
LGBTQ+ parent families: ART legal parentage at risk, 236, 238–239, 243–244, 248–249; assisted reproductive technologies as facilitating, 243–244; Uniform Parentage Act recognizing, 246. See also family, diversity of forms facilitated by assisted reproduction; lesbian couples; trans reproduction
LGBTQ+ people: chosen family as longstanding practice of, 126–127, 128; eugenics movement seeking to limit reproductive autonomy of, 135; gay men's support for HPV vaccine, 32; high rates of STIs among male adolescents, 37, 38; IVG process for children related to both women in lesbian couples, 147; male adolescent preferences in clinician characteristics, 39; and reemergence of status inequalities, 249; sexual relations as right, attack on, 244; and thermic testicular contraception, 174–175, 184, 184n4, 185–186n14; trans organizations fundraising to assist access for trans reproductive care, proposal for, 138; as under siege in wake of *Dobbs*, 238–239, 244, 249. See also LGBTQ+ parent families; same-sex marriage
—DISCRIMINATION AGAINST (HOMOPHOBIA): internal, 220; and lack of same-sex friendships among cisgender heterosexual males, 41; transphobia, 290–291, 293
lifestyle: as factor in global decline of sperm counts, 93–94; as risk factor associated with male infertility, 87–88
liver disease, cisgender men's higher rates of, 54

McCaughey, Martha, 57
MacKinnon, Catherine, 115
male, as term, 5, 12. See also men, as term
male contraception: as act of caring about women's well-being, 162–163; the Affordable Care Act and exclusion of, 27, 33, 44, 159, 169; condoms and vasectomies as only options on market, 25, 168; expansion of access to, and building of male reproductive identity, 169; as gendered term, and need for a gender-sensitive approach to fertility prevention, 174–175, 184n1; as percentage of contraceptive use globally, 168; as underfunded research field, 176; views on gender-equitable behavior and interest of men in, 25, 160, 167, 170; withdrawal, 168; *Zeugungsverhütung* ("procreation prevention") as nongendered term for and conceptual shift in, 174–175, 183–184. See also condoms; contraception; male contraceptive efficacy; vasectomy
—DEVELOPMENT OF NEW METHODS: overview, 1, 7, 168–169; approaches to sperm suppression, generally, 168, 175–176; burden of failures borne by women, 180, 181, 183; and male reproductive identity, building of, 168–169; marketing, questions about, 33; none are on the market, reasons for, 175, 184n5; nonhormonal types, generally, 175; pharmaceutical companies as resistant to investing in, 25, 184n5; putative difficulty of development for the male body, 177–178. See also thermic testicular contraception

male contraception (*cont.*)
—HORMONAL METHODS: overview, 176; acceptability shown in surveys, 25, 160, 168; clinical trials, 25, 179; earliest reports of, 176; health care provider for, as not yet established, 25, 170; as hegemonic form in development, 176; and the human right not to have a child, 65; interaction with gender-affirming hormone therapies, and suggestion to use nonhormonal methods, 185–186n14; none are on the market, 25, 175, 184n5; "nonresponse" phenomenon, 181–182; side effects in clinical trial accepted by patients but not by trial monitors, 160, 184n5; as "The Male Pill," 176

male contraceptive efficacy: clinical trials, steps in, 179–180, 182–183, 185n9, 185n10; *Zeugungsverhütung* and wider array of sexes and genders in research design, 184
—PREGNANCY RATE AS "BEST CLINICAL ENDPOINT" (PEARL INDEX): "efficacy phase" of clinical trials and requirement of, 179–180, 182–183, 185n10; exclusion of female with impaired fertility, 183; as indirect measure, and complexities of relationship status, infidelity, and sexual activity, 182; as indirect measure of male (in)fertility, 180; "nonresponse" phenomenon and inadequacy of, 181–182; sperm counts considered "surrogate parameters," 180
—SPERM COUNT SUPPRESSION: accepted threshold by activists and users (≤1 million of sperm/ml), 180–181; accepted threshold by consensus of experts (≤1 million of sperm/ml), 179, 185n11; costs and sample sizes reduced in, 182–183; as direct measure, simplifying complexity, 182; healthy/normal concentration amounts, and putative difficulty of developing male contraceptives, 177–178; repeated assessments of sperm counts to overcome the "nonresponse" phenomenon, 181–182; scientists recommending as "surrogate parameter," 180; suppression levels with pregnancy rates comparable to female methods (≤3 million of sperm/ml), 179; time savings speeding up development, 183; zero sperm (azoospermia) not necessary, 178–179, 185n11

Male Contraceptive Initiative, 168, 174–175; trials on and sales of thermic ring (AndroSwitch), 181, 185n12

male factor infertility: overview, 72; CDC meeting on (2010), 85; childlessness resulting from, as increasing globally, 263; conflated with erectile dysfunction, 262; conflated with sexual failure, 255–256; as crisis, 76; four major categories of sperm defects, 262; IVF cycles per year due to, 73; lack of male evaluation prior to couple entering infertility treatment, 72–73, 74; low-income men and the human right to treatment of, 65; Male Reproductive Health Ecosystem, 76, 77; Male Reproductive Health Initiative, for research, 75–78, 80n3; men's embarrassment, guilt, and grief feelings about diagnosis, 84–85, 255–257; men's sense of isolation after diagnosis of, 256–257; as most stigmatizing of all male health conditions, 262; as negatively impacting maternal and infant wellness, 76; percentage of infertility caused by, 71–72, 84, 255, 257, 262; percentage of infertility caused by, in the Middle East, 263; public awareness, building of, 255, 258–259; socioeconomic data, need for, 75, 78–79, 80; WHO panel recommendations for clinical and basic research due to lack of data, 71, 79; women bearing burden of treatment for, 72, 73, 256. *See also* infertility; infertility investigation process; sperm/semen testing
—BARRIERS IN ACCESS TO CARE: overview, 79–80; CDC lack of men's health division, 85; communication style as barrier, 78; cultural beliefs, 75; educational achievement, 75; geographic location, 75; inadequate numbers of MRH specialists, 73–74, 75, 80, 257; inclusivity of men in clinical settings, 78, 79–80; insufficiency in medical education and training of specialists, 74–75; insurance coverage lacking, 73, 85; as missed opportunity to diagnose infertility-related health conditions, 73; profit-motivation of direct use of ART as barrier, 85; racial inequalities, 75; social awareness, proposals for increasing, 78–79; state laws mandating insurance coverage for, as few, 73; support groups as typically limited to women's issues, 85, 258

—CATEGORIES OF: defects of sperm morphology (teratozoospermia), 262; genetic abnormalities known to be cause of severe cases, 263–264; low sperm count (oligozoospermia), 262; poor sperm motility (asthenozoospermia), 262; total absence of sperm in ejaculate (azoospermia), 262, 263, 265, 270; very low sperm count and poor motility (oligoasthenozoospermia), 263

—OTHER MEDICAL PROBLEMS ASSOCIATED WITH: overview as biomarker for current and future health, 1–2, 79, 85, 93; as global crisis, 76, 93; informing patient of risks of, 87; lack of insurance coverage for male infertility as missed opportunity to find, 73; medical evaluation of male infertility as revealing, 73; types of diseases and problems, 73, 76, 85, 87, 88, 93; and the urgency of need for social awareness of MRH, 78–79

—TREATMENTS: caution against using testosterone monotherapy, 88; clinical guidelines (AUA and ASRM), 86–89; medications to increase testosterone, 88; varicocele(s), surgical varicocelectomy for, 88, 269. *See also* assisted reproductive technologies (ART); ICSI (intracytoplasmic sperm injection)

Male Reproductive Health Ecosystem, 76, 77
Male Reproductive Health Initiative (MRHI), 75–78, 80n3
male reproductive identity: and the barrier of gendered construction of reproductivity as sole responsibility of women, 166–167; benefits of men's engagement to maternal and newborn health, 31, 46, 167; definition of, 166; emotions, thoughts, and behaviors of men and, 166; and engagement with preventive health care, 170; lack of or "neutrality" on engagement, as reinforcing female reproductive burden, 167–168

—BUILDING ENGAGEMENT: education and awareness efforts, 169–170; equal family leave and, 169–170; expansion of access to existing contraceptive methods, 169; expansion of new male contraceptive methods, 168–169, 170–171

Man Up Checkup campaign, 54, 55–56
marriage: consensual adult sex outside of, Catholics' approval of, 192; and reemergence of status inequalities, 249; state parentage laws protecting only married couples with donor-conceived children, 248–249; Supreme Court finding against different rules for married same-sex and different-sex couples with donor-conceived children, 232. *See also* same-sex marriage

Martin, Emily, "The Egg and the Sperm," 96
Mascaro, Christopher, 58
masculinity: adolescent SRH strategies promoting many ways to be male, 42; the aesthetics of hybrid masculinities used by direct-to-consumer digital health companies, 283, 285; media literacy and development of better forms of, 42; the multitude of, and concept of queer sperm, 221; significant caregiving responsibilities as different kind of investment in, 55. *See also* masculinity beliefs, traditional; public health campaigns—"healthy masculinity strategies"

masculinity beliefs, traditional: the child support system and outdated breadwinner model of masculinity, 117–118; communication style and reticence to volunteer information, 78; and COVID-19 diagnosis and death rates, 55; as cultural scripts (vs. biology) that hurt themselves and others, 55, 58–59; endocrine-disrupting chemicals and male infertility as crisis of, 95; factors reinforcing, 41, 56; the patriarchy as social system maintaining, 212n13, 220; pharmaceutical companies' marketing of sexual health conditions by appealing to anxieties of, 282–283; and refusal to see a doctor, 39, 41, 46, 54; risky health behaviors and, 41, 54–55; sexual script of active sperm and passive egg, 96, 157, 215, 216; sperm as potent symbol of Western hegemonic masculinity, 95–98; sperm donor perceived as "metaphorically having sex" with partner, 257; therapy as cultural "feminization," 256; white supremacist "white-genocide" conspiracy theory of declining sperm counts, 95–96; women's bodies as reproductive and men's as not, as barrier to research in sperm count trends, 98–99. *See also* direct-to-consumer digital health companies—marketing of erectile dysfunction (ED) and premature ejaculation treatments; misogyny; public health campaigns—"healthy masculinity strategies"; violence; virility

masculinity beliefs, traditional (*cont.*)
—ADOLESCENTS AND: "boy code," 41–42; as cultural script, 41–42, 45–46, 142; double standards about sexual behavior, 41; engaging in higher risk behaviors, 41, 142; females as responsible for contraception, teen pregnancy, and STI prevention, 41; homophobia and, 41; lack of emotional expression, 41; media literacy and unlearning, 42; and refusal to see a doctor, 39, 41, 46; risky health behaviors and, 41; and same-sex friendships, lack of, 41; socioecological framework for adolescent SRH and unlearning, 42, 45–46; SRH strategies to promote multiple masculinities, 42

masturbation: as haram in the Muslim world, 267, 270; for ICSI, 266–267; for IVF, 265; for sperm/semen analysis, 256

maternal effects on reproductive outcomes: adverse childhood events, 31; epigenetic transformations, 105; paternal partner involvement improving outcomes, 31; smoking cessation, 31; smoking, cited as factor in global decline of sperm counts, 94. *See also* environmental exposures

maternal mortality in pregnancy and childbirth: overview of inherent risk as burden, 276; Black fathers' trauma and challenges due to, could be ameliorated with prevention of deaths, 31–32; Black women's rate as significantly higher, 31–32, 276; homicide as leading cause of pregnancy-associated death in the US, 31; rate in the US as highest of any wealthy nation, 31; systemic factors affecting women of color, 276

media literacy, 42

media. *See* news media; social media

Medicaid programs, and trans fertility preservation, 125, 137, 138

medical schools and residencies: male infertility fellowship training programs in US, 75, 85–86; need for integrating the evidence that male infertility portends future general health issues, 78; need for training in male factor infertility, 74–75; need for training in men's and adolescents' SRH, 43–44, 47; need for training vasectomy providers, 159; sperm health not taught in, 140. *See also* physicians

"men as partners," public health messaging, 7–8

men, as term, 12, 166. *See also* male, as term

men of color: eugenics movement seeking to limit reproductive autonomy of, 135, 161–162; gendered disparity in likelihood to be sterilized, 159–160; sperm bank practices disproportionately excluding, 231, 247; as sperm donors, 231; vasectomies of, 161–162. *See also* Black men; Indigenous people; Latine people

men's rights groups and ideology, 10; antiabortion sentiment driven by, 64

mental health: of donor-conceived persons, knowing the identity of donor and improvement in, 210; and gendered differential in focus of direct-to-consumer digital health companies, 285–286n1; men's struggle with, after diagnosis of male factor infertility, 255–257; self-help literature limited for male factor infertility, 256–257; support group access for male infertility patients, limited due to focus on women's issues, 85, 258; therapy, men's discomfort with, 256; of trans youth, gender-affirming care as improving, 121. *See also* mental health professionals; mental illness; suicide; support groups

mental health professionals: in assessment of need for trans fertility preservation, 122, 124, 125; bringing awareness of male infertility to, 259; lack of graduate programs with coursework in infertility counseling, 257–258; lack of male therapists, 257

mental illness: eugenics movement seeking to limit reproductive autonomy of people with, 135; and genetics testing for ART procedures, 225

Merck, HPV vaccine, 32

metabolic disorders, associated with male-infertility, 73, 76

Middle Eastern Muslim men, and male factor infertility: overview, 261–262, 270; adoption as haram, 267–268, 270; childlessness due to, as deeply troubling, 263; depleted uranium exposures in US-led Iraq wars, as cause, 264–265, 269; genetic abnormalities as cause of severe male infertility, 263–264; ICSI as "only hope" for, 267–268; and "local moral worlds," 262; male infertility as percentage of all infertility (60–90%), 263; patrilineal organization of, and paternity as critical, 263; as recalcitrant to prevention and chronic, 264; as running in families, probably due to consanguineous marriage, 264; sperm donation

as haram, 267, 270. *See also* Arab America; ICSI (intracytoplasmic sperm injection)
migration status, and stratified reproduction, 63
military servicemembers, exposure to depleted uranium (Iraq wars), 264–265, 269
Miller, Steven, 259
Mincy, Ronald, 118
Minio-Paulello, Mika, 290–291
miscarriage. *See* pregnancy loss (miscarriage and stillbirth)
misogyny: and hypervolence against transgender women, 293; as motivating antiabortion sentiment, 64; of stigma surrounding abortion decisions, 275; and "white genocide" conspiracy theory of declining sperm counts, 95–96. *See also* sexism; violence against pregnant people; violence, sexual
mortality rates: of cisgender men, and cultural scripts of masculinity, 54–55; infant, 31. *See also* maternal mortality in pregnancy and childbirth
Movember movement for men's health issues, 57–58

Nagy, Beáta, 275
Najari, Bobby B., 73–74
narrative medicine, 205, 208, 211–212
National Association of Social Workers, 259
National Institutes of Health (NIH), inclusion of females in biomedical research and clinical trials, 6–7
National Survey of Family Growth, 45, 74
Nazi Germany, and eugenics, 206, 225–226
neurological issues, associated with male infertility, 85, 87
New Zealand, declines in sperm counts, 90
news media: Black sperm donor shortage, 107; and the donor conception community, 199; global decline in sperm counts as crisis, 92–93, 94–95, 97, 103, 105; in history of donor insemination, 206; and media literacy, importance of, 42; reproductive justice coverage in wake of *Dobbs*, 62; "shrinking penis" coverage, 105; transgender women as mothers, 290–291
Nieschlag, Eberhard, 98
nonbinary people: and thermic testicular contraception, 174–175, 184, 184n4, 185–186n14; tucking, 184n4. *See also* trans and gender diverse youth
North American Society for Pediatric and Adolescent Gynecology, 42

Nuclear Family (Russo-Young) (documentary), 211–212
nutritional deficits, and maternal mortality and morbidity risks, 276
nutritional supplements, informing male infertility patients of limited utility of, 87–88

Obama, Barack, "1 is 2 many" campaign, 56–57
Obamacare. *See* Affordable Care Act (ACA)
obstetrician-gynecologists: in exodus from states with increasing legal liability (post-*Dobbs*), 203n9, 248; expertise in SRH not available to males, 22; as gatekeepers for infertility investigations, 72; tubal ligation immediately postpartum as expected practice of, 159
obstetrics and gynecology, EMERGE Framework as based on, 23, 24
Office of Population Affairs, *Providing Quality Family Planning Services,* 42–43
oropharyngeal cancers, HPV vaccines and prevention of, 24
Our Father (documentary), 245

Pacey, Allan, 97
Pancoast, William, 243
Parens, Erik, 224
parental leave, paternal: denial of, and female partners assuming childcare responsibilities, 26; provision of, and building of male reproductive identity, 168–169
parenting: incarcerated men and separation from children, 66; mapa (gender-neutral term combining "mama" and "papa"), 66; reproductive justice and the right to raise children in a safe and healthy environment, 10, 62, 66, 121–122, 127. *See also* child support system; child welfare system; family; fathers/fatherhood; pregnancy and related reproductive burdens—mental load
paternal effects on reproductive outcomes: overview, 7; age, 1, 7, 25, 87; age, and birth defects as risk, 87; health insurance policies do not cover paternal genetic testing, 25; health risks to children, 1, 7; informing the parents on risks of, 87; lack of programs for behavioral change, 25; lack of warnings on medications or substances, 7; mental health care, 25; pregnancy loss, 1; smoking, 7; smoking cessation, 25; toxic exposures, 7. *See also* environmental exposures; epigenetic transformations within sperm due to environmental toxicants

paternity testing, and child support, 117, 276. *See also* child support system—the afterlife of incarcerated fathers

Path 2 Parenthood, 258–259

patriarchy: and ART as queering sperm, 220; sperm as stuck in reproductive normativity of, 288, 289–290. *See also* gender, dualistic/binary view of; heteronormativity; masculinity beliefs, traditional; misogyny; sexism; white supremacy

Pearl Index. *See* contraceptive efficacy, pregnancy rates as principal metric of—the Pearl Index; male contraceptive efficacy—pregnancy rate as "best clinical endpoint" (Pearl Index)

Pearl, Raymond, 177

Pence, Mike, 228

people of color. *See* Black men; Black women; ethnicity, and inequalities; Indigenous people; Latine people; men of color; reproductive justice; women of color

Peters, Torrey, *Detransition, Baby,* 292–293, 295

pharmaceutical companies: marketing sexual health conditions by appealing to masculine anxieties and widening the population of medicalized penises, 282–283; resistance to investing in male contraception research, 25, 184n5. *See also* direct-to-consumer digital health companies—pharmaceutical sales

pharmaceuticals: guidelines to inform male infertility patient of risks to fertility, 88–89; lack of warnings on paternal effects of, 77. *See also* male contraception—hormonal methods

physicians: characteristics of, preferred by patients, 39, 46; female clinician discomfort with male SRH exams, 43–44; inadequate numbers of men's reproductive specialists, 42, 43–44, 73–74, 75, 80, 159, 257; lack of medical specialty in men's reproduction, 42, 158; loss of, in wake of *Dobbs,* 202, 203n9, 245, 248; racial bias of ("Black women can't be infertile"), 230; as rarely discussing sperm health, 140; as rarely providing preconception and contraception counseling, 22, 43; reproductive endocrinologists, 72; showing adolescent males their sperm under a microscope, 142; telehealth, 281. *See also* andrologists (male reproductive health specialists); clinical recommendations and guidelines; medical schools and residencies;

mental health professionals; obstetrician-gynecologists; primary care; urologists

pituitary abnormalities, associated with male infertility, 85, 87, 88

Planned Parenthood of Southeastern Pennsylvania v. Casey, 30, 228

Plume (direct-to-consumer digital health company), 285–286n1. *See also* direct-to-consumer digital health companies

podcasts, 259

police violence, as reproductive justice issue, 66

Pollentree.com, 231

postgenomic perspectives, 103. *See also* environmental damage; environmental exposures

poverty: and abortion decisions, social perception of, 275; access to abortion limited by, 9–10; basic resources denied to those in, 8, 9; disabilities, disparities in rates for people with, 230; and eugenics movement seeking to limit reproductive autonomy, 135, 161; of formerly incarcerated fathers with child support debt, 115–118; and maternal mortality and morbidity risks, 276; punitive reproductive landscape and, 33–34; trans women of color and, 136. *See also* class; gendered social inequalities; racialized inequalities

preconception counseling: genetic testing, recommendations for, 225; men as rarely provided, 22

pregnancy: EMERGE Framework and paternal involvement in, 25–26; as fundamentally social as well as biological, 7; immediate postpartum tubal ligation as expected sterilization choice, 159; maternal factors as focus in, 25; paternal involvement in, and improvements in health of infant, mother, and father, 31, 46, 167; teen pregnancy, and risk of maternal mortality and morbidity, 276. *See also* breastfeeding; conception; maternal effects on reproductive outcomes; maternal mortality in pregnancy and childbirth; paternal effects on reproductive outcomes; pregnancy and related reproductive burdens; pregnancy loss (miscarriage and stillbirth); pregnancy, unintended; violence against pregnant people

pregnancy and related reproductive burdens: overview, 273, 278; the EMERGE framework aiming for alleviation of, 23–27; men and male partners as unaware of the full extent of, 21–22, 26, 274; "neutral" men and male

partners as reinforcing, 167–168; terminology of gender and, 273; (white) male policymakers unable to grasp full extent of the burdens, 22, 169, 278
—BIOLOGICAL/PHYSICAL LOAD AS INHERENTLY UNEQUAL: overview, 157–158, 273–274; breastfeeding as, 277; conception as coequal act, 273, 278; doctor's visits, 274–275; prenatal vitamins, 274; race and class as systemic factors in, 276; risk of mortality and morbidity, 31–32, 276; socioeconomic burdens of, 274–275, 276, 277. *See also* bodily autonomy—of pregnancy-capable people; maternal mortality
—MENTAL LOAD: overview, 273; as beginning at conception, 273; cognitive labor for the family, 274; decision to discontinue a pregnancy and, 275–276, 278; definition of, 274; egalitarian couples reverting to traditional gendered roles, 168, 274; emotional labor for the family, 274; equitable division of labor, development of, 169–170, 277–278; state elimination of choice and exacerbation of, 162, 273, 278; as unseen time and energy, 273, 274
pregnancy loss (miscarriage and stillbirth): effect of paternal age on, 1; IVG research revealing men's influence on, 151; loss of practitioners for high-risk pregnancies in wake of *Dobbs*, 203n9, 248; recurrent, and evaluation for male infertility, 86–87; subpar care in abortion-hostile states, 162
Pregnancy Poems (cárdenas), 293, 295
pregnancy, unintended: adolescent males and, 37, 38, 41, 141; defined as in the eye of the beholder, 275; educational framing by health care providers and, 26; factors contributing to male partner's labeling of, 275; intersectional inequalities in perception of, 275; male partner's lack of empathy in recognizing decisions should be female partner's, 26; and male partner's vocal advocacy for abortion, importance of, 26; public health campaigns aimed at women, 158; stigma and shame feelings of male partners, 26; stigma and "slut" shaming of women, 26, 275; "stud" celebration of the male partner in, 275–276. *See also* abortion decisions
premature ejaculation, 282. *See also* direct-to-consumer digital health companies—marketing of erectile dysfunction (ED) and premature ejaculation treatments
Preventative Services Task Force, US, STI screening recommended for women but not men, 23–24, 32
primary care: adolescent services, clinical guidelines and failure to provide, 36–37, 42–43; female clinicians shown to provide better quality care, 43–44; gendered differential in well visit patterns, 44, 84; sexual and reproductive care, burden on women for, 32, 33. *See also* physicians
privacy, medical, 201–202, 247, 250n4
Project Hombre, 45–46
Providing Quality Family Planning Services (CDC and Office of Population Affairs), 42–43
public awareness and education: male celebrities speaking on male factor infertility, 255, 258–259; male factor infertility, urgency of need for, 78–79; male reproductive identity, 169–170; MILES (Men, Infertility, and Life Experiences) podcast, 259. *See also* public health campaigns
public health campaigns: breastfeeding promotion, 277; "ending teen pregnancy" as focused on girls, 158; HPV vaccine for men and male partners, 24–25, 32–33; "men as partners," 7–8; paternal effects on pregnancy, need for, 7; promotion of the multiple ways there are to be male, 42
—"HEALTHY MASCULINITY STRATEGIES": overview, 56; alternative proposal: question negative impacts of masculinity instead of reinscribing, 55, 59; Man Up Checkup campaign, 54, 55–56; as masculinizing men's health-seeking behavior while reinscribing and essentializing negative aspects, 55, 56, 57–59; Movember movement for men's health issues, 57–58; research showing cisgender men more likely to engage in risky health behaviors, 41, 54–55; sexual violence prevention campaigns, 56–57
Public Service Announcements, federal resources for, 79

queer, definition of, 215–216
queer identity: defined as reclaimed derogatory term, 216; and sexual and gender identities, 220. *See also* LGBTQ+ people

queer sex, as lens of understanding the heteronormativity reinforced by direct-to-consumer men's digital health companies, 284–285
queer theory, on reproduction as antiqueer, 292
queering of sperm by ART, 215–221

race, as social (vs. biological) category, 8–9
racialized health inequalities: overview of social processes that produce, 8–9; in access both to providers and to quality of care, 9; adolescent males and high rates of STIs, 37, 38; adolescent males and high rates of unintended pregnancies, 37, 38; age of first sex experience, 38; female factor infertility care, 230; male factor infertility care, 75; maternal mortality and morbidity risks, 276; sperm donor access, 108, 224, 230, 239–240, 247–248; trans reproductive care and, 127–128, 137–138; vasectomy access, 159–160, 161–162. See also Black men; Black women; Indigenous people; Latine people
racialized inequalities: and abortion decisions, social perception of, 275; in hiring, and untenable position of formerly incarcerated fathers with child support debt, 118; hyperfertility trope imposed on Black women, 230, 294; sperm banks as reproducing, 108. See also reproductive justice; stratified reproduction
racism, systemic: overview, 8–9; basic resources denied due to, 8, 9. See also white supremacy
Ramsey, Gordon, 255
regenerative medicine, 148
religious institutions: and federal law allowing religious entities to restrict reproductive services, 190–191. See also Catholic health systems
religious people: Catholics Bishops as leaning further right than their parishioners, 192; IVF and other reproductive freedoms as normalized and utilized, 192. See also Arab America, male infertility in; Middle Eastern Muslim men, and male factor infertility
reproductive endocrinologists, 72
reproductive health services, increasing men's health care seeking: communication strategies, 78; inclusivity of men in clinical environments, 78, 79–80; Office on Men's Health (proposed), 78–79; provider education of adolescent and adult males, 78; Public Service Announcements, 79. See also health care, reluctance of men to obtain; sexual and reproductive health (SRH), and men
reproductive justice: overview, 10, 62; abortion rights, as matter of access not just choice, 127; assisted reproduction regulation argued as, 233–234, 235, 239; assisted reproduction regulatory proposals in need of intersectional analysis, 244–245, 247–249; balancing the virtue of access to fertility preservation with the value of nonnormative family relations as central tenet of, 127; bodily autonomy of women and pregnancy-capable people as sacrosanct, 10–11, 61, 127; capitalization as Reproductive Justice in the text, 61; developed by Black women activists, 62; establishment due to intersectional oppressions faced by women of color and marginalized women, 10, 62–63; as human rights framework, 62; and ICSI (intracytoplasmic sperm injection), 269–270; post-*Dobbs* attacks on, 244; the right to have a child, 10; the right to not have a child, 10; and the right to parent their children in safe and healthy communities, 10, 62, 66, 121–122, 127; and sperm donation, 108; and trans fertility preservation, 121–122, 127–128, 136–138; and trans women, hyperviolence against, 65, 293; *Zeugungsverhütung* ("procreation prevention") as nongendered term for and conceptual shift in "male contraception," 174–175, 183–184
—INJUSTICES FACED BY WOMEN OF COLOR: birthing disproportionately in hospitals with religious constraints on care, 191; classist logics structuring, 63; eugenics-influenced barriers to trans reproductive care, 135–138; eugenics movement seeking to limit reproductive autonomy, 135; involuntary sterilization, 10, 135, 161, 162; mass incarceration effects on health and family life, 10, 66, 115; termination of parental rights, 10; in violation of human right to parent children in safe and healthy communities, 66; white supremacist logics structuring, 63
—FOR MEN: may not limit women's right to bodily autonomy, 10–11, 27, 29, 30–31, 34, 64–67; may not sacrifice commitment to women of color, marginalized women, and all pregnancy-capable people, 61, 63–64, 65–67; no diversion of resources from

women's SRH programs, 27, 29, 34. *See also* —stratified reproductive justice, *below*
—STRATIFIED REPRODUCTIVE JUSTICE: overview, 61–63; for application to egg-producing people not from multiply marginalized populations, 61–62; for application to sperm-producing people, 61–62; and the context of stratified reproduction, 62–64; example of application by researchers, 66–67; the human right to have a child, 64–65; and human right to not have a child, 65–66; and human right to parent their children in safe and healthy environments, 66; and the intersectional context of embodied difference, 62–63; may not sacrifice commitment to women of color, marginalized women, and all pregnancy-capable people, 61, 63–64, 65–67; as rejecting obfuscation of power and inequity in calls for "reproductive justice for all," 64, 66
reproductive normativity, 288, 289–290
reproductive rights movement: as failing to adequately address the needs of Black and marginalized women, 62. *See also* reproductive justice
Resolve (infertility support organization), 85, 258
Rigó, Adrien, 275
Ro (direct-to-consumer digital health company), 280–281, 285, 285–286n1. *See also* direct-to-consumer digital health companies
Robertson, Lindsey G., 274
Robinson, Zandria, 62
Rodsky, Eve, *Fair Play* (program, book, documentary), 277–278
Roe v. Wade: *Casey* decision reaffirming, 30, 228; overturned by *Dobbs*, 9–10, 244. *See also Dobbs v. Jackson Women's Health Organization* (2022)
Ruppanner, Leah, 274
Russo-Young, Ry, *Nuclear Family* (documentary), 211–212

same-sex marriage: Catholic Americans and majority approval of, 192; right to, at risk, 244; Supreme Court finding against different rules for married same-sex and different-sex couples with donor-conceived children, 232
same-sex parent families. *See* LGBTQ+ parent families

schizophrenia, 225
Seeger, Matthew W., 91
Sellnow, Timothy L., 91
sex and gender, traditional categories of: and conflation of reproduction with female bodies, 7; as cultural beliefs, 5, 96, 157; definition of, 5; egalitarian couples reverting to in pregnancy and childcare, 168, 274; inclusion of females in biomedical research and clinical trials and, 6–7; paternity leave denied, and default to women as childcare givers, 26; rejection of, as methodology, 5–6. *See also* biological fables; burdens of reproductivity as gendered inequality; gender, dualistic/binary view of; gendered social inequalities
sex education: the active sperm and passive egg story taught in, 157. *See also* public awareness and education; public health campaigns
—AND YOUNG MEN: age to begin teaching, 38; gender-based discrepancies in, 45, 259; lack of data on breadth and depth of, 45; lack of federal mandate for comprehensive teaching, 44–45; as teaching they do not need to understand women's bodies or experiences of reproduction, 23
sexism: internalized, 220; patriarchy as social system maintaining, 220; as system of oppression, 62. *See also* misogyny
sexual and reproductive health (SRH), and men: definition of, 36; expansion of male services in family planning clinic and increase of demand for, 39; lack of expert providers for, 22, 42, 43–44; "male involvement" and "male responsibility" introduced as concepts in, 142, 143; no single medical specialty focused solely on, 42; traditional masculinity beliefs and refusal to see a doctor, 39, 41, 46. *See also* adolescent male sexual and reproductive health—socioecological framework for; EMERGE (Expanding Male Engagement in Reproductive and Gender Equity) Framework; health care, reluctance of men to obtain; reproductive health services, increasing men's health care seeking
sexual minority persons. *See* LGBTQ+ people
sexually transmitted infections. *See* STIs
Seymour, Frances, 205–206
Shapiro, Dani, *Inheritance* (memoir), 207–208
Sharpe, Richard, 93
Siegel, Reva, 249

single-parent families: and reemergence of status inequalities, 249; and risk of maternal mortality and morbidity, 276
—AND DONOR CONCEPTION: ART legal parentage at risk, 238–239, 243–244, 248–249; in history of insemination, 206; and the movement to tell children they are donor-conceived, 212–213n4; as socially infertile, 230; Uniform Parentage Act recognizing, 246. *See also* family, diversity of forms facilitated by assisted reproduction

SisterSong Women of Color Reproductive Health Collective, 10, 62, 127. *See also* reproductive justice

Skakkebaek, Niels, 90

smoking: cessation of, 25, 31; cisgender men and health risk-taking behavior, 54; as factor in global decline of sperm counts, 93–94; as producing paternal effects on reproductive outcomes, 7

social media: Man Up Checkup campaign, 56; media literacy and unlearning negative masculinity roles, 42; support groups for donor-conceived people, 208, 213n5; support groups for male factor infertility, 258; teen content, as factor reinforcing traditional masculinity beliefs, 41. *See also* sperm donation (DIY/informal market)

Society for Adolescent Health and Medicine, 42

socioecological framework for adolescents. *See* adolescent male sexual and reproductive health—socioecological framework for

sperm: overview of nexus of sperm, health, and politics, 1–3; as biological sentinel, 96, 103–104, 105–106; biological structure of, 216; dictionary definition of, 3; as "exposed biology" in need of protection, 105; as fundamentally social as well as biological, 3–4, 11, 84; gendered metaphor of active sperm and passive egg, 96, 157, 215, 216; global population of persons who produce, 166; Google searches for, 1; as main symbol of virility, 96, 97–98, 215, 216; nested dolls metaphor of, 3–4, 4; as queered by assisted reproductive technologies, 215–221; spermarche, lack of data about, 141. *See also* IVG (in vitro gametogenesis)

sperm banking for preservation of fertility (cryopreservation): by cisgender youth with cancer, 122, 126, 128–129, 129n4; cost of, as prohibitive for many trans women, 136; due to epigenetic influences of toxic environments, 105; due to medications that can affect sperm quality, 88–89; informing patient of advisability of, 89. *See also* trans people's fertility preservation

sperm banks (sperm donation): overview as formal market, 229; barriers to care as pushing people into DIY/informal sperm market, 230–231, 239; class and racial disparities in access to, 108, 224, 230, 231, 239–240, 247–248; commodification of sperm and, 217–218, 223, 224, 225, 233; competition for clientele, 223; cost of, 230–231, 235, 236, 239; COVID-19 pandemic and shortage of donors, 107, 108, 224; disabilities, disparities in access for people with, 230; donor, defined, 202n1; insurance coverage, 230, 239; interests of donor-conceived people may be ignored in, 233, 236–237, 239; legal parentage and protection of all families formed through (Uniform Parentage Act), 246; legal parentage of diverse family forms at risk, 238–239, 243–245, 248–249; legal parentage security, as reason to choose the formal vs. informal market, 231; no legal relationship with donor, 231; no public banks in US, 225; non-cisgender sperm-producing people as donors, 229; processing and handling of sperm, 218–219. *See also* donor-conceived people; egg donation; sperm donation (DIY/informal market)

—BLACK DONOR SHORTAGE: explanations offered by sperm banks as failing to explain, 107, 108, 109; lack of studies of, 108–109; lighter skin tone donors as alternative, as criticized for colorism, 108; mistrust of the medical profession blamed for, 107, 108, 109n1; and reproductive justice, questions of, 108; same-race sperm donors and norms of what family "should" look like, 108; sperm bank practices as perpetuating, 108, 109, 224, 231, 247; statistics showing underrepresentation, 107, 231; waitlists for Black women seeking Black donor, 107–108

—DONOR ANONYMITY: ASRM and other professional organizations opposed to abolishing, 203n8; calls for mandatory disclosure of identity, 199; Colorado abolishing (Donor-Conceived Persons Protection Act), 200, 203n7, 203n8, 209,

228, 245, 246–247; direct-to-consumer DNA testing as revealing identities, 199, 201, 208–209, 210; fertility industry fear of lost profits, 208, 210, 212; Fourteenth Amendment equal protection clause, 201; HIPAA privacy, 201–202, 250n4; origins of: in eugenics, heteronormativity, and preservation of masculinity, 205, 206–207, 211, 212, 213n7, 243, 245; other countries that abolished, 200, 208, 209, 235; other states proposing to abolish, 200–201
—DONOR ELIGIBILITY STANDARDS: overview, 203n2; the FDA as setting, 200; FDA attempts to enforce, 234; FDA standards as relatively minimal, 225, 230, 231–232; gay male donors excluded by FDA, 231–232, 235; gay male donors, recommendation to include, 239; infectious disease screening, 203n2, 223, 225, 230, 232; professional organization guidelines, 223, 230, 233
—DONOR IDENTITY DISCLOSURE: balancing of interests among donors, recipients, and donor-conceived people, 201–202, 234–235, 236–237, 239–240; clarity and intention in writing of regulations, 202; cost and, 235, 236, 239; critical concerns about majoritarian values, 238–239; donor registries, 200, 202; donor updates to contact information, 209; exceptionalizing ART, 238; family-limit (number of donations) regulations, 203n7, 233, 235, 236, 237, 239; fewer practitioners/chilling effect resulting from, 202, 203n9; and genetic essentialism, 237–238, 244, 249; increases in donors in countries with mandatory, 209, 235; intended families opposing, 236; intersectional reproductive justice lens needed for, 244–245, 247–249; legal parentage of diverse family forms at risk, 238–239, 243–245, 248–249; out-of-state donors, 203n7, 209; parental rights of intending parents must be secure, 239; and reproductive autonomy, 235–237, 244; reproductive justice argument for regulations, 233–234, 235, 239; state laws allowing disclosure by agreement between gamete provider and intended parents (at age 18), 246; state laws requiring disclosure (at age 18), 239, 246–247; state laws requiring disclosure during childhood and facilitating contact, proposed, 247, 248–249; states allowing by request of donor-conceived person, 200, 203n6; states allowing parents to request nonidentifying medical information at any time, 246; and supply of donors, 202, 235; the Uniform Parentage Act and, 200, 245–247
—DONOR'S MEDICAL HISTORY: expanded liability potential for donors, 245, 248; law requiring medical privacy must be waived, proposed, 247, 250n4; law requiring release of last five years of medical care, proposed, 247; mandates for banks to maintain and share, 200, 203n8; racial equity issues raised by, 247; verification requirement, 203n8
—FERTILITY FRAUD: expanded liability potential for donors, and potential reduction of supply, 245, 248; expanded potential liability laws targeting providers, and loss of services, 245, 248; failure to disclose genetic information, 203n3; history of fraudulent behavior, 243, 245, 247, 250; narrowly written laws, 245; retroactive penalties, 245; state laws, 203n8, 245
—GENETIC TESTING OF DONORS: overview, 203n2; and asymmetric donor-recipient relationship, 224; class and racial disparities in access to, 224; competition for clientele and, 223, 224; diseases to exclude via, 224, 225–226; dominant conditions not tested for, 223; donor-conceived persons and need to know, 208, 210; eugenic and "fittest" sperm, 224, 225–226; general population preconception testing as comparison, 224–226; guidelines from professional organizations (ASRM), 223, 230; guiding philosophy of, options for, 226; as increasingly comprehensive, 223; polygenic risk scoring, 223; for recessive disorders, 223, 226; recipients undergoing same level of testing, proposal for, 225; single-payer health care systems and, 225–226; US health care system and, 225, 226

sperm count suppression. *See* male contraceptive efficacy—sperm count suppression

sperm counts in global decline: overview, 1, 90; causes and meaning of, as knowledge gap, 71, 79, 97, 104; climate change science

sperm counts in global decline (*cont.*)
compared to, 90, 104; as measurement issue vs. actual decline, 97; media reports on, 92–93, 94–95, 97, 103, 105; prospective studies needed, vs. the existing retrospective meta-analyses, 98–99; in "Western" countries, 90, 95. *See also* male factor infertility; male factor infertility—other medical problems associated with; sperm/semen testing
—AS CRISIS: overview, 76, 90–91, 92; definition of crisis and political nature of designation as, 91–92, 97–99; as environmental crisis (endocrine-disrupting chemicals), 94–95, 97, 149; as extinction crisis, 90, 92–93, 104–105; as male health crisis, 93; as masculinity crisis, 95–98; as modern lifestyle crisis, 93–94; popular science fiction narratives invoked, 90; as set of interconnected crises, 90–91, 92, 96; and sperm as biological sentinel, 96, 103–104; as white supremacist "white-genocide" conspiracy theory, 95–96
sperm donation (DIY/informal market): overview, 108–109, 229; barriers to care in formal sperm donation as pushing people into, 230–231, 239; Black women turning to, 108, 231; cost as much more accessible, 230–231; ease of collecting sperm, 229; networking among friends, 230, 231; online/social media sperm donation, 107, 108–109, 230, 231, 232–233; regulation proposed for, 233–234; reproductive justice and, 233–234. *See also* sperm banks (sperm donation)
—DONORS: benefits to donors in, 231–232; Black donors, 109, 231; gay male donors in, 231–232; men of color as, 231; pool of donors may include those excluded from sperm banks, 211–212, 231–232; relationship with donor, desire for, 231
—LEGAL PARENTAGE: donation without medical assistance as risk, 232; general attacks on nontraditional families, 238–239, 243–245, 248–249; known donors as risk, 211–212, 232–233, 249; sperm donor found to be legal parent, 232–233, 249; state health care may not be available, 232; Supreme Court finding against different rules for married same-sex and heterosexual couples, 232
—RISKS OF: conception less certain, 232; enforcement of contracts, lack of, 234; health screening incomplete, 232, 234; intercourse demanded by donor, 232; interests of donor-conceived people may be ignored in, 233, 236–237; sexual violence, 232; sperm analysis not done, 232
Sperm Donation USA, 231
sperm extraction methods. *See* ICSI (intracytoplasmic sperm injection)—sperm extraction methods
sperm/semen testing: abnormal parameters, clinician informing of associated health risks, 87; abnormal parameters should be evaluated by men's reproductive health specialist, 86; adolescent anxiety about sperm health and, 142; direct-to-consumer "home sperm tests," 84–85, 185n13; failed ART cycles or recurrent pregnancy losses, and evaluation of, 86; fear and embarrassment experienced due to need for, 84–85, 256; healthy/normal concentration amounts, 177–178; initial infertility evaluation and concurrent male/female testing, 86; measurement standards as uncertain, 97; the microscope as DIY method, 142, 185n13; specimen collection, 256; for thermic testicular contraception (male contraceptive), 185n13
spermatogenesis: IVG as research tool for understanding, 148–151. *See also* male contraceptive efficacy—sperm count suppression
spinal muscular atrophy, 223
sports, as factor reinforcing traditional masculinity beliefs, 41, 56
standards of care: assaults on reproductive care and difficulty following, 10. *See also* clinical recommendations and guidelines
state law and policy: abortion bans, 10, 22, 278; adoption, open, 210, 238; anti-trans legislation (proposed or ratified), 66, 121; ART restrictions proposed, 228; book bans, 121; contraception restrictions, 10; fertility fraud, 203n8, 245; gender-affirming care bans, 66, 121, 136; gender-affirming care restrictions, 10, 66; infertility coverage mandated by law, 73, 85; injunctions by men to block abortion (proposed), 30; paternity testing, 276; Uniform Parentage Act, 200, 232, 238, 245–247; in vitro fertilization restrictions, 10; (white) male policymakers unable to grasp full extent of burdens of pregnancy making decisions on, 22, 169, 278. *See also* child support system; incar-

ceration; law and policy; Medicaid; sperm banks (sperm donation); sperm donation (DIY/informal market)

STDs. *See* STIs (sexually transmitted infections)

stem cell research: as regenerative medicine, 148. *See also* IVG (in vitro gametogenesis)

sterility. *See* infertility

sterilization: Affordable Care Act as covering female, but not vasectomy, 159; Catholic health systems prohibiting, 191; gendered disparity in statistics on, 158–159; race and class disparities in, 159–162. *See also* hysterectomy; tubal ligation; vasectomy

—FORCED AND COERCED: eugenics campaigns and, 135, 161–162; as mid-twentieth century requirement for those seeking gender-affirming care, 135; reclaiming of practices used in, 162; as reproductive justice issue, 10

stigma: and abortion decisions, 26, 275; individualization of responsibility for health and, 9; male infertility as most stigmatizing of all male health conditions, 262; types of, 275

stillbirth. *See* pregnancy loss (miscarriage and stillbirth)

STIs (sexually transmitted infections): condoms as underused by men in new sexual relationships, 23; gamete donors tested for, 203n2, 223, 225, 230, 232; policy defining as female burden (gender disparity in official recommendations for screening), 23–24, 32–33; rates in the US as rising, 23; traditional masculinity beliefs defining as female burden, 41. *See also* HIV infection; HPV (human papillomavirus) vaccine

stratified reproduction: definition of, 63, 160; gendered disparity in, 161; trans people's fertility preservation and, 127–128, 135–138; vasectomy and, 161–162; white middle-class women's access and, 160; women of color and coercive practices, 160–161. *See also* reproductive justice—stratified reproductive justice

stress, chronic: as factor in global decline of sperm counts, 93–94; maternal mortality and morbidity risk and, 276

Strolovitch, Dara Z., 91

structural violence. *See* homelessness; incarceration; poverty; racial inequalities

substance use: adolescent concern about sperm health due to, 142; adolescent male need for help with, 40; arrest and prosecution of low-income and women of color for perinatal use, 33

suicide: cisgender men's higher mortality rates, 54–55; trans and gender diverse youth and, 121; trans people in general, 121; of US high school students, 121

Sullivan, Will, 103, 104

support groups: for donor-conceived people, 208, 213n5; for donor conception community members, generally, 199; male infertility patient access, limited due to focus on women's issues, 85, 258

Supreme Court: finding against different rules for married same-sex and different-sex couples with donor-conceived children, 232; *Planned Parenthood of Southeastern Pennsylvania v. Casey*, 30, 228. *See also Dobbs v. Jackson Women's Health Organization* (2022); *Roe v. Wade*

surrogacy, 229, 230, 239

Swan, Shanna, and Stacey Colino, *Count Down*, 90, 94, 95

Switzerland, groups experimenting with thermic testicular contraception, 184n2

systemic racism. *See* racism, systemic

Talking Heads, 297

Tan, Catherine, 55

Tay-Sachs disease, 203n2

Test Tube Babies (Connell) (exploitation film), 206–207, 212n2

testicles: surgical varicocelectomy for infertility patients, 88, 269; "tucking," 175, 184n4. *See also* thermic testicular contraception

testicular cancer, associated with male infertility, 73, 76, 85, 87, 93, 95

testicular dysgenesis syndrome, 93

testicular sperm extraction. *See* ICSI (intracytoplasmic sperm injection)—sperm extraction methods

testosterone, and sperm count: medications to increase, 88; as shutting off sperm production, caution against monotherapy with, 88; sperm count decline and changes in circulating levels of, 93. *See also* gender-affirming care

That Fertile Feeling (Davis) (video), 294–295

thermic testicular contraception (artificial cryptorchidism): overview of method, 175, 176; accepted sperm count efficacy threshold by activists and users (≤1 million of sperm/ml), 180–181; activist men's groups and men's* groups in Europe and the U.S. for, 175, 184n2, 185n12; Andro-Switch device, clinical trials and sales of, 181, 185n12; andrological associations advising against using, 180–181; cis men, queer folk, trans women, and nonbinary persons among users of, 174–175, 184, 184n4, 185–186n14; clinical trials as small, 176, 181; clinical trials, steps for, 179–180, 185n9, 185n10; devices can be used for tucking, 175, 184n4; DIY devices, 176; earliest reports of (1950s), 176; heat effects other than sperm counts, 185n6; jockstraps, silicon rings, and androgynous contraceptive fashion as devices used to achieve, 175; "nonresponse" phenomenon, 181–182; sperm analysis (by medical specialist, DIY, or at-home tests), practical merit of, 185n13; sperm counts, practical merit of, 181–182; users, number of, 180, 185n12; as *Zeugungsverhütung* ("procreation prevention"), nongendered term for and conceptual shift in "male contraception," 174–175, 183–184. *See also* male contraception

Thomas, Clarence, 244
Thunberg, Greta, 105
Title X (1970), 42–43, 141
Tober, Diane, *Romancing the Sperm*, 212–213n4
traditional views of sex and gender. *See* masculinity beliefs, traditional; sex and gender, traditional categories of
trans and transgender people: capitalization of Trans in the text, 129n1; rights of, the Catholic Church's advocacy against, 192; suicide rates and, 121. *See also* gender-affirming care; trans and gender diverse youth; trans reproduction; transgender people's fertility preservation
—TRANS MEN: IVG process allowing biologically related children to, 147. *See also* pregnancy and related reproductive burdens
—TRANS WOMEN: breastfeeding by, 277, 290–291; of color, disproportionate burden of structural violence experienced by, 136; and human right to have a biological child and raise them in safety, 65, 127; hyperviolence against, as reproductive justice issue, 65, 293; persistent bias against, in reproductive sciences, 136; and thermic testicular contraception, 174–175, 184, 184n4, 185–186n14; and transphobia, 291, 293; tucking, 175, 184n4

trans and gender diverse youth: book bans, 121; and chosen family, importance of, 126–127; homelessness and family rejection experienced by, 126; suicide rates among, 121; as the target of punitive laws, 66, 121, 136. *See also* gender-affirming care; transgender people's fertility preservation—trans and gender diverse youth

trans reproduction: gender-neutral language as necessary but insufficient, 288–289; hyperviolence against transgender women as reproductive justice issue, 65, 293; reproductive desires rendered as invalidating of transgender identity, 125, 292, 293–294; sperm as stuck in reproductive normativity of patriarchal white supremacy, 288, 289–290; sperm as stuck, and transgender women as breastfeeding mothers, 290–292. *See also* transgender people's fertility preservation; transgender people's fertility preservation—trans and gender diverse youth
—UNSTICKING SPERM: overview, 291–292; approximating cis intimacy with it (Torrey Peters), 292–293, 295; creating a trans future with it (micha cárdenas), 293–294, 295; exaggerating a racialized absence with it (Vaginal Creme Davis), 294–295, 295; sperm as metonym for reproductive intimacy, 288, 292, 295; sperm as tool of speculative reproductive desire, 288, 294, 295–297

transgender people's fertility preservation: in adulthood, cryopreservation (freezing) of sperm or eggs, 136–137; in adulthood, data needed on effects of puberty blockers and hormone therapy started in a person's youth on adult fertility, 123, 124, 136, 137; in adulthood, discontinuing estrogen can lead to viable sperm production, 124, 293; fear that expressing desire to preserve fertility may jeopardize access to gender-affirming care, 125; gender dysphoria as risk of hormonal medication and procedures required for, 123–124, 125; IVF for cisgender women partners of trans women, 137, 138; race and class dispari-

ties as heavily influencing access to, 127–128, 135–138; recommendations to assess patients' desire for fertility preservation (WPATH and US Endocrine Society), 122, 124, 126–127, 129n2, 129n4, 134, 135; as reproductive justice issue, 121–122, 127–128, 136–138
—COST OF: as creating eugenics-influenced barriers to care, 135–138; dollar amounts, 136; insurance coverage, need for guarantee of, 125–126; insurance coverage, reforms of, 137, 138; insurance coverage, uncertainty of, 136–137; Medicaid coverage, 125, 137, 138; proposals for moving beyond reproducing inequalities, 137–138
—TRANS AND GENDER DIVERSE YOUTH: access to gender-affirming care must be guaranteed, 125–126; chosen family as longstanding queer and trans practice, avoidance of privileging "biological family" over, 126–127; cisgender youth with cancer as "control group" for, 122, 126, 128–129, 129n4; cryopreservation (freezing) of ovarian or testicular tissue with subsequent in vitro maturation, data needed on success of, 123, 126, 129n4; as embodiment of (racial) futurity, 128; as insurance for an "open future," 128; percentage of trans youth pursuing, 122; puberty blockers and hormone therapy block development of sperm or eggs, 122–125, 129n3, 134; safety from discrimination as community concern, 127
transphobia, 290–291, 293
Transgender Legal Defense and Education Fund, 136
tubal ligation: forced sterilizations, 10, 135, 161; health insurance covering, but not vasectomy, 27; immediate postpartum, as expected practice by obstetrician-gynecologists, 159; as likely permanent contraceptive method, 26–27, 159; statistics on use of, 158; vasectomy as cheaper, safer, and more effective than, 26, 158. *See also* hysterectomy as sterilization; vasectomy
Turnaway Study, 30–31
23and Me. *See* direct-to-consumer DNA testing
Tyler, Edward T., "Artificial Insemination," 212–213n4

Ulmer, Robert R., 91
Umamaheswar, Janani, 55

Uniform Law Commission, 245, 246–247
Uniform Parentage Act (UPA), 200, 232, 238, 245–247
unintended pregnancy. *See* pregnancy, unintended
United Kingdom (UK): donor anonymity abolished, 208, 209; HIM Fertility, 258; Men's Fertility Forum, 258; servicemen exposed to depleted uranium in Iraq wars, 264; transphobic responses to trans women as mothers, 290–291
unmarried couples: ART legal parentage at risk, 236, 238–239, 243–244, 248–249; Uniform Parentage Act recognizing, 246. *See also* family, diversity of forms facilitated by assisted reproduction
urgent care centers: as access point for health care, 56; Man Up Checkup public health campaign in, 54, 55–56
urologists: erectile dysfunction claimed for treatment domain of, 282; inadequate number available for male infertility care, 73–74, 75; insufficient medical training for male infertility care, 74–75; as specialists in acute conditions, 22. *See also* andrologists

vasectomy: access to, increasing, 169; the Affordable Care Act excluding from coverage, 27, 33, 44, 159, 169; Catholic health systems prohibiting by policy but facilitating for patients, 191, 192–193; as cheaper, safer, and more effective than female sterilization, 26, 158; and condoms, as only male contraceptive methods on market, 25, 168; cost without insurance coverage as barrier to care, 159–160; efficacy of (Pearl Index number), 177; forced, as rhetorical tactic in wake of *Dobbs*, 161–162; forced, via state-sanctioned eugenics campaigns, 161–162; as gold standard in contraception, 158; health insurance not covering, 27, 33, 159; and the human right not to have a child, 65; vs. male hormonal methods, 160; as option later in life, 143; providers, inadequate number of, 159; race and class disparities and, 159–160, 161–162; rate of use increasing in wake of *Dobbs*, 162–163; as side-effect free, 160; statistics on usage, 158; stratified reproduction and, 161–162; as underutilized, 26–27. *See also* male contraception
Vereecke, Gertjan, 124

violence: against transgender women, as reproductive justice issue, 65, 293; as factor reinforcing traditional masculinity beliefs, 41; gun violence, as reproductive justice issue, 66; intimate partner, adolescent males experiencing, 40; police violence, 66

violence against pregnant people: homicide as leading cause of pregnancy-related death, 31; risk as higher in women who wanted an abortion but were denied access, 30–31; women of color and higher rates of, 31; women who received a wanted abortion and reduction of, 30

violence, sexual: adolescent males experiencing, 40; "healthy masculinity" campaigns for prevention of, 56–57

violence, structural. *See* homelessness; incarceration; poverty; racial inequalities

virility: ART as aid to lifelong pursuit of, 216; ART technoscientific reproduction as effeminizing and queering sperm, 215–221; envisioned as ever-present and never changing, 103, 216; as essential trait of "Western" hegemonic masculinity, 96, 215, 216; linkage with fertility, 262; sperm as main symbol of, 96, 97–98, 215, 216, 293. *See also* masculinity beliefs, traditional

Vora, Kalindi, 296

Wahlberg, Ayo, 105
water, racism and poverty precluding access to clean and safe, 9
We Are Donor Conceived, survey, 213n6
(white) male policymakers unable to grasp full extent of burdens of pregnancy making decisions on law and policy, 22, 169, 278
white middle-class: couples as "worthy" insemination recipients (eugenics), 207; focus on ART access in wake of *Dobbs*, 228; women's disproportionate access to reproductive care, 160
white supremacy: global decline of sperm counts as "white genocide" conspiracy theory, 95–96; sperm as stuck in reproductive normativity of patriarchy and, 288, 289–290; as structuring logic of reproductive injustice, 63. *See also* eugenics; racism, systemic

women of color: as disproportionately birthing in hospitals with religious constraints on care, 191; eugenics movement seeking to limit reproductive autonomy of, 135, 161; gendered disparity is likelihood to be sterilized, 159–160; homicide rate during pregnancy, 31; punitive reproductive landscape for, 33–34; racial disparity in reproductive care options, 160–161; trans women of, disproportionate burden of structural violence experienced by, 136. *See also* Black women; reproductive justice

women. *See* bodily autonomy; burdens of reproductivity as gendered inequality; misogyny; pregnancy; pregnancy and related reproductive burdens; reproductive justice; violence against pregnant people

women who are sexually active, eugenics movement seeking to limit reproductive autonomy of, 135

World Health Organization (WHO): clinical trials of hormonal male contraception (1990s), 179; global rates of infertility, 259; healthy/normal sperm concentration, 177–178; infertility classified as disease, 73, 199; male infertility panel recommendations for basic and clinical research, 71

World Professional Association for Transgender Health (WPATH): proposal to enshrine reproductive justice in trans medicine, 137; recommendations to assess patients' desire for fertility preservation, 122, 124, 126–127, 129n2, 129n4, 134, 135

Young Men's Clinic, 141

Zeugungsverhütung ("procreation prevention"), as nongendered term for and conceptual shift in "male contraception," 174–175, 183–184. *See also* male contraception